HUMOUR AND HUMANISM
IN CHEMISTRY

HOCUS POCUS
OR SEARCHING FOR THE PHILOSOPHERS STONE.

1. HOCUS POCUS
or Searching for the Philosophers Stone.
T. Rowlandson, 1800.

HUMOUR
AND HUMANISM
IN CHEMISTRY

BY

JOHN READ

PH.D. (ZÜRICH), M.A. AND SC.D. (CAMB.), F.R.S.
PROFESSOR OF CHEMISTRY IN THE UNITED COLLEGE
OF ST. SALVATOR AND ST. LEONARD IN THE
UNIVERSITY OF ST. ANDREWS ; FORMERLY
PROFESSOR OF ORGANIC CHEMISTRY,
PURE AND APPLIED, IN THE
UNIVERSITY OF SYDNEY

London 1947

G. Bell and Sons Ltd.

First published 1947

PRINTED IN GREAT BRITAIN
BY R. & R. CLARK, LIMITED, EDINBURGH

TO MY PUPILS

Science is not an abstraction; but as a product of human endeavour it is inseparably bound up in its development with the personalities and fortunes of those who dedicate themselves to it.

EMIL FISCHER

I have seen many phases of life; I have moved in Imperial circles, I have been Minister of State; but if I had to live my life again, I would always remain in my laboratory, for the greatest joy of my life has been to accomplish original scientific work, and, next to that, to lecture to a set of intelligent students.

JEAN BAPTISTE ANDRÉ DUMAS

CONTENTS

CHAPTER V

CHAPTER VI

CHAPTER VII

CHAPTER VIII

CHAPTER IX

CHAPTER X

CHAPTER XI

CHAPTER XII

TITLES AND DESCRIPTIONS
OF THE ILLUSTRATIONS

The numbers in heavy type refer to illustrations reproduced in the plates, those in ordinary type to illustrations in the text; the plates face the pages indicated.

xi

PAGE

Tailpiece: Bush-Sprite and Eucalyptus Leaf. From an original drawing by May Gibbs (copyright).

PREFACE

In the introduction to *Prelude to Chemistry* the author referred to 'his original design of filling in the outlines of a further sequence of alchemical and chemical scenes, dealing partly with later times'. To complete that design has been the task of the present book, the main object of which, dovetailing into that of the *Prelude*, is to offer a broad and humanistic presentation of the development of alchemy and chemistry. About one-fifth of the present work (Chapters I to V) deals with alchemy; one-fifth (Chapters VI and VII) with chymistry—that transition from alchemy to chemistry, falling in the seventeenth and eighteenth centuries; and the remaining three-fifths (Chapters VIII to XII) with chemistry. Chapter I forms a connecting link between the two books, and the earlier part of this second book contains many references to the *Prelude*, although the narrative is complete in itself.

The survey of alchemy closes with an account of certain romantic episodes in which the leading parts are played by James IV of Scotland, amateur of medicine, surgery, physiology, psychology, and alchemy; his court alchemist, John Damian, the flying Abbot of Tungland; that mysterious Scot, Alexander Seton, 'the chief martyr of alchemy', known also as 'The Cosmopolite'; his rescuer, Michael Sendivogius, the noble Polish goldmaker, to whom Rudolph II erected a marble tablet at Prague; van Helmont, iatrochemist and mystic; Helvetius, physician to the Prince of Orange and author of 'The Golden Calf'; and that elusive alchemic messiah, 'The Artist Elias', with his five great Golden Pendants and 'shoes dropping wet with snow'.

The transition from alchemy to chemistry, in the course of the seventeenth and eighteenth centuries, is brought home in an unusual and realistic way by tracing the evolution

of chymical text-books during this period, opening with
Beguin's *Tyrocinium Chymicum* (1610), and leading on
through the later works of Davidson, Glauber, le Febure,
Glaser, and Lemery, to the monumental and epoch-making
Elementa Chemiae of Boerhaave (1732). This method of
survey has the advantage of presenting a series of contemporary impressions of the theory and practice of chymistry,
told largely in the language of the day and illustrated by
drawings reproduced from the original texts: such first-
hand impressions must necessarily possess a sharpness of
outline often lacking in a more formal and exhaustive treatment of historical chemistry. An added advantage is the clear
picture that emerges of the gradual change in the character
of chemical apparatus, practical operations, and laboratories.

Another interesting feature of this contemporary view
of chemistry in the seventeenth and early eighteenth centuries is the absence of the orthodox emphasis attached
nowadays to such outstanding figures as Boyle, Hooke,
Mayow, and Hales. The full recognition of the ideas and
work of these eminent men came only in a later age. In
their own period, teachers and writers like le Febure,
Glaser, and Lemery exerted a much greater influence than
Boyle, Hooke, and Mayow in diffusing a wide appreciation
of the nature and scope of chymistry. Moreover, in the
words of the *Prelude* (p. 31), 'Modern chemistry did not
spring fully equipped from between the covers of *The
Sceptical Chymist*. . . . It is true that the outer defences of
the alchemical citadel were breached by Boyle, but some
four generations elapsed before its main works were carried
by Lavoisier.' It is fitting to add that the present book, like
the *Prelude*, does not profess to offer a formal treatment of
historical chemistry ; and that its plan does not call for
an addition to the innumerable accounts that have been
written of the experiments and views of Boyle and Mayow
at the beginning of the phlogistic era and of the even more
important activities of Lavoisier and Dalton at its end.[1]

In the chemical cavalcade now presented, the birth of
modern chemistry late in the eighteenth century is heralded

[1] See *e.g.* the author's *Textbook of Organic Chemistry*, London, 1946, p. 19 *et seq.*

by the appearance of Joseph Black. The ensuing story, so full of humour and humanism to the discerning student, is traced partly in the pages of Mrs. Jane Marcet and John Scoffern, who were two of the most entertaining writers on chemistry in the first half of the nineteenth century, although their names may be unknown to most chemists of the present age. The rise of chemistry is also bound up intimately with the development of our knowledge of gases, and in the forefront of a reference to this subject some care has been taken in tracing the curiously interesting train of circumstances that led up to the discovery and collection of coal gas by that brilliant but little-known amateur of seventeenth-century science, the Rev. Dr. John Clayton, 'parson of *James* city, *Virginia*', 'Rector of Crofton, at Wakefield, in Yorkshire', and later Dean of Kildare.

The humanistic element in chemistry, like the elements of the Periodic System, has to be sought after in the laboratory. Hence, in tracing the occurrence in modern times of this much-neglected element, we visit in turn the laboratories of Berzelius, Gay-Lussac, Bunsen, Baeyer, and other eminent chemists of the nineteenth and twentieth centuries. Like the formal historian, we are interested in the researches going on in these laboratories; but we find an equal attraction in the personalities of the directing geniuses, in their pupils, and in their environment. In this section of the book the author has deemed it of interest to record some first-hand impressions of two celebrated modern laboratories in which he was so fortunate as to work as a research student.

In the twentieth century, research in every branch of science has advanced in a kind of geometrical progression. The consequent expansion of knowledge has imposed great burdens upon teachers, students, and research workers alike. It is difficult for the teacher to present, and for the student and research worker to cope with, the vast stores of information; and it is difficult for any of them to take a broad view of a particular branch of science, to say nothing of science as a whole. In the background looms the even greater problem of acquiring a balanced education, a cultured outlook, and a sound acquaintance with the world of men and affairs, of things and ideas. So long ago as 1871, Clerk-Maxwell wrote: 'I do not myself believe in Science of any kind as the principal pabulum of the half-cultivated mind'; and he went on to suggest that 'for beginners the best mental pabulum is some kind of history about people, expressed in good style. These things remain in the mind. . . . And even in Science it is when we take some interest in the great discoverers and their lives that it becomes endurable, and only when we begin to trace the development of ideas that it becomes fascinating.'

In other words, the full value of science as an educative and cultural influence cannot be exercised by presenting it baldly as a regimented system of facts, laws, and theories. In chemistry, for example, isomerism is *ipso facto* a phenomenon of great interest; but it becomes of manifold interest when related (p. 340) to the experiences and discoveries of Wöhler and Liebig, to the dramatic scene between Pasteur and Biot at the polarimeter, to the visions of Kekulé, and to the coincidence in time of the ideas of Le Bel and van 't Hoff. Again, all chemists have a richly humanistic birthright of history, literature, and art: is this heritage to be entirely neglected, or, at the best, dismissed as something less in value than a mess of pottage?

This book touches upon a few only of the multitudinous aspects, incidents, and personalities of chemistry; yet the survey should be sufficient to show that, throughout its long history, chemistry has been bountifully endowed with humanism, besides being seasoned and mellowed with humour. Humour is, indeed, the golden thread which runs through the whole tapestry of chemistry: it is the real Philosopher's Stone; the universal catalyst. Let no chemist undervalue the importance of humour.

It is not too much to claim that the study of chemistry, if approached befittingly, may reasonably take rank beside the so-called humanities as a broadly educative, cultural, and humanising influence; and that the specialised outlook which is becoming increasingly bound up with the trend of scientific research may be alleviated by the cultivation of an interest in the broad humanistic aspects of science. As

Richard Semon, the naturalist, wrote in 1899, science, at that time advancing so proudly, threatened 'to produce an unlimited number of specialists, each of whom is blind to everything but the narrow sphere of his chosen department'. The importance of cultivating a wider outlook, he added, 'is to a naturalist what migration to the sea is to a young salmon'.

This last sentence points to another consideration. The development of an interest in historical science is naturally only one of many avenues leading to a widening horizon: for, in the words of Tennyson, 'all experience is an arch wherethro' gleams that untravell'd world, whose margin fades for ever and for ever when I move'. The development of broad interests in science, as well as in other fields of intellectual activity, was formerly helped by courses of foreign study and research. An account of one such course has been included in this book, in order to afford an intimate picture of an experience of the kind. In chemistry the practice of going abroad for post-graduate research fell largely into desuetude after the war of 1914–1918, as a consequence of the development of strong schools of chemical research in Great Britain. An ideal of the future should be an extensive interchange of students, research workers, and teachers, not only between Great Britain and the continent of Europe, but also between Great Britain, the Dominions and Colonies, and the United States—as well as interchange between the universities of Great Britain. In the penultimate chapter of this book an attempt has been made to indicate the widening horizons greeting a migrating chemist who is imperceptibly forced to readjust his mental outlook, and to learn to think also in terms of geography, biology, and economics.

Coming at last to our closing chapter, if perchance any chemist shall ask soberly why a work on chemistry should end in a pure flight of the imagination, he may be reminded of Kekulé's exhortation (p. 341), 'Lernen wir träumen!' and Baeyer's aphorism (p. 261), 'So viele Chemiker haben nicht genügend Phantasie'. Baeyer's reproach could not have been levelled at Sir Humphry Davy, in whom that 'shaping spirit of imagination', characteristic of the poet, 'found wings in another region, the region of science'; for Davy's 'mind had the true poetic impulse, and habitually tended *upwards*, from the visible to the invisible, from form to origin, from matter to spirit . . . a tendency which accounts for the charm that Coleridge found in his conversation even when he first came to Bristol, a raw Cornish boy'.[1]

The creative science of chemistry, like the creative arts, calls for a constant cultivation and exercise of the imagination. Apart from this truism, as Edmund Blunden has observed in his charming book, *Cricket Country*,[2] 'we do not quite trust to the Euclidean treatment of a subject for its full appeal to our hearers': sometimes it is a virtue in a writer on a seemingly specialised field to 'be found reminiscent, recreational, intent on seeing and making you see what a wealth of nature, in man and round him, has been accessible through this separate field'.

The many illustrations which form an integral part of the work have been prepared mainly from books, manuscripts, engravings, specimens, etc., in the collection of the Chemistry Department of the United College of St. Salvator and St. Leonard, in the University of St. Andrews. The publication of a book containing so much pictorial matter, at a price designed to bring it within reach of the average reader, would have been impracticable without the aid of a generous grant from the Walker Trust of the University of St. Andrews and also from Imperial Chemical Industries Limited: it is a pleasing duty to acknowledge with gratitude the practical help and encouragement derived from these sources.

Some of the material has formed the subject-matter of lectures given in many centres in Great Britain; some has been broadcast; and some has appeared in the form of contributions to various journals in Great Britain and abroad: acknowledgments are offered in particular to the

[1] Mrs. H. Sandford, *Thomas Poole and his Friends* (2 vols., London, 1888), **2**, 283.
[2] London, 1944, pp. 110, 111.

editors of *Ambix, Endeavour, Nature, Scientia, The Chemist and Druggist, The Chemistry Leaflet* (State College, Pennsylvania), *The Listener*, and *The Sydney Morning Herald;* also to the British Broadcasting Corporation. Further acknowledgments, concerning the reproduction of certain of the illustrations, are included under the heading of 'Titles and Descriptions of the Illustrations'. Fig. 77 is appearing simultaneously as an illustration in another new work by the author, entitled *A Direct Entry to Organic Chemistry*, published by Messrs. Methuen & Co., London.

The author's colleague, Professor H. J. Rose, M.A., F.B.A., has again aided him with interpretations of various Latin passages; his son, Mr. J. H. Read, B.Sc., has lent help with some of the illustrations; Mr. R. B. Pilcher, O.B.E., of the Royal Institute of Chemistry, has supplied valuable information about some of the engravings. To all of them the author expresses his gratitude and thanks ; also to Mr. F. Lodge, Secretary of the Wakefield Gaslight Company, the Very Rev. G. F. Graham, M.A., Dean of Kildare, and Mr. J. D. Griffith Davies, M.A., Assistant Secretary of the Royal Society, for information respecting Dr. John Clayton; furthermore, to Principal Sir James Irvine, C.B.E., F.R.S., University of St. Andrews, Sir David Russell, LL.D., Markinch, Fife, Professor Dr. Hans Rupe, Basel, Switzerland, Professor F. T. Brooks, C.B.E., F.R.S., Cambridge, Mr. G. H. Bushnell, University Librarian, St. Andrews, Dr. W. Douglas Simpson, University Librarian, Aberdeen, Professor A. Killen Macbeth, C.M.G., M.A., D.Sc., Adelaide, Messrs. F. H. Faulding & Co., Adelaide, Miss May Gibbs, Sydney, and Sir David Rivett, K.C.M.G., F.R.S., Melbourne.

J. R.

The University,
  St. Andrews, Scotland

CHAPTER I

THE LIGHTER SIDE OF ALCHEMY

ALCHEMICAL HUMOUR

IT is not usual to suppose that alchemy or alchemists have anything to do with humour. The alchemist is viewed as a strange and almost inhuman being, aloof and abstracted, and wholly absorbed in activities incomprehensible to the common man. Alchemical writings, likewise, are dismissed as a meaningless jargon or empty farrago of words, carrying no message or interest for the ordinary reader. These views are not unreasonable; yet to the discerning and sympathetic mind the alchemist is by no means lacking in human traits, and alchemical writings have a distinctive fascination and even a characteristic humour. It is true that alchemical humour is of an unusual kind; but it might be found abundantly, 'would men observingly distil it out' from the recondite matrix in which it lies embedded.

The alchemists prided themselves upon that 'noble practise' which led them to 'vaile their secrets with mistie speach'. Their extensive use of every conceivable form of cryptic and mystical expression gave rise to a limitless ocean of literature calculated to discourage and dismay even the most ardent explorer. Alchemical humour does not float upon the surface of these strange seas of thought. Like the precepts and maxims of alchemy, it is wont to lie hidden in those annotated manuscripts and fire-stained tomes of a bygone age which form alchemy's written records. Often it lies hidden also in time, like a wine of rare vintage which mellows and reaches perfection only with age. Alchemical humour, indeed, is to a large extent unconscious humour, concealed even from the alchemists themselves. It is marked by a robust extravagance of conception; it has a noble luxuriance; it is closely akin to the gross mediaeval humour of Rabelais. Sometimes it smacks strongly of Alice in Wonderland.

Humour has a time-element, being often, although not always, tied to a period: the truth of this statement may be tested in a simple way by a glance at old numbers of *Punch*. What was humorous to the seventeenth-century mind may no longer be humorous to us, and contrariwise we may find humour in what appeared to intelligent men of that age as sober sense. In general, it is impossible to apply a modern yardstick to the literary, artistic, or scientific fabric of a bygone age. The historian must possess, above all, the faculty of immersing himself in the atmosphere of the age which he attempts to appraise.

THE ALCHEMICAL HIERARCHY

The alchemists often referred to themselves as 'sons of Hermes'. Hermes (Mercury) was the Greek counterpart of Thoth, the god of healing in ancient Egypt. The famous precepts of Hermes Trismegistos, or Hermes the Thrice-Great, forming in effect the articles of association of the esoteric brotherhood of alchemists, were a typical outcome of the capacious alchemical imagination. These thirteen precepts[1] were reputed to have been engraved by Hermes in Phoenician characters on an emerald slab, the legendary Emerald Table (*Tabula Smaragdina*) said to have been discovered in Hermes' tomb in a cave near Hebron.

In order to lend authority to the legend it was considered necessary to have the Table brought to light by a personage of standing. Christopher Columbus was then unknown. According to some alchemists the ceremony of discovery was performed by Alexander the Great; but others favoured a lady, in the person of Sarah the wife of Abraham, whose sepulchre in the cave of Machpelah at Hebron was conveniently near to the reputed place of Hermes' tomb. Presumably Abraham had joined his forefathers at the time of the unveiling; so that the choice

[1] *Prelude*, 54.

of the *ad hoc* resurrected Sarah was peculiarly apposite, for the Emerald Table (Fig. 2) served as an unfailing widow's cruse to generation after generation of alchemists in search of quotations or texts for their literary works or the walls of their laboratories.

Among other functions, the precepts were supposed to afford a cryptic guide to the preparation of the Philosopher's Stone; for this purpose particular importance was attached to the fourth precept—'Its father is the sun, its mother the moon: the wind carries it in its belly, its nurse is the earth'. The thirteenth precept is equivalent to 'Message ends', the virtual end being the grandiloquent pronouncement of the twelfth precept: 'Therefore am I called Hermes Trismegistos, having three parts of the philosophy of the whole world'. The idea of the Emerald Table is a characteristic alchemical conceit, permeated with a latent and unconscious humour that took a thousand years or so to mature.

The beginnings of chemistry are often attributed to ancient Egypt; indeed, it has been supposed that the word *alchemy* may signify *al Khem*, the art of Egypt, otherwise Khem, the country of dark soil. Egypt, or Khem, was the Hebrew 'Land of Ham', and Ham was one of the sons of Noah. Possibly it was by some such route that certain devious alchemical minds settled upon Shem or Chem— likewise a son of Noah—as the founder of alchemy. At times, Shem and Ham seem to have formed a merger. 'Others have called it *Alchamia*,' wrote le Febure in 1660, 'supposing *Cham* one of the Sons of *Noah*, to have been after the Flood inventer and restorer òf Chymical Arts, but chiefly Metallick.'

To go further, alchemy may be pictured as possessing a standing committee charged with the selection of prominent and influential personages, real or imaginary, for addition to the roll of honorary membership of the fraternity. Like a modern advisory committee on honorary distinctions, these fishers used a net of fine mesh and cast it far and wide. Their extensive and peculiar haul included Tubal-cain, an expert on the working of brass and iron; Jason and Moses, two well-known workers on gold; Solomon, whose Song was

held to possess an inner alchemical meaning; the Queen of
Sheba, who came to Solomon with much gold and absorbed
his wisdom; Cleopatra, another early woman chemist who
studied the action of vinegar on pearls;[1] Hercules and
Mahomet, elected under a special statute for conspicuous
general services; and, of course, Hermes, chief patron of
'the Divine Art' and reputed author of 36,000 contributions
to alchemical literature.

It is remarkable that such personages were seriously
credited with an expert knowledge of alchemy, even so late
as the days of Robert Boyle, and by a writer so level-headed
and practically-minded as Nicasius le Febure. 'We are
taught', wrote le Febure, 'that even in the Worlds Infancy,
Tubal-Cain the eighth of Mankinde from *Adam*, descended
of *Cain's* line, was an expert Artist in all Brass and Iron
works, which he could not have been without a previous
knowledge of Minerals, and without being well acquainted,
that the Mineral nature contains in it self and comprehends
the Metallick, as the purest part of its essence. But this
knowledge cannot be attained unto, but by the help and
skill of *Chymistry*; since it is by this Art we are informed,
how a metallick, malleable and ductile body, may be extracted
out of brickle and inform minerals. Whence we do safely
conclude, that he did receive this noble Art from his Predecessors, or being himself the inventor of it, left it to
Posterity, as the richest Jewel they could inherit from him.
This Assertion may be proved by the most ancient of
Authors, and most worthy of credit; and so we have upon
record, that *Moses* took the Golden Calf, an Idol of the
Israelites, did calcine it, and being by him reduced to powder,
caused those Idolators to drink it, in a reproach and punish-
ment of their sin. But no body, how little soever initiated
in the mysteries of this Art, can be ignorant, that Gold is
not to be reduced to Powder by Calcination, unlesse it be
performed either by immersion in Regal Waters, Amamul-
gation with Mercury, or Projection; all which three Operations are only obvious to those which are fully acquainted
both with the Theorical and Practical part of Chimistry.'

[1] Pliny, *Natural History*, Book IX.

ALCHEMICAL SYMBOLISM

The earliest writings having a purely alchemical interest are a heritage from the Alexandrian centre of Greek culture; the oldest surviving manuscripts of this era date from the opening centuries of Christianity, but there are many later transcripts of such writings. Alchemical symbolism makes an early appearance in some of these literary remains, one of the most interesting examples being the so-called Formula of the Crab, recorded by Zosimos in the third or fourth century A.D. This puzzling sequence of symbols was regarded by the alchemists as a cryptic record of the secret of transmutation; in reality, it appears to have been used as a workshop cipher by Egyptian craftsmen, who were enabled thereby to impart a gold finish to metal articles by means of certain preparations containing copper.[1]

As alchemy developed, its symbolism became more and more elaborate and intriguing. A great deal of the pictorial symbolism was bound up with the sulphur-mercury theory in its manifold guises. In its simplest and most primitive expression, the sulphur-mercury theory amounted merely to a distinction between opposites: it may be traced back to the doctrine of the Two Contraries, which prevailed in various forms among the ancient civilisations of China, Mesopotamia, and Egypt. The celebrated theory of the Four Elements, which held sway as the leading theory of physical science from the time of Aristotle until the eighteenth century, is itself an elaboration of this fundamental conception. As laid down by Aristotle, it postulates the existence of two pairs of contrary properties of bodies: heat and cold, dryness and wetness. When conjoined in pairs, these give rise to two pairs of opposed elements: *fire* (hot and dry), and *water* (cold and wet); together with *earth* (cold and dry), and *air* (hot and wet). Of these two pairs of elements, the first is by far the more important in alchemy; many alchemists, indeed, drew little or no distinction between the fire-water and sulphur-mercury appositions. Both the theory of the four elements and the sulphur-

[1] *Prelude*, 40.

mercury theory are evident in the fourth precept of Hermes quoted above, the father (or sun) being sulphur and the mother (or moon) mercury.

The blending, or incorporation, under ideal conditions of these two opposed elements or principles—whether considered as fire and water or as sulphur and mercury—constituted the Great Work of alchemy, leading to the preparation of the Philosopher's Stone. For this purpose a menstruum was often held to be needful: this fluid medium was symbolised sometimes by a dragon, sometimes by the Hermetic Stream of 'heavy water' or mercuric spirit of metals, sometimes by the Philosopher's Bath, and sometimes even by 'the bloud of *Infants* gathered up, and put in a great vessell, wherein the *Sunne* and *Moone* came to bathe themselves'.[1]

Pictorial alchemy thus abounds in representations of the two opposed principles, or proximate materials of the Great Work, known in the esoteric terminology as sophic (or philosophical) sulphur and sophic mercury. The great variety of these ideographs is not surprising when the wide prevalence of the doctrine of the Two Contraries—both in space and time—is called to mind. This doctrine lay behind the conceptions of Hara-Parvati in ancient India, Yin-Yang in ancient China, and Isis-Osiris in ancient Egypt. It was thus linked inseparably with fundamental ideas of religion and sex. Osiris and Isis, gods of fecundity and fertility in the pantheon of ancient Egypt, ranking as father and mother deities, and sometimes associated with the sun and moon, found their counterparts in Sol and Luna of the alchemists.[2] Sol and Luna in turn were interpreted as gold and silver, masculine and feminine, brother and sister, fixed and volatile, positive and negative, active and passive, giver and recipient, Hermes' seal and wax, and in many other ways.

The two contraries were often depicted as animals, sometimes engaged in combat or frolicking, such as the maned lion and the feathered lioness, the lion and serpent, the toad and eagle, and the two dragons. Classical mythology

[1] *Prelude*, 62.   [2] *Op. cit.* 20.

2. The Emerald Table of Hermes.

From *Amphitheatrum Sapientiae Æternae*, H. Khunrath, Hanau, 1609. The thirteen precepts are set out in Latin and German. (See p. 2.)

3. The Birth of Eve.

From the MS. *Philosophorum Praeclara Monita*, early 18th century. The original
painting is delicately coloured.

provided a rich field for Michael Maier and others, who regarded its picturesque narratives as allegorical cloaks for the concealment of alchemical truths. Such mythological fables were utilised with striking effect in the pictorial propaganda of some of the later alchemical writers. One of their favourite allusions was to Hermaphroditus, a bisexual being resulting from the union of the nymph Salmacis, whilst bathing in a fountain, with the beautiful son of Hermes and Aphrodite. Thus, some of the quaintest of these alchemical drawings depict hermaphroditic figures, often shown in the company of a dragon, representing the liquid vehicle or bath. Even Adam, Eve, and the Serpent were brought into such pictorial representations of alchemical doctrine (Fig. 3).

The modern reader may be disposed to dismiss such representations of alchemical ideas as idle conceits unworthy of a second thought; but it is a striking reflection that the ionic and electronic theories of matter—in which modern science takes so much pride—are merely contemporary phases of a fundamental conception drawn from prehistory. The electron and the positron are direct descendants of Isis and Osiris, of ancient Egypt, or, if you will, of Yin and Yang, of ancient China. One of the many bizarre illustrations of the Hermetic Androgyne[1] might be used with entire propriety as a design for the cover of an up-to-date work on the electronic theory: the figure is, indeed, an early representation of the neutron—although Thomas Norton would have described it in the fifteenth century as 'the faire White Woman married to the Ruddy Man'. Of scientific theory it may be said with justice that *Plus ça change, plus c'est la même chose*—the more it changes, the more it is the same thing. The human mind, like the electron, seems to move as a rule in closed orbits.

In a work entitled *Atalanta Fugiens* ('Atalanta Fleeing'), Count Michael Maier, physician and private secretary to the Emperor Rudolph II at Prague, published in 1618[2] a series of fifty copper engravings designed as symbolical representa-

---

[1] See *e.g. Prelude*, Plate 16.
[2] A few copies (with flaws) are known, bearing the date 1617.

C

tions of alchemical ideas. Many of them depict the sulphur-mercury theory in such guises as brother and sister, Sol and Luna, Mercury and Venus (Hermes and Aphrodite), two eagles, wolf and dog, and two lions. To an undiscerning modern mind Maier's illustrations and the accompanying text convey little beyond a ludicrous appeal and an impression of the limitless credulity of the alchemical brotherhood. The discovery that Sir Isaac Newton, the foremost thinker of his age, went to the trouble of making detailed manuscript notes of the titles and import of these fifty engravings throws a flood of light upon the contemporary attitude of mind towards such seemingly absurd ideas. Newton's extant transcriptions from this book, written in his characteristic fine hand, occupy eight pages (19·6 by 15·2 cm.).

The transcribed title (Fig. 4) of the representation of two lions indulging in frolicsome horseplay,[1] which is No. 16 in Maier's series of emblems, reads: *Hic Leo, quas plumas non habet, alter habet.* The maned lion without feathers represents Sol, gold, sophic sulphur, or the fixed masculine principle; the plumed lion is Luna, silver, sophic mercury, or the volatile feminine principle. Maier provided each of the fifty emblems with an explanatory Latin epigram in elegiac couplets, which he set to a peculiar form of music: he termed this a 'fuga', but in reality these remarkable musical settings consist of canons in two parts against a repeated *canto fermo*, for three voices in all. More than three hundred years after their publication, some of them were sung in London by a student choir from the University of St. Andrews, in 1935. Four of these 'numbers' (2, 27, 18, 45) were recorded for the gramophone, together with a modern example of this pleasant method of inculcating chemistry without tears:

Aëre cum crasso tenuis componitur aër;
Adde Iouis fulmen, fit sonus, unda manet.

With a dense gas a thin gas is mixed; pass the
electric spark, and pop! you have water.

$$2H_2 + O_2 = 2H_2O.$$

[1] A closely similar contemporary engraving of the two lions, taken from another source, is reproduced in *Prelude to Chemistry* (Plate 57).

Newton had a profound interest in alchemy, and he devoted much thought and experiment to the possibility of effecting metallic transmutation. It may be surmised that he would have been particularly interested in the musical rendering of Fuga XVIII, for his manuscript bears an index finger drawing attention to his transcript of the title of this emblem and the accompanying notes. The emblem concerned (Fig. 5) has a direct bearing upon the problem of gold-making; since it depicts an alchemist engaged at his hearth with a large bowl of coins beside him, it was well calculated to attract the close attention of Newton in his capacity of Master of the Mint. The title of this emblem— *Ignire ignis amat, non aurificare, sed aurum*—may be freely translated: 'Fire loves to fire, but gold it maketh not; Gold maketh gold, but fireth ne'er a jot.' The epigram states that every active principle in nature sends out its force in all directions and loves to multiply the same, thus pointing the alchemical maxim that a thing multiplies only in its own species.

With the exception of the sentence in brackets ('Gold cannot be made from herbs, etc.'), Newton's manuscript notes on this emblem are copied from Maier's discourse following the epigram. They refer to the specific possibility of preparing a lead-making Stone, capable of transmuting quicksilver into lead, and to the wider possibility of the transmutation of metals in general, 'in the same time in which one might eat an egg'.

THE ORIGIN OF DRAGON'S BLOOD

Count Michael Maier, the author of *Atalanta Fugiens* and many other works of the same general type, was an indefatigable collector of mare's-nests. He ransacked the archives of antiquity in search of allegorical images of alchemy. He was sublimely uncritical, and his large-hearted credulousness rose superior to all the canons of common sense. An amusing example of his ingenuous acceptance of cock-and-bull stories is to be found in the account which he published in 1618, in his *Viatorium* or 'Traveller's Companion', of the origin of Dragon's Blood.

These deep-red resins occur as exudations from so-called dragon trees, notably *Dracaena draco* of the Canary Islands and *Calamus draco* of the East Indies.   Maier adopted without question a much more picturesque version of their origin which he reproduced, without acknowledgment, from Pliny's *Natural History*.   From his 'Description of Dragon's Blood', written in Latin and rendered below in English, it will be seen that the cock and bull are replaced in this hoary narration by two less familiar animals:

'Here [in Africa], to say nothing of other things, is seen an elephant, taking the foremost place among the other beasts as being remarkable not only for its size of body but also for its intelligence (some hold that it has a power of understanding, speaking and writing second only to that of man).   As naught attains to perfect bliss,[1] a vast dragon presents itself straightway as its ill-wisher and implacable foe.

'This dragon, not daring to wage open warfare upon so huge a creature, to whose strength its own is far from equal, in hopes of injuring it resorts to guile, as follows.   It notes by what way the elephant will return from drinking water; it takes possession of this way where it narrows, and hides itself in a lower part, until the elephant, swollen with water, comes near.   It then winds its coils or circles about the elephant's legs, and tastes and sucks its blood.

'When at length the elephant's strength is exhausted— the dragon being now twisted about it, filled full of blood and free from all anxiety regarding its victory over its enemy—it (the elephant) falling to the ground and taking vengeance by its very death, crushes and annihilates the dragon by its weight, and so all its blood is vomited up and spilt.   This is now known as dragon's blood, although the most part of it is the elephant's, and is of considerable use in medicine and for other human needs.   One should carefully identify this dragon, whose blood is used for philosophic medicine, lest someone substitute something earthy [cinnabar] or taken from the depths of the ground, or otherwise unsuitable, in its place.'

[1] Horace, *Odes*.

Maier provided an illustration (Fig. **6**) entirely worthy of this combat, which he seems to have regarded as an encounter carried out solely in the interests of alchemy by the two protagonists. There is little doubt that in his mind the combat had an allegorical significance similar to that of his sixteenth emblem of the two sportive lions. The elephant and dragon represent sulphur and mercury, respectively: the resulting dragon's blood, red in colour, is a symbol of the Philosopher's Stone of esoteric alchemy, and of cinnabar (mercury sulphide) of exoteric alchemy.

In the eighth book of his *Natural History*, Pliny gives two versions of the combat, in which the serpent anticipates the tactics of the dive-bomber and the submarine respectively, by lying in ambush for the elephant either in a lofty tree or submerged in a river; later in the same work he states that the gore from dragons and elephants, obtained in this way, is a valuable pigment, and that it is used also as a remedy under the name of cinnabar.

Richard Hakluyt, who was a contemporary of Maier, had included a somewhat different version of the same conflict in *The Principall Navigations, Voyages, Traffiques and Discoveries of the English Nation*, issued in 1588. In this 'prose epic of the English nation' the relation occurs in a quaint and attractive form as part of an account of a voyage to Guinea 'in the yere 1554, the Captaine whereof was M. John Lok':

Elephants—which rather surprisingly 'are made tame by drinking the juise of barley'—'have continual warre against Dragons, which desire their blood, because it is very cold: and therfore the Dragon lying awaite as the Elephant passeth by, windeth his taile (being of exceeding length) about the hinder legs of the Elephant, & so staying him, thrusteth his head into his tronke and exhausteth his breath, or else biteth him in the eare, wherunto he cannot reach with his tronke, and when the Elephant waxeth fainte, he falleth downe on the serpent, being now full of blood, and with the poise of his body breaketh him: so that his owne blood with the blood of the Elephant runneth out of him mingled together, which being colde, is congealed into that substance which the Apothecaries call Sanguis Draconis, (that is) Dragons blood, otherwise called Cinnabaris, although there be an other kinde of Cinnabaris, commonly called Cinoper or Vermilion, which the Painters use in certaine colours. . . . Of other properties & conditions of the Elephant . . . who so desireth to know, let him reade Plinie, in the eighth booke of his naturall history.'

ALCHEMICAL ALLEGORY 'À LA MODE'

There are striking similarities between Michael Maier and the so-called Basil Valentine, the 'Mighty King' of alchemy, who seems to have been a contemporary writer. Basil Valentine was an exponent of the theory of the *tria prima*, or three principles of sulphur, mercury, and salt, which is usually linked with the name of Philippus Aureolus Theophrastus Paracelsus (1493–1541): this expansion of the sulphur-mercury theory, although nominally demolished by the Honourable Robert Boyle in *The Sceptical Chymist* (1661), lingered on to the time of Lavoisier in the late eighteenth century.

Both Maier and Valentine delighted in bizarre emblems and extravagant conceptions; but Brother Basilius, unlike the musical Count, often gave clear and genuine working directions for laboratory operations of great interest, notably in his *Triumphal Chariot of Antimony*. Upon occasion, however, this enigmatical 'Monke of the Order of St. Bennet' could indulge in fantasies of the wildest and most ludicrous kind. As an example, in an introduction to his celebrated *Twelve Keys*, an illustrated work which purports to unlock the doors barring access to the Philosopher's Stone, he gathers a number of eminent patrons of 'the Divine Art' to take part in a kind of Garden Party of Alchemical Mad Hatters and the like, and the account of their freakish proceedings forms one of the most extraordinary episodes in the vast literature of alchemy.[1]

The alchemical imagination was so active, so quick to interpret its limited stock of ideas in every conceivable medium, that a latter-day alchemist might well be credited

[1] *Prelude*, 198.

with having recourse to that modern microcosm of life, cricket, and devising a series of Alchemical Test Matches, with the aim of bringing the leading exponents of his craft effectively into the public eye. A typical report of such a contest might run as follows:

HERMES TRISMEGISTOS' XI *v.* THE REST

Played on the Ark. Noah lost the toss. HERMES THE THRICE-GREAT won it for the third time running in these contests.

An eventful game ended in a win for the visitors by 13 runs. These were scored by HERMES THE THRICE-GREAT, who also finished off the match in 3 balls, symbolising the *tria prima*.

Scores:—
HERMES TRISMEGISTOS' XI

Fr. B. Valentine, not out .	101	(taken to the pavilion in the Triumphal Chariot)
Count M. Maier, c Minerva b Pythagoras . .	50	(canons)
HERMES TRISMEGISTOS (capt.), c & b Aphrodite .	13	(precepts)
Shem, st Noah b Moses .	6	(for lost ball—rolled off the Ark)
Atalanta, c Hippomenes b Aphrodite. . .	3	(golden apples)
Aristotle, c Lavoisier b Boyle . . .	4	(elements)
P. A. T. Paracelsus, c Lavoisier b Boyle .	3	(the *tria prima*)
Hercules, lbw b Jupiter .	36	(in one six-ball over—thereafter effective work by Umpire Ham)
Fr. B. Schwarz, retired hurt	0	(oiled his bat with nitroglycerine)
T. Norton, absent . .	0	(in search of the Red Lion)
Cleopatra, did not bat .	0	(exceeded time limit in coming out: pavilion mirror taken away by Aphrodite)
Extras: byes (due to planetary influence) . .	7	
Total .	223	

The Rest

Jupiter, c & b Cleopatra .	4	(signature number)
Pythagoras, c & b Cleopatra	10	(the tetractinal $1 + 2 + 3 + 4$)
Noah (capt.), c & b Cleopatra	6	(for lost ball)
Osiris, c & b Cleopatra .	6	(for lost ball)
Neptune, retired . .	6	(for lost ball: went overboard after 3 lost balls, and exceeded time limit in surfacing)
Aphrodite, run out . .	99	(fast work by Atalanta)
Hippomenes, run out .	0	(fast work by Atalanta)
Minerva, st Paracelsus b Hermes . . .	61	(the Thrice-Great's first ball)
A. L. Lavoisier, not out .	0	(obsessed by O-theory and thus failed to score)
Hon. R. Boyle, st Paracelsus b Hermes . . .	0	(the Thrice-Great's second ball)
Moses, st Paracelsus b Hermes	0	(the Thrice-Great's third ball, completing the usual hat trick —Solomon umpiring at square leg)
Extras: wides (due to Cleopatra losing pace and direction against Aphrodite and Minerva)	18	
Total .	210	

Umpires: Solomon (nominated by Hermes Trismegistos)
Ham (nominated by Noah)
Scorers: Bacon (R.), (Somerset)
Bacon (F.), (Middlesex)

Such a latter-day son of Hermes as we have envisaged would not scruple to exalt the glory of his patron by adding an extra precept (borrowed from Andrew Lang without acknowledgment) to the Emerald Table:

The Fourteenth Precept of Hermes Trismegistos, the Thrice-Great

I am the batsman and the bat,
I am the bowler and the ball,
The umpire, the pavilion cat,
The roller, pitch, and stumps, and all.

4. A Transcription from *Atalanta Fugiens*, by Sir Isaac Newton. (See p. 8.)

From the original MS.

5. 'Fire loves to Fire, but Gold it maketh not.'

Emblem XVIII from *Secretioris Naturae Secretorum Scrutinium Chymicum*. M. Maier, Frankfurt, 1687 (reprinted from *Atalanta Fugiens*, M. Maier, Oppenheim, 1618). (See p. 9.)

SANGVINIS DRACONIS DESCRIPTIO.

6. The Origin of Dragon's Blood.

From *Viatorium*, M. Maier, Oppenheim, 1618. (See p. 11.)

References

Festugière, A. J., 'L'Hermétisme et l'Alchimie', in *La Révélation d'Hermès Trismégiste*, Paris, 1944.

Hakluyt, R., *The Principall Navigations, Voyages, Traffiques and Discoveries of the English Nation*, with an introduction by J. Masefield, 8 vols., Everyman's Library, London and New York.

Maier, M., *Atalanta Fugiens*, Oppenheim, 1618.

Idem.   *Viatorium*, Oppenheim, 1618.

Read, J., *Prelude to Chemistry* 2nd edn., London, 1939.

CHAPTER II

A FLYING ALCHEMIST

In mediaeval times the kings and princes of western Europe often attached alchemists and astrologers to their courts. Early in the thirteenth century, for example, the celebrated Michael Scot became court astrologer and philosopher to the Emperor Frederick II in Sicily. Frederick II was a patron of learning, with a strong interest in the science of his day, and Michael Scot was a veritable Wizard of the North, who achieved fame in Spain and Italy as a master of Latin learning, of Hebrew, and of Arabic. In most of these instances, however, the princes were actuated by avarice and credulity, rather than by an intelligent interest in science; and the court astrologers and alchemists were charlatans, who achieved a precarious livelihood—and sometimes an untimely death—by imposing upon the credulity of their employers in the matter of goldmaking, or multiplying. Alchemy became identified in the popular mind with goldmaking, and fell gradually into disrepute by reason of the wild claims and fruitless activities of the puffers and impostors.

A ROYAL ROAD TO RESEARCH

Of the more intelligent princes of this period, whose interest in alchemy was not solely mercenary, James IV, King of Scotland from 1488 to 1513, furnishes a worthy example (Fig. 7). Although James was not above trying to turn an honest penny, or to achieve spectacular cures by alchemical means, he must be regarded, according to the standard of his day, as an enlightened amateur of science. He had an active and enquiring mind, and, like Frederick II, sought to extend his knowledge by observation and experiment. His

interests included medicine and surgery, physiology, alchemy, and even psychology.

Thus, dabbling in physiology, James arranged for a
pair of united twins, born in Scotland during his reign, to be
brought up at the court, under his notice. 'In this meane
tyme thair was ane great marwell sene in Scottland', wrote
the celebrated chronicler, Lindesay of Pitscottie; '. . . the
kingis maiestie gart [caused] tak great cure [care] and
deliegence wpoun the wpbringing of thir two bodyis in ane
personage, gart nurische them and leir [teach] them to pley
and singe wpon the instrumentis of musick quho [who]
war become in schort tyme werie ingeneous and cunning in
the art of musick quhairby [whereby] they could pleay and
singe tuo pairtis, the on[e] the tribill the wther the tennour
quhilk [which] was werie dulse and melodious'.

In the realm of psychology, James's experimental *tour
de force* dealt in a very direct way with the problem of that
'primitive tongue' which Ben Jonson, in a jocular mood,
supposed to be High Dutch.[1]   Lindesay of Pitscottie gives
an account of this historic experiment, started in 1493:

'The king gart tak ane dum woman and pat hir in
Inchekeytht [Inchkeith island in the Firth of Forth] and
gaif hir tua zoung bairnes [two young children] in companie
witht hir and gart furnische them of . . meit, drink, fyre and
candell, claithis [clothes], witht all wther kynd of necessaris
. . . desyrand [desiring] . . . to knaw quhat langage thir
bairnes wald speik quhene they came to lauchfull aige. Sum
sayis they spak goode hebrew bot as to my self I knaw not
bot be [except by] the authoris reherse [narration].'

According to the canny Lindesay, James IV was well
learned in the art of medicine and was also a cunning surgeon.
The generous monarch, in his eagerness to secure practical
experience in surgery and dentistry, reversed the normal
procedure, and paid fees to his patients. Thus, an entry in
the accounts of the Lord High Treasurer of Scotland, in
1491, runs as follows: 'Item, to Domynico, to gif the King
leve to lat him blud, xviijs'. That the King also indulged
in dental practice is shown by an entry of 9 February

[1] *Prelude*, 39.

1511/12, noting the payment of 14*s*. to 'ane fallow, because the King pullit furtht his tootht'. These official accounts also contain many entries of grants made by James to various physicians; they show also that he was in the habit of laying in considerable stocks of medicaments and also of materials for alchemical experiments.

It is likely that James IV's excursions into alchemy were determined largely by his interest in medicine, because of the potent medicinal virtues which were ascribed at that time to the Philosopher's Stone. This, the ultimate goal of alchemy, viewed in the light of the doctrine of the unity of all things, was pictured not only as a transmuting agent for the perfecting of base metals into gold, but also as an infallible remedy for the ills of imperfect man.

The medicinal and rejuvenating effects sometimes ascribed to the Stone were perhaps inspired by the physiological action of that marvellous spirit of wine which was often regarded as the perfect solvent for the Stone, in the preparation of the Elixir of Life. 'The patient shall think he is no longer a man, but a spirit', wrote Isaac of Holland, referring to the rejuvenating action of the Stone, or Elixir. 'He shall feel as if he were nine days in Paradise, and living on its fruits.'

SCOTLAND'S FIRST RESEARCH LABORATORY

James IV's chief associate in his alchemical studies and experiments was a certain John Damian, an ingenious and personable foreigner who had been attracted to the Scottish court from either Italy or France. Damian included a practical knowledge of medicine and alchemy among his numerous accomplishments: 'in pottingry he wrocht grit pyne', wrote William Dunbar, referring to his prowess in the art of the apothecary. Under Damian's inspiration and direction James established an alchemical laboratory in Stirling Castle, which, incidentally, was the King's birthplace. Considerable sums of money were needed to sustain these activities, and Damian figures repeatedly in the contemporary accounts of the Lord High Treasurer of Scotland under such names as 'the Franch leich' and 'Franch Maister

Johne'. These references date from 1501, in which year alchemical experiments were already in progress, and the King and Damian had become so intimate as to play cards together.

It appears from these accounts that, quite apart from the cost of his furnaces, apparatus and materials, and the wages of his 'ministers', an alchemist was an expensive adjunct to a mediaeval court.[1] Thus, in February 1501/02, 'Maister Johne' was provided with garments befitting his position, at a total cost of £22 : 16s. The separate items were: a long damask gown lined with lambskin, £15 : 16s.; 'London scarlat to be tua [two] pair of hos', £3; and 'wellus [velvet] to be brekis [short hose]', £4. Among other disbursements made at this time on behoof of Maister Johne were 24s. for linen sheets, 18s. for a pair of blankets, and further sums for a Kentdale frieze and a tapestried bed. Moreover, beyond the running expenses of his researches, our 'Franch leich' drew frequent sums 'be the Kingis command' for unspecified purposes: the total amount which he absorbed in this way during the six months following 26 August 1503 exceeded £150.

At about this time the King married Margaret Tudor, daughter of Henry VII of England. This important event, which led to the union of the English and Scottish crowns a hundred years later, took place amidst great rejoicings, mirrored by William Dunbar in his poem 'The Thistle and the Rose'. The King was then in his thirty-first year, his youthful bride only in her fourteenth. Hitherto, the King had taken great pride in his remarkably fine and ample beard; but on 9 August 1503, the day after his marriage, there is an entry in the Lord High Treasurer's accounts recording an honorarium paid to the English Countess of Surrey and her daughter, Lady Gray, when they 'clippit the Kingis berd'. This was apparently done, in the absence of the rejuvenating principle of the quinta essencia, in an attempt to reduce the difference in years between the King

---

[1] It is notably a matter of great difficulty to correlate the currencies of different eras. A multiple of 3 or 4 may be applied in order to convey a rough idea of the modern (1938) equivalents of the costs here set out.

and his bride. The removal of the royal beard was almost as costly as the pursuit of the Philosopher's Stone, for the two fair barbresses received an honorarium, paid in cloth of gold and damask gold, of no less than £510.

A little later, a significant entry occurs in the accounts, under date 12 March 1503/04: 'Item, payit, be the Kingis command, to Bardus Altovite, Lumbard, for Maister Johne, the Franch medicinar, new maid Abbot of Tungland, quilk he aucht [owed] to the said Bardus, xxv*li*. [£25]'. This brief note, in the Treasurer's prim and precise phraseology, records a dramatic move by the King, who had transmuted his alchemist into an abbot in order to endow him with an emolument and provide him with the necessary leisure for his alchemical projects.

The new ecclesiastical dignitary preferred the smells of his laboratory to the odour of sanctity, and feared the effects of the laboratory smoke upon religious vestments which were far more costly than his alchemical garb; for William Dunbar, the poet, who had cast longing eyes upon the vacant appointment at Tungland, in Galloway, wrote acidly of the Abbot:

> Unto no mess pressit this prelat,
> For sound of sacring bell nor skellat.[1] . . .
> On him come nowthir stole nor fannoun,[2]
> Ffor smowking of the smydy.

The Lord High Treasurer's accounts show that the new prelate was indeed very active during the next few years in the laboratory at Stirling Castle; but it seems that the adequate leisure appertaining to his appointment was accompanied by a less adequate emolument. Such an inference may perhaps be drawn from a plaintive entry of 27 July 1507, referring to a sum of £33 : 6s. 8d.: 'Item, lent, be the Kingis command, to the Abbot of Tungland and can nocht be gottin fra him'.

The expenses incurred for the actual materials which Damian used for alchemical and medicinal purposes must have reached an impressive total, especially as many of them

---

[1] Little bell.
[2] Scarf worn on the left arm of a priest officiating at mass.

had to be fetched from abroad. For example, on 30 May 1502 the 'Franch leich' was given a sum of 300 French crowns, equivalent to £210 in Scots money, to cover the expenses of a visit to the Continent in connection with his work.

The accounts of the Lord High Treasurer of Scotland from 1501 to 1513 throw some interesting light upon the nature and cost of the specific materials which Damian and his associates used in their attempts to prepare the quinta essencia, or Quintessence. The precise information here recorded is indeed of exceptional value, since the alchemists were invariably secretive regarding their materials, apparatus, and running expenses. So pronounced was their reticence in these matters that a mere glance at a pictorial representation of an alchemical interior by such an artist as Brueghel, Stradanus, or Teniers often affords a better idea of the equipment and operations of these early laboratories than can be gathered from an exhaustive examination of dozens of written expositions of alchemy and its reputed achievements.

As a rule, the term 'quinta essencia', as used in these accounts, may be taken to denote either the Philosopher's Stone or the related Elixir of Life; but upon occasion it seems to be used as a slightly mocking nickname for Damian. According to the general dictates of alchemical theory, the 'primitive materials' regarded as essential for the operations of the Great Work, or preparation of the Stone, were usually gold, silver, and quicksilver. All of these find a place in the accounts of James IV's treasurer.

Gold was provided chiefly in the form of gold coins, such as the four 'Hary nobles' which were sent 'to the leich for to multiply' on 3 March 1501/02, and the four ducats of gold, valued at 76s., contributed by the King 'to put in to the quinta essencia' in October and November 1512. 'Brint silvir', costing 14s. an ounce, was possibly silver which had been purified for the Great Work by cupellation. Quicksilver was used in quantities which show that it was fairly easy to obtain, and that it played an important part in the operations. The 5 pounds entered on 20 February 1502/03 cost 20s.; and a further 25½ pounds was sent to Stirling, 'to mak quinta essencia thare', about a month later.

Another material consumed in large quantities by the alchemists of Stirling appears in the accounts under the name of 'aqua vite'. This term, in Scotland, probably meant whisky at that time, since the Exchequer Rolls of 1494/95 show that a certain pioneer of the Scottish distilling industry, known as Friar John Cor, was supplied with eight bolls of malt for making aqua vitae. The preparation of strong alcohol by the repeated distillation of wine and other fermented liquors was a well-known process at the beginning of the sixteenth century: thus, the title-pages of Brunschwick's *Liber de arte Distillandi de Compositis* (Strassburg, 1507) and *Das Buch zu distillieren* (Strassburg, 1519) bear a woodcut illustrating the use of a water-cooled 'serpent', or primitive fractionating column, for this purpose (Fig. 8).

The physiological properties of strong alcohol made a great impression upon the early alchemists who handled and investigated it. 'The taste of it', wrote the pseudo-Lully in his enthusiasm, 'exceedeth all other tastes, and the smell of it all other smells.' It was prepared from living material, capable of germination and growth; moreover, it appeared to combine the properties of the opposed elements, fire and water, or sulphur and mercury.[1] In alcohol, the alchemists beheld a combination of fire with its ancient enemy, water. The alchemical lion had lain down with the lamb. The two contraries had at last become reconciled. To certain mystics this squaring of the alchemical circle betokened the approaching end of the world. Thus, spirit of wine which had reached 'myche hignes of glorificacioun' by distillation 'unto a thousand times' was identified by some of the alchemists with the Elixir of Life, quinta essencia, or 'mannys hevene'. The Abbot of Tungland's interest in aqua vitae is easily understandable by the student of alchemy, if not indeed by others.

Although in the strange Scotland of James IV whisky

---

[1] In burning, it thus separates again into fire and water. In the era of phlogiston, alcohol was similarly regarded as a compound of phlogiston and water.

7. James IV of Scotland.
(See p. 16.)

8. Distillation of Spirit of Wine in the time of James IV.

From the title-page of *Das Buch zu Distillieren*, H. Brunschwick, Strassburg, 1519.

(See p. 22.)

must have been a rare drug reserved mainly for medicinal purposes, Damian and his collaborators were able to secure and find uses for surprisingly large amounts of it. An early entry of 10 March 1502/03 records the application of 'aqua vite to the curyis [researches] of quinta essencia'. Later entries show that it was procurable in various strengths: in June 1508 'David, barbour' sent six quarts of 'aqua vite thryis drawin' to Stirling at a cost of £3 : 12s., and a gallon of 'small aqua vite to the Abbot of Tungland' is entered at 24s.

The small aqua vitae cost 6s. a quart, the ordinary 8s., and the thrice-drawn (possibly known also as 'mannys hevene') 12s. Still another source of the magic fluid is recorded in an entry of 13 October 1507, when £6 was paid 'for ane punschioun of wyne to the Abbot of Tungland to mak quinta essencia'; but whether this raw material was devoted wholly to the Great Work or partly to 'the refreshment of wearied Servants of Laboratories' is not clear from the Treasurer's accounts.

The wine of those days was obtainable in puncheons of different sizes, and, like the aqua vitae, in various qualities. The brethren of St. Andrews, judging from an entry of 19 March 1505/06, were less successful than the Abbot of Tungland in arranging for the conjunction of a good wine with a generous container; for a mere trifle of 35s. was paid 'for ane punschioun of wyne to the chanons of Sanctandrois, be the Kingis command'. It is only fair to the King to add that the St. Andrews puncheon was delivered carriage paid at the door, for the succeeding entry records a disbursement of 8d. 'for carying the samyn fra the toun to the Abbay'.

Reliable data concerning the cost of specific and serious attempts to prepare the Philosopher's Stone are so exceedingly rare that it is of interest to summarise some of the information embodied in the accounts of the Lord High Treasurer of Scotland during the period of Damian's researches. The appended list gives, in contemporary Scots money,[1] the prices of certain alchemical materials

[1] See footnote, p. 19.

D

and apparatus used in Scotland between 1501 and 1508. Items marked with an asterisk are taken from painters' expenses, except sulphur, which was bought as an ingredient of gunpowder. The prices were liable to fluctuation: alum, for example, cost 7*d*. per lb. at one time and about 11½*d*. on a later occasion.

Prices of Alchemical Materials and Apparatus in Scotland 1501–08, in contemporary Scots Money

	£	s.	d.
Alchemists' attire:			
damask gown	15	16	0
velvet short hose.................	4	0	0
scarlet hose	1	10	0
Alembic, silver, 10¾ oz. (bos hed to ane stellatour).........................	6	19	9
Alum (allum)......................			7 lb.
Aqua vitae (aqua vite):			
small.............................		6	0 quart
ordinary..........................		8	0 quart
thrice-drawn		12	0 quart
Bellows, small (bellisses)...............		1	0
Cauldrons, 18 gallons..................	1	1	0
*Cinnabar (synaper)		16	0 lb.
Flasks, large glass (gret flacatis).........		4	0
and		6	8
Flasks, small glass (urinales)............		2	0
Glass, cakes of.......................		5	0
Gold	6	10	0 oz.
*Linseed oil (oly lingeat)		8	0 quart
Litharge (litargiri auri)................		5	0 lb.
*Mastic (masticot).....................		4	0 lb.
Mortar, metal, 53 lbs.	3	9	0
Mortar, brass, with pestle (brassin mortar with pestell)........................	1	0	0
*Orpiment (orpement)		6	0 lb.
Pitchers, earthenware (pecharis)			4½
and		1	3
Pots, large earthenware (pottis of lame)..		1	0
Quicksilver (quyk silvir)...............		4	0 lb.
*Red lead (rede lede)		2	6 lb.
Sal ammoniac (sal aramomakle).........	1	15	0 lb.
Saltpetre (sal-petir)			3 oz.

	s.	d.	
Silver (brint silvir)	14	0	oz.
Silver, wrought	13	0	oz.
Sugar (succour)	1	6	lb.
*Sulphur (bryntstane)	8	0	stone
Tin (fyne tyn)	1	2	lb.
*Verdigris (varngreis)	6	0	lb.
*Vermilion (vermeloun)	6	0	lb.
Vinegar (vinakir)	4	0	gallon
*White lead (quhit lede)	2	0	lb.

The materials and apparatus for the work in the Stirling laboratory were often supplied to Maister Alexander Ogilvy, also described as 'doctour', who was evidently an active participant in the operations. Another name which occurs frequently in the accounts is that of the Captain of Stirling Castle, Andrew Ayton. Caldwell, the keeper of the furnaces, received a wage of a shilling a day. These furnaces were in constant operation; fuel for heating them, and the wages of the laboratory staff who attended to the firing, etc., figure prominently in the accounts. Thus, on 'the penult day of March' in the year 1503 'ane boy that kepit the furnes fire' (Fig. 9) received 6s. 8d. 'be the Kingis command'. The fuels mentioned are charcoal, wood, peat, and coal.

In 1506 the laboratory staff was augmented by the temporary appointment of 'ane Johne Balbyrny', who was paid £3 : 10s. for 'keping of the furnes for quinta essencia' for a space of ten weeks, ending in November: his wage was thus the same as Caldwell's. Even the smith of Cambuskenneth was pressed into the service of the all-absorbing quinta essencia: among several items in which he is mentioned there is one, dated 22 December 1507, in which a payment of 14s. is noted 'to the smyth of Cambuskenneth for making of ane irne kist [iron chest] for quinta essencia'.

This historic laboratory was the first to find any mention in the annals of Scotland. Its situation in Stirling Castle—a fortress built upon a steep and dominating crag—was both secure and picturesque. In appearance and equipment it was probably very similar to the laboratory depicted by

Hans Weiditz in his spirited woodcut of about twenty years
later.   There are many references in the accounts to the
apparatus and equipment of Damian's laboratory, some of
which find mention in the summary given above.   There
were metal mortars of various sizes, large cauldrons, and
apparatus made of earthenware or glass.   Earthenware was
cheap, since pots were obtained at 1s. and pitchers at 4½d. and

9. 'Ane boy that kepit the furnes fire.'   A furnace and stills with Rosenhut
condensers.   From *Das Buch zu Distillieren*, H. Brunschwick, Strassburg, 1519

1s. 3d. each.   Glass was much more expensive: five 'cakes'
of glass were bought for 25s., large flasks for 4s. to 6s. 8d.,
and small ones for 16d. to 2s. each.   These last, known as
'urinales', were used in large numbers, being the alchemical
equivalent of the test-tube: for example, seven were entered
on 8 February 1505/06, and twenty-four more a week later.

These were all common pieces of apparatus; but there
must have been great excitement in the Stirling Castle
laboratory on 28 July 1508, when the equipment was
brought thoroughly up to date by the addition of a silver

helm, or alembic, at a cost of nearly £7. This 'bos hed to ane stellatour of silvir weyand x unce iij quartaris of his aun stuf', was made by Matho Aucklek, the King's goldsmith in Stirling, and delivered 'to Maister Alexander Ogilvy for quinta essencia', at a cost of 13s. per ounce.

The normal personnel of the laboratory apparently consisted of Damian as director, with Ogilvy as his chief assistant, supplemented at times by one 'Johne Mosman, potingair in Strivelin'. The head of the laboratory staff was Caldwell, the keeper of the furnaces. Other 'ministers' included occasional helpers, such as John Balbirnie; there were also interested amateurs, among them Andrew Ayton, the Captain of the Castle, who were pleased to lend a hand at odd times. The laboratory boys, 'that kepit the furnes fire', fetched fuel, and performed other minor duties, were well to the fore; as in later days, they were of a tautomeric disposition, the accounts indicating that this section of the staff was subject to sudden changes in composition.

Doubtless this laboratory, in which such portentous operations were being conducted, was provided with the mediaeval equivalent of a 'Keep Out' notice; but there were occasional privileged visitors. It is certain that the King came in frequently, to enquire after the quinta essencia and to take part in the work; for it is unimaginable that this inquisitive and active monarch, who took so much delight in acquiring practical experience of all kinds, would be content to play a passive rôle in exercises so intriguing as those of an alchemical laboratory. Possibly, indeed, various unexplained payments to Damian were requitements for the privilege of helping in the alchemical operations—a kind of alchemical drinksilver (transmuted of course into gold)—just as on 7 February 1507/08 a payment of 14s. was made 'to the smyth quhar the King straik at the stedy [anvil] in Leith'.

THE POTINGAIR OF SANCTANDROIS

In July of 1506 the Stirling Castle laboratory welcomed one who may be claimed as the mediaeval forerunner of the St. Andrews school of chemistry. Skilled in the distillation of 'waters' perfumed with essential oils, and also in the primitive 'succour' [sugar] chemistry of those times, he was the unwitting prototype of the St. Andrews research chemists of a later era. Looking back to those far-away days, we may dimly picture the worthy Broun, master potingair [apothecary] of Sanctandrois, emerging through the Swallow Port on a summer forenoon in 1506, with a led packhorse carrying his precious potingaries. Master Broun had been patronised by the King in the foregoing spring, with results so satisfying that a royal call to Stirling followed. Spending a couple of days on the painful journey of some fifty miles, he passes at last over the high arch of the Auld Brigg of Striveling, and puts a stout heart to the stey brae leading up to the Castle. In this lofty eyrie, perched on its rock high above the town, he enters the secret den of the Abbot of Tungland, where he unpacks his wares and enlists the good offices of Caldwell, the grimy Vulcan of that 'smowking smydy'.

10. A Scottish Alchemist. From the Erskine alchemical MSS. (early 17th century)

What like (to adopt the local idiom) was this worthy potingair of Sanctandrois? His portrait was not—like that of Margaret Tudor —painted by Mabuse; but we may surmise that he was not vastly different in appearance from an intriguing and somewhat wistful figure shown in one of the alchemical manuscripts of Sir George Erskine of Innertiel (Fig. 10). How long he stayed in Scotland's first research laboratory, and what feats of skill he 'wrocht in pottingry', may be assessed to some extent from contemporary entries in the Lord High Treasurer's accounts. On 3 July 1506 there is an entry of 27s. 'to the potingair of Sanctandrois to remane in Strivelin to still wateris'; a second expenditure of 11s. appears under the same date

'to by him stuf at nedit to him'. On 20 July two gallons
of vinegar are entered for 8s. and four pounds of sugar for
6s. Six days later the potingair of Sanctandrois is credited
with £6, 'be the Kingis command'; and in the following
month he obtains two pounds of sugar for 3s. 'to mak
conserva of borage'.

Potingair Broun's repeated use of sugar at so early a
date is an interesting detail. Sugar seems to have first
appeared in Scotland in 1319, in the form of sugar-loaves,
costing 1s. 9½d. per lb. A coarser kind was later imported
in barrels from Italy, Cyprus, and Egypt. Alexandria was
known for its coloured sugars. The chief use of sugar in
mediaeval Europe was for sweetening and softening the
acid wines of those days.

To what extent the worthy potingair's materials were
used in the quest of quinta essencia is not disclosed; but
when he appears for the last time, some four years later
(23 November 1511), at home in St. Andrews, he is revealed
as an unequivocal apothecary, supplying the King with
expensive remedies for a disordered royal stomach: to wit,
a pound of diambra at 48s. and a pound of dragalanga at
16s. At this point the quick curtain falls upon this indispensable dispenser of mediaeval St. Andrews, leaving us
to hope that he lived long and prosperously at the sign of
'The Goldin Pestell' by the Swallow Gate, concocting
soothing remedies, fragrant 'wateris', and sugary confections
for the proud ecclesiastics and nobles, the learned regents and
doctors, the scarlet-gowned scholars, and the solid burgesses
who trod the narrow wynds and cobbled ways of the old
grey city at the beginning of the sixteenth century.

'AIR CRASH IN SIXTEENTH CENTURY'

The Abbot of Tungland's attempts to achieve transmutation suffered an interruption in 1507, after some six
years' experimentation, as a result of another spectacular
activity of this versatile man. His ingenious mind was wont
to stray beyond matters medical, alchemical, or ecclesiastical,
in order to dwell upon the possibilities of artificial flight.
Here again, sharing his august master's habit of mind, he

resolved to put his ideas to the test of experiment. Why
he suddenly turned from alchemy to flying is not evident;
but other specialists in chemistry have been known to
undergo equally unexpected transitions in more modern
times. Possibly he grew tired of 'ever climbing up the
climbing wave' of unsuccessful alchemical experimentation;
perhaps in the course of his alchemical reading he had come
across Roger Bacon's confident prediction of flying machines
that should traverse the air.

The considerations that determined the unique form of
Damian's demonstration are also unknown. Since his
alchemical experiments were conducted in the security and
secrecy afforded by Stirling Castle, the lofty battlements of
this fortress (Fig. 11) would become a natural taking-off
ground for his flying. Perhaps, too, he was familiar with
the legend of Michael Scot's ambassadorial flight through
the skies from Scotland to Paris on a magic black horse,
to fulfil an important mission with the French king.

Whatever the dominating motives may have been,
Damian's courageous attempt to take off from the heights of
Stirling Castle for a flight to Paris constituted the first
serious flying experiment ever made in Scotland, if not,
indeed, in the whole history of experimental flight. His
bold conception was modelled upon bird flight, with movable
wings, and the courageous executive attempt is described as
follows by Bishop Lesley, in a manuscript history of the
period which he gave to Mary Queen of Scots in 1571:

'The xxvij day of September [1507] the Archebischopp
of Sanct Androis and the Erle of Arrane wer send ambassadouris to the King of France, and past be sey [passed
by sea], for obteaning of certane privilegeis for the commone
weill of the realme, speciallie towart the garde and gentlemen
of armes in France, and the weill of merchantis.

'This tyme thair wes ane Italiane with the King, quha
[who] wes maid Abbott of Tungland, and wes of curious
ingyne. He causet the King believe that he, be multi-
plyinge and utheris his inventions, wold make fine golde of
uther mettall, quhilk science he callit the quintassence;
quhairupon the King maid greit cost, bot all in vaine. This

11. Stirling Castle.
Drawn by G. F. Robson.   Engraved by E. Findon.

Abbott tuik in hand to flie with wingis, and to be in Fraunce befoir the saidis ambassadouris; and to that effect he causet mak ane pair of wingis of fedderis [feathers], quhilkis beand fessinit apoun him [which being fastened upon him], he flew of the castell wall of Striveling [Stirling], bot shortlie he fell to the ground and brak his thee bane [thigh bone]; bot the wyt thairof he asscryvit [ascribed] to that thair was sum hen fedderis in the wingis, quhilk yarnit [yearned] and covet the mydding and not the skyis.'

If this historic venture took place on or about 27 September 1507, as Bishop Lesley's account suggests, it was doubtless witnessed by the King: the court moved from Edinburgh to Stirling on 21 September 1507, and on 27 September the friars of Stirling brought the King a gift of pears and plums. That James would have missed the spectacle of his alchemist-abbot taking off from the battlements of Stirling Castle for a non-stop flight to Paris is inconceivable; moreover, had the attempt succeeded, it is easy to picture the impetuous monarch ordering 'ane pair of wingis of fedderis' for himself and challenging his flying favourite to an air-race.

Judging from his explanation of the mishap, it seems that the alchemical airman had accepted a tender for wings made entirely of eagles' feathers, which would, in his opinion, have had a natural longing to soar into the skies. Apparently, however, the unscrupulous or uncomprehending contractor, finding eagles' feathers scarce, had turned to the homely hen to eke out his raw material and feather his own nest. The base feathers of the lowly fowl, because of their hankering after the middens frequented by their former owners, were thus the obvious cause of this 'air-crash' of the early sixteenth century (Fig. 12). The intrepid Abbot's idea of hens' feathers having an affinity with middens, and those of eagles with the skies, bears the impress of the doctrine of signatures,[1] and is also in keeping with the conception of sympathy, as entertained later by Sir Kenelm Digby and others.

William Dunbar celebrated this incident with unnecessary

[1] *Prelude*, 97.

but amusing gusto in a satirical poem entitled 'The Fenyeit
Freir of Tungland, how he fell in the myre fleand to Turki-

12. Alchemy in the Modern Press (1932)

land'. There is some soul of poetry in all good alchemists
and chemists, who will therefore appreciate the force, if
not the language,[1] of Dunbar's spirited lines:

[1] *Fenyeit*, feigned; *freir*, friar; *seir fassonis he assailyeit*, he tried various
fashions; *failyeit*, failed; *nocht*, naught; *fedrem*, a coat of feathers with wings; *schupe*,
tried; *schewre*, tore, or shore; *schene*, bright; *glar*, mud, or dirt; *dirkit*, darkened;
come, came; *zawmeris and zowlis*, yammers and yowls; *walknit*, wakened.

Me thocht seir fassonis he assailyeit,
To mak the quintessance, and failyeit;
And quhen he saw that nocht availyeit,
    A fedrem on he tuke,
And schupe in Turky for to fle. . . .

He schewre his feddreme that was schene,
And slippit owt of it full clene,
And in a myre, up to the ene,
    Amang the glar did glyd.

In pursuing his theme, the poet describes with great relish how the fowls of the air made mock of this clumsy intruder into their element:

The air was dirkit with the fowlis,
That come with zawmeris and with zowlis,
With skryking, skrymming and with scowlis,
    To tak him in the tyde.
I walknit with the noyis and schowte,
So hiddowis beir was me abowte;
Sensyne I curss that cankerit rowte
    Quhair evir I go or ryde.

                 Ffinis quod Dumbar

Men are apt to suspect, and even to fear and hate, what they do not understand. It is often the lot of the bold pioneer and venturer, both in the realms of thought and action, to be treated with contumely and derision by men of lesser faith and vision. Notwithstanding contemporary jibes, and the later condemnation of Damian as an arch-impostor, anybody who has peered over the battlements of Stirling Castle will agree that the man of metals was also a man of mettle, endowed with the courage of his convictions, and deserving of the lucky star which had let him down with nothing worse than a broken thigh-bone. To evaluate the achievements of mediaeval experimentalists is even more difficult than to express mediaeval prices of labour and materials in modern currencies. Judged by the standards of his day and generation, Damian appears to have been an enterprising and enlightened exponent of the experimental method in science.

The unsuccessful court alchemist often received short shrift from his disappointed patron; but the broad-minded Scottish king, comprehending Damian's sincerity of purpose, and knowing from his own experience that experiments 'gang aft agley', treated him with characteristic generosity. By this time, indeed, the King had admitted his alchemist-in-chief to a degree of friendship which must have appealed particularly to a specialist in the art of multiplying gold. They played cards, dice, and other games together, and a scrutiny of the Lord High Treasurer's accounts shows that the stakes were wont to run unusually high when the King played with the Abbot. Contests of this kind seem to have been particularly frequent during the Abbot's convalescence, whilst the broken 'thee bane' was healing.

On 12 November 1507 the King lost £4 : 4s. 'at the cartis with the Abbot of Tungland'; on 18 December following he lost £6 : 12s.; and the night before he had lost £4 : 18s. to the Abbot 'at the hasard of dis [dice]'. On 2 March 1507/08, playing at the Irish game, a kind of backgammon, with 'the Erle of Ergile eftir none', the King lost 29s.; but 'that samyn nycht' playing 'eftir soupir with the Abbot of Tungland', he lost 42s. There were also trials of practical skill, such as that of 15 April 1508, when 'the King schot in the hall of Strivelin and tynt [lost] with the Abbot of Tungland, xxviijs.' These entries do not necessarily indicate that the King never won, since the accounts deal only with disbursements; but the frequent debit items suggest that he lost steadily and royally.

Judging from the Treasurer's records, work proceeded apace in the Stirling laboratory during the first half of 1508. Then, on 8 September 1508, 'Damian, Abbot of Tungland, obtained from the King a licence to pass out of the realm and remain in what place he pleases at the study, or any lawful occupation during the space of five years'. The object of the Abbot's travels is not specified, but it may be inferred that he had planned a visit to some of the Continental centres of alchemical activity, in order to gather new inspiration and to purchase manuscripts, books, and materials for the continuance of the Great Work.

Damian returned to Scotland in 1512. Notwithstanding his absence, the work on quinta essencia seems to have been prosecuted with vigour in the interim, judging from an entry in the Lord High Treasurer's accounts for 1512: 'Quinta Essencia: Item, to Maister Alexander Ogilvy, for his ordinar expens fra the x day of September bipast to the xiij day of August . . .' £214 : 4s. Presumably this item included the acting director's stipend for the period, and the very large sum concerned throws a significant light upon the King's action in promoting Damian to a sinecure as Abbot of Tungland.

FAREWELL TO STRIVELING

Soon after his return a grant of £20 was made on 29 March 1513, 'to the Abbot [of] Tungland, to pass to the myne in Crawfurdmure', from which a certain amount of gold had been obtained. But now the sands were running out, and Damian was destined to see little more of the laboratory in Stirling Castle. During these last days of its glory, the work on quinta essencia seems to have remained chiefly in the hands of a new alchemist, one Robert Maklellane, or McCllane, 'the man that makis the watter in Striveling to the quintessence'. The last entry referring to this work occurs on 5 August 1513: 'deliverit to the Constable of Striveling xlij*li*. allem [alum], to put in the quinta essencia, price tharof, xl*s*. . . . Item, to Valentyne McLellane that suld mak the quinta essencia, lvj*s*.'

Fate now intervened. Little more than a month afterwards, on 9 September 1513, the interest of the Scottish crown in alchemy came to an untimely end with the death of James IV on the tragic field of Flodden. It was a century and a half before this interest in science found a rebirth in two of James's distant descendants—Prince Rupert of Bavaria and King Charles II.

REFERENCES

Compota Thesaurariorum Regum Scotorum: Accounts of the Lord High Treasurer of Scotland, 11 vols., Edinburgh, 1877–1916. Vols. **1-4** cover the period from 1473 to 1513.

Lesley, J., *The History of Scotland from* 1436 *to* 1561, Edinburgh, 1830.

Lindesay of Pitscottie, *The Historie and Cronicles of Scotland*, Edinburgh and London, 1899.

Read, J., 'Alchemy in Scotland', *The Chemist and Druggist*, 25 June 1938; 'Alchemy under James IV of Scotland', *Ambix*, 1938, 2, 60; 'Michael Scot: a Scottish Pioneer of Science', *Scientia*, Oct.-Nov. 1938, 190; 'Scottish Alchemy in the Seventeenth Century', *Chymia*, 1948, 1 (Philadelphia).

CHAPTER III

THE TRAGEDY OF THE COSMOPOLITE

IT seems to be inherent in the Scot to infuse at times into his actions a picturesque or dramatic quality calculated to touch the heart or appeal to the imagination. This characteristic, reflected so clearly in the novels of Sir Walter Scott, accounts largely for the spirit of romance with which the history of Scotland is imbued. The romantic element has often been tinged with tragedy, as in the lives of Wallace, James IV, Queen Mary, and Montrose. Although remarkable, it is therefore not surprising that in alchemical history Scotland should have produced, in the person of the mysterious Alexander Seton, a figure of high romance and tragedy—one, indeed, who has been termed 'the chief martyr of alchemy'.

THE CURTAIN RISES

Scottish alchemy reached its zenith in the seventeenth century, which opened upon the alchemical epic of a reputed Scotsman, the story of whose romantic wanderings through Europe as a goldmaker led up to a climax no less artistic than tragic. Alexander Seton shoots across the records of alchemy 'like a streamer of the northern morn', between the years 1601 and 1604, a century after the activities of James IV's flying alchemist in Stirling Castle. Within this brief space of less than three years, his doings have been described with a wealth of circumstantial and documented detail unsurpassed in the history of alchemy. The number of actors in Seton's alchemical drama was so great, and the scenes were so varied, that the narrative may well be prefaced by a summary of the chief persons and places concerned, after the manner of the formal drama :

The Tragedy of the Cosmopolite

Persons
(in the order of their mention)

ALEXANDER SETON, the Cosmopolite, *a Scots alchemist and goldmaker*
JACOB HANSSEN, *captain of a Dutch ship*
JOANNES VAN DER LINDEN, *a Dutch physician*
J. ANTONIDES VAN DER LINDEN, *a medical bibliographer*
DANIEL GEORG MORHOF, *a man of very great learning*
JOHANN WOLFGANG DIENHEIM, *Professor at Freiburg*
WILLIAM HAMILTON, *a red-haired Scotsman*
DR. JACOB ZWINGER, *Professor of Greek at Basel*
GÜSTENHÖVER, *a goldsmith of Strassburg*
KOCH, *a merchant of Frankfurt*
ANTON BERDEMANN, *an alchemist of Cologne*
MASTER GEORGE, *a Scots surgeon of Cologne*
CORNELIUS MARTINI, *Professor of Philosophy at Helmstedt*
GRETEL, *the beautiful daughter of a burgher of Munich*
CHRISTIAN II, *the young Elector of Saxony*
MICHAEL SENDIVOGIUS, or SENSOPHAX, *a Polish nobleman*
GOLDSMITHS, GAOLERS, SOLDIERS OF THE ROYAL BODY-GUARD, POSTILLIONS, INNKEEPERS, etc.

Scenes

The sea-coast near Edinburgh

Enkhuysen in Holland

Amsterdam, Rome, Zürich, Basel, Strassburg, Frankfurt, Cologne, Hamburg, Munich

The tavern of the Golden Stork at Basel

The tavern of the Holy Ghost at Cologne

The Saxon court at Crossen and Dresden

A dungeon and torture-chamber at Dresden

Cracow

Time

From the summer of 1601 to January 1604

Seton's dramatic story is given very fully by the nine-teenth-century historians of chemistry, K. C. Schmieder and L. Figuier. Schmieder's *Geschichte der Chemie*, like Figuier's *L'Alchimie et les Alchimistes*, although uncritical and often marked by great credulity, is full of interest and easy to read. These works, indeed, now so little known, would provide delectable material for chemists and others seeking reading practice of an entertaining kind in German and French.

The curtain rises upon the first act of the Setonian drama in the summer of 1601, to disclose the wreck of a Dutch vessel upon the Scottish coast. The captain of the ship, Jacob Hanssen, and his crew were succoured by the owner of the adjacent estate, whose name is given as Alexander Seton, with such variations as Sethon, Sethonius, Sidon, Sitonius, Suethonis, and Scotus. Seton also became known as 'the Cosmopolite', owing presumably to his many appearances in various countries. In spite of extensive research, the identity and earlier life of one whose doings between the years 1601 and 1604 have been described in such detail have remained an unsolved enigma. Similarly, the locality of the shipwreck has remained in doubt, although it has usually been identified with Seton, or Seatown, near Edinburgh; this conclusion, however, seems to have been based upon the name of the hero of the drama, so that the uncertainties so typical of alchemical narratives are evident from the outset.

THE MYSTERY OF ALEXANDER SETON

Alexander Seton is one of the most typical Scottish names that could be found or imagined, and it is therefore remarkable that in the circumstantial story of Seton's alchemical Odyssey his native land, Scotia, should be disguised under the pseudonym of 'Molia'. The different spellings of Seton are understandable: for example, in the matriculation and graduation rolls of the University of St. Andrews, from 1413 to 1579, the name is written in no fewer than ten different ways. The noble Scottish family of Seyton figures in *The Abbot*, by Sir Walter Scott, and the fifth Lord Seton was 'The Loyal Seton' who sheltered

E

Queen Mary at Seton House after the murder of Rizzio
and on other occasions. Seton House, situated on the coast
to the east of Edinburgh, would agree with the supposed
site of the shipwreck; moreover, one of the sons of the
fifth Lord Seton was named Alexander. This Alexander
Seton cannot, however, be identified with the Cosmopolite,
as he became Chancellor of Scotland and Earl of Dun-
fermline, and lived until 1622. In short, it has not proved
possible to identify any historical Alexander Seton with
'the chief martyr of alchemy'.

ENKHUYSEN

According to the story, Seton and the rescued Dutch
captain became very friendly, and early in 1602 the Scotsman paid the Dutchman a visit at Enkhuysen in Holland.
At this point the first mention occurs of Seton's interest in
alchemy and particularly in goldmaking. He revealed
himself to his host as a master of the Hermetic Art, and
proceeded to give an experimental demonstration of his
claims. He converted a small piece of lead into an equal
weight of gold. Then, in the meticulous and dramatic
manner of the successful transmutationist, he borrowed a
needle, marked the alchemical gold with the date and time
of the experiment—13 March 1602, 4 P.M.—and gave it to
Hanssen as a memento of the occasion.

Hanssen presented a piece of the gold to his physician,
Joannes van der Linden. A son of this physician, Joannes
Antonides van der Linden, achieved a reputation as a
professor of medicine and medical bibliographer. His son,
in turn, became a physician at Amsterdam. Some seventy
years after the Enkhuysen transmutation, this grandson of
Hanssen's physician showed his grandfather's fragment of
the alchemical gold to the celebrated Daniel Georg Morhof,
'a man of very great learning and of sound critical judgment', who is the authority for this part of the history
of the Scottish gold-maker: the details are given in a
Latin work which he published at Hamburg in 1673
(Fig. 13).

149

Iodami lamina quædam aurea, à Joḣ
bannis Antonide van der Linden Medici
Profefloris Clariffimi filio Medico, quę
particula erat auri, quod Scotus ille
Enchufæ, ubi medicinam faciebat Pater
Jobannis Antonide , Amftelodamenfis
Medici Avus, in ædibus nautæ Jacobi
Hanſſen, è plumbo confecerat, à quo
habuit particulam illam Medicus En-
chufanus. Tempus verò ille manu fuâ
accuratè fignaverat : Annum 1602. diem 13. Martii, horam quartam pomeri-
dianam. Occafio notitiæ, quæ Scoto
cum nautâ fuit, è naufragio orta eft.
Nautæ enim ad littus Scoticum eð tra-
ctu, quo prædia illo habebat ejectus,
humaniter ab illo habitus, hofpitio
Enchufam venientem exceperat. Is po-
ftea in Germaniâ plura artis fuæ fpeci-
mina oftendit, ut pene exitium fibi i-
pfi ftruxerit, à quo per Sendivogium,
Polonum, vel Moravum, ut alii volunt,
liberatus præmii loco pyxidem pulve-
re aurifico plenam illi obtulit. Diem
interea Setonius obiit. Sendevogius
viduâ ejus in uxorem ductâ, quam ar-
K 3   tis

13. Morhof tells of Seton. From *De Metallorum Transmutatione*, D. G.
Morhof, Hamburg, 1673. The extract may be completed by prefixing
the words 'Ostensa mihi fuit Amste-', and adding 'habere notitiam
putabat, magna spe excidit: nec praeter donatum pulverem quicquam
habuit'.

BASEL

In the next act of the drama the scene changes from Scotland and Holland to Basel, in Switzerland, which Seton reached in the following year. His itinerary is not clearly defined, but he seems to have visited Amsterdam, Rotterdam, and Italy in the meantime, accompanied by a Scots retainer named William Hamilton. At Basel the narrative is taken up by a man of learning and wide reputation, Johann Wolfgang Dienheim, doctor of laws and of medicine, professor at Freiburg im Breisgau, and a declared opponent of the Hermetic philosophy. From him an eyewitness account of Seton's most celebrated experimental demonstration has come down to us. Dienheim's story, originally published in 1610, is related in a clear and circumstantial manner unsurpassed in the literature of transmutation, as may be judged from the following English translation made from Schmieder, and which may be entitled *The Narrative of Johann Wolfgang Dienheim, Professor at Freiburg im Breisgau:*

'In the high summer of 1603, as I was returning from Rome to Germany, I became acquainted with a fellow-traveller of a middle age, intelligent and very modest in his demeanour, and of a sanguine temperament. Though of small stature, he was robust; his complexion was fresh, and he had a chestnut-brown beard, trimmed after the French fashion. He wore a habit of figured black satin. He was accompanied by a single servant, who would have been obvious in a multitude by reason of his red hair and beard. The traveller, if he spoke sooth, was called Alexander Setonius. He came from Molia, an island kingdom of the ocean.

'At Zürich, where Pastor Eghlin gave him a letter addressed to Dr. Zwinger at Basel, we hired a boat and went on to that city by water. When we had taken up our quarters at the tavern of the Golden Stork in Basel, my acquaintance said to me: "You will recall how, throughout the journey, and especially on board the boat, you have censured and discredited alchemy and the alchemists. You

will remember, too, how I promised to reply to you not with
philosophical syllogisms, but with a philosophical fact. I
am now only awaiting the arrival of another witness, so that
the opponents of alchemy may have still less reason to
doubt the genuineness of the demonstration.''

'A man of standing was then called in, whom I knew
only by sight, and who dwelled not far from the Golden
Stork. I learned later that he was Dr. Jacob Zwinger, a
member of a family of natural philosophers of high repute.
The three of us went together to a goldsmith's, Dr. Zwinger
bringing with him several plates of lead. We procured a
crucible from the goldsmith, and we had bought some
ordinary sulphur on the way.

'Alexander touched nothing. Upon his instructions,
a fire was kindled, the lead and sulphur were arranged in
layers in the crucible, the bellows were brought to bear, and
the mass was mixed by stirring. While this was doing, he
cracked jokes with us. After quarter of an hour had passed
he said to us: "Now throw this little paper into the molten
lead, but take care that it goes well into the middle, and not
into the fire nearby!"

'The paper enclosed a heavy, greasy powder, citron-
yellow in colour; but only the eye of a lynx could have
discerned so small a quantity if placed on the point of a
knife. Although as full of doubts as St. Thomas himself,
we carried out his behest. The mass was then heated for a
further quarter of an hour, being stirred meanwhile with a
glowing iron rod. The goldsmith was then directed to pour
out the contents of the crucible. But no lead was left. We
found in its place the purest gold, which according to the
goldsmith's assay surpassed by far the native gold of
Hungary and Arabia. Its weight was the same as that of
the original lead.

'There we stood, gaping at one another and hardly
daring to believe our eyes. But he laughed at us and said
mockingly, "Now away with your pedantries and subtle
arguments pursued at your own sweet will! Here you see
the truth in the deed, and that overrides all your syllogisms."
Then he cut off a fragment of the gold and gave it to Zwinger

as a souvenir. I got a fragment too, weighing nearly four ducats, which I keep in memory of this great demonstration.

'What is there in this for you to turn up your noses at, you sceptics? Here am I, still alive, and a living witness to what I saw. Moreover, Zwinger is still alive, and will not refuse to bear witness to the truth if he is asked to do so. Also Setonius and his servant are still alive, the latter at present in England, and the former in Germany, according to reports. I.could easily add where Setonius dwells, were it not for the need to guard against any untoward happening to that great and sacred man—that demigod!'

Dienheim made play with the scepticism of St. Thomas; but his last paragraph shows that he had become a seventeenth-century Saul among the prophets, reproaching the opponents of alchemy for maintaining the sceptical attitude which he himself had only recently abandoned. His fellow witness, Dr. Jacob Zwinger (1569–1610), was professor of Greek at Basel and an authority on medicine. He, too, accepted the evidence of the practical demonstration; his independent account of Seton's demonstration, recorded in 1606 in the form of a Latin letter, and afterwards printed at Nuremberg, substantiates Dienheim's narrative.[1]

After this, it seems that Seton rapidly became a legendary figure on the Continent. He is said to have appeared under various names in many places, and if he took part in all the alchemical incidents with which he has been credited he must have owned a much more efficient pair of 'wingis of fedderis' than those of his predecessor, John Damian!

STRASSBURG

Under the name of Hirschberger he is said by Schmieder to have brought trouble upon a worthy goldsmith of Strassburg, called Güstenhöver, in the summer of 1603. As a return for the goldsmith's hospitality, Hirschberger left him a little of his red powder of projection, which Güsten-

---

[1] Five years after this incident, Thomas Coryat spent the last two days of August 1608 in Basel. In his *Crudities* he records that: 'In a certaine roome of Erasmus Colledge I heard a very learned Greeke lecture read in one of Homers Iliads by Mr. Zuinggerus the publike professour of the Greeke tongue, who was the sonne of that famous Theodorus Zuinggerus a great Philosopher of this University'.

höver applied successfully in transmuting metals into gold. The modest goldsmith, after his transmutation into a proud goldmaker, tried to hide at least some of his light under a bushel, and imparted his results only to his friends and neighbours. As Schmieder aptly remarks, however, every neighbour had a friend, and every friend had a neighbour. In brief, all Strassburg was soon agog with the cry, 'Güstenhöver knows how to make gold!' Güstenhöver became embarrassingly popular.

The affair was investigated by an *ad hoc* sub-committee of the city council, consisting of three members, each of whom is said to have produced gold under Güstenhöver's direction by throwing a little of the powder, wrapped in paper, into molten lead contained in a crucible. A specimen of alchemical gold, reputed to have been made on this occasion, was shown in Paris so late as 1647.

Güstenhöver's fame now began to multiply in a truly alchemical manner, and eventually the alarmed celebrity was haled off to Prague at the command of the Emperor Rudolph II, whose interest in alchemy had earned him the title of 'the German Hermes'.[1] Here, Güstenhöver had to confess that his supply of the powder was exhausted, and that he was unable to replenish his store. Rudolph, convinced that the luckless goldsmith knew more than he cared to say, kept him permanently imprisoned in the White Tower.

FRANKFURT

Seton appears next in Frankfurt am Main, where he is said to have posed as a French count. Here he became friendly with a merchant named Koch, and showed him how to transmute quicksilver into gold with the aid of a brownish-red powder. In a letter to Ewald van Hoghelande, which was afterwards published, Koch described the testing of the gold in his presence by a jeweller, who submitted it to five successive fusions followed by cupellation. Koch added that he had a shirt-stud made out of half of this alchemical gold. Both the gold and a little silver which was

[1] *Prelude*, 22, 229.

produced simultaneously were described as possessing a peculiar brilliance.

COLOGNE

It is said that during his succeeding stay in Cologne, Seton's apostolic zeal in the cause of alchemy was raised to fever-heat by the associations of that city with Albertus Magnus, Denis Zachaire, and Leonhart Thurneisser. As a sign of this fervour he seems to have abandoned the caution which had hitherto characterised his movements in Germany; for he and his servant, William Hamilton, enquired openly after local devotees of alchemy. As a result, they left the tavern of the Holy Ghost for the house of an alchemist named Anton Berdemann, who entertained them for a month. On 6 August 1603 Seton accomplished spectacular transmutations of antimony, lead, and tin on the premises of Hans Löhndorf, a goldsmith who lived near the church of St. Laurence. Again, after repeated tests, the product was found to consist of 'the best gold'.

A few days later, Seton encountered a fellow Scotsman in the person of a surgeon known as Master George, who dwelt in the Katzenbochgasse. Master George, although hitherto an inveterate adversary of alchemy, changed his views abruptly on 11 August 1603, after witnessing the conversion of iron and lead into gold by the triumphant Seton. This was done on the premises of the goldsmith Hans von Kempen, in the presence of his son, four workmen, and an apprentice. As the two Scots emerged, after the demonstration, from the sign of the Golden Anchor into the Market-place, the Cosmopolite remarked to Master George:

'Berdemann tellit me, laddie, that ye were a declared enemy of alchemy, and I ettled yon wee bit proof for ye. I ganged the same gait, ye ken, at Rotterdam, Amsterdam, Basel, Strassburg, and Frankfurt.'

'Tak' tent, brither Scot,' replied Master George, now a convinced adherent of Seton. 'Ye maun be daft to show your hand sae kenspeckle. Gin yon lang-nebbit German lairdies jaloused your gowdmaking, they wad rin like auld

Nicky Ben to grab ye and fleech or ding oot the secret, hilt and hair!'

'Och, awa', Geordie!' cried the adept, brushing aside the warning. 'Cologne is a free city, and I dinna fash mysell wi' worriecows. But gin ane o' yon birkies e'en fanged me the noo, he wadna gar me gie ower my secret. A thousand times liefer wad I dee. Forbye, ye ken, I wadna swither to gie yon bit proof of my art—aiblins to mak' up to fifty or sixty thousand ducats' worth o' gowd.'

Seton's host, the good Berdemann, calculated that in the Cologne transmutations the tincture had converted 2820 times its weight of base metals into gold. Seton replied that under proper conditions this proportion could be increased to 80,000. He added that during the past three years he had fabricated gold weighing more than himself and his red-headed servant put together!

A detailed account of Seton's doings in Cologne was sent by Theobald van Hoghelande, who happened to be staying in the city at that time, to his brother, Ewald van Hoghelande, by whom it was published in 1604.

HELMSTEDT

Seton is next heard of at Hamburg, where he is said to have made several astonishing projections. At about this time also, according to Schmieder, he made a dramatic appearance at a lecture given in the University of Helmstedt by the professor of philosophy, Cornelius Martini. The professor was retailing his well-worn arguments against the possibility of transmutation when a stranger entered, stepped forward, and asked for permission to intervene. This being granted, he called for a brazier of charcoal, a crucible, and a piece of lead. Forthwith transmuting the base metal in the usual way, with the aid of a pinch of his potent powder, he broke the reeking crucible and handed the warm ingot of gold to the nonplussed professor, exclaiming in the grand Setonian manner: 'Solve mihi hunc syllogismum!' The ingot proved to be a nut too hard for the professor to crack, and the learned syllogiser was unable to meet the challenge. As Schmieder remarks, the mode of action smacks strongly of Seton, the chief object of whose travels seems to have been the dramatic confutation of antagonists of alchemy.

GRETEL 'HITTS THE MARKE'

An unwonted lull fell upon Seton's alchemical activities when at last he reached Munich in the course of his wanderings. Not a single transmutation is reported during his sojourn in the Bavarian capital; but, as Figuier remarks, a philosopher cannot always work for his idea. Seton's apparent inactivity is easily explained. For the nonce he had transferred his interest from the golden beads of Hermes in the crucible to the golden arrows of Cupid in his heart. These missiles were directed at the wandering Scot with unerring aim by the fair daughter of a burgher of Munich. We do not know her name, but we may call her Gretel. She is said to have been related to a certain Adam Rockosch, of Munich. Figuier, seizing upon the essential point with true Gallic insight, says: 'L'histoire nous dit qu'elle était jolie; voilà tout ce que nous savons sur elle'. Gretel was beautiful, and, in alchemical phraseology, she 'hitt the Marke' :[1] that is all we know, or need know, about her.

So, for a while, the crucibles of the Cosmopolite remained cold. His bellows remained still. The anti-transmutationists held the field unrefuted. Lead remained lead. Iron preserved its identity. Quicksilver continued to flow unmolested. The goldmaker had been brought low by golden darts—*similia similibus curantur!*

At this place, to use an apt turn of phrase to be found in an English edition of Glauber's *Works*, published in 1689, 'we may fitly subjoyn this sutable Poesie, making for our present Purpose, and expressing the same in few Words':[2]

> With anxious Doubts and Fears oppreſt
> Fond Gretel claſps her Chymiſt's Breaſt;
> Those tender Fears he would remove,
> Yet fighs for Glory as for Love.

[1] *Prelude*, 130.
[2] *Op. cit.* 138; J. Read, *Cluster-o'-Vive*, London, 1923, 60.

HAMILTON GOES HOME

Such tender fears were soon justified by events; for the career of the Cosmopolite was now nearing its tragic climax. Soon after his marriage, Seton decided upon the unwise course of extending his alchemical apostolate to Saxony. In the autumn of 1603, possibly in response to an invitation from the Elector, he went to Crossen, where the Saxon court was then in residence. Not having yet returned to his crucibles and base metals, the newly wed adept entrusted his servant, William Hamilton, with some of the powder of projection, and appointed him to give a demonstration. Hamilton appeared before the Elector and a company of distinguished guests, and successfully converted lead into excellent gold, which, according to Güldenfalk, sustained every test. At this point the rufescent Hamilton drops out of the story. Soon after his demonstration he left discreetly for Holland, and returned to his native land; but whether his departure was due to Seton's marriage or to a canny anticipation of ill is uncertain.

IN THE DRESDEN DUNGEON

Upon the invitation of the Elector, then only twenty years of age, the Cosmopolite and his wife accompanied the court to Dresden. Christian II of Saxony was young, cruel, and avaricious. Schmieder likened his behaviour towards Seton to that of an incipient Nero. Unlike his predecessors, Augustus and Christian I, who were sympathetic patrons of alchemy, Christian II held the 'Divine Art' in derision. Hamilton's fateful transmutation aroused his cupidity, and Seton was soon faced with the grim consequences of neglecting Master George's warning at Cologne.

At first the Elector fawned upon the adept, now completely in his power, with the object of extracting his secret of secrets. Unsuccessful flattery gave way to threats. Finally, the reticent and resolute Scot was consigned to the torture chamber. Here, time after time, he was put on the rack and also burned with red-hot irons; but all to no avail. The Cosmopolite, fortified by his belief in the Divine inspiration of his mission, proved himself a worthy fellow-countryman of Patrick Hamilton and George Wishart, and maintained an unyielding silence. At length the Elector, fearing that his victim would die without disclosing the secret, removed him from the torture chamber to a loathsome dungeon, in which he was put under the observation of a changing guard drawn from a detachment of forty soldiers of the bodyguard. In this dreich and unhealthy prison he languished for three months in solitary confinement. Not even his young wife, who waited anxiously upon events in a neighbouring inn, was allowed to visit him.

ENTER SENDIVOGIUS

The curtain now rises upon the last and most dramatic scene in the life of this surprising Scot. There was staying in Dresden at that time a certain Michael Sendivogius, or Michal Sensophax, whose description as a Polish nobleman seems to have been based upon his possession of a domicile in Cracow. According to another account, he was the natural son of Jacob Sendimir, a gentleman of Moravia. The date of his birth is given as 1556 or 1566, so that he was apparently about the same age as Seton. As an amateur of alchemy he took a lively interest in the famous Cosmopolite, to whose rescue he now addressed himself. Gaining the ear and confidence of the Elector, he obtained permission to visit the prisoner in his dungeon, with the ostensible object of extracting from him the secret of transmutation.

Seton met the approaches of Sendivogius with reserve, until his persevering visitor found an opportunity of broaching the subject of a possible deliverance from captivity. What would Seton give him, asked Sendivogius, if his escape could be contrived. Ample for Sendivogius and his dependants for life, replied Seton. A plan was concerted between them, and Sendivogius raised the necessary funds by travelling to Cracow and selling his house there.

THE ESCAPE FROM THE DUNGEON

Upon returning to Dresden, the Pole visited the prison daily and established himself on intimate and popular terms with the soldiers of the guard, in the usual way. On the chosen evening—according to some accounts during the celebration of a festival—he plied them all so freely with their favourite beverages that they relapsed to a man into drunken slumbers, under cover of which Sendivogius succeeded in removing the maimed and crippled adept to a carriage which was waiting near the prison gates. They drove off hurriedly to Sendivogius' lodging; here they were joined by Seton's wife, who collected the tincture from a secret hiding-place of which the adept informed her. Travelling night and day in desperate haste, they crossed the frontier and eventually reached Cracow in safety.

THE CURTAIN FALLS

Seton's story ends in tragedy. His deliverance came too late. Even the potent tincture, when administered in the form of the Elixir, was powerless to repair the ravages of the unnatural and barbarous treatment to which the adept had been subjected. He died at Cracow in January of 1604, less than two years after making his public début in Holland as a goldmaker.

Alexander Seton, as portrayed in these picturesque records, is a nebulous and enigmatical figure, and his animating motive is difficult to discern. Figuier commends him for his disinterestedness. The circumstantial accounts of his alchemical peregrinations indicate that he was not prompted by dreams of wealth or power. Like other adepts of his time, he seems to have regarded himself as a missionary, crusader, or apostle of alchemy. He ended by becoming its chief martyr.

REFERENCES

Dienheim, J. W., *Medicina Universalis*, Argentorati [Strassburg], 1610.
Ferguson, J., *Bibliotheca Chemica*, 2 vols., Glasgow, 1906.
Figuier, L., *L'Alchimie et les Alchimistes*, 3rd edn., Paris, 1860.
Güldenfalk, S. H., *Sammlung von mehr als hundert wahrhaften Transmutationsgeschichten*, Frankfurt and Leipzig, 1784.
Morhof, D. G., *De Metallorum Transmutatione*, Hamburg, 1673.
Schmieder, K. C., *Geschichte der Chemie*, Halle, 1832.
van Hoghelande, E., *Historiae aliquot Transmutationis metallicae*, Coloniae, 1604.

CHAPTER IV

THE MANTLE OF THE COSMOPOLITE

THE romantic story of Alexander Seton does not end even with his death. It continues in an equally romantic way for many years in the recorded activities and adventures of his rescuer, Michael Sendivogius, who lived to a ripe old age. Sendivogius' brief association with the Scots adept changed the whole tenor of his life and raised him to a vicarious eminence in the annals of alchemy, which he would not have otherwise attained.

Before his death, Seton is said to have rewarded Sendivogius by the gift of an ounce of the magic powder; but he refused to impart to him the secret of its preparation, which he regarded as a Divine mystery entrusted to him by God. Sendivogius' first inheritance from Seton was the fair daughter of the burgher of Munich, whom he shortly espoused; his second, her share of the remaining store of the powder of projection; his third, the adept's alchemical writings; his fourth, the cognomen of ' Cosmopolite '. The mantle of the Cosmopolite had fallen fair and square upon the shoulders of Sendivogius.

RISE OF A GOLDMAKER

Both Figuier and Dufresnoy, following a hint thrown out by Morhof, made the ungallant suggestion that Sendivogius married the beautiful young widow in order to obtain from her the secret of preparing the potent powder; but in this event his expectation was not realised. According to a calculation made by Schmieder, and based upon a transmuting power of 5000, the original ounce of tincture which Seton gave to Sendivogius was worth 120,000 thalers. On this basis the transmuting effect of his full store would have been very considerable. With it, he began to make gold; this he sold to a Jew, who was said to be still living at Cracow in 1651, in a letter dated 12 June of that year and quoted by Dufresnoy.

Sendivogius took great precautions with the precious powder, and when travelling concealed most of it in a secret receptacle fashioned in the step of his coach. His retainer, Johann Bodowsky, habitually carried a small quantity of it in a golden capsule suspended beneath his garments by means of a golden chain passing around his neck. This was drawn upon, as occasion demanded, to fabricate gold for defraying current expenses—the problem of transporting large amounts of the metal being thus solved in a very simple manner. Sendivogius, as might be anticipated, now became increasingly extravagant, and began to make a prodigal use of his tincture in public demonstrations which gratified his vanity. Ignoring his position as the temporary master of a wasting asset, soon he assumed the port and carriage of a wealthy adept, possessed of the secret of preparing the Stone.

THE MARBLE TABLET OF PRAGUE

His fame was bruited abroad, and in 1604 he was called by the Emperor Rudolph II to Prague. Here, under the guidance of Sendivogius, with the aid of some of Seton's powder of projection, 'the German Hermes' justified his alchemical pseudonym by accomplishing a transmutation with his own hands. This delighted him so much that instead of sending 'the noble Pole' to join the unlucky Güstenhöver, who was still languishing in the White Tower, he presented him with a medal and made him a counsellor. Moreover, he caused to be affixed to the wall of the room in which the transmutation had been achieved a marble tablet bearing an inscription of his own composition:

> *Faciat hoc quispiam alius,*
> *Quod fecit Sendivogius Polonus!*

('Let another do that which Sendivogius of Poland has done!')

Schmieder considered this *Tabula marmorea Pragensis*, which was still to be seen in the room in 1650, to have been far more important to alchemy than the famous *Tabula Smaragdina*, or Emerald Table of Hermes.

ROMANTIC ADVENTURES OF A GOLDMAKER

Sendivogius' progress now began, as might also be anticipated, to excite envy and greed. On his way back to Cracow he was seized and imprisoned by a Moravian count who was eager to learn his secret. With the aid of a file, and a rope made from his attire, the resourceful alchemist managed to escape through a window of his prison in a half-clad condition. The Emperor, upon hearing of the outrage, caused the count to transfer to Sendivogius the estate of Gravarna, which he is said to have given eventually to his only daughter as a dowry.

Another adventure followed some striking demonstrations of goldmaking made before the Duke of Würtemberg in 1605. The ducal alchemist, von Müllenfels, was a man of parts who had earned his spurs by representing himself to the Emperor Rudolph II as a bullet-proof goldmaker. He did not explain that the bullets were made of amalgamated lead and that he was an expert conjurer capable of producing gold from a crucible as easily as a rabbit from a hat. Seeing his position now threatened by his too successful 'Fachgenoss', von Müllenfels decoyed Sendivogius away from Stuttgart, seized him secretly, immured him in a castle, and appropriated his transmuting powder. With this he effected a series of impressive transmutations, thereby inducing the Duke to convey to him the estate of Neidlingen which had been intended for Sendivogius, now unaccountably missing.

After undergoing eighteen months' imprisonment, Sendivogius again escaped through a window—this time fully clothed, as he had improved with practice upon his original technique, by making a rope from his bedclothes rather than from his garments. Having achieved his freedom, Sendivogius demanded that justice should be done upon von Müllenfels. Meanwhile his wife had lodged a complaint with the King of Poland. Strong representations were made to the Duke of Würtemberg, and as a result von Müllenfels was arrested and threatened with the rack. He confessed, and was hanged upon a gilded gallows in a robe covered with tinsel from head to foot. This occurred in 1607.

The resident alchemist should have taken warning from the fate of one of his predecessors, Jörg Hanover, who had been hanged in a precisely similar way ten years earlier, on 2 April 1597, after obtaining more than 200,000 thalers from the Duke of Würtemberg, on the pretence that he could make gold from iron. A curious work published at Hamburg in 1706, by an anonymous writer calling himself 'Alethophilo', contains an engraving of Jörg Hanover, and of his hanging upon the gilded gallows, to the end that (as the ironical inscription runs) he should be able to improve his method of making gold ('er soll besser lernen Gold machen').

FALL OF A GOLDMAKER

Sendivogius now found himself in a parlous plight. Owing to his extravagant use of the powder of projection, his stock had become alarmingly low at the time of his imprisonment by von Müllenfels. He is said to have dissipated part of it in fruitless attempts to multiply it, by means of experiments based upon wrong interpretations of Seton's obscure writings. He also tried the effect of triturating the powder in oil, instead of enclosing it in wax as Seton had done. Little by little, in spite of all his efforts, the precious heritage dwindled. The final blow came with von Müllenfels' theft of practically the whole of the remaining powder. It is stated that the despairing alchemist eked out the last residues by using them as a potent medicine in admixture with rectified spirit of wine. When his last grains had gone, he began to borrow money from confiding friends. As their confidence followed the precedent of the powder, and dwindled, he descended a stage lower, and the alchemist-actor became a common charlatan.

One of the devices which Sendivogius used in his degenerate days, in attempting to keep up appearances, became known as one-sided transmutation ('einseitige Veredlung'). A specially prepared coin, the 'head' and 'tail' of which were composed of gold and silver respectively, was treated carefully with mercury, so as to give it a uniform silvery appearance. In the demonstration which followed, the 'head' was moistened with a 'secret' liquid (probably water), after which the whole coin was heated to dull redness. The mercury having volatilised, the coin was allowed to cool, and its 'head' was shown to consist of the purest gold!

In such ignoble ways the once famous Sendivogius sank gradually into a dubious obscurity. He appears to have maintained a decaying practice as an alchemical charlatan until his death, which is supposed to have occurred at Gravarna in 1636 or 1646, when he was eighty years old.

A MYSTERIOUS MANUSCRIPT

The powder of projection, which became a kind of Pandora's box in the hands of Sendivogius, formed only part of his heritage from Seton. It was accompanied by an alchemical manuscript which came into Sendivogius' possession when he married the adept's widow. That this manuscript might afford a clue to the method of preparing the mysterious powder was a natural supposition; but Sendivogius pored over the adept's writings, like an alchemical Tantalus, without being able to extract from them any grain of useful information. Nevertheless, the remarkable story of Seton and Sendivogius would be incomplete without some account of the manuscript purporting to have originated from one of alchemy's most elusive figures.

Unfortunately, the writings ascribed to Seton throw no light upon his history or personality. Altogether, in fact, they are singularly colourless and quite out of keeping with the vivid happenings of Seton's meteoric career as a goldmaker. It is usually stated that the alchemical manuscript which Seton left to his widow was the one that Sendivogius published, soon after Seton's death, under the title *Novum Lumen Chymicum* ('A New Light of Alchemy'). Unfortunately, the bibliography of the works ascribed to Sendivogius is confused, owing partly to his use of anagrams and to the transference of the pseudonym of 'Cosmopolite' to him from Seton. The *Novum Lumen Chymicum* was usually printed in company with other tracts entitled *Aenigma philosophicum, Dialogus Mercurii, Alchymistae et Naturae,* and *Tractatus de Sulphure.* These other tracts are generally ascribed to Sendivogius, although it is sometimes stated that the *Dialogus* was written by Seton.

'*A NEW LIGHT OF ALCHYMIE*'

The *Novum Lumen Chymicum,* said to have been written by Alexander Seton and appropriated by Michael Sendivogius, is a work that belies its name. Although it has a mild interest, the only light that it sheds upon alchemy is reflected from other sources. It cannot be claimed beyond doubt that Alexander Seton wrote it; but the repeated attribution of this work to Michael Sendivogius by alchemical writers was due largely to the usual occurrence on the title-page of an anagram of his name. This example of misplaced ingenuity took the form *Divi Leschi genus amo,* 'I love the race of the divine Leschi', in which the meaning of the last word is obscure, although it may possibly signify Hermes. According to Lenglet Dufresnoy, who attributed the work to 'Le Cosmopolite' and thus begged the question, it was published at Prague and at Frankfurt in 1604, at Paris in 1606, and at Cologne in 1610; but the earliest edition now extant would appear to be one of 1608, issued at Paris at the instance of Jean Beguin, to whom, indeed, the authorship has sometimes been wrongly ascribed.[1]

It is somewhat surprising that the sensible and practical Beguin could see fit to characterise the *Novum Lumen* as a work 'filled with so much learning and erudition', and to hail its author as a philosopher than whom none could 'have written more clearly and concisely of the power of art and nature'. That the book was prized in the seventeenth and eighteenth centuries may be inferred from the issue of numerous printed editions and from the existence of manuscript copies, made at the expense of much time and

---

[1] T. S. Patterson, *Annals of Science,* 1937, **2**, 245.

labour. The St. Andrews collection contains one such vellum-bound copy of the Geneva edition of 1628, in Latin, written in the early eighteenth century and filling 244 pages; this includes *De Sulphure* and the other tracts.

The character of the *Novum Lumen* may be gauged from a brief examination of John French's English translation, which appeared in 1650 under the title *A New Light of Alchymie* (Fig. 14). In a preface addressed to 'the Searchers of *Alchymie*', 'the true Sons of *Hermes*', or 'the Sonnes of Art', the author refers scathingly to the puffers: 'that wicked swarm of smoke-fellows, whose delight is to cheat . . . who most unworthily defaming the most commendable Art of *Alchymie*, have with their Whites, and Reds deceived almost the whole world'.

The writer develops his theme in a series of twelve short treatises, followed by an Epilogue, or Conclusion. Nature, he says, works in sperm, or seed. The sperm is the Elixir or Quintessence, 'or the most perfect decoction, or digestion of a thing'. We do not doubt him when he adds that 'there might truely be made a large discourse of this sperme'; for the alchemical writers were certainly adepts at making bricks without straw—and even without clay. The four elements (earth, air, fire, and water), by their incessant motion, 'cast forth a sperme into the Center of the earth, where it is digested, and by motion sent abroad'. All metals have a common seed: 'the same is found in Saturne [lead] which is in Gold, the same in Silver which is in Iron'.

A version of the sulphur-mercury theory of the composition of metals follows. The first and principal matter of metals 'is the humidity of the aire mixed with heat; and this the Philosophers called Mercury, which is governed by the beams of the Sunne, and Moon in the Philosophicall sea:[1] the second is the dry heat of the earth, which they called Sulphur'. The theory of the formation of divers metals from these two principles is expounded on the lines laid down in such works as the *Semita Recta* and *Speculum Alchemiae*, written some four hundred years earlier.[2]

Nature makes seed out of matter received from the four

---

[1] *Prelude*, 219.   [2] *Op. cit.* 24, 46.

A NEW LIGHT

John OF ~~Alchymie~~

ALCHYMIE:

Taken out of the fountaine of
NATURE, and Manuall
Experience.

To which is added a TREATISE of
SVLPHVR:

Written by _Micheel Sandivogius_:
_i.e._ Anagram matically,
DIVI LESCHI GENVS AMO.

Also Nine Books _Of the Nature of Things,_
Written by _PARACELSVS_, viz.

Of the
{ _Generations_
Growthes
Conservations
Life : Death }
{ _Renewing_
Transmutation
Separation
Signatures }
of Naturall things.

Also a Chymicall Dictionary explaining hard places
and words met withall in the writings of _Paracelsus_,
and other obscure Authors.

All which are faithfully translated out of the
Latin into the _English_ tongue,

By _J. F._ M.D.

London, Printed by _Richard Cotes_, for _Thomas Williams_, at the
Bible in Little-Britain, 1 6 5 0.

14. Title-page of the English edition of _Novum Lumen Chymicum_,
London, 1650

elements, and 'every thing that hath seed is multiplyed in
it'. There are three kinds of seed: the mineral (known by
philosophers alone), the vegetable (common and vulgar),
and the animal (known by imagination). The Philosopher's
Stone is regarded simply as the seed of gold, which, like
other seeds, can multiply and breed more gold—'Are not
Metalls of as much esteem with God as trees?' If metals
have seed, 'who is so sottish to think they cannot be multiplyed in their Seed?' The only difficulty, of course, is to
get this metallic seed. 'Why doth not Gold, or any other
Metall bring forth seed?' asks our author. Just because it is
unripe; 'by reason of the crudity of the air, it hath not
sufficient heat'.

The elaboration of this point smacks of Sendivogius the
Pole, who was accused by Dufresnoy of altering the original
text of the passage and adding some local colour: 'As for
example, wee see that Orenge trees in *Polonia* doe indeed
flourish as other trees; in *Italie*, and elsewhere, where their
naturall soil is, they yeeld, and bring forth fruit, because
they have sufficient heat. . . . The same happens in Metalls:
Gold may yeeld fruit, and seed, in which it multiplyes it
self by the industry of the skilful Artificer.' Gold, nevertheless, cannot be ripened and made to seed by the mere application of heat. 'The naturall is this, that the pores of the body
be opened in our water [sophic mercury], whereby the seed,
that is digested, may bee sent forth, and put into its proper
Matrix.'

This is the substance of the twelve treatises, written 'in
love to the sonnes of Art, that before they set their hand to
the worke they may know the operation of Nature'. The
author is plainly reluctant to lay down his quill at this point,
lest, as he says, 'any should complain of my briefnesse'.
He proceeds accordingly to relate a so-called 'Parable'.

AN ALCHEMICAL PARABLE

This continuation of the *New Light* is in essence an
alchemical refresher course cast in the form of a vision, in
which the dreamer was led by Neptune into 'a most pleasant
Iland'. Situated towards the south, this country was peopled

by a choice assortment of alchemical hares and hatters which
seem to belong to the world of Lewis Carroll's 'Alice'.
Some of their misty yet familiar forms were shown to the
dreamer, appropriately enough, by means of 'a Looking-
glasse, in which'—as the Parable states—he 'saw all Nature
discovered'.

The chief figure in this nightmare gallery was 'a great
man, upon whose forehead was written the name of *Saturne*.
This man taking the vessell drew ten parts of water; and
tooke presently of the tree of the Sun, and put it in; and I
saw the fruit of the tree consumed, and resolved like ice in
warm water. I demanded of him; Sir, I see a wonderfull
thing . . . wherefore is all this? But he answered mee
most lovingly. My Son . . . this water is the Water of
life, having power to better the fruit of this tree so that . . .
only by its own odour it may convert the other six trees into
its own likeness.' The Parable here deals with the transmutation of the other metals into gold by virtue of the
Philosopher's Stone, obtained by conjoining the seed of
gold (fruit of the sun-tree) with sophic mercury.[1]

This passage seems to have been regarded by contemporary adepts as the high light of the *New Light*. Thus,
it forms the setting for the illustration of Sendivogius in
Maier's *Symbola Aureae Mensae Duodecim Nationum* of 1617
(Fig. 15). The engraving was reproduced in 1624 by
Daniel Stolcius[2] in his *Viridarium Chymicum*, with a Latin
epigram which may be rendered as follows:

Michael Sendivogius, of Poland

Although he lived in silence, with his name kept secret, yet fame
has brought it out of the black darkness.
Prague the triple city saw his first writing, and the work which he
teaches in his twice six writings.
'Saturn', he said, 'moistens the earth so as to have thy flowers,
Phoebus, and thine, wandering moon.'

It is of interest that this contemporary epigram, written
by one who had graduated at Prague itself in 1618,[3] con-
firms the statement that the *Novum Lumen Chymicum* was

---

[1] *Prelude*, 133.   [2] *Op. cit.* 223, 256.   [3] *Op. cit.* 314.

first published at Prague. Moreover, in this epigram Stolcius definitely attributes the authorship of the 'twice six writings', or twelve treatises of the *Novum Lumen Chymicum*, to Sendivogius. That he was also regarded as the author of the 'Parable' is clear from the composition of the picture.

Saturn (lead), the slow and melancholy planet, is depicted in the engraving as the aged wooden-legged man of the First Key of Basil Valentine,[1] who is watering the sun-tree with the 'Water of our Sea, the Water of life not wetting the hands, or Philosophicall Water', as it was variously termed. This phase of the Saturn mysticism in alchemy is bound up with the *opus mulierum* motive—the labour of 'the woman that washes clothes'.[2] Sometimes also saturnine wetness was symbolised by representations of springs or deep wells: thus, an illustration[3] in the *Musaeum Hermeticum* of 1625 shows the 'Chymic Choir' of the seven metals or 'planets' performing beside a well, like a ruddy and musical David dispersing the melancholy of a dark and saturnine Saul.

MERCURY PLAYS THE ALCHEMICAL ASS

The 'Parable or Philosophicall Ridle' was afterwards reprinted in other works, without any indication of its original source.[4] Even after the reader has escaped from its mazes, he still finds the author clinging to him after the manner of the Ancient Mariner and exposing him to another dazzling beam of the *New Light*, in the form of 'A Dialogue between *Mercury*, the *Alchymist* and *Nature*'. This dialogue was published as a separate tract at Cologne, so early as 1607, under the anagrammatised name of Michael Sendivogius as it appears on the title-page of the *New Light*. The *Dialogus* can only be regarded as a feeble *jeu d'esprit*, representing the primitive alchemical humour of the early seventeenth century.

The Alchymist, in his search for the Stone, heats Mercury in a glass. 'The Mercury as it is wont to do, vapoured away, the poor silly Alchymist not knowing the

---

[1] *Prelude*, Plate 37(i), pp. 91, 143, 201.   [2] *Op. cit.* 238.
[3] *Op. cit.* Plate 31.   [4] *Op. cit.* 268, 316, 317.

15. Michael Sendivogius, of Poland.
From *Viridarium Chymicum*, D. Stolcius, Frankfurt, 1624.
(see p. 61.)

16. Michael Sendivogius.
Engraved
by I. C. de Reinsperger,
anno 1763.
(See p. 64.)

nature of it, beat his wife, saying: No body could come hither besides thee, thou tookest the Mercury out of the glass.' Later in the proceedings the tormented Mercury assumes the rôle of Balaam's ass. 'Mercury began to laugh, and to speak to him saying, What wilt thou have, that thou thus troublest mee my Master Alchymist? *Alch.* O ho, now thou callest me Master, when I touch thee to the quick, now I have found where thy bridle is.'

Nature then appears on the scene, and acts as a combined buffer and buffoon between Mercury and the Alchymist, reproving each of them in turn. The Alchymist eventually admits that he knows nothing, but dare not say so for fear of losing both his reputation and his livelihood: 'yet will I say', he continues, 'that I doe certainly know, or else no body will give mee so much as bread: for many of them hope for much good from mee. . . . I will feed all of them with hope.' Nature then enquires, 'What wilt thou doe at last?' 'Ha, ha, ha,' replies the Alchymist, 'there be many countryes, also many covetous men, to whom I will promise great store of Gold, and that in a short time, and so the time shall passe away, till at last either I, or they must die Kings, or Asses.' The curtain descends upon Nature as she exclaims, 'Fie upon thee, make hast and be hanged, and put an end to thy self, and thy Philosophy'.

So ends the much-vaunted *New Light of Alchymie* and its appendages; leaving the modern reader to wonder how Seton, or Sendivogius, or any other alchemist, could have been anxious for his name to appear on the title-page, even in the form of an anagram. That the book could win the strong approval of Beguin and attract a wide public throughout the seventeenth and early eighteenth centuries is a circumstance which throws a vivid light upon the mentality of that age. In his introductory remarks to the English edition of 1650 John French, the translator, went so far as to say: 'If any one should ask me, What one book did most conduce to the knowledge of God and the Creature, and the mysteries thereof; I should speake contrary to my judgment, if I should not, next to the sacred Writ, say *Sandivogius*'.

Even Sir Isaac Newton treated these publications with

great respect.   Among the extant alchemical manuscripts in
his own hand (amounting to the surprising total of 650,000
words), there are two, of some 16,000 words, containing
notes and abstracts, mostly in English, of the *Novum
Lumen Chymicum*, 'Y* Philosophick Ridle', etc.[1]   Such
evidence shows how seriously the *New Light* was regarded
for more than a hundred years after its first publication.

AN ALCHEMICAL AFTERGLOW

It shone for a long time.   Besides the numerous issues
in Latin and French quoted by Schmieder, there were
German editions dated 1613, 1628, 1681, 1718, and 1750;
and a 'popular' illustrated edition was issued at Nuremberg
so late as 1766.   Two notable features of this edition are a
prefixed summary of its contents ('Kurzer Inhalt dieses
ganzen Tractats'), in a diagrammatic and versified form,[2]
and a folding plate bearing what is described on the title-
page as an accurate portrait of the author.   Besides the
'Leschi' anagram, a new one appears on this title-page:
Angelvs doce mihi jvs, 'Angel, teach me the right'.

The portrait (Fig. 16) bears a Latin inscription stating
that 'the original of this copy is preserved in the private
apartment of a certain Prince of the Holy Roman Empire,
and is a copper-plate engraving, fourteen inches high by
nine inches wide'.   It is described as 'A true portrait of that
Noble Pole, the Famed Hermetic Philosopher, Michael
Sendivogius.   Engraved by I. C. de Reinsperger, anno
1763.'   In it is depicted *inter alia* the famous medal given
to Sendivogius by the Emperor Rudolph II.

As a rule, alchemical portraiture is highly imaginative
and peculiarly unreliable; but the portrait here reproduced
bears a marked resemblance to the engravings of Sendivogius
published during his lifetime on the title-page and in Book
XII of Michael Maier's *Symbola Aureae Mensae Duodecim
Nationum* (1617).   In that work[3] Maier pays Sendivogius
the great compliment of including him among the 'twelve
chosen Heroes of Chymistry' under the pseudonym Anony-

---

[1] *Catalogue of The Newton Papers*, London, 1936; *Prelude*, 307.
[2] *Prelude*, 209.   [3] *Op. cit.* 222.

mus Sarmata, 'to whom', he says, 'a certain person gives this testimony, that he is *Heliocantharus Borealis*, the Sun-Beetle of the North [another pseudonym of Sendivogius], and that the witness has seen with his own eyes the remarkable power of his tincture when projected upon divers metals, also the conversion of the same into first-rate gold . . . the man himself and his dissertations are available and before the eyes and minds alike of very many persons'.

The portrait, and this contemporary testimony of Maier, bring back to us in a striking way the strange figure of Michael Sendivogius, the rescuer and disciple of that romantic and forgotten son of Scotia, Alexander Seton, the Cosmopolite.

REFERENCES

Alethophilo, *Hermetis Trismegisti Erkäntnüss der Natur und des darin sich offenbahrenden Grossen Gottes*, Hamburg, 1706.
Dufresnoy, L., *Histoire de la Philosophie Hermétique*, 3 vols., Paris, 1742.
Sandivogius, M., *A New Light of Alchymie*, trans. J. F[rench], London, 1650.

CHAPTER V

ELIAS COMES TO THE GOLDMAKERS

IT is impossible to read the descriptions of the transmutations attributed to Seton and Sendivogius without being impressed by their air of reality. Taken in their entirety, the episodes provide the most considerable and consistent body of documentary evidence which alchemical literature is able to provide in support of the alleged practicability of metallic transmutation. The reports of such fancied transmutations are surprisingly numerous. Güldenfalk, for example, published in 1784 (p. 51) a collection of more than a hundred references to stories of this kind, including those of Dienheim, Güstenhöver, and Martini. Of all such accounts, only two can compete for verisimilitude with those relating to Seton: one is concerned with the illustrious iatro-chemist, Johannes Baptista van Helmont, and the other with the celebrated physician, Johannes Fredericus Helvetius.

VAN HELMONT MAKES GOLD

Neither of these operators claimed to have prepared the Stone himself, like Seton; in both instances the powder was handed to them by a mysterious stranger. 'He who first gave me the Gold-making Powder', wrote van Helmont in his *Ortus Medicinae*[1] (translated into English under the title *Oriatrike or Physick Refined*), 'had likewise also, at least as much of it, as might be sufficient for changing two hundred thousand Pounds of Gold . . . he gave me perhaps half a

---

[1] A posthumous work, edited by his son Franciscus Mercurius van Helmont, and first published at Amsterdam in 1648, four years after the author's death (2nd edn., Amsterdam, 1652). Van Helmont was a scion of a noble family in the Netherlands, and the quaint frontispiece to *Ortus Medicinae* (Fig. 17) shows him with his son, surrounded by ancestral heraldic bearings.

grain of that Powder, and nine ounces and three quarters of
Quick-silver were thereby transchanged: But that Gold,
a strange Man, being a Friend of one evenings acquaintance,
gave me.'

'I have at distinct turns', wrote van Helmont in the same
place, 'made projection with my hand, of one grain of the
Powder, upon some thousand grains of hot Quick-silver;
and the buisiness succeeded in the Fire, even as Books do
promise; a Circle of many People standing by, together with
a tickling Admiration of us all.' His account of an experiment which is said to have taken place in 1618, in his
laboratory at Vilvorde, near Brussels, is given in another
section of his book:

'I therefore contemplate of the New-birth or renewing of
those that are to be saved, to be made in a sublunary and
earthly Nature, just, even as in the Projection of the Stone
which maketh Gold: For truly, I have divers times seen
it, and handled it with my hands: but it was of colour,
such as is in Saffron in its Powder, yet weighty, and shining
like unto powdered Glass: There was once given unto me
one fourth part of one Grain: But I call a Grain the six
hundredth part of one Ounce: This quarter of one Grain
therefore, being rouled up in Paper, I projected upon
eight Ounces of Quick-silver made hot in a Crucible; and
straightway all the Quick-silver, with a certain degree
of Noise, stood still from flowing, and being congealed,
setled like unto a yellow Lump: but after pouring it
out, the Bellows blowing, there were found eight Ounces,
and a little less than eleven Grains of the purest Gold:
Therefore one only Grain of that Powder, had transchanged 19186 Parts of Quick-silver, equal to it self, into
the best Gold.'

Because of his great and merited reputation as a leading
man of science of his day, van Helmont's testimony concerning the possibility of transmutation carried great weight
in the seventeenth century and later, especially as it was
supported some twenty years after his death by a similar
experience described by the renowned Helvetius.

Johannes Fredericus Helvetius (or Schweitzer) was

physician to the Prince of Orange and a man of great reputation in Holland. In 1667 he created a sensation by publishing at Amsterdam a modest sedecimo booklet of 72 pages, entitled *Vitulus Aureus* ('The Golden Calf'), in which he gave a detailed and most circumstantial account of the transmutation of lead into gold. This work, which is very rare and valuable, contains a fine engraved portrait of the author ostensibly at the age of thirty-six (in 1667), but actually at the age of thirty (in 1661), as an earlier impression of the plate shows (Fig. **18**); there is also a folding plate depicting a famous medal reputed to have been made of alchemical gold and exhibited at Prague in 1648. A German translation was published at Nuremberg in 1668, and an English one soon followed.

The English version is entitled 'The Golden Calf, Which the World adores, and desires: In which is handled The most Rare and Incomparable Wonder of Nature, in Transmuting Metals; *viz.* How the intire Substance of Lead, was in one Moment Transmuted into Gold-Obrizon, with an exceeding small particle of the true Philosophick Stone. At the *Hague*. In the Year 1666.' This tiny book of 128 pages, measuring only about 5 by 3 inches, was possibly the greatest 'thriller' of the seventeenth century in England. It was 'Printed for *John Starkey* at the *Mitre* in *Fleetstreet* near *Temple-Barr*, 1670', and is now extremely rare. A bound copy, originally sold for a shilling in the seventeenth century, might realise eight or ten guineas in a modern auction-room.

In his dedicatory epistle to three friends whom he names and describes quaintly as 'most Accurate Inspectors of the *Vulcanian Anatomy*', Helvetius states categorically that he had himself transmuted lead into gold, but that in so doing he had merely acted as an agent of an art which he knew not. He seemed to regard the publication as necessary 'for the propagation of the Glory of the most Wise, and most powerful God our Creator', and it is significant that he opened his account with a quotation from van Helmont's *De Arbore Vitae*. The relation is very picturesque, but too lengthy to be reproduced here in full.

THE ARTIST ELIAS COMES TO HELVETIUS

There came to Helvetius' house at the Hague, on 27 December 1666, a man 'planely unknown' to him, 'but endued with an honest gravity', and 'cloathed in a *Plebeick Habit*', whose appearance he describes minutely, even to 'some Pock-holes here and there dispersed' in his visage. This picturesque visitor, whom Helvetius designates as a 'Phænix, or Bird most rare to be seen in this Land', was known as the Artist Elias. His shoes were dropping wet with snow, and he wore a cloak and country coat. He removed these, to reveal under his shirt 'five great Golden Pendants' bearing inscriptions of a mystical religious nature: these were copied down and reproduced by Helvetius.

In due course the mysterious visitor 'pulled out of his Pocket an Ivory Box, in which he had three ponderous Fragments, in magnitude scarcely equalizing a small Walnut; these were Glass-like, of the colour of pale Sulphur'. Helvetius seems to have reverenced the exhibit as if it had been a sacred relic. 'After I had plighted my Faith,' he continues, 'I held that pretious Treasure of this *Stone*, within these my hands, for almost a quarter of an hour, and from the Philosophick Mouth of the Owner, I heard many things worthy of note, touching the Wonderfull Effect of the same, for humane and Metallick bodies.'

During a second visit, three weeks later, the stranger responded very grudgingly to Helvetius' repeated entreaties by giving him a small particle of the material, with the promise, 'To-morrow at nine of the Clock, I will return, and shew you, how your Medicine must be used to transmute Lead into Gold'. Although anticipated 'with a most vehement desire', Elias the Artist failed to appear, leaving Helvetius 'most sad in expectation' and reluctant to try the crucial experiment in his absence. At this point, however, Helvetius' wife—whom he describes as 'a very curious Searcher in the Art of that Laudable man'—came to him, troubling him and saying, 'Go to, let us try, I pray thee, the Verity of the work, according to what that man said. For otherwise, I certainly shall not sleep all this night.'

There was no withstanding this seventeenth-century Eve, and so the experiment was put in train. Helvetius ordered his son to kindle the fire. He proceeds: 'I commanded yellow Wax to be brought, wherein to wrap the Matter, and finding Lead, I cut off half an Ounce, or six Drachmes. My Wife wrapped the Matter of the Stone in the Wax, and when the Lead was in Flux, she cast in that little Mass, which, with Hissing and Flatuosity, so performed its Operation in the Crucible well closed, as in one quarter of an hour, the whole Mass of Lead was transmuted into the best Gold.

'Certainly, had I lived in the Age of *Ovid*, I could not have believed, any *Metamorphosis* more rare, than this of the Chimical Art; but if I could behold things with the hundred eyes of *Argus*, I should scarcely see any work of Nature more admirable. For this Lead, mixt with the Stone of the Wise, and in the Fire melted, demonstrated to us a most beautiful colour, yea, I say, it was most green; but when I poured it out into a (Cone, or) susory Cup, it received a colour like blood, and when it waxed cold, shined with the colour of the best Gold: I, and all who were present with me, being amazed, made what haste we could with the Aurificate Lead (even before it was through cold) to a Gold-Smith, who after a precious Examen, judged it to be Gold most excellent, and that in the whole world, better could not be found; withall, adding, that for every Ounce of such Gold, he would give 50 Florens.

'The next day, the rumour of this wonderful Metallick Transmutation was spread all over our *Hague;* whence many illustrious men, and lovers of Art, made hast to me . . . and we went together to the house of a certain very curious Silver-Smith, by name *Brechtelius*, in whose Workhouse, the Excellency of my Gold was evidenced.'

Helvetius describes the assay of his specimen by fusion with three or four parts of silver, followed by treatment with aqua fortis. This perfectly genuine method of assaying the gold by 'parting' led to the remarkable conclusion that it was more than a hundred per cent. pure! Helvetius explained this strange result by assuming that the excess of

Helmont

Ranst

Bauw

Vilain

Ioannes Baptista Van Helmont

Franciscus Mercurius von Helmont

Staßart

Halmale

Reniahne

Merode

17. Ioannes Baptista van Helmont and his Son.
From his *Ortus Medicinae*, Amsterdam, 1652. (See p. 66.)

IOHANNES FRIDERICUS HELVETIUS,
ANHALTINUS CÖTHÖNENSIS DOCTOR atq̃
Practicus Medicinæ HAGÆ COMITIS. Æt 30. Aͦ.1661
Contra vim Mortis est panacea Radix Iesse mea Iesu

18. Iohannes Fridericus Helvetius. Æt. 30. Aͦ· 1661.
From his *Theatridium Herculis Triumphantis*, 's Graven-Hage, 1663.
(See p. 68.)

tincture present in the alchemical gold had transmuted some of the silver into a further quantity of gold.

'Behold!' writes Helvetius in conclusion, 'thus have I exactly, from first to last, commemorated this History. The Gold I indeed have, but where, or in what Land or Countrey *Elias* the *Artist* is at this day hospited, I am wholly ignorant, for he told me, his purpose was to abide in his own Country no longer then this Summer; that after he would travil into *Asia*, and visit the *Holy-Land*. Let the most wise King of Heaven (under the Shadow of whose divine Wings he hath hitherto layn hid) by his Adninistratory [*sic*] Angels accompany him in his intended Journey, and prosper it so, as he living to a great Age, may with his inestimable Talent greatly succour the whole Republick of Christians, and after this Life gloriously behold, and partake of the prepared Inheritance of Life Eternal. *Amen*.'

THE RIDDLE OF ALCHEMICAL TRANSMUTATIONS

The case for the possibility of metallic transmutation, as it has been argued from time to time, has been based to a large extent upon the narratives of van Helmont and Helvetius, with a backing provided by the earlier stories of Seton and Sendivogius. Arguments for the acceptance of these accounts at their ostensible value have usually been marked by enthusiasm and credulity rather than by the severely critical attitude demanded by statements so revolutionary in their implications. 'These records', observes von Meyer, 'afford the most remarkable testimony to the power of alchemistic illusion'; but it is interesting that other reputable historians of chemistry have not hesitated to consider the episodes seriously. Schmieder, admittedly one of the least critical of such historians, remarks that the records of Seton's activities provide all that the historian can demand; that the testimony of expert witnesses of the standing of Dienheim and Zwinger cannot be dismissed lightly; and that trickery, chemical deception, and the lust for gain are all equally untenable as explanations.

Much more weight must be attached to the opinion of Kopp, one of the greatest authorities on alchemy and historical chemistry, that it is unreasonable to impugn the accuracy of men like van Helmont and Helvetius. 'The story of this transmutation is one of the most remarkable on record', wrote Kopp in 1843, referring to van Helmont's experiment. 'It is difficult to see how van Helmont could have been mistaken, as he was a good chemist; or how any deception could have been practised in his own house and in the absence of the alchemist from whom he obtained the transmuting agent. This occurrence is to be numbered with many others in the history of science, in which it is almost as hard to assume the existence of a deception as to accept a statement.'

Since Kopp's day, modern science (or modern alchemy, to use the apt expression of a distinguished physicist) has provided many examples of the limited transmutation of certain elements into others; further, in 1945, an example of rapid transmutation, induced artificially and taking place on a large scale, was provided by the atomic fission of the uranium isotope of atomic weight 235 (U 235). The atomic disintegration of U 235 is due to a chain reaction which sets in as the result of an initiating bombardment with excessively minute subatomic particles known as neutrons. Each disintegrating atom of U 235 liberates further neutrons; these, in turn, affect neighbouring atoms of U 235; and so a progressive atomic decay spreads through the material. Atoms of other elements of lower atomic weight are thereby formed from the heavy uranium atoms, and at the same time there is a partial conversion of matter into energy, taking place with inconceivable rapidity and leading to explosive effects of a stupendous order.

From an alchemical point of view, the neutron may be regarded as a form of the Philosopher's Stone. It is, indeed, a potent transmuting agent, which, in keeping with the common alchemical idea expressed so picturesquely by George Ripley (1415–1490), canon of Bridlington, may be multiplied 'infynytly'; so that ten parts 'beyng multyplyed lykewys, Into ten thousand myllyons, that ys for to sey, Makyth so grete a number I wote not what yt is'.[1] Truly, the ancient conception of the existence of a Philosopher's Stone commands sympathy from the latter-day discoverers of the marvellous powers of the neutron, of inorganic catalysts, and of enzymes, hormones, and vitamins. In the words of a discerning poet,[1] 'Every thing possible to be believ'd is an image of truth. . . . What is now proved was once only imagin'd.'

The doctrine of transmutation lingered on into the eighteenth century, and is still heard of occasionally in its alchemical form; but the pretensions of its adherents gradually ceased to find acceptance in a more enlightened and critical age, possessed of precise scientific methods and criteria. Thus the career of Dr. Price, the last English transmutationist of any repute, ended in tragedy in 1783, when he found himself unable to vindicate his claims before the Royal Society; while in Germany the curtain fell upon the farcical story of the worthy Professor Semler of Halle, whose servants, in their eagerness to please him, introduced first gold and then brass into his preparations.

Modern science does not accept the validity of transmutations of the kind attributed to Seton, Sendivogius, van Helmont, and Helvetius. Must it be concluded, therefore, that these men were charlatans? If not, how are their statements to be viewed?

Of the four figures concerned, that of Seton remains shadowy, elusive, and unidentifiable with any known person. The remaining three are definite historic individuals, van Helmont and Helvetius having been men of outstanding reputation in their day, while Sendivogius was admittedly addicted to charlatanism. Any attempt to answer the above questions must therefore deal mainly with van Helmont and Helvetius.

An outstanding feature of all the narratives is their air of verisimilitude. It must be recalled, however, that they were written in an age of literary verisimilitude, which found its culmination somewhat later in Defoe's *Robinson Crusoe*, and in his *Memoirs of a Cavalier* and *History of the Plague*. In such writings the fabrication of circumstantial, but fictitious, detail into vivid and convincing narratives became a fine

[1] William Blake.

art. Another noteworthy point is that the various narratives are in some respects curiously alike. Both Seton and Helvetius adopted periods of a quarter of an hour for the heating operations; the resulting gold was usually equal in weight to the original base metal; and the quality of the product excelled that of 'ordinary' gold. Even similarities in phraseology may be found. Thus, Flamel, in describing an alleged transmutation in 1382, mentions his 'exceeding great pleasure and delight, in seeing and contemplating the *Admirable workes of Nature*, within the *Vessels*'; similarly, Helvetius wrote in 1667, 'I should scarcely see any work of Nature more admirable.' There are also points of resemblance in the rôles played by Helvetius' wife and Perrenelle, the wife of Nicolas Flamel.[1]

A factor of primary importance was the prevailing attitude towards transmutation in the seventeenth century. In general, the possibility of transmutation was accepted as a matter of course. Alchemical theory demanded transmutation; adepts and puffers alike strove incessantly to achieve transmutation; mystical alchemists made transmutation a pillar of their religious beliefs; and everywhere, credulity and superstition were rampant, and ready to welcome marvellous stories of goldmaking. There was, indeed, a virulent goldmaking germ in the air of the seventeenth century. Even Robert Boyle caught the infection and imagined that he had solved the great secret of 'multiplying'; this he entrusted in writing to his friends Sir Isaac Newton and John Locke, both of whom had a keen interest in alchemy. After Boyle's death, however, some of the relevant papers proved to be missing, and so the method could not be put to the proof: 'I feare I have lost ye first and third part out of my pockett', wrote Newton, in his naïve way, to Locke on 7 July 1692. It is not surprising that in such a favourable soil goldmaking weeds grew apace.

THE SEED OF GOLD

The method adopted in all the experiments described was fundamentally the same. It was based upon the current

[1] *Prelude*, 66.

alchemical theory of the origin and constitution of metals, as laid down, for example, in the *Novum Lumen Chymicum*. Stolcius' illustration of Michael Sendivogius (Fig. **15**) shows the main idea very clearly. Metals, like trees, grow from seed. Just as the seed of a tree has to be nurtured with ordinary water in order to germinate and grow, so the seed of gold (or Philosopher's Stone) has to be nurtured with its appropriate 'water' in order to multiply. In the picture, 'the grand old gardener' with the wooden leg is attending to this need of the sun-tree, with its crop of golden flowers. In strict accordance with theory the 'water' should be sophic mercury; but in their actual experiments the alchemists under notice used as a rule either molten lead or liquid quicksilver as the 'water' or pabulum for their powder of projection.

It can be seen at once how strongly such a theory would appeal to van Helmont, whose celebrated 'tree experiment' became so famous. He allowed a willow-tree, weighing originally five pounds, to grow in a known weight of dry earth, water being supplied to it regularly in the form of rain-water or distilled water. After five years the tree had gained 164 pounds, not including the weight of the shed leaves, and the soil had lost only two ounces in weight. Thus he concluded quite logically (but erroneously, as we now know) that the roots, wood, and bark of the tree had grown from the water alone. 'Are not Metalls of as much esteem with God as trees?' asked the author of the contemporary work *Novum Lumen Chymicum*. Would not van Helmont's experiment fortify him in the belief that gold could grow from its appropriate 'seed' and 'water'?

There was another influence which operated very strongly upon van Helmont and certain other contemporary believers in transmutation. In van Helmont, with all his genius, there was a curious blend of elements almost as incompatible as fire and water. In some respects his work was marked by an accuracy of observation and a power of logical deduction unsurpassed in the seventeenth century; at the same time, his thoughts and activities were deeply tinged with mysticism, superstition, and strong religious sentiments. Thus, his references to transmutation, which, if substantiated, would have been of such tremendous import to science and civilisation, are interposed casually in disquisitions on 'the Tree of Life' (*Arbor vitae*) and 'Life Eternal' (*Vita aeterna*). His interest in the alleged transmutation appears to have been concerned with its bearing upon mysticism and religion rather than upon science. His comment on the crucial experiment runs, indeed, as follows: 'The Soul therefore, and Body, are thus regenerated by Baptisme, and the communion of the unspotted Body of the Lord; so that a just heat of Devotion of the Faithful shall be present. . . . I have said, that Baptisme doth bring with it a real Effect of Purity perceivable by Sense, and that the holy-sacred Communion of the Eucharist, hath something like it in earthly things, whereby we may the more easily believe Regeneration.'

THE ALCHEMIC MESSIAH

To van Helmont, and also to Helvetius and others, a firm belief in transmutation became almost a tenet of their religion. Here, too, there is still another significant circumstance that has been neglected, if not indeed overlooked, in discussions of the supposed metallic transmutations of the seventeenth century. A hundred years or so earlier, Paracelsus, whose word and writings carried so much authority, had foretold the coming of one whom he called Elias the Artist. This prophecy had been disseminated by other writers; so that, in the words of Glauber: '*Many Philosophers, besides* Paracelsus, *have predicted the coming of* Elias the Artist . . . *who, he saith, when he comes, will teach the way by which the Transmutation of Metals may be effected. Here Men imagine Wonders, and generally regarding the words themselves, expect the coming of a certain Man sent from GOD, whom they believe, shall in the later Ages of the World, discover occult Arts, and make known the Secrets of Nature.*'

Doubtless many alchemists supposed the mysterious Seton, or Cosmopolite, to be this forerunner of a new dispensation; it was natural, therefore, for stories of marvellous transmutations to crystallise around this shadowy figure. The *deus ex machina* of one evening's acquaintance, who gave the powder of projection to van Helmont, can legitimately be identified with the same Elias in another guise. Helvetius openly proclaimed his own mysterious visitor to be Elias the Artist. The new day had dawned; the heavens had opened; and the advent of the Alchemic Messiah heralded the establishment of a New Reign, or Fifth Monarchy, of Alchemy.

Zwinger referred to Seton, almost ecstatically, as 'that great and sacred man—that demigod!' Helvetius, in a similar vein, mentioned the intended journey of Elias the Artist to the Holy Land. A messianic motive had found recognition in alchemy. With the coming of the Alchemic Messiah,[1] metallic transmutation was a foregone conclusion to men imbued with the influences of mystical religion and at the same time actuated by an alchemical theory that demanded transmutation. 'Let there be transmutation!' The adept, dominated by his mystical fervour, tuned in to a fiat inaudible to ordinary man: and there *was* transmutation! Here was a new miracle to set beside the turning of water into wine and the multiplication of loaves and fishes. The picturesque accounts of alleged transmutations in the seventeenth century, although irreconcilable with experience when removed from their context and examined in a twentieth-century frame, become intelligible when relegated to their proper environment in time, thought, and belief.

Jung, and other psychologists, have pointed out that in the course of a chemical experiment the operator may pass through psychic experiences which to him form part of the chemical process: there is little doubt that a psychological explanation must be sought for the strange alchemical episodes of the seventeenth century, as well as for the verisimilous accounts of the experiments, operators, and incidents that have come down to us from that fascinating age. Perhaps mass-hypnotism, as well as self-hypnotism, played a part in these episodes. Moreover, the spirit of the

---

[1] Robert Child, in letters written to John Winthrop, jun., in New England (1648–1650), referred to a current report that Elias the Artist, the Messiah of Alchemy, had appeared in the flesh.

seventeenth century was infected with credulity and super-stition to a degree difficult of understanding in modern times.

Glauber, obsessed by his discovery of *sal mirabile* (sodium sulphate) and his interest in salts generally, brushed aside the obvious interpretation of the Paracelsian prophecy. Pointing out solemnly that 'if the word *Elias* be read back-wards, and E changed into A', the result is '*Salia* (that is, salts)', he concluded 'that to him to whom Salts are known, hath Elias appeared'. In brief, as Mr. Micawber might have said if he had been a Latinist, *Elias alias salia!*

Glauber neglected to observe that by an extension of this process *Elias* may be transmuted into *Midas*. Elias was the Midas of seventeenth-century alchemy.

REFERENCES

Glauber, J. R., *Works*, trans. C. Packe, London, 1689.
Helvetius, J. F., *Vitulus Aureus, Quem Mundus adorat & orat*, Amsterdam, 1667; *The Golden Calf, which the World Adores, and Desires*, London, 1670.
Jung, C. G., *Die Erlösungsvorstellungen in der Alchemie*, Zürich, 1937.
Kopp, H., *Die Alchemie in älterer und neuerer Zeit*, 2 vols., Heidelberg, 1886; *Geschichte der Chemie*, 4 vols., Braunschweig, 1843–1847.
Meyer, E. v., *History of Chemistry*, trans. M'Gowan, G., London, 1891; 2nd edn., London, 1898.
van Helmont, J. B., *Ortus Medicinae*, Amsterdam, 1652; *Oriatrike or Physick Refined*, trans. J. C[handler], London, 1662.

CHAPTER VI

A CENTURY OF CHYMICAL ARTISTS

FROM ALCHEMY TO CHYMISTRY

Throughout the long ages of alchemy there were usually men who found more satisfaction in carrying out practical operations in their laboratories than they derived from writing in their studies upon the theoretical, allegorical, and religious aspects of the subject. It is fortunate that many of these skilled practicants left written records of their work and views. In the fifteenth century, for example, Thomas Norton[1] of Bristol was such a man: his *Ordinall of Alchimy* contains much valuable information about the organisation and working of an efficient laboratory, together with an account of the important materials and apparatus in use at that time. It was largely through the work and records of such men that chemistry eventually arose, phoenix-like, from the ashes of alchemy. It was through them that in the nineteenth century Liebig was able to look back and say that alchemy was never at any time anything different from chemistry.

Long before Norton's time the pseudo-Geber, probably in the early years of the fourteenth century,[2] had recorded much clear and accurate chemical knowledge in his *Summa Perfectionis*, or 'Sum of Perfection', a work which Sarton has called 'the main chemical text-book of mediaeval Christendom'. Somewhat later, the *Codex Germanicus*, compiled about 1350, afforded an invaluable account, with fascinating illustrations, of the position which technical chemistry had then reached. With the passage of time and the accumulation of practical knowledge, works of a more specialised type began to appear.[3] Among these were

---

[1] *Prelude*, 179.   [2] *Op. cit.* 48.   [3] *Op. cit.* 75-80.

Brunschwick's *Buch zu Distillieren*, or Book of Distillation, which greeted the opening of the sixteenth century; Biringuccio's *Pirotechnia* (1540), the first printed work on practical metallurgy;[1] and Agricola's *De Re Metallica*, a lavishly illustrated work dealing with mining and metallurgy, first published in 1556.

Towards the end of this century Libavius (1540–1616) produced, in his *Alchymia*, a work of a more general type, in which he laid down the principles of chemistry as then understood and also gave in clear language descriptions of individual chemical processes and products. This work is also of particular interest because he included in it an account of some of his own discoveries, together with a written and pictorial description of his ideal 'chemical house', or laboratory. Ferguson, whose statements on historical chemistry always merit close attention, says of Libavius that 'he was among the first to describe chemical actions in plain language, and he has the credit ascribed to him of writing the first real text-book'. At the same time, there was another side to Libavius. He was deeply imbued with alchemical lore and imagery, and in his *Commentariorum Alchymiae*, or Handbook of Alchemy, he dived almost as deeply as Michael Maïer into mystical alchemy.[2]

However, Libavius had driven in a little further the thin end of the wedge which was now beginning to bring about a cleavage between chemistry and alchemy. The rift gradually became more evident in a notable succession of chemical works published during the seventeenth century. Although for the most part unknown to modern chemists and students, these works may well be regarded as precursors of our present-day text-books of chemistry. As such, they are undeserving of the obscurity to which they have been relegated for so many generations. In considering some of them, we must bear in mind that throughout the seventeenth century and in the early part of the eighteenth century, 'Chymistry', as it was called, was viewed essentially as an Art. In those days it was

[1] *Nature*, 1943, 151, 569.   [2] *Prelude*, 214.

often called the Noble Art, and its skilled practitioners were usually referred to as 'Artists', or 'Chymical Artists'.

Le Febure expressed the contemporary point of view when he wrote in 1660: 'For as it is the only scope of a Science to contemplate, and its end to attain knowledge by that contemplation, wherein it doth rest satisfied without putting the minde to a further inquiry: So Art is only bent to operation, and never ceaseth untill it hath brought the purposes of the Artist to a desired accomplishment'. He concluded that '*Chymistry* may be called both Science and Art in several respects, and so consequently *a practical or operative Science*'. In this period the rank and file of 'Chymists' were interested chiefly in the operative or practical aspect of 'Chymistry', and they took little or no heed of the revolutionary views of a Boyle or a Mayow. This attitude of mind finds repeated expression in the standard chemical works of the period, written by operative masters of the Noble Art.

BEGUIN'S 'CHYMICAL BEGINNER'

Jean Beguin, who sponsored the edition of the *Novum Lumen Chymicum* published at Paris in 1608, was born in Lorraine in the second half of the sixteenth century and died about 1620. He became interested in chemistry and pharmacy, and eventually made his way to Paris in the reign of Henri IV (1589–1610). Here he found a patron in Jean Ribit, sieur de la Rivière, first physician to the king, and a powerful and enthusiastic supporter of science. About the year 1604, aided by Ribit, as also by Turquet de Mayerne, he opened in Paris a school for the teaching of chemistry and pharmacy. Besides his lectures, constituting the first public exposition of chemistry in Paris, he gave practical instruction in the preparation of chemical drugs. This novel combination of lectures and practical work was developed somewhat later by William Davidson, again under Ribit's patronage, at the Jardin du Roi, in Paris.

As a help to his students in their practical operations, Beguin issued privately in 1610 a modest work entitled *Tyrocinium Chymicum*, or 'The Chymical Beginner'. In an expanded form, and under various titles, this work became the most popular chemical text-book of the seventeenth century: between 1612 and 1690 nearly fifty editions[1] were published, mostly in Latin. The first French edition was issued in 1615 under the title *Les Elemens de Chymie*. No English version appeared until Richard Russell's translation of 1669, which bore the title 'Tyrocinium Chymicum: or, Chymical Essays, acquired from the Fountain of Nature, and Manual Experience'.

Written in clear and intelligible language, the *Tyrocinium* provides a refreshing contrast to the obscure outpourings of Beguin's contemporary, Michael Maier, and other mystical alchemists of the time. It consists mainly of straightforward directions for carrying out a long series of pharmaceutical preparations. These directions form the substance of the second and third books, the first book being concerned with a general discussion of chemistry, chemical remedies, and chemical terms. The very rare French edition of 1615 is a neat and modest volume of duodecimo size, bound in vellum, and without illustrations. On the title-page (Fig. 19) Beguin is designated as Almoner to the King. The first book occupies only 73 pages out of a total of 290, showing that the author's main interest lay in the practical work.

Beguin takes the iatro-chemical or spagyric view of chemistry, defining it as the art of separating and recombining natural mixed bodies so as to produce agreeable, salubrious, and safe medicaments. His discussion of chemical theory is commendably brief for a writer of his time. In referring to the Paracelsian principles, mercury, sulphur, and salt, he discriminates between them and the common substances bearing these names; moreover, he emphasises the importance of basing all chemical theories and operations upon these three principles. With regard to the composition of metals, he states (in Russell's words): 'Hydrargyry [mercury] is said to be the Mother of metals, and sulphur the Father. And in these are represented the four Elements, which are the remote matter of all natural bodies.'

[1] For details see T. S. Patterson, *Annals of Science*, 1937, **2**, 243.

LES ELEMENS DE CHYMIE,

DE MAISTRE IEAN BEGVIN AVMOSNIER du Roy.

Seigneur vous m'auez delecté en l'étre des choses qu'auez faictes, & me resiouiray és œuures de vos mains. Psal. 91.

A PARIS.

Chez MATHIEV LE MAISTRE, ruë S. Iean de Latran à l'Arbre sec.

Auec priuilege du Roy.

M. DC. XV.

19. Title-page of *Les Elemens de Chymie*,
by Jean Beguin, Paris, 1615

The second book would have made a strong appeal to the worthy Broun, potingair of Sanctandrois, who had distilled his fragrant 'wateris' a hundred years earlier in Stirling Castle. It opens with an account of such waters, prepared from plants by distillation—a process to which Beguin attaches particular importance. Water of fennel, for example, was obtained by distilling crushed fennel seeds with water containing a little salt: upon distillation, says the French edition of 1615, 'l'eau passera auec l'huile qu'il faudra separer'. Waters are followed by 'strong waters', ordinary aqua fortis being made by distilling saltpetre with dried vitriol (presumably ferrous sulphate).

The last-named preparation is a typical example of the imperfect practical methods of the seventeenth century. Other examples of the kind occur in the list of eight 'spirits', comprising those of wine, tartar, turpentine, sulphur, vitriol, common salt, nitre, and Saturn. Spirit of wine was obtained from wine by repeated rectification. In making spirit of sulphur, the sulphur was burnt in an earthenware vessel placed beneath a glass bell-jar, with the entry of sufficient air to maintain the flame. A pound of sulphur treated in this way yielded only an ounce of spirit, which evidently consisted of a mixture of sulphurous and sulphuric acids. As usual, the remedial uses of the product are set out in some detail. It was mixed with waters, syrups, electuaries, and pills, besides being applied externally to ulcers and skin eruptions. 'Externally also', in Russell's quaint language, 'it is profitable for dealbation of the teeth'; it seems to have achieved a great reputation for this purpose in the days before tooth-powders and tooth-brushes.

Spirit of vitriol was apparently a somewhat similar preparation, perhaps richer in sulphuric acid. It was made by calcining vitriol, dry distilling the solid, and rectifying the distillate. Spirit of nitre, obtained by distilling saltpetre with an inert bolus, was commended, in the words of Russell, as 'the true Balsamick fire of nature, and in the Cholick, Pleurisie, and Quinsey, is very beneficial'.

A particular interest attaches to the 'Esprit ardant de

Saturne', or Burning Spirit of Saturn, since this product must be identified with acetone, the original discovery of which is therefore credited to Beguin. This very precious spirit, he says, may be used for diverse maladies, internal as well as external. As the name implies, he regarded it as a liquid principle derived from lead. He made it by digesting minium, or calx of Saturn, with vinegar, and distilling the resulting crude acetate of lead from a sand-bath. The odour, no less than the inflammability, of this liquid evidently created a sensation in Beguin's laboratory, for he writes that if a capacious recipient is not well luted to the retort 'tout le laboratoire se remplira d'vne si grande & si suaue odeur, que ie croy fermemēt qu'elle surpasse de beaucoup les odeurs de tous les vegetables odoriferans mis ensemble' —or, in Russell's words, 'so great a fragrancy (filling the whole Laboratory) will be lost, as I doubt not but if the odours of all odorate Vegetables were gathered together, and mixed, it would far exceed them'. What Beguin would have thought if he had stumbled upon thio-acetone is hard to imagine.

The nomenclature is often confusing. Sometimes sensibly identical materials made in different ways are given different names, as with spirit of sulphur, spirit of vitriol, and oil of vitriol. For the last-named, vitriol was carefully recrystallised three times, dried, and warmed for three days with spirit of wine. The spirit of wine was then removed by distillation, after which the residue was distilled from an ash-bath.

Beguin's rudimentary attempt at classifying his products is based upon similarities in physical properties and preparative methods. Besides his waters, strong waters, spirits, tinctures, balms, and extracts—which were all liquids—Beguin gives directions for making solid preparations, such as calcination products, salts, flowers, and magisteries. Calcination products were often of uncertain composition; but sometimes definite substances resulted, as in the so-called calcination of saltpetre, when flowers of sulphur were added carefully to the molten salt. The resulting potassium sulphate seems to have been a worthy forerunner of Glauber's *sal mirabile*, as it was recommended for use 'in all diseases, both internal and external'.

Among the salts appear cream of tartar, salt of corals, and salt of Saturn. Salt of corals, made by dissolving corals in distilled vinegar, is extolled for its many virtues, including purification of the blood. Salt of Saturn (lead acetate) is more wonderful still, for 'if six grains be given in white wine in the Pest, it cures the sick in twenty-four hours'. Such frequent claims of remarkable curative effects probably had a good deal to do with the wide circulation of Beguin's book and of other similar works of that era.

One of the most interesting preparations falling under the general heading of Flowers is benzoic acid, appearing in the guise of 'Fleurs de Benioin', or 'Flowers of Benjamin'. This was made by subliming coarsely powdered benjamin (gum benzoin) in a round pot surmounted by a paper cone. The flowers are described as a sovereign remedy for asthma and all affections of the lungs, if half a scruple be taken in a suitable liquor or syrup; they are also excellent for pimply and red faces.

Beguin's definition of a magistery—like so many definitions of the modern student—begins with the over-worked words 'is when'. Russell's translation runs: 'A *Magistery* is when the mixt body is so prepared by chymical artifice without extraction ; as all its homogeneal parts are preserved, and deduced to a more noble degree, either of substance or quality, the exteriours of impurity being segregated'. Magistery of Tartar, for example, was made by adding an ounce of spirit of vitriol, drop by drop, to four ounces of oil of tartar, and evaporating the product to dryness with the help of three or four additions of spirit of wine. Since oil of tartar was a calcined cream of tartar (potassium carbonate) which had been allowed to deliquesce, the resulting white and fixed Vitriolate Tartar must have been the same as the product obtained in the calcination of saltpetre with sulphur (potassium sulphate), but this identity was not realised.

The short third book of *Les Elemens de Chymie*, occupying only 20 pages in the edition of 1615, is devoted to the

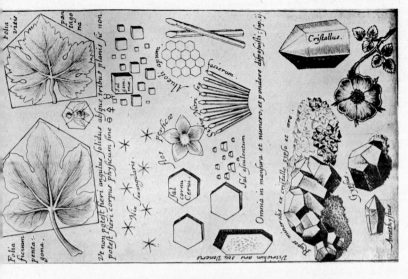

21. A plate from *Les Elemens de la Philosophie de l'Art du Feu, ou Chemie*, W. Davissone, Paris, 1657.

(See p. 90.)

20. Willielmus Davissonus, Nobilis Scotus. Æt. 60. D. Schull pin. P. Lombart sculp.

(See p. 88.)

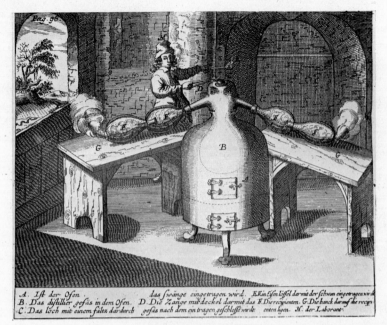

A. Ist der Ofen.
B. Das distiller gefäs in dem Ofen.
C. Das löch mit einem fältz dardurch
das schwänge eingetragen wird.
D. Die Zange mit deckel darmit das
gefäs nach dem ein tragen geschlossen wirde
E. Ein Löffel darmit der schwan eingetragen wird
F. Die recipienten. G. Die banck darauf sie recip
enten ligen. H. der Laborant.

22. Glauber's 'Iron Man'.

From Glauber's *Works*, ed. C. Packe, London, 1689. (See p. 95.)

A. Ist der Ofen darin das holtz gebresset wirde.
B. Der deckel darmit der Ofen geschlossen wirde.
C. Die thur in dem Ofen dardurch man die kohlen aus nimbt.
D. Seind die rohren darinnen sich der holtz safft
Condensirt vnd heraus runt.
E. Ist ein fas darin der hole essig laufft.

23. The Destructive Distillation of Wood.

(After Glauber.) (See p. 98.)

preparation of the quintessences of human blood, wine, corals, and pearls. Beguin regards a quintessence as an ethereal, celestial, and very subtle substance composed of the three principles of the original body deprived of their gross, corruptible, and mortal qualities. This extreme refinement seems to have depended mainly upon repeated distillation, the corals and pearls being first dissolved in distilled vinegar. The blood, drawn from a man who is healthy and in the flower of his age, has to be boiled continually 'iusques à ce que le dragon ait deuoré sa queuë'. The dragon devouring his own tail is a familiar alchemical image;[1] Beguin, however, uses the phrase not as a mystical expression, but as a practical direction to continue the process until nothing but a dry solid is left, that is, until the attainment of complete coagulation or fixity.

Viewed as a production of the early seventeenth century, Beguin's book is remarkably clear and intelligible. In it he made a very definite step forward from the mysticism of alchemy towards the precision of chemistry, and for this reason the book is a landmark in the history of the development of chemistry. Nevertheless, it would be unreasonable to suppose that Beguin was able to cut himself free from alchemical influences. That he did not do so is evidenced by his enthusiastic commendation of the *Novum Lumen Chymicum*. Moreover, the time was not ripe for the abandonment of alchemical terms and modes of expression. Thus Beguin uses such terms as 'the Celestial Eagle more white than snow', and designates the metals by the names of planets. He appears to accept the precepts of the Emerald Table of Hermes, although he does not necessarily interpret them in the alchemical sense. Thus, referring to the second precept, he writes: 'That which is superiour, is as that which is inferiour. For by the same reason as nature doth produce Plants, and other vegetables in the superficies of the earth; so doth she in subterranean places generate metals, though more slowly and in longer space of time.'

Finally, like van Helmont and other contemporaries,

---

[1] *Prelude*, 108, 216, 241.

H

Beguin associates religion with chemistry. He begins and ends *Les Elemens de Chymie* with a quotation from the ninety-second Psalm. The title-page bears the French version of 'For thou, Lord, hast made me glad through thy work: I will triumph in the works of thy hands'. The last page ends: 'A brutish man knoweth not; neither doth a fool understand this'. The book is dedicated 'Au Roy des Cieux, immortel, invisible . . . auquel ie voue et dedie ce petit mien labeur'.

DAVIDSON'S 'PYROTECHNIC PHILOSOPHY'

In the early days of Beguin's *magnum opus*, probably during the second decade of the seventeenth century, there appeared in Paris a very remarkable Scotsman (Fig. **20**). William Davidson, Davison, or Davisson (1593–c. 1669), was the first of his countrymen to show how to extract a safe and respectable livelihood from the teaching of that 'slippery science' which even in the days of Chaucer had made many so bare. Appropriately enough, Davidson was an Aberdonian, and he claimed descent from several noble Scots families, including those of Forbes, Leslie, Huntly, and Argyll. Soon after graduating at Marischal College, Aberdeen, in 1617, he went to Paris, probably as a physician[1] and apothecary, and according to Hoefer at the instance of Jean Ribit, sieur de la Rivière, to whom Beguin also had owed his establishment in the French capital. Davidson's knowledge of chemistry enabled him to continue the lecturing tradition established by Beguin, and eventually led to his appointment to the first chair of chemistry to be founded in Paris; he also became a physician to the King of France, Louis XIII.

Davidson's chair was possibly the earliest of all chairs of chemistry, although other chairs were founded at Marburg and Jena at about the same time. The Paris chair was associated with the Jardin du Roi, where a chemical laboratory had been in existence for some years before the official opening of the Jardin and its buildings in 1640. Davidson

---

[1] His Aberdeen degree was M.A.: King's College first conferred the M.D. degree in 1654, Marischal College not until 1700.

also became professor of botany. In the chemical laboratory, pleasantly situated in the old garden of Guy de la Brosse, the professor's public teaching of the theory of chemistry was eventually supplemented in a later generation by the practical illustrations of a demonstrator attached to the post. The progress of chemistry in France was closely bound up during the next two hundred years with the activities of the professor and demonstrator of chemistry at this institution, known later as the Jardin des Plantes, and since 1792 as Le Musée d'Histoire Naturelle. Among the eminent chemists who held office there were Glaser, Bourdelain, the brothers Rouelle, Macquer, Gay-Lussac, and Chevreul; moreover, the great Lavoisier was a pupil of Guillaume Rouelle, and in a later age Frémy and Moissan worked on fluorine in the same institution. Through such men France exerted a profound influence upon the general development of chemistry.

The teaching of this first Scots professor of chemistry attracted pupils from many countries, and it was for their benefit that Davidson published, in 1633–1635, what was essentially an early text-book of chemistry, under the title *Philosophia Pyrotechnica, seu Curriculus[1] Chymiatricus* ('Pyrotechnic Philosophy, or a Course in Spagyric Chymistry'). This was issued in several editions, first in Latin and afterwards in French; but it was never translated into Davidson's native language. Hellot's French translation[2] is entitled 'Les Elemens de la Philosophie de l'Art du Feu, ou Chemie'. The author is described on the title-page as the 'sieur Davissone, Escuyer, Conseiller, Medecin du Roy, & Intendant de la Maison & Jardin Royal des Plantes Medicinales, au Fauxbourg S. Victor, à Paris'.

The Latin edition is an octavo volume of more than six hundred pages. It opens with a nicely executed engraving of an Emblem of the Complete Work, in the best alchemical tradition. The first two parts of the book reflect to a large extent the general ideas of Paracelsus. They are devoted to theoretical and speculative considerations, and contain many

---

[1] Changed to *Cursus* in the Latin edition of 1641.
[2] Paris, 1651 (1st edn.), 1657 (2nd edn.).

references to the Aristotelian and Galenic philosophies, together with a complex geometrical diagram based upon the concentric representation of the cosmos so characteristic of mediaeval science. The short third part, prefaced by a summary in the form of a folding table, is concerned with explanations of chemical terms. The fourth part deals with the apparatus and operations of chemistry; for example, with the preparation and medical uses of corrosive sublimate, flowers of benjamin, and the quintessence of wine. An engraved plate shows various kinds of distilling apparatus employed in the practical processes.

Thus, after describing the sublimation of flowers of benjamin, Davidson states that the substance is used for diseases of the lungs, for coughs, and for asthma, as also in the preparation of cosmetics for ladies. 'After the same fashion', he continues, 'I will proceed to show various specifics which have a distinctive odour and will delight my hearers.'

This part of the book also contains one of the earliest contributions to crystallography—'a new subject', as Davidson says, 'which, so far as I know, none before me has elaborated'. Besides crystals, he includes in his considerations various plant and animal forms, such as the stalks, leaves, and flowers of plants, and the bee and its cells. One of two engraved plates illustrating this subject shows a selection of twenty regular solids, headed by the cube, octahedron, tetrahedron, icosahedron, and dodecahedron, which Davidson associates severally, according to Plato, with the four elements—earth, air, fire, and water—and the quintessence.

The second plate (Fig. 21) is intended to illustrate the statement that the Platonic doctrine is sufficient to explain 'the true cause of the different forms, numbers and sundry proportions in bodies, as the figure of the hexagon, the cube, the pentagon, the octahedron and the rhomb', in the objects depicted, and also in the emerald, diamond, and so forth. The representations include crystals of common salt (*sal esculentum*), rock salt (*sal gemmae*), copper sulphate or 'vitriol of Venus' (*vitriolum aeris seu Veneris*),[1] gypsum,

----

[1] *Prelude*, 88.

Styrian nitre, 'hexagonal snow' (*nix sexangularis*), and the so-called carbonate of ammonia (*sal cornu Cerui*); leaves enclosed in pentagons; a bee enclosed in a hexagon; a series of bees' cells shown in section, and curiously resembling the modern formula of a complex aromatic hydrocarbon; and a peach blossom and one other flower.

The first of two inscriptions on this plate states that 'as a solid angle cannot be made without three planes, so a natural body cannot be made without salt, sulphur and mercury'. The second is a quotation from the Wisdom of Solomon:[1] 'Thou hast ordered all things in measure and number and weight'. This dictum summarises Davidson's views, which are based upon the Pythagorean and Platonic conceptions of the importance of number, geometrical form, and harmonies in the interpretation of Nature and the Cosmos.[2]

Although imbued with the theoretical ideas of his alchemical predecessors, and given to associating the doctrines of chemistry with those of religion, in his practical outlook William Davidson has claims to be called a chemist rather than an alchemist. In this respect he has affinities with Beguin and Glauber, as one looking ahead to chemistry rather than backwards to alchemy after the general fashion of his age. An alchemist in theory, he was a chemist in practice.

Davidson's great reputation led to his appointment as councillor to the King of France, and in 1648 he became keeper of the Jardin du Roi. John Evelyn mentions in his diary that on 21 October 1649, during a visit to Paris, he 'went to hear Dr. D'Avinson's lecture in the physical garden, and see his laboratory, he being Prefect of that excellent garden, and Professor Botanicus'. Davidson prided himself on his ancestry, and styled himself 'Nobilis Scotus'; moreover, he gallicised his name, which fortunately began with the right letter, to d'Avissone, and obtained for himself and his descendants all the rights and privileges of a gentleman of France. Although he resigned his French

---

[1] In *The Apocrypha according to the Authorised Version*, xi, 20.
[2] *Prelude*, 247.

appointments in 1650, in order to become physician and chemist to John Casimir, King of Poland, he maintained a close association with France, and his descendants appear to have become completely gallicised.[1]

GLAUBER'S 'WORKS'

The greatest practical chemist of the seventeenth century was Johann Rudolph Glauber (1604–1670), the son of a Franconian barber of Karlstadt. Most of his original laboratory work was carried out before the middle of the century, during the difficult period of the Thirty Years War, after which he added a voluminous literary output to his experimental activities. Glauber seems to have gained his extensive knowledge through his own experimentation and reading, in the course of a busy life interspersed with much travel.

It seems likely that Glauber's career was influenced by a striking cure which he experienced in his twenty-first year, after falling into 'a burning Feaver, known by the name of *The Hungarian Disease*', on the way to Vienna. Some eight miles from that city, following the counsel of the local inhabitants, he drank of the mineral water of a neighbouring well, which completely restored him. 'I asked them what kind of water that was?' wrote Glauber. 'They answered that it was water of Salt-petre, which I believed, being then unskilful in such things. . . . Now it is certainly evident to me, that that Fountain contained that Salt which *Paracelsus* called *Sal Enixam*, and I *Sal Mirabile*, and also that it is the nature of that to shoot into long Crystals, and yet not to conceive flame.' After his later discovery of *sal mirabile*, Glauber was wont to regard it as a universal remedy: there is no evidence that he established its presence in the potent waters of Neapolis Viennensis, as some (including even Ferguson) have stated. This salt (sodium sulphate) is still known as *sal mirabile Glauberi*, or 'Glauber's salt'.

In 1646 Glauber reached Amsterdam in the course of

---

[1] *Proceedings of the Society of Antiquaries of Scotland*, 1875, **10**, 265; *J. Chem. Education*, 1941, **18**, 503.

his wanderings. Here, save for travels in Germany during the years 1649 to 1655, he spent the rest of his life. At Amsterdam, in 1650, was completed the publication of his first and most important book, *Furni novi Philosophici*. This was translated into English with surprisingly little delay, for those days, Dr. John French's version being issued at London in 1651 under the title *A Description of new Philosophical Furnaces*. The title is somewhat misleading, since the description of each kind of furnace is merely a preliminary to detailed accounts of its uses in 'making Spirits, Oyles, Flowers, and other Medicaments'. There are also directions showing 'how to make and prepare Iron, Earthen, Glass, and other kind of Instruments necessary for the aforesaid four furnaces, as also other necessary, and most profitable Manuals'. In brief, the work is a compendium of chemical preparations, set out in clear terms, together with descriptions of the necessary apparatus and manipulative methods. In its day it was, in effect, an up-to-date text-book of practical chemistry, consisting to a large extent of original work.

Glauber wrote his works in German, with Latin titles. About thirty treatises, covering the period 1648 to 1660, were published in 1661 under the title *Opera Omnia*, at Amsterdam. Altogether Glauber published some forty distinct treatises, an astounding performance for one who devoted so much time to laboratory work and to travel. An English edition of *Opera Omnia* was issued by Christopher Packe, in 1689, about twenty years after Glauber's death. This large folio volume, comprising some 750 pages, with illustrations printed from Glauber's original copperplates, bears the following descriptive title-page: 'The Works of the Highly Experienced and Famous Chymist, John Rudolph Glauber: containing Great Variety of Choice Secrets in Medicine and Alchymy In the Working of Metallick Mines, and the Separation of Metals: Also, Various Cheap and Easie Ways of making Salt-petre, and Improving of Barren-Land, and the Fruits of the Earth. Together with many other things very profitable for all the Lovers of Art and Industry.' It is of interest that the list of subscribers given in the book contains the name of 'The Honourable *Ro. Boyl*, Esq;'.

The collection opens with French's translation, *Philosophical Furnaces*; other outstanding treatises are *The Mineral Work*, *Miraculum Mundi*, *A Treatise of the Nature of Salts*, and *The Prosperity of Germany*. The writings are disconnected and often redundant and unduly discursive; at the same time they contain much sound sense and new information of a practical nature. On the whole, the volume may be viewed as a precursor of the modern chemical encyclopaedia, suggestive also in some respects of a book of workshop recipes and processes. The writer combines the superstitions and extravagances of the thorough-going alchemist with unusual practical skill, accurate observation, and a keen appreciation of the possibilities of applied chemistry. In one place he shows himself to be an ardent believer in the doctrine of signatures;[1] in others he is anxious to apply chemistry in the arts and industries, including agriculture, as well as in medicine. He is at the same time an economist, and in his lengthy treatise on *Teutschlands Wohlfarth* ('The Prosperity of Germany') he emphasises the importance of the proper development of raw materials in his native country. Glauber thus has a two-fold character: situated in time midway between Paracelsus and Scheele, he partakes of the characteristics of both.

Glauber accepted the fundamental theoretical conceptions of alchemy, and used alchemical phraseology freely in expressing his experimental results. His admirable method of preparing silver chloride, for example, is described in the following quaint terms: '*The Feather or Wings are thus found and acquired*. Dissolve one pound of pure Silver in *Aqua Fortis*. If to this Solution you pour good Spirit of Salt, in which Common Salt is dissolved, all the *Luna* will be precipitated from the *Aq. Fortis* in the form of a white Calx. In which Precipitation the Silver acquires the aforesaid white Pidgeons Feathers from the Salt-water, and submergeth them, together with it self, in the bottom of the Vessel. In this Precipitation also the *Aqua Fortis*

[1] *Prelude*, 89, 96, 182.

perisheth not, but passeth into good *Aqua Regia*. This white Calx of *Lune*, which I have otherwise called *Mercury* of *Lune*, if it be diligently edulcorated and dried, then are the Feathers prepared.'

In an interesting passage of his *Miraculum Mundi*, Glauber sets out by describing a process in alchemical terms, thereafter rendering it in contemporary chemical phraseology, because, as he says, 'this Enigma is a little too obscure for the unskilful'. The process deals with 'the manner of concentrating and amending of Metals by Nitre', and Glauber's description is illustrated by a plate (Fig. 22) of the celebrated apparatus known as the Iron Man or Fiery Man.

'First', he writes, 'a Man is to be made of Iron, having two noses on his head, and on his crown a mouth, which may be opened, and again close shut. This, if it be to be used for the concentration of Metals, is to be so inserted into another man, made of Iron or Stone, that the inward head only may come forth of the outward man, but the rest of his body or belly may remain hidden in the belly of the exteriour man. And to each nose of the head, glass receivers are to be applied, to receive the vapours ascending from the hot stomach. When you use this man, you must render him bloody with fire, to make him hungry and greedy of Food. When he grows extreamly hungry, he is to be fed with a white Swan: When that Food shall be given to this Iron man, an admirable Water will ascend from his fiery stomach into his head, and thence by his two noses flow into the appointed Receivers; a Water, I say, which will be a true and efficacious *Aqua-vitae;* for the Iron man consumeth the whole swan by digesting it, and changeth it into a most excellent and profitable Food for the King and Queen, by which they are corroborated, augmented, and grow. But before the Swan yieldeth up her spirit, she singeth her Swan-like song, which being ended, her breath expireth with a strong wind, and leaveth her roasted body for meat for the King, but her *anima* or spirit she consecrateth to the gods, that thence may be made a *Salamander*, a wholsome Medicament for men and metals.'

This description is strongly reminiscent of Basil Valentine, and, indeed, Glauber associates it with the Sixth Key of Basilius.[1] His interpretation is given in the following words:

'The Iron man is the destilling Vessel, which I have described in the Second Part of my Furnaces. This is put into another Iron or Stone Furnace, and the fire under it. To the noses or pipes of the upper part, some Receivers are to be so applied, that at least three Glass-Receivers may be applied to one nose, the first of which is to be firmly luted to the nose; the second must enter the perforated belly of the first Glass, by a Pipe; and in like manner the third must be inserted into the belly of the second; the Pipe of the second Glass, which entereth the belly of the first, is to be well luted; the third is not to be luted to the belly of the second, but to remain open, that the expiring gass may go out of the second into the third. To the other nose also three or four Receivers are to be applied after the same manner, but so that the last may remain unluted. The white Swan is the *Amalgama* of Tin and *Argent-vive*, to which Nitre is added. . . . This powder is *The Swan of Basilius*, of which he prepareth Meat for the King; but I call it *The Fulmen of Jove*, by which all Metals are destroyed and reduced into nothing. And from this nothing, Metals much better and more noble are generated *de novo*.'

Glauber explains that 'the noxious and superfluous Sulphur of the Tin is burnt by the Salt-Petre, which being separated, the rest of the Tin acquireth a more compact and better body'. A wordy disquisition follows, in the enigmatical style of Basil Valentine; but a careful winnowing of Glauber's statements in this place reveals that he had more than a glimmering of the processes now known as oxidation and reduction, and of their complementary relationship.

'The mass remaining in the stomach of the Iron man', he continues, when at length he descends again to earth from his cloud of Basilian verbiage, 'cannot be reduced to its former body by Fire alone. . . . Nevertheless, by the

[1] *Prelude*, 196.

following operation it may be reduced to its pristine Body: Put it into a very strong Crucible, which cover, and set in a Wind-Furnace that will give a very strong Fire (such as is my Fourth Furnace) the Fire being raised by degrees, let it be made white-hot, and when it is so, the Cover being a little removed, throw into the fiery mass a little Sulphur, Antimony, or Coals in fine powder, put on the Cover again, and lastly, cover the Crucible over with Coals, that all the matter may flow well. In this operation the combustible Sulphur will enter the fixt Nitre, and separate it from the fixed Metal, and with the same, whatsoever of Sulphur, Antimony, or Coals was added, will be turned into black Scoria. The Tin . . . returneth into a metallick body, which after it is poured out and cold, is to be separated from the Scoria. Jupiter hath the aspect of his former body, but is amended, as the proof will shew him that pleaseth to make it; the remaining Scoria are to be kept, because an excellent universal Medicine may be made of them.'

Besides discovering new substances, such as sodium sulphate and arsenic trichloride ('butter of arsenic)', potassium acetate, and ethyl chloride, Glauber improved the methods for preparing many others, especially mineral acids and salts. He also noticed the formation of certain other substances which he could not collect owing to their volatility: these included the gases now known as sulphur dioxide, nitrogen peroxide, and hydrogen chloride. Moreover, he began to perceive the fundamental nature of a salt, to grasp the essential character of a double decomposition, and to visualise dimly the idea of chemical affinity. An example of his acumen is to be found at the opening of his *Philosophical Furnaces*, where he describes the preparation of 'spirit of salt' (hydrochloric acid) by dry distilling a mixture of common salt, green vitriol, and alum. 'Thou wilt object', he writes, 'that the spirit made after this maner is not the true spirit of salt by reason of the mixture of vitriall and allome, but mixed, and compounded. I answer; There can by this way distill no spirit of vitrioll, and allome, being that which I often tryed, casting vitriol, or allome into the furnace, where I received no spirit at all.'

In *Miraculum Mundi* there is an interesting account of the destructive distillation of wood in a brick oven (Fig. **23**), the smoke or fume being forced out through an air condenser formed of an earthen channel or pipe. Glauber notes that the acid vinegar of wood carries with it 'a sharp hot Oyl of a dark reddish colour'. With his keen eye for applications, he points out that the oil (tar) is useful for preserving wood from rotting. Also, hedge stakes impregnated with it will repel wild beasts, seeing that the latter shun all strong odours. Better still, if hempen cords soaked in this oil are bound about fruit-trees, 'it will hinder the creeping up of Spiders, Ants . . . and other the like Insects, which are wont to damnifie Fruit; inasmuch as those Insects plainly abhor such hot Oils'.

Glauber records two ways of concentrating the acid constituent of the aqueous distillate from wood. Referring to distillation, he says: 'If this acid Spirit be rectified . . . it much exceedeth the common Wine, and Beer Vinegar in sharpness'. Further, he found that the acid could be concentrated by freezing out water, as the following passage shows: 'This Vinegar of Wood being exposed in Hogsheads to the cold in Winter, that it may be frozen to Ice, the Phlegm only freezeth, but the sharp spirit, with the Oil, is not turned into Ice, but remaineth in the middle of the Hogshead so sharp, that it corrodeth metals like *Aquafortis*'.

So early as 1648, in the destructive distillation of coal, Glauber obtained a black oil from which he distilled fractions evidently consisting of crude benzene hydrocarbons and crude middle oil; the more elusive coal gas, however, seems to have escaped his notice.

Glauber took a sorry view of his contemporaries, whom he considered to be envious, wicked, and ungrateful. 'All good manners are turned into bad,' he lamented; 'women turn men, and men women in their fashion and behaviour, contrary to the institution and ordinance of God and Nature.' He complained of the deceit and dishonesty of servants, as Norton had done some two hundred years earlier, and even of collaborators whom he had taken into his laboratory.

'Scarce one in ten can be found', he wrote, 'that you may give credit to, and trust . . . my own thirty years of experience hath taught me.' For this reason his practical directions, usually so clear, occasionally become obscure when he fears that he is on the point of disclosing a particularly valuable secret. Thus the description, in *Miraculum Mundi*, of the preparation of his cherished *sal mirabile* begins: 'R. of common salt two parts, dissolve it in a sufficient quantity of common water; pour *A*. upon the solution; put the mixture into a glass Body . . . set on an Head, and begin to distil with Fire of sand, encreasing your Fire gradually'. The products are spirit of salt and *sal mirabile*, so that *A*. is evidently spirit of vitriol.

Glauber seems to have been obsessed with the 'wonderful Virtues' of this salt. Among its many uses in medicine he declares that 'in the *Tooth-ach* it performs Wonders, drawing out the Humours causing dolour in the Teeth'; further, 'against green Wounds of the Body and old Fistula's . . . this salt is egregiously useful'. The long list of its 'utilities' in various arts and in alchemy provides examples of Glauber's superstitions and fantastic notions, as well as of his keen observation and practical ability. Thus, he states that dogs, cats, mice, and insects drowned in water 'by help of it may again be restored to life'. The page containing this startling claim also bears entries showing that Glauber had studied the hydration and dehydration of sodium sulphate, for he writes: 'It suddenly coagulates River-Water, Rain-Water, or any destilled Water, so as it becomes Ice, and may be carried in Paper, a Sack, or Wooden-Box or Chest, wheresoever you will, and be dissolved when need is, so as the salt may be separated from the Water'. Here he evidently refers to the action of heat on the crystalline hydrate. He had also used the salt as a drying agent, for he adds: 'It separates the Phlegm from subtile Mineral-spirits, whence they are made volatile and more powerful'.

Glauber was even inclined to regard his marvellous salt as the Philosopher's Stone. In discussing its possible transmuting powers he observes ingenuously 'That here is nothing of impossibility, I have obscurely in this and

other places shewed; but which way the Operation is to be
instituted, I have not yet declared: because I my self have
not as yet obtained a perfect understanding of the same'.
Glauber was a firm believer in transmutation, as also in
the existence of an alkahest, or universal solvent; but
fortunately for the progress of chemistry he did not allow
himself to become a slave of the Stone. With his highly
developed faculty for finding practical uses for his products,
he applied one of his unsuccessful transmuting tinctures
as a hair restorer: 'My bald head', he wrote, 'began to be
cover'd with black curl'd hairs, from which I am verily
perswaded, that had I more of the like Tincture, it would
have wholly renewed me.'

Glauber's applications of his discoveries may truly be
described as extensive and peculiar. On one page of
Miraculum Mundi, for example, he gives practical hints
alleged to be of benefit to clockmakers, smiths, pewterers,
cabinetmakers, tailors, shoemakers, weavers, dyers, and
potters. He describes how to remove corns and warts, how
to make women's skins of a beautiful whiteness by means
of 'an Egregious Cosmetick', and how to perform certain
'waggish tricks', such as throwing doped seeds to birds, so
that they may be taken with one's hand. But some of his
suggestions are remarkably apt. Thus, he describes how
to prepare a varnished linen cloth, with the aid of linseed
oil boiled with a drier, so that soldiers, merchants, and
others may travel dry in the rain. He also anticipated
chemical warfare by preparing 'firey Waters' for use against
the Turks: 'by this Invention of mine', he says, 'no man is
slain, and yet the victory wrested out of the Enemies
hands'. At the same time he condemns the 'diabolical
abuse' of gunpowder, which he calls a 'mischievous composition'.

Neither his chemical discoveries and inventions nor his
books brought Glauber any adequate material return. 'By
all that ever I writ', he says, 'I never gained one half-peny.'
It is a melancholy reflection that after a lifetime devoted
to chemistry he died in poverty. Chemistry undoubtedly
owed him a great debt; but there was no reward in his

day for a research chemist, however skilled, who possessed no wealthy or influential patron, and was not a qualified medical man, an apothecary, or a charlatan. Nevertheless Glauber, like Scheele in the following century, maintained his enthusiasm for experimental chemistry in spite of all material cares. For the last four years of his life he was bedridden, probably as a result of unguarded operations on compounds of mercury, arsenic, and antimony. At the end of his *Spagyrical Pharmacopoeia* he wrote, lying on a sick-bed: 'If the most wise God will prolong my life untill the next Summer, and enable me to write out of Bed, my purpose is to publish some other new wonderfull Works'.

To the seeker after new chemical knowledge Glauber said: 'It is easier to add to things already found out, than to become the first Author of new inventions. . . . He that seeks shall find. Wherefore rise from your soft Pillows, and with Smutted Hands touch black Coals, and accurately give heed to the institutions of Art. For with Idleness, Eating, Drinking, and playing on Musick, you shall never approach to great Mysteries.'

LE FEBURE'S 'COMPLEAT BODY OF CHYMISTRY'

Soon after William Davidson's departure from Paris to Poland in 1650, a certain Nicolas le Fevre, or Nicasius le Febure,[1] was appointed demonstrator in chemistry at the Jardin du Roi. Like Beguin and Davidson before him, le Febure (Fig. 24) came to Paris and gave public lectures and demonstrations on chemistry, probably at the same time conducting a business as an apothecary. His reputation is evident from entries in the diary of John Evelyn, who in 1647 'frequented a course of chemistry, the famous Monsieur Lefevre operating upon most of the nobler processes'. After nearly ten years at the Jardin he became 'Royal Professor in Chymistry' to Charles II in 1660, a few months after the Restoration; he was also appointed Apothecary-in-Ordinary to the royal household. In 1663 he was elected an original

[1] The entry in *The Record of the Royal Society of London* (1940) is 'Le Febure Nicasius'

Fellow of the newly founded Royal Society. He died in London in 1669.

Le Febure had been in London only a short time when his *Traicté de la Chymie* (1660) was published in Paris. This work achieved a wide and lasting reputation. For the next hundred years it ranked as a standard treatise on chemistry, an augmented French edition in five volumes being published so late as 1751. It was also translated into German, Latin, and English. The first English edition (London, 1664) was issued under the title (Fig. 25) *A Compleat Body of Chymistry*, and dedicated to Charles II: it consists of two books of small quarto size, usually bound together, and amounting to some 700 pages, with eight folding copper-plates of chemical apparatus and symbols.

The book was written in the first place for the use of apothecaries. As a compendium of medicinal preparations it would appeal also to a much wider public, and would even find a place in the still-rooms of many of the large house-holds of the seventeenth and eighteenth centuries. Le Febure mentioned indeed that he wrote the treatise in the vulgar tongue, rather than in Latin, because he hoped that it might be useful 'not only to the Apothecaries, but likewise to men of other professions'.

Le Febure was an admirable pharmacist, and the *Compleat Body* contains the results of some thirty-five years' practical experience in the preparation of remedies 'from vegetables, animals, and minerals'. For the more general parts of his treatment of 'Theorical and Practical Chymistry' he acknowledges his indebtedness to 'the *subtil Van Helmont* lately deceased, the *laborious Glauber*, yet living, and *Paracelsus*'.

He recognises three kinds of Chymistry: Philosophical, or wholly Scientifical; Iatrochymy, or Medicinal Chymistry, which depends upon the first kind; and Pharmaceutical Chymistry, belonging to the Apothecary's profession, which depends upon the second kind. Apart from a preliminary discussion of chemical theory and other matters of general interest, occupying somewhat more than the first hundred pages, le Febure devotes his book almost exclusively

Nicolas Le Févre

24. Nicasius le Febure.
Edelinck sculp. (See p. 161.)

The Calcination of Antimony
by the Sun.
2ᵈ part   Page 241.

a the Table.
b the Glaße with its up
    holder by which ye may
    rayse it higher or lower.
c the Stone or Plate on wᶜʰ
    yͤ Antimony in powder is
    layd.
d yͤ Artist yͭ orders yͤ Glaße &
    stirs about yͤ Antimony.
e yͤ light yͭ is centerd by the
    Glaße.

27. A Chymical Artist calcining Antimony.
After N. le Febure, 1664.   (See p. 107.)

A

COMPLEAT BODY

OF

Chymiſtry:

Wherein is contained whatſoever is neceſſary for the
atiaining to the curious knowledge of this Art; Comprehending in general the whole practice thereof:
and teaching the moſt exact preparation of *Animals*, *Vegetables* and *Minerals*, ſo as to preſerve their
eſſential Vertues.

Laid open in two Books, and dedicated to the uſe of all Apothecaries, &c.

By *Nicaſius le Febure*, Royal Profeſſor in Chymiſtry to his Majeſty of *England*, and Apothecary in Ordinary to His Honorable Houſhold.

Rendred into Engliſh by *P. D. C.* Eſq. one of the
Gentlemen of his Majeſties Privy Chamber.

Part. I.

LONDON,

Printed by *Tho. Ratcliffe*, for *Octavian Pulleyn* Junior, and are
to be ſold at the ſign of the Bible in St. *Pauls* Church yard near the
little North-door. 1664.

25. Title-page of *A Compleat Body of Chymistry*, by Nicasius le Febure,
London, 1664

I

to a description of pharmaceutical preparations and their medicinal applications.

The 'Chymical Artist', he writes in the course of his introductory survey, resolves 'the mixt bodies in their several substances, which he separates and purifies afterwards'. Having studied these 'homogeneal' constituents, he is better able to judge 'their Office whilest yet joyned in their Mixt', or compound. His function is 'to joyn *homogeneal* and separate *heterogeneal* things by the means of Heat'. He increases the heat 'untill he findes no *heterogeneity* (or *Dissimilar parts*) left in the Compound'. This, in brief, is the seventeenth-century conception of chemical analysis and synthesis.

By pushing his analysis to the end, the Artist finds 'last of all five kinde of substances, which Chymistry admits for the Principles and Elements of natural bodies'. These are Phlegm, or Water; Spirit, or Mercury; Sulphur, or Oyl; Salt; and Earth. Some give them other names, says the author, and some call Earth and Water Elements and give the name of Principles to the other three. Earth and Water are commonly called passive Principles; Mercury, Sulphur, and Salt are reckoned active Principles. Later in the book, Fire and Air are also included among the Elements, although the fire in 'mixts' is held to be 'nothing else but their Sulphur'. Le Febure shows no interest in transmutation: he considers it to be possible, but adds that 'the difficulty of success is almost insuperable'.

The many pharmaceutical preparations are arranged according to their origin from animal, vegetable, or mineral materials. The mineral class is the most numerous, followed closely by the vegetable; animal preparations take a subordinate position, although they are considered first. Only a limited number of the preparations have any real chemical interest, but chemical processes and apparatus are usually needed in carrying out the recipes. Distillation enters largely into the processes, since 'fire is a potent agent, which easily drives upwards, evaporable, sublimeable, and volatile Substances, such as Phlegm, Spirit and Oyl'.

Many of the remedies seem to be 'endowed with almost

innumerable Vertues'. Among typical preparations from animal sources are 'the Igneous Spirit of Urine', and 'Remedies out of Harts-horn'. The former, obtained by distilling urine, is said to be 'of a soverain efficacy in allaying the pain of all parts of the body', and is also 'a very excellent remedy against Epileptical, Apoplectical, Maniacal Diseases, and all other of the like nature'. Discoursing on the virtues of vipers—an obsession of that age—le Febure refers to the authority of Galen, and commends those undaunted English ladies who, in the reign of the Merry Monarch, made 'no scruple to drink of that Wine, wherein living and intire Vipers have been suffocated, to keep themselves in their plumpness, sound disposition of Body, and quickness of Spirits, hinder the injury of wrinckles, and preserve their flying beauty'.

Vegetable preparations include such varied items as 'Syrups of the Juyces of Plants', 'the unctuous Balsom of the Oyl of Angelica Root', 'the true Essence of Roses', and 'the Queen of Hungary's Water with the Flowers of Rosemary'. The 'Spirituous Water and Ætherial Oyl of Aniseeds, Fennel, Parsley, and the like' were prepared by steam distillation, and 'the Elixir of Limon and Orange Peel' were alcoholic extracts, sugared, and perfumed with musk and ambergris. Laudanum, turpentine, 'Flowers of Benjuin', and 'Camphire' are also described.

Camphor is regarded as a wonderful natural production, 'the nearest of all resembling light', owing to 'the subtilty, quickness, transparency and whiteness of this unparallel'd mixt'. When kept in a knot of taffeta upon the breast, 'towards the upper Orifice of the stomack, where the first sensations of joy or grief are raised', it was capable of over-coming 'Tertian Agues', provided that certain conditions were strictly observed. 'The knot must be worn nine days, without intermission, and the ninth day thrown, without examining what remains in, in a running water, and that without omitting any of these circumstances, if you look for a recovery.'

The last part of the book contains directions for making a large number of preparations derived from the seven metals, and from antimony, arsenic, and sulphur, typical examples being Crocus Martis (by moistening and calcining iron filings), vitriol of Mars (by dissolving iron filings in spirit of vitriol), vitriol of Venus, sugar of lead, corrosive

26. The Preparation of Spirit of Sulphur *per campanam*.
After N. le Febure, 1664

sublimate, aqua fortis, regal water (aqua regis), allom, and spirit of brimstone.

Le Febure gives an illustration (Fig. 26) of 'the Bell to make the Eager or the Spirit of Sulphur' *per campanam*, according to the method described in Beguin's *Tyrocinium Chymicum* (p. 84) and much earlier still in Biringuccio's

Pirotechnia (1540); he advises the Artist to work in moist or rainy weather, 'because if the ayr be too dry you shall draw very little spirit from lib. j. of Brimstone'.

Another illustration (Fig. 27) depicts 'the Solar Calcination of Antimony', by means of 'Magical and Celestial Fire, drawn from the Rayes of the Sun by the help of a Refracting or burning Glass'. Both 'mineral or common Antimony' (stibnite) and 'the Stellat or starry Regulus' (metallic antimony), in a finely divided condition, were used in this process, which le Febure termed 'a kind of Calcination Philosophical indeed, and worthy a son of Art'. Presumably it was when working with the latter material that he noticed an increase of weight: this, in the quaint language of the day, he attributed to the fixation of light, or Promethean Fire: 'this noble Mineral hath a kind of natural Magnes in it self, which makes it capable to attract from the highest Heavens this noble kin and similar light, by which it is produced and supplyed with its vertue'.

The burning-glass, three or four feet in diameter,[1] was made by joining together two concave pieces of glass with fish-glue, the space being filled with water through a hole. The Artist wore a pair of green glass spectacles to preserve his sight while he led 'the edge of the Sun beams upon the Antimony'. Since the Artist is left-handed, it would appear that le Febure's engraving was executed in reverse from a right-handed original drawing. The illustration was redrawn and reproduced in Valentini's *Museum Museorum* (Frankfurt, 1704), the Chymical Artist being made right-handed and fitted out with up-to-date attire in the process.

Le Febure was a skilled practicant, but his work does not reveal the originality which stamps the writings of Glauber. At the same time he avoided Glauber's extravagances of thought and expression. Le Febure is at his best in describing the apparatus and operations of the laboratory: indeed, the chief value of the *Compleat Body* at the present day lies in its clear and accurate accounts of a practical technique which held sway in chemistry laboratories from

---

[1] This size is prescribed in the text, although 'the Glasse with its upholder' shown in the accompanying illustration (Fig. 27) is of more modest dimensions.

the middle of the seventeenth century for a hundred years
or so. Le Febure sometimes helped out his descriptions with
copperplate engravings remarkable for their clear delinea-

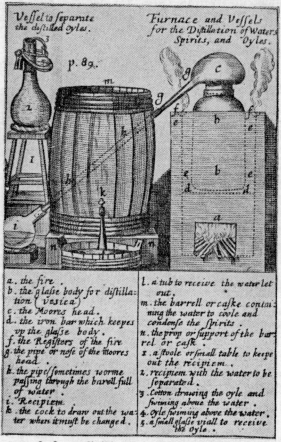

28. Steam-distilling Essential Oils of Plants.
After N. le Febure, 1664

tion and working value. 'The Figure here annexed', he
rightly observed in one place, 'will demonstrate all what
belongs to this Operation much more natively and plainly
then our Pen can represent.'

A good example is provided by Fig. 28, which represents
the apparatus le Febure used in extracting the essential oils

of plants by steam distillation. This lettered and annotated drawing is so remarkably informative that it requires little further explanation. The plants were gathered soon after sunrise, cut very small with 'Cizzars', and put into the body of the still with water. The 'Moores head' was luted on 'with Paper fillets pasted with Pap made of Flower and Water', and the fire was regulated by adjusting the door and registers of the furnace. At the end of the distillation the upper layer of oil in the receiver was separated 'by the help of a Cotton, which will draw it to it self, and cause it to run into the Viol, which should be tyed to the upper part of the Neck of the Recipient, as it will appear more clearly in the annexed Plate'. Le Febure used a similar furnace for the dry distillation of plants, but for this purpose a two-beaked alembic, removable by means of a cord and pulley, replaced the simple still-head.

Like Glauber and other ardent chymical practicants, le Febure devoted a good deal of attention to furnaces, which he defined as 'Instruments destinated to those Operations, that are performed by the help of Fire, that heat may be as it were kept in awe and bridled, to submit it self to the judgement, skill, and intention of the Artist'. He described the athanor, the distillatory furnace, the furnace of cementation, the reverberatory furnace, the wind-furnace, and last of all the 'Lamp-Furnace, used by the most curious [careful] Artists for many Chymical Operations'.

Le Febure evidently agreed with Thomas Norton[1] that

A parfet *Master* ye may him call trowe,
Which knoweth his Heates high and lowe.

The Lamp-Furnace (Fig. 29) permitted the Chymical Artist of le Febure's day to control his lower 'Heates' with a precision unknown to Norton. In this furnace the source of heat was an adjustable oil-lamp, fixed to a movable screw; moreover, 'by putting more or less wieks to burn in the Lamps; and augmenting or lessening the number of threds in the wieks, the heat is multiplyed or lessened, according to the nature of the Operations'.

1 *Prelude,* 181.

There was an even greater refinement, in the form of a rudimentary air thermometer. 'He that will proceed with more nicety in observing the exact degrees of heat', con-

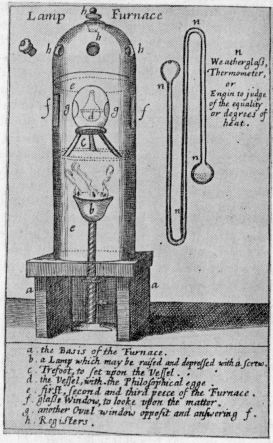

29. The Lamp-Furnace and Weather-Glasse.
After N. Le Febure, 1664

tinues le Febure, 'must have recourse to the *Thermometer* (commonly called *A Weather-glasse*) wherein the water inclosed, doth by its raising and depressing, exactly shew the degrees of heat.' An illustrative drawing of this 'Engin' (Fig. 29) shows a double U-tube with a bulb at each end;

the lower bulb contains some water, the upper bulb is perforated, and there is a thread of water in the bottom bend of the tube. It is interesting to compare this early

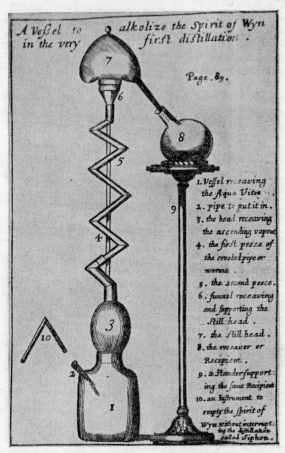

30. The Rectification of Spirit of Wine.
After N. Le Febure, 1664

form of air thermometer with the forms devised by Galileo, at the end of the sixteenth century, and by le Febure's contemporary, Robert Boyle.

For preparing 'the Alkool of Wine' le Febure describes a still provided with a long zigzag 'worme' (Fig. 30);

'in this Vessel of invention', he says, 'it is impossible the phlegm should ever ascend'.

Charles II showed a great interest in the laboratory

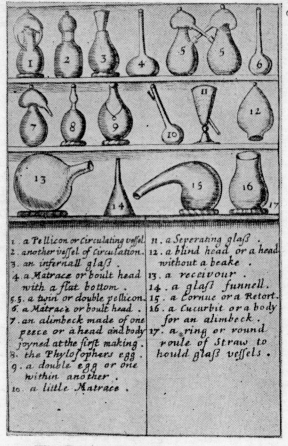

1. a Pellicon or Circulating vessel.
2. another vessel of Circulation.
3. an infernall glaß.
4. a Matrace or boult head with a flat bottom.
5.5. a twin or double pellicon.
6. a Matrace or boult head.
7. an alimbeck made of one peece or a head and body joyned at the first making.
8. the Phylosophers egg.
9. a double egg or one within another.
10. a little Matrace.

11. a Seperating glaß.
12. a blind head or a head without a beake.
13. a receivour.
14. a glaß funnell.
15. a Cornue or a Retort.
16. a Cucurbit or a body for an alimbeck.
17. a ring or round roule of Straw to hould glaß vessels.

31. What Pepys saw in 'the King's little elaboratory'.
After N. Le Febure, 1664

which le Febure used at St. James's Palace, and often took visitors to see it. On 20 September 1662 Evelyn wrote: 'I presented a petition to his Majesty about my own concerns, and afterwards accompanied him to Monsieur Lefevre, his chemist (and who had formerly been my master in Paris), to see his accurate preparation for the composing Sir Walter Ralegh's rare cordial: he made a learned discourse before his Majesty in French on each ingredient'. Soon afterwards le Febure published a discourse in French on this celebrated cordial.

Explanation of the Chimical Characters p.99.

Steele iron or mars	celeſtial ſigne.	Gumme	Crocus =
Loadſtone	Cancer :	Hower	martis
Ayre	another 69	Oyle	Sagitari. a celeſtial ſign
Lymbeck	Aſhes	Day	Soap
Allom	Pot Aſhes	Gemini a celeſtial ſigne	Scorpi. a celeſtial ſign
Amalgama aaa	Calx	Leo another ſigne	Salt alkali
Antimony	Quick lime	Stratū ſuy ſtratū or	Armoniac Salt
Aquarius a ſigne of the zodiack	Cinnabar or.	lay upon lay.	Comōn Salt
Silver or Luna	Vermillion	Marcaſſite	Salgemme
Quickſilver or	Waxe	Precipitate of Quickſilv	Brimſto or ſulph
Mercury	Crucible	Sublimate	Black ſulphur
Aries another	Calcinated copper	Moneth	Philoſophers ſulphur
celeſtial ſigne	as uſbt or crocus	Niter or Salt peter	To ſublimate
Arsenith	veneris	Night	Talck
Balneum	Note of Diſtillation	Gold or Sol	Tartar
Balneum =	Water	Auripigmentū	Taur. a Celeſtial ſigne.
Maris	Aqua fortis	Lead or Saturne	Earth
Vaporous =	aqua Regaliſ	Piſces a Celeſtial ſigne	Caput Morruū
Bath	Spirit	Powder	Tuty
Libra another	SP.	To precipitate	Glaſſe
celeſtial ſigne	Spirit of Wyn	To purify	Vert degriſe or ſlower. of Copper
Borax	Tinne or Jupiter	Quinteſſency QE	Vinegar
Bricks	Powder of Bricks	Realgar	Dyſtilled Vinegar
capricornus another	Fire	Retorte	Vitriol
		Sand	Urine

32. Chemical Symbols in 1664. After N. le Febure

Samuel Pepys also made a note of a visit to the laboratory on 15 January 1669: 'Through the Park, where I met the King and the Duke of York, and so walked with them', he wrote. 'Then down with Lord Brouncker to Sir R. Murray, into the King's little elaboratory, under his closet [study], a pretty place; and there saw a great many chemical glasses and things, but understood none of them.' These 'chemical glasses' are shown in one of le Febure's illustrations in the *Compleat Body* (Fig. 31). One can picture the inquisitive Pepys juggling with the 'infernall glass': 'that Instrument which is called *a Hell*, because whatsoever is put in it can never go out again'.

A representative list of symbols used by the 'chymicall Artists' of le Febure's day is shown in Fig. 32.

GLASER'S 'COMPLEAT CHYMIST'

When le Febure resigned his demonstratorship at the Jardin du Roi in 1660, there was living, at the sign of 'la Rose Rouge' in the Faubourg St. Germain, a certain Christophle Glaser, an apothecary. Glaser was born at Basel, and after graduating in medicine in his native city, he eventually made his way to Paris. Here he gained a reputation which led to his appointment as successor to le Febure; he was also Apothecary to the King and the Duke of Orleans. It was not long before he followed the example of his two predecessors by writing a book dealing with his activities at the Jardin; for the first edition of his *Traité de la Chymie* was published in Paris in 1663. His tenure of the post came to an abrupt end in 1672, owing to his connection with the notorious Brinvilliers poisoning case, Glaser having innocently supplied quantities of white arsenic to Sainte-Croix. Glaser had to leave Paris, and it is said that he died at Basel in 1678.

Glaser's book achieved considerable popularity during the succeeding fifty years, for it appeared in thirteen or fourteen editions between 1663 and 1710. These were mainly in French, but there were five German and one English editions. The English translation was published in London in 1677, under the title *The Compleat Chymist, or, A New Treatise of Chymistry*. Fig. **33** shows the ornamental title-page of the third French edition, of 1673. This has an alchemical flavour, with the symbol of fire surmounting representations of the armillary sphere of Hermes and a symbol of the Stone.[1] The date at the foot, appearing in the editions of 1663 and 1667, has been erased.

---

[1] *Prelude*, 209, 223, 211. This particular copy bears the following inscription on the flyleaf: 'Bought in Paris the 20 of 9be, By me Thomas: Worthington cost 2s 1d Ano Dom 1674.'

The English edition has a plain title-page. It is a modest book of 285 pages, which easily slips into the pocket. The general plan is similar to that of le Febure's earlier book; but Glaser gives more prominence to the mineral preparations. In detail, also, the two books have much in common; but Glaser is more succinct than le Febure, and his descriptions of practical operations, although precise and accurate, do not create so vivid an impression as le Febure's. Among the writers of his time, Glaser mentions only van Helmont.

Theory occupies only a few pages. The rest of the first book of 46 pages deals with operations and apparatus, with the help of three copperplates. The second book is in three sections, of which, in Glaser's own words, 'The First shall treat of the Preparations of *Metals, Metallick Bodies, Stones, Vitriols, Salts, &c.* The Second shall teach the Preparation of *Vegetables.* And the Third that of *Animals*; to which we shall join some Preparations of things not comprehended in these three Families, as *Manna, Honey, Wax, &c.*'

Glaser thus emphasises the operative aspect of 'Chymistry'. For the rest, Mercury, Sulphur, and Salt are active Principles, and Flegm and Earth passive ones. In his account of the calcination of lead Glaser adopts, without acknowledgment, Boyle's theory of the absorption of igneous particles: 'The *Calx* of a Pound of *Lead* will be found encreased above two ounces, by reason of the Particles of Fire incorporated with it, and by their activity reducing it into very subtle parts'.

It is sometimes stated that Glaser gave the first account of the preparation of potassium sulphate by heating sulphur and saltpetre together; but Beguin appears to have used the method much earlier (p. 85). Glaser named the salt *Sel Polycreste*, 'or of many uses', and it became known as *sal polychrestum Glaseri.* 'The Figure of this Salt is square, much like that of common Salt', wrote Glaser. "Tis used against obstructions of the *Liver, Spleen, Pancreas,* and *Mesentery*; it unloosens *Viscous* matter and Purges gently downwards. The Dose is from two Drams to six. 'Tis usually dissolved overnight with Spring Water, and taken the next morning.'

LEMERY'S 'COURSE OF CHYMISTRY'

One day there came to Glaser in Paris a young man from Rouen named Nicolas Lemery, who was destined to achieve an unparalleled reputation as a popular expositor of the chemistry of that age. Lemery, who was born in 1645, had been trained as an apothecary, and he came to Paris to enlarge and perfect his knowledge of chemistry. He became a pupil of Glaser, but left him at the end of a couple of months, according to Fontenelle because he found him reactionary in his ideas and of an unsociable temperament. Nevertheless, it is clear that Lemery obtained and made good use of an intimate knowledge of the demonstrations and also of Glaser's *Traité*. After several years of absence, including a period of study at Montpellier, Lemery returned to Paris in 1672 as an apothecary, and proceeded to give public lectures and demonstrations in chemistry, eventually in a laboratory of his own. He was not appointed demonstrator at the Jardin du Roi, as sometimes stated, although his son afterwards achieved that distinction; Glaser was succeeded by Charas.

Lemery quickly achieved fame as a remarkably clear and attractive lecturer and experimentalist, and his *Cours de Chymie*, first published in 1675 as a small octavo volume, was phenomenally successful. This book, indeed, did more to bring chemistry to the popular notice than any other work published before the birth of modern chemistry at the end of the eighteenth century. By 1712 no fewer than ten editions had been issued in French, and the final French revision appeared so late as 1756, forty-one years after the author's death. There were four English editions (Fig. 34), and the book was also translated into Latin, German, Spanish, and Italian. Besides its popular appeal, it exerted a good deal of influence upon the chemical thought of the period; for it contained original theoretical ideas as well as original contributions to experimental chemistry.

The work, especially in its early form, smacks strongly of the Jardin du Roi. For the general plan, and some of the details, Lemery owes much to the immediately pre-

A
COURSE
OF
Chymiſtry.

CONTAINING
The Eaſieſt Manner of per-
forming thoſe *Operations* that are in
Uſe in *PHYSICK.*

ILLUSTRATED
With many Curious Remarks and
Uſeful Diſcourſes upon each
OPERATION.

Writ in *FRENCH* by Monſieur
NICHOLAS LEMERY.

Tranſlated by *WALTER HARRIS,*
Doctor of *PHYSICK.*

LONDON,
Printed for *Walter Kettilby* at the *Biſhop's*
Head in St. *Paul's* Church-Yard, 1677.

34. Title-page of *A Course of Chymistry*, by Nicholas Lemery,
London, 1677

ceding *Traité de la Chymie* of Glaser; but the debt is no-where acknowledged.   The unexampled popularity of the later work was due partly to the simplicity of the exposition and to Lemery's easy and entertaining style.   'My design', he wrote, 'is simply to facilitate the means of working in *Chymistry*, and to take away, as much as lies in my power, those things that render it mysterious and dark.'   This, however, had also been the aim of Glaser and others; and in Lemery's treatise there are important contributory factors that have been largely overlooked.   Sober statements of fact are occasionally enlivened by short anecdotes, and the narrative often becomes pleasantly discursive and at times mildly argumentative.   Care is taken in successive editions to keep the text up to date and to give prominence to matters of current interest: thus, the third English edition of 1698 devotes nearly fifty pages to a picturesque discussion of phosphorescent materials, and refers to an observation made so recently as 1696.   At the end of the same edition there is a list of 'the vertues of the several remedies described in this book', covering a vast array of all conceivable ailments, and followed by an unusual alphabetical index to the whole book, enabling a quick reference to be made to any specific remedy.   This feature would make a strong appeal to the multitudes who must have bought the book as a kind of home-doctor.

The decorative and discursive features of the book were gradually added in the later additions.   Thus, the first English edition (London, 1677) had only 323 numbered pages, with an addition of 140 pages in an appendix published three years later (London, 1680).   These issues contained neither the section on phosphorescent materials nor the list of remedies.

These varied features eventually led to a book of considerable bulk.   The English edition of 1698 ran to 815 pages, exclusive of introductory matter and index. This edition was clearly printed on excellent paper and well illustrated with cuts of apparatus.   The editor, James Keill, who attended Lemery's lectures and demonstrations, stated that the course occupied three or four days a week for eight

TRAITÉ
DE LA CHYMIE
Enseignant par une brieue et facile
methode toutes ses plus necessaires
preparations.
Par
CHRISTOPHLE GLASER
Apothiquaire ordinaire du ROY
et de Monseigneur le Duc
D'Orleans.

Auec priuilege du ROY.

33. Title-page of *Traité de la Chymie*, by Christophle Glaser,
Paris, 1673.
(See p. 114.)

Docte et Laborieux Artiste,
Des Agents naturels il connut les ressorts:
Et pour l'Analyse des corps,
Aucun ne Surpassa cet Illustre Chymiste.

35. Nicolas Lemery, 1645–1715.
L. Ferdinand pinxit.   C. Vermeulen sculpsit.   (See p. 122.)

weeks. In this edition Keill gives details of a programme extending over thirty-four days.

On the first day, Lemery 'explained the Principles of *Chymistry*, shewed his Furnaces, Vessels and Instruments, and gave their Names and Uses'. He performed from two to seven demonstrations in a meeting. Thus, on the second day he distilled wine into brandy, distilled spirit of wine in two ways, distilled vinegar, purified saltpetre, purified vitriol, and calcined vitriol. On the thirty-fourth day he ended up triumphantly by preparing the oil and spirit of vipers.

Lemery stated that '*Chymistry* is an Art that teaches how to separate the different substances which are found in mixt Bodies'. Like Glaser and le Febure before him, he arranged 'mixt Bodies' and the preparations made from them under the heads of minerals, vegetables, and animals; like them also, he recognised Spirit, Oil, and Salt as active Principles, and Water and Earth as passive ones. Lemery, however, possessed theoretical views of a commendably elastic nature. 'Some prejudiced *Chymist*', he wrote in one place, 'may not relish perhaps this my explication, because I do not season it with *Salt* enough, and *Sulphur*'; he added that he never used the five Principles 'but when they are necessary to explicate some effect; for whensoever I find I cannot satisfie my reason, nothing shall hinder me from pursuing my thoughts farther, and searching otherwhere for some better explication'.

In fact, Lemery was a chemical freethinker: a rare and refreshing phenomenon among the 'Chymical Artists' of the seventeenth century. Although his theories may appear crude to the modern reader, his attitude was fundamentally scientific.

Lemery's independence of view, and his complete freedom from alchemical mysticism, are shown in his adoption of a primitive kind of atomic theory, in which he correlates the properties of substances with the imagined shapes of their particles. Acid particles have sharp points which tear open metals; the spikes penetrate the fine metal particles, so that the light acid particles buoy up the heavy

K

metal ones in the resulting clear solution, 'like so many Finns'. A precipitant, such as an alkali, 'by its motion and figure is able to engage the *acids* enough to break them', and so the metal particles are precipitated by their own weight, carrying down the broken and embedded spikes of the acid particles with them.

The increase in weight of a metal upon calcination is ascribed to the entry of igneous particles into its pores: 'these igneous particles do also much rarefie *Lead;* for the more it is Calcined and reduced into a *Calx*, it still grows larger'. In discussing the effect of heat on Salt of Saturn (lead acetate), Lemery states 'these Pores must needs be so disposed as to shut again like *Valvules*, and hinder the return back of those fiery parts'. Here, as often, he pays close attention to the weights of the materials concerned in the changes.

Sometimes, to lighten his discourse, Lemery throws in a taking trifle to suit the popular taste, afterwards apologising for the digression. Thus, a couple of paragraphs on 'Inks called Sympathetical' is followed by the remark: 'These Operations are indeed of no use, but because they are somewhat surprizing, I hope the curious will not take it ill'. Withal, he then goes on to 'explicate well the effects I have now related'.

Like other writers of the period, Lemery paid much attention to vipers. He thought he knew a good deal about them. ''Tis good to take *Vipers* in the Spring, or Autumn', he informs the aspiring Artist, and adds in a burst of confidence, 'The Cold kills 'em'. Presumably for the instruction of those about to take 'em, he says: 'Being taken up by the Tails, they can't wind themselves like Serpents, to make such circumvolutions about the Arm'. He omits to say that their Tails should first be seasoned with *Salt* enough! Nevertheless, the 'Chymical Artist' was credited with a good 'yield' in this preliminary practical operation; for the account of the subsequent distillation of the catch opens with the confident direction: 'Take twelve dozen of *Vipers* dried in the shade'. After surmounting so many difficulties, the Artist might well experience a certain revulsion on finding the chief virtue of oil of vipers summed up in the sentence: 'Hysterical Women may smell to this last, to allay vapours, and Paralytical parts may be anointed therewith; but its smell is so offensive that it is hard to endure it'.

One of Lemery's anecdotes deals with a related subject. '*Vipers* flesh', he remarks, 'and the flesh of *Scorpions* do cure the poison themselves do give, as I shall shew hereafter, when I come to speak of the *Viper*. And hereupon the Reader will not take it amiss if I give him a short story that is very pertinent to this subject.

'One day I put two living *Scorpions* into a glass-bottle, and then added a little Mouse to their company. Which Mouse running over the *Scorpions* provoked them to bite her till she cried out. Half a quarter of an hour after, I saw her die of Convulsions. Some hours after this, I threw in another Mouse (a little bigger and more active than the first) to the same *Scorpions*. She leapt upon the *Scorpions* as the other had done before, and was bit by them in like manner, she cried aloud, and was so provoked to revenge her self, that she eat up both the *Scorpions*, leaving only the head and the tail. I would needs observe the end of this Tragedy; I left the Mouse in the bottle, four and twenty hours, and during all that time she had not the least appearance of being hurt, and was only concerned at the being imprisoned. I intended to have dissected her, in order to see whether there were no change in the parts, or in the blood: But a stander by hapning to take up the bottle too carelessly let it fall, and broke it, so the Mouse escaped . . . but let every body explicate this experiment according to his own principles, I shall resume the thread of my discourse.'

As aforesaid, at the end of this third English edition of *A Course of Chymistry* (1698) there are lists of remedies for a surprising variety of human ills; these range from *Tetters* to *Tooth-ach* and from *Corns* to *the Kings-evil*. Judging from the array of some forty remedies, *Vapours and Palpitations* loomed large in the contemporary consciousness, followed closely by *Hypochondriack Melancholy*. The first remedy

given for the latter ailment is from eight to sixteen drops
of 'Burning Spirit of Saturn', otherwise acetone. For
Madness, Powder of Vipers, or Powder of Toads, might be
tried; for *the Hiccough*, Cinnamon Water; and against
Deafness, Oil of Paper, 'dropt in the Ear'. This last preparation was obtained by the dry distillation of paper pellets.
Incidentally, 'Paper has some use in Physick; pieces of it
are lighted in a room, and Hysterical women are made to
receive the fume of it; they are commonly relieved with
this disagreeable smell, as by many others of the like
nature'.

Lemery's experimental skill and precise directions are
well illustrated in his account of the preparation of 'the
Volatile salt of Ambar' (succinic acid), which he was the
first to recognise as an acid: 'Put two pounds of *Ambar*
powdered into a large glass or earthen Cucurbite, let it be
filled but the fourth part, set this Cucurbit in sand, and
after you have fitted a head to it, and a small Receiver, lute
well the junctures, and light a little fire under it . . . when
you see the vapours rise no longer, you must put out the
fire, and when the vessels are cold unlute them. Gather the
volatile salt with a Feather, and because it will be but
impure as yet, by reason of a little Oil that is mixed with it,
you must put it into a Viol big enough that the salt may fill
only the fourth part of it, place the Viol in sand, after you
have stopt it only with paper, and by means of a little fire,
you'l sublime the pure salt in fair Crystals to the top of the
Viol. When you perceive the Oil begin to rise, you must
then take your Viol off the fire, and letting it cool, break it,
to separate the salt; keep it in a Viol well stopt, you'l have
half an ounce.'

Lemery (Fig. **35**) had a shrewd idea of the immensity
of his subject and of the limitations of human effort. In
his discussion of Vegetables he remarks: 'It is more than
probable, that every Plant has some Vertue or other to cure
one or other Disease; but as yet we know only the use of
some few: Nor do we know all the Vertues of any one'.
And in a sentence reminiscent of Glauber he adds: 'The
life of Man is too short to try all. Men mind only what is

most necessary, and love to follow the common road of others.'

REFERENCES

Beguin, J., *Les Elemens de Chymie*, Paris, 1615; *Tyrocinium Chymicum: or, Chymical Essays, acquired from the Fountain of Nature, and Manual Experience*, trans. Russell, R., London, 1669.

Bugge, G. (ed.), *Das Buch der grossen Chemiker*, 2 vols., Berlin, 1929–1930.

D'Avissone, W. [Davidson, W.], *Philosophia Pyrotechnica, seu Cursus Chymiatricus*, Paris, 1633–1635; *Les Elemens de la Philosophie de l'Art du Feu ou Chemie*, trans. Hellot, J., Paris, 1651.

Dobson, A. (ed.), *The Diary of John Evelyn* (Globe edn.), London, 1908.

Glaser, C., *The Compleat Chymist, or, A New Treatise of Chymistry*, 'faithfully *Englished* by a *Fellow* of the *Royal Society*', London, 1677.

Glauber, J. R., *A Description of new Philosophical Furnaces*, trans. J. F[rench], London, 1651.

Idem.   *Works*, trans. Packe, C., London, 1689.

Le Febure, N., *A Compleat Body of Chymistry*, trans. P. D. C., London, 1664.

Lemery, N., *A Course of Chymistry*, 1st English edn., trans. Harris, W., London, 1677–1680; 3rd English edn. from 8th French, Keill, J. (ed.), London, 1698.

de Milt, C., 'Early Chemistry at Le Jardin du Roi', and 'Christopher Glaser', *J. Chem. Education*, 1941, **18**, 503; 1942, **19**, 53.

Smith, G. G. (ed.), *The Diary of Samuel Pepys* (Globe edn.), London, 1925.

CHAPTER VII

CHEMISTRY COMES TO THE TEXT-BOOKS

RETROSPECT

I<small>N</small> the first half of the sixteenth century, Paracelsus (1493–1541) gave a new direction to applied chemistry, and greatly enlarged its scope, by allying it with medicine. The ensuing period of iatro-chemistry, or chemistry applied to medicine, persisted throughout the sixteenth and seventeenth centuries. The alliance overcame to a large extent the stultifying effect of generations of transmutationists: it brought to alchemy, which now began to blossom into chemistry, a new orientation and a new life. Indeed, the interaction stimulated both chemistry and medicine, although the effect on individual patients subjected to heroic chemical medicines was not always so favourable!

The general adoption of iatro-chemistry, coming as a reaction to the ancient Galenic order, led in its turn to excesses and extravagant views. To Paracelsus, as to van Helmont (1577-1644) and de le Boë (Dubois) Sylvius (1614–1672), the human body was essentially a chemical microcosm, susceptible only to chemical remedies. As a consequence, the apothecary was transmuted from a Galenic herbalist into an iatro-chemical pharmacist, or maker of chemical medicines. Paracelsus and van Helmont blended mystical and spiritualistic conceptions with iatro-chemistry. These were swept away by Sylvius, who adopted a still more rigid view of medicine, as nothing more than applied chemistry. Van Helmont had stressed the use of acid or alkaline medicines to counteract the opposite condition in the body; Sylvius, developing this idea, classified diseases into those proceeding from either acid or alkaline 'acridities'. Further, he regarded both physiological and pathological processes as purely chemical, and prescribed for internal use such heroic medicines as zinc sulphate and the redoubtable *lapis infernalis* (silver nitrate).[1] 'In the human body', wrote Thomas Thomson, the historian of chemistry, Sylvius 'saw nothing but a magna of humours continually in fermentation, distillation, effervescence, or precipitation; and the physician was degraded by him to the rank of a distiller or brewer.'

Iatro-chemistry attracted more restrained followers in such men as Libavius (d. 1616), Glauber (d. 1670), and the distinguished physician Turquet de Mayerne (d. 1655); but the extravagant views of its extreme exponents, in particular Sylvius and his pupil Tachenius, led ultimately to a revulsion of opinion. Iatro-chemical doctrines met with an early assault in the *Sceptical Chymist* (1661), in which Robert Boyle struck a shrewd blow at the roots of the system by questioning the existence of the very Principles of the spagyrist or iatro-chemist. Later, other antagonists arose, and the end of the seventeenth century found iatro-chemistry on the wane.

During the sixteenth and seventeenth centuries the iatro-chemists, with all their faults, had kept chemistry alive and growing. To a large extent they had taken over the rôle fulfilled in the earlier age of alchemy by metalworkers and artisans, whose practice had found expression in the *Codex Germanicus* and in the published works of Brunschwick, Biringuccio, Agricola, and others.[2] The laboratory practitioners of iatro-chemistry were the solid party of the centre, standing, in the seventeenth century, midway between the esoteric mysticism of Khunrath and Michael Maier and the adventurous originality of Boyle and Mayow. Thus Beguin, at the opening of the century, applied his chemical skill in the preparation of agreeable, salubrious, and safe medicaments, and his example was followed by a

---

[1] 'This *lapis infernalis* is a most powerful cautery,' wrote Boerhaave in 1732, 'and by a bare touch instantly burns the parts of a live body to an escar . . . hence skilful chirurgeons highly extol the virtue of this stone. . . . If given internally in this form, it is an immediate corrosive poison; and therefore never to be used in this manner. I have known it prove pernicious to the artist that prepared it.'

[2] *Prelude,* 75.

succession of others, culminating in Lemery at the close of the century. Men like Beguin, Glaser, and Lemery are not usually numbered among the leaders of iatro-chemistry: yet by their lectures and practical demonstrations they brought chemistry home in a new and effective way to large circles of enthusiastic auditors; and they reached out to a still wider public by means of their books, all of which were made available in the vulgar tongue. Their activities, like the practical work of Glauber in its published form, developed a new and growing interest in the everyday applications of chemistry.

These Chymical Artists of the seventeenth century showed that chemistry had more solid benefits to offer than the incomprehensible jargon of the mystical alchemists or the illusive experiments of the goldmakers. They were essentially practical workers with little enthusiasm for aspects of the subject which seemed to them to have no immediate bearing on their laboratory operations. Their views were derived largely from observations made on the organic materials which entered so largely into their processes. They noticed, for example, that plant and animal materials gathered from the most diverse sources could be resolved by destructive distillation into phlegm and oil (aqueous and oily distillates), salt (sublimed matter), earth (residue), and spirit or air (vapour or gas). These products were accordingly regarded as the fundamental principles of all bodies, and they comprised the Aristotelian quartette and the Paracelsian *tria prima*. These practical iatro-chemists doubtless viewed Boyle's idea of elements as a new-fangled and ornamental superfluity—if, indeed, they troubled to think about it at all.

Until the eighteenth century, the operations of practical chemistry were applied chiefly in metallurgy and pharmacy. It is clear to us now that chemistry could not arise as a distinct science until clear notions had been formulated concerning the composition of substances. Hence it is of interest to discern the dim beginnings of chemical analysis in the iatro-chemical period, particularly in the work of Tachenius and Boyle, both of whom had a rudimentary idea of qualitative analysis.

Tachenius defined a salt as a compound of an acid and an alkali, and by means of tincture of galls and other reagents he devised tests for certain metals in solution. Such methods clearly had a bearing upon Boyle's views concerning the fundamental importance of gaining a knowledge of chemical composition. Boyle himself developed the wet method of analysis: he applied coloured plant juices in testing for acids, bases, and salts; moreover, he described a variety of other tests, including the formation of characteristic precipitates, the fuming of ammonia with mineral acids, and the green flame produced by copper salts. It was not until the era of phlogiston, however, that the qualitative work of such masters as Scheele, Bergman, and Gahn provided a firm basis for qualitative analysis, and thus opened the way for the succeeding age of quantitative chemistry. The Swedish chemists, in particular, developed the use of the blowpipe in mineral analysis, and eventually in the hands of Berzelius this simple instrument became the symbol of qualitative analysis in the dry way.

Returning to the position of chemistry at the beginning of the eighteenth century, it may be seen that men's minds had begun to expand, and that a more critical attitude towards the old ideas had set in. True, the doctrine of the fundamental principles, in various forms, lingered on into the second half of the eighteenth century; but, in general, there was a disposition early in that century to depart from the restricted iatro-chemical view of chemistry. A new method of chemistry was sought—to quote a contemporary judgment—'differing very widely from what has been observ'd by the most celebrated chemists of *Europe* in their courses, and lectures. . . . A tumultary mass of pharmaceutical processes, without any certain design or coherence, is all they afford. . . . But how hard and unjust is this on poor chemistry! To make an art a drudge to physic, which, in reality, is the principal part of all philosophy!'[1] The new method found its expression *par excellence* in Herman Boerhaave's *Elementa Chemiae*, published at Leyden in 1732.

[1] Boerhaave, as reported in the preface to the English edition (1727) of *Institutiones et Experimenta Chemiae*.

HERMAN BOERHAAVE

Herman Boerhaave (1668–1738) was probably the most erudite and versatile figure of his day. Ferguson describes him as 'the most distinguished teacher of his time, and a man of immense and varied learning in languages, philosophy, theology, mathematics, botany, chemistry, anatomy and medicine'. In the opinion of Thomas Thomson, himself a doctor, Boerhaave was perhaps the most celebrated of all physicians, Hippocrates excepted. Boerhaave was born at Voorhout, near Leyden, being one of thirteen children of the village pastor. After the death of his father in 1682 he managed with difficulty to obtain a university education; eventually, indeed, he was obliged to eke out his slender patrimony by giving instruction in mathematics. He intended originally to enter the Church, but in the course of his later studies he developed a great interest in medicine, chemistry, and botany. In 1693 he graduated in medicine, and soon afterwards began to practise as a physician. It is of interest that in 1691 Boerhaave attended the lectures of Dr. Archibald Pitcairne of Edinburgh, who for a short time was professor of medicine in the University of Leyden; Richard Mead was also a member of the class. Pitcairne opposed the extravagances of the later iatro-chemists, and impressed Boerhaave with this point of view.

In 1701 Boerhaave became lector in medicine in the University of Leyden, and by 1709 his reputation was such that he was appointed to the chairs of medicine and botany. Instead of falling to the ground between these two stools, according to the proverb, he strengthened his position on a third in 1718, when he was elected to the chair of chemistry. In his inaugural address as professor of chemistry, delivered at Leyden on 21 September 1718, his theme was that the errors of an earlier generation of chemists are always corrected by a later generation, his leading examples being the fixing and weighing of fire and the acid-alkali theory in physiology and medicine.

'Such was the activity, the zeal, and the ability with which he filled all these chairs,' wrote Thomson, 'that he raised the University of Leyden to the very highest rank of all the universities of Europe. Students flocked to him from all quarters. . . . So great was the number of students, that it was customary for them to keep places, just as is done in a theatre when a first-rate actor is expected to perform.' His position in early eighteenth-century science has been likened to that which Voltaire held for so long in eighteenth-century literature. Through his pupils and his writings, Boerhaave also exerted an influence upon later chemical thought and practice, which endured until the downfall of the phlogiston theory towards the end of the century.

Although he does not rank as an eminent exponent of chemical research, Boerhaave settled authoritatively by his experiments a number of uncertainties which had for long impeded the progress of chemistry. Thus, he refuted alchemical claims by showing that mercury could neither be fixed by heating it for fifteen years, nor rendered more volatile by distilling it five hundred times in succession! He showed also the falseness of other claims alleging the preparation of mercury from sugar of lead and other lead salts. Furthermore, he illustrated his teaching of chemistry by a wealth of original experiments bearing upon various points at issue in his day: many of these are described in his *Elementa Chemiae*.

In medicine,[1] Boerhaave became the first great exponent of clinical teaching. He raised the Leyden school to the premier position in Europe; moreover, the Edinburgh school, to which the cause of medicine in the English-speaking world owes so much, rose to fame largely through the exertions of certain of his pupils. The progress also of pure and applied chemistry in Scotland owed much to certain pupils of Boerhaave and even more to the succeeding generation of chemists whom they drew around them, including Cullen, Black, and Roebuck.[2] Boerhaave's debt

---

[1] That Humphry Davy respected Boerhaave's medical ability is shown by a remark in his anonymous work *Salmonia* (2nd edn., London, 1829, 127): 'All anglers should remember old Boerhaave's maxims of health, and act upon them: "Keep the feet warm, the head cool, and the body open" '.

[2] See A. Clow, *Nature*, 1945, **155**, 159.

to Dr. Archibald Pitcairne, the Edinburgh physician, was richly repaid.

Although Boerhaave (Fig. 36) became very wealthy, he preserved an unostentatious mode of life. Like Cavendish, later in the century, he paid no attention to the dictates of fashion, and went about in shabby clothing, an ancient hat, and rough shoes. Indeed, contemporary writers described him as a florid-complexioned, snub-nosed man, with untidy brown hair, who lived like a poverty-stricken brewer. 'For the rest,' runs one account, 'in medicine, chemistry, botany, latinity, theology, physic, and mathematics, as pretty a man as you shall see. Has also the biggest classes.' There was no limit to his application and patience, in search of the truth.

DR. JOHNSON, CHYMISTRY, AND BOERHAAVE

Dr. Samuel Johnson's omniscience is not usually held to embrace a knowledge of chemistry; but it is an interesting circumstance that one of his earliest literary ventures was a 'Life of Dr. Herman Boerhaave', which he contributed to the *Gentleman's Magazine* as a serial narrative in the first four months of 1739, soon after Boerhaave's death. His sketch followed very closely Schultens' Latin eulogy published in the preceding year, and this in turn was based upon some of Boerhaave's own notes.

According to Boswell, it was in this contribution that Johnson 'discovered that love of chymistry which never forsook him'. Thus, in 1763, Johnson had 'an apparatus for chymical experiments' in his garret; in 1772, he sent Mr. Peyton to a chymist's shop in Temple-Bar to buy an ounce of oil of vitriol at a cost of a penny; in 1781, during a journey to Bedfordshire, we find him 'chiefly occupied in reading Dr. Watson's second volume of *Chemical Essays*,[1] which he liked very well, and his own *Prince of Abyssinia*, on which he seemed to be intensely fixed'; and, in 1783, 'he attended some experiments that were made by a physician at Salisbury, on the new kinds of air'. Moreover, in a self-portrait, Johnson once wrote: 'His daily amusement is chymistry. He has a small furnace which he employs in

---

[1] Published at Cambridge in 1781.

distillation, and which has long been the solace of his life. He draws oils and waters, and essences and spirits, which he knows to be of no use; sits and counts the drops as they come from his retorts, and forgets that whilst a drop is falling a moment flies away.'

Of the young Boerhaave, Johnson says that 'at intervals, to recreate his mind, and strengthen his constitution, it was his father's custom to send him into the fields, and employ him in agriculture, and such kind of rural occupations, which he continued thro' all his life to love and practise'. This love of country life and pursuits led to 'a robust and athletic constitution of body, so harden'd by early severities, and wholesome fatigue, that he was insensible of any sharpness of air, or inclemency of weather'. In appearance, says Johnson's account, 'he was tall, and remarkable for extraordinary strength. There was in his air and motion something rough and artless, but so majestick and great at the same time, that no man ever looked upon him without veneration, and a kind of tacit submission to the superiority of his genius. The vigour and activity of his mind sparkled visibly in his eyes. . . . He was always chearful, and desirous of promoting mirth by a facetious and humourous conversation.'

In discussing Boerhaave's character, Johnson stressed his unwearying diligence and added the shrewd reflection: 'Statesmen and generals may grow great by unexpected accidents, and a fortunate concurrence of circumstances, neither procured, nor foreseen by themselves: but reputation in the learned world must be the effect of industry and capacity'. In an appreciation of his unusual versatility, Johnson remarked that 'Boerhaave lost none of his hours, but when he had attained one science, attempted another: he added physick to divinity, chemistry to the mathematicks, and anatomy to botany'. But his learning, although so great, was eclipsed by his virtue and the beauty of his character: 'he was an admirable example of temperance, fortitude, humility and devotion. His piety, and a religious sense of his dependance on God, was the basis of all his virtues, and the principle of his whole conduct.'

BOERHAAVE AS 'L'AUTEUR MALGRÉ LUI'

The fame and popularity of Boerhaave's lectures on chemistry brought him, in 1724, face to face with a disconcerting and extremely disagreeable situation. In the eighteenth century, as later (and, for that matter, earlier), students often took great pains over their lecture notes. As a consequence, the views of Stahl, Black, and other celebrated teachers of the century were disseminated far beyond the bounds of their own classes, through the circulation of sets of such notes. Boerhaave's students went further. Some of them, possibly incited by an enterprising publisher, surreptitiously edited and published a complete version of his chemistry lectures, in Latin, under the title *Institutiones et Experimenta Chemiae*. The two octavo volumes were issued in 1724 under the name of Boerhaave as author, and it is supposed that the edition, assigned ostensibly to Paris, was actually prepared in Leyden.

The preface suggests that this printed version of the teachings of the most illustrious Boerhaave will save his own students a good deal of time, besides conferring a great benefit upon strangers; and the unblushing pirates end by regretting the impracticability of arranging for the most illustrious author to put a final polish upon the work by revising it! In spite of Boerhaave's energetic disclaimers and protests, the work achieved immediate popularity, and was reissued several times within the next few years.

An English translation appeared in London, in 1727, as a large quarto volume of more than 700 pages, with two copperplates and numerous annotations introduced by the translators. It bears the title: 'A New *Method* of Chemistry; including the Theory and Practice of that Art. . . . Written by the very Learned *H. BOERHAAVE*, Professor of *Chemistry*, *Botany*, and *Medicine* in the University of *Leyden*, and Member of the Royal Academy of Sciences at *Paris*. Translated from the Printed Edition, Collated with the best Manuscript Copies. By *P. Shaw*, M.D. and *E. Chambers*, Gent. With additional Notes and Sculptures.'

This spurious work afforded, in fact, a very competent

presentation of Boerhaave's exposition of chemistry; but the distress and indignation which its publication caused him can well be imagined. As a fastidious scholar, he would be shocked by every misrepresentation or mistake; even more, as a teacher, he would feel bitterly the inconsiderate action of students to whom he had given so much. The matter might perhaps have been composed, but for the embarrassing success of a work on chemistry bearing the great name of Boerhaave. 'The book thus vilely publish'd', wrote Boerhaave, 'found plenty of purchasers. . . . Hence I frequently lay under a necessity of seeing the detested piece, even in the hands of my auditors; who, to my face, were daily comparing my words, as I delivered them, with the text thereof.' As part of their labour-saving plan, the students were obviously confining their lecture notes to marking the day's programme in the printed version and taking down any supplementary matter. However innocent their action, it served to acerbate Boerhaave's feelings. Finding it impossible to ban the publication, he resigned the chair of chemistry.

The printed version continued to find a ready market. Boerhaave's friends pointed out to him the urgent necessity of publishing an authentic account of his method of chemistry: everywhere, they insisted, the spurious edition was 'applauded, much call'd for, and sold dear; and . . . would quickly come to a new impression'. Boerhaave then likened himself to Petrarch, who bewailed 'the unhappiness of his age, upon finding himself ranked among the chief poets of it'. At length, however, he recognised that his hand had been forced. He interrupted his medical teaching, and between September 1731 and March 1732 wrote his famous *Elementa Chemiae*, 'quae Anniversario Labore docuit, in Publicis, Privatisque, Scholis, Hermannus Boerhaave'.

This work (Fig. **37**) was published in two quarto volumes at Leyden, in 1732, with 17 copperplates. 'I publickly declare', wrote Boerhaave at the end of the preface, 'that the Book with which I now trouble the World, was forced from me much against my Inclination.' As a token of his abhorrence of the spurious edition, he printed a certificate of authenticity upon the back of the title-page of the first volume of his own edition: *Ut certus sit Lector, hunc librum a me editum prodire, propria manu nomen adscribendum putavi: nec pro meo agnosco, ubi haec adscriptio abest* ('To assure the reader that this book is put out by me, I have thought it well to sign my name in my own handwriting, and I refuse to acknowledge any copy which lacks this signature'). He then wrote his name, 'H. Boerhaave', at the end of this declaration, in each copy issued (Fig. 38).

Boerhaave's *Elementa Chemiae* at once became the standard text-book of chemistry, a position which it held until the end of the era of phlogiston. Besides Latin

Ut certus sit Lector, hunc librum a me editum prodire, propria manu nomen adscribendum putavi: nec pro meo agnosco, ubi haec adscriptio abest. H. Boerhaave.

38. Boerhaave's signed certificate of authenticity. From a copy of his *Elementa Chemiae*, Leyden, 1732, in the University Library, St. Andrews

editions published at Leyden, London, Paris, Leipzig, Venice, and elsewhere, there were other editions in English, French, and German, the latest of which was issued only seven years before Lavoisier's *Traité*. Boerhaave was the last chemist of note who wrote habitually in Latin.

Of the English versions, the best are those of Dr. Timothy Dallowe (*Elements of Chemistry*, London, 1735) and Dr. Peter Shaw (London, 1741). Shaw's translation, which is the more interesting, was published as a second edition of the *New Method of Chemistry* of 1727; it is, however, a careful rendering of the authentic edition, although many of the translators' annotations are taken over from Shaw and Chambers' earlier work, and supplemented by others, thus making Shaw's English version considerably larger than the Latin original. It appeared, four years after Boerhaave's death, in two large quarto volumes, altogether exceeding a thousand pages, and containing 25 copperplates. It is entitled: 'A New Method of Chemistry; including the

36. Herman Boerhaave, 1668–1738.
From an engraving by F. Anderloni and G. Garavaglia. (See p. 130.)

ELEMENTA
CHEMIAE,

QVAE

ANNIVERSARIO LABORE DOCUIT,

IN PUBLICIS, PRIVATISQUE,

SCHOLIS,

HERMANNUS BOERHAAVE.

TOMUS PRIMUS.

QUI CONTINET HISTORIAM ET ARTIS
THEORIAM.

CUM TABULIS AENEIS.

LVGDVNI BATAVORVM,
Apud ISAACUM SEVERINUM.
M. D. CCXXXII.

37. Title-page of *Elementa Chemiae*, by Herman Boerhaave, Leyden, 1732.
(See p. 133.)

History, Theory, and Practice of the Art: Translated from the Original Latin of Dr. *Boerhaave's Elementa Chemiæ*, as Published by Himself. . . . By *Peter Shaw*, M.D.'

The two English versions of Boerhaave's lectures, with the common title of *A New Method of Chemistry*, bear a close resemblance to each other. Both are racy of the mid-eighteenth-century soil, and engaging to read. The spurious version is more intimate and less formal than the other, and is lightened with anecdotes and colloquial illustrations which a professor would retail to his classes but withhold from his printed text. For example, the preface to the spurious edition refers to 'Monsieur *Lemery*, whose performance has gone thro' I don't know how many editions, in various languages; and yet nothing could be worse concerted for such as study the art: He begins with the very hardest part, metals; a great number of his processes are merely calculated for the preparing of remedies; and his view, throughout the whole, is rather to furnish the shops with medicines, than to instruct his readers in the knowledge of chemistry'. This is a downright criticism of a contemporary which Boerhaave avoided sedulously in his published work, and there is no reference of the kind to Lemery in his *Elementa Chemiae*.

A GENERAL VIEW OF BOERHAAVE'S 'NEW METHOD'

Chemical historians have united in paying homage to Boerhaave's treatise. Kopp, who entered more than ninety references to Boerhaave in his celebrated history, wrote that 'if ever a text-book of chemistry contributed to spreading a knowledge of the subject, raising its status, and enlarging its scope, that book was Boerhaave's'. Restrained in tone, and of a clarity hitherto unequalled, it was at the same time the most complete and the least biased exposition of chemistry known to the pre-oxygen era. As one of the editors remarked, late in the eighteenth century, Boerhaave 'seemed to be born to place chemistry in a clear light'. As a man of wide culture, he depicted it liberally as a science as well as an art, and showed its bearing upon the activities of everyday life. He gave for the first time in the history of chemistry an orderly exposition of its theory and a detailed account of its practice. With the immense industry and application which characterised him, Boerhaave collected his data from every conceivable source, and the main criticism that can be levelled against him is a certain lack of critical discrimination, leading in turn to diffusiveness. His narrative, 'rich with the spoils of time', is certainly set out on an 'ample page'. Even this weakness is counterbalanced by his ability to collate diverse chemical observations and focus them into a synoptic picture.

The modern student of historical chemistry may thus use the *Elementa Chemiae* as a window enabling him to take a backward look into eighteenth-century chemistry, using the eyes of an informed and reflective observer of that day. In the wider world of 1732, seen only in one aspect through this magic casement, Bentley, Swift, and Congreve, like Boerhaave himself, were approaching old age; Bach, Handel, Pope, Voltaire and Hogarth were in their prime; Benjamin Franklin, Fielding, Linnaeus, Chatham, Johnson and Rousseau were young men; David Garrick, Joshua Reynolds and Adam Smith were boys; Goldsmith, James Cook, Black, Cavendish, Haydn and George Washington were infants. It was a world of good literature, good architecture, and good music. For chemistry, it was an age of suspense, an age which might well be called the induction period of the chemical revolution.

In taking this backward look, it must always be remembered that Boerhaave lived in a world of physical science no less alien to the modern mind than his social and economic background, his views on philosophy and religion, his clothes, his conversation, and a hundred and one trivialities of his daily life. For reasons of this kind it is always dangerous to attempt to render the scientific ideas of a bygone age in the parlance of modern science. At the best, even if the main idea of a passage is conveyed, the effect will be akin to that of an English rendering of one of Barnes' poetic masterpieces in the Dorset dialect: there will be a sacrifice of the subtle charm and fine shades of meaning of the original. Accordingly, in attempting to give an outline of Boerhaave's classical text-book, it is advisable to express his views largely in his own language, as interpreted in Shaw's contemporary translation: in other words, one who gazes through an eighteenth-century window should wear eighteenth-century spectacles.

THE 'NEW METHOD' UNFOLDED

Shaw's translation is set out in three parts, like the original. Parts I and II are included in the first volume, and Part III takes up the whole of the second volume. Part I (*De Historia Artis*) deals with the History of Chemistry, Part II (*De Theoria Artis*) with the Theory of Chemistry, and Part III (*Quae ipsas Artis Operationes Exhibet*) with the Processes, or Operations of the Art.

'My Design', begins Boerhaave, 'is to initiate students in the knowledge of chemistry.' To this end, both theory and practical operations must be explained, 'so that both head and hand may come qualified for the effectual treatment of it'.

The opening historical introduction with its copious footnotes added by the translator occupies sixty-four pages, as compared with twenty-five pages of the Latin original. It testifies to Boerhaave's great erudition; but according to present-day standards, the treatment shows little critical judgment. Boerhaave deals tenderly with the alchemists, but is more severe on the iatro-chemists. Basil Valentine's 'chief failing was the ascribing medicinal virtues to every thing procured from antimony; than which nothing can be more absurd, fallacious, or pernicious. Yet the same fatal error has hence infected all the tribe of chemists to this day.' He intersperses some racy anecdotes of Paracelsus (for whom also he shows little love), including the story of the 'noble canon of *Liechtemfels*', who, to escape paying his doctor's bill, affected to believe that the three most effective laudanum pills with which Paracelsus had dosed him were 'nothing but three mice-turds'.

Part II, on the theory of chemistry, opens with the following impressive definition: '*Chemistry is an art which teaches the manner of performing certain physical Operations, whereby bodies cognizable to the senses, or capable of being render'd cognizable, and of being contain'd in vessels, are so changed, by means of proper instruments, as to produce certain determined effects; and at the same time discover the causes thereof; for the service of various arts'.* As Thomas Thomson remarks drily, 'This definition is not calculated to throw much light on chemistry to those who are unacquainted with its nature or object'. As an image of the contemporary view of chemistry, the definition must nevertheless be kept in mind in appraising Boerhaave's system.

The treatment of chemical theory opens with a brief description of the chief substances or materials with which chemistry deals. These are classified according to their origin, as mineral, vegetable, or animal, and it is noticeable that they do not include any gases. The seven Metals come first.

To take an example: Gold is said to be the heaviest and densest of all bodies; it is also the simplest, and the most fixed in air or fire. It is 'the only body that resists the force of antimony and lead . . . being melted with them, it sinks to the bottom'. Thus, gold is 'the least changeable of all bodies hitherto known'. It is also the most ductile, and 'is soft, and scarcely elastic or sonorous'. It melts by fire, unites very readily with quicksilver, 'nor ever wastes it self by emitting *effluvia*, or exhalations'. Further, 'it is not liable to rust; because *aqua regia* and spirit of sea-salt do not float in the air'. The only other reference to its chemical properties lies in the statement that 'when dissolved in *aqua regia*, and precipitated with salt of tartar, it has a fulminating property'. The account ends with short notes on the natural occurrence and separation of gold.

Boerhaave's tenderness towards the alchemists becomes comprehensible when it transpires that he still regarded metals in the light of the sulphur-mercury theory of the mediaeval era.[1] Gold consists, he says, 'of a most pure, simple matter, like mercury, fixed by another pure, simple, subtile principle, diffused thro' its minutest parts. . . . This the chemists mean when they say it consists of mercury and

[1] *Prelude,* 17, 24.

sulphur.' The other metals also contain an intermixture of 'earth', and perhaps some 'crude sulphur'. Boerhaave holds transmutation to be possible, although difficult: 'the quantity of gold procured from any other metal, by transmutation, can only be in proportion to the quantity of mercury it before contained'.

The next heading, of Salts, comprises only common salt (divided into *sal gemmae* or rock-salt, that of salt-springs, and sea-salt), salt-petre, borax, sal-ammoniac, and alum; but other salts are mentioned elsewhere in the text.

Sulphurs, which come next in the arrangement, comprise sulphur itself, orpiment, and arsenic. Also petroleum, naphtha, asphaltum, pit-coal, and amber are classified as bituminous sulphurs. These are 'unctuous bodies . . . in the composition whereof sulphur appears to have the predominant part'.

Stones and Earths are treated very briefly and perfunctorily. Stones are classified as transparent or gems (diamond, emerald, etc.), semi-transparent (agate, chalcedony), and opake (asbestos, marble, lime-stone). Some Earths are 'native fossils [minerals], usually somewhat unctuous', which may be made into a paste with water, and so are called boles, such as white clay and fullers-earth; but others are 'of a dryer, and leaner kind; as chalk, ochre, and marl'. No hint is given of the chemical nature of Stones or Earths.

The Semi-Metals include antimony, bismuth, and zinc. These are held to be 'composed of a true metal and a sulphur combined together', and accordingly cinnabar is included among them. The same term is applied to vitriols, which are held to be 'composed of a true metal combined with a salt'; and also to 'the generality of native ores in mines, and numerous other bodies', among them lapis lazuli and load-stone.

A note on Vegetables contains indefinite references to plant juices, honey, balsam, oil, rosin, and gums. Chemical operations 'produce an infinite number of beautiful and useful things' from plant materials; but such operations bring about changes 'in the particular texture of each body, and the medicinal virtues dependant thereon, that the utmost caution must be used before the cause of their action can be assigned'.

'The third kind of bodies considered by chemists includes the Animal kingdom; we mean the bodies of animals, and the parts thereof.' Boerhaave points out here that 'a great agreement' appears between plants and animals, in that 'they are both sustained with the same food'. This is gradually changed 'by the organical structure of the animal . . . into various other forms'. He alludes cursorily to animal salts and oils, and also to various 'humors', such as milk, fat, lymph, serum, saliva, blood, and urine; but makes no remark on their chemical nature.

Having surveyed his raw materials, Boerhaave proceeds to consider how they are affected by the operations of chemistry. He reiterates part of his earlier definition by saying that 'Chemistry is employed in changing the bodies contained in the three classes above specify'd'. These changes are mostly brought about by heat, or fire. The translator introduces footnote references to Newton's view that all bodies seem to be composed of hard particles or atoms, and to Boyle's attack on the common doctrine of the so-called elements; but Boerhaave himself comes to the conclusion 'that fire, air, water, earth, alcohol, mercury, the presiding spirit in each body, and several others, do, when absolutely simple, appear to be fine, permanent elements'.

It is significant that Boerhaave's list of elements represents essentially a conglomeration of Aristotle's quartette with the alchemical sulphur and mercury: alcohol replaces sulphur as the principle of inflammability, and the 'salt' of Paracelsus' *tria prima* is thrown overboard, in token of Boerhaave's disapproval of iatro-chemistry.

Boerhaave regards these elements as entities beyond the reach of chemical art. 'No human art', he says, 'can produce the least drop of pure water, and much less any of the rest, as air and earth, or the like . . . even alcohol, it self, in burning, separates into different parts.' So much for analysis, applied to the elements; but in synthesis there is a similar barrier, for 'by re-compounding the chemical elements extracted from any body, we very rarely produce the primitive compound'.

Boerhaave's liberal view of chemistry finds an expression in his ensuing exposition of its manifold applications in natural philosophy, in medicine, and in the arts. In the last group he specifies painting, enamelling, staining glass, dyeing, the making of glass and imitation gems, metallurgy, the art of war, natural magic, cookery, the art of wines, and brewing.

The art of war, he observes, has turned entirely upon the one chemical invention of gunpowder. 'God grant', he adds, 'that mortal men may not be so ingenious at their own art, as to pervert a profitable science any longer to such horrible uses. For this reason I forbear to mention several other matters far more horrible and destructive.' He closes an account of the use of chemical knowledge in producing effects which appear magical to the layman by remarking: 'How little men may safely pronounce concerning the powers of bodies, in whatsoever age they live: there being still more surprizing things hidden in the secret powers of nature'.

THE SIX INSTRUMENTS OF CHEMISTRY

The real theoretical discussion begins on page 205 under the heading 'Instruments of Chemistry'; but of the 389 pages comprising the rest of Shaw's first volume only the last 13 pages deal with 'Chemical Apparatus, and Vessels'. Boerhaave regards instruments as 'certain bodies by whose means the requisite actions are produced. These, with the best chemists, we usually reduce to six principal ones: fire, water, air, earth, menstruums, and utensils.' He next proceeds to consider them in this order, 'beginning with fire, by reason no chemical operation ever was, or can be hereafter performed, to which fire does not contribute'.

Boerhaave's classical account of Fire occupies 173 pages, and is interspersed with descriptions of his own experiments and the conclusions he drew from them. It bears witness to the bewilderment with which the chemists of this era viewed

the phenomena associated with fire; to their vague and
contradictory conceptions of the nature of fire and heat,
which they usually regarded as equivalent terms; to their
complete ignorance of gases; and to their fruitless attempts
to arrive at a consistent and satisfying theory of combustion
—a costly failure which held up the progress of chemistry
for more than a century. It is not surprising that the
cautious Boerhaave was unwilling to commit himself to a
definition of fire, although this was an instrument of such
importance in chemistry that some chemists called themselves 'philosophers of fire'. Boerhaave adopted the method
of 'the algebraists, who, when they seek an unknown thing,
suppose nothing at all known in it'. Such caution is
necessary, however, because 'the elements of fire are found
everywhere; in the most solid gold, as well as in the most
empty *vacuum* of an air-pump'.

The small particles that constitute the ultimate elements
of fire are of excessive minuteness and great penetrative
power; they 'appear to be the most solid of all bodies'.
Boerhaave does not consider these particles to be ponderable:
fire, he says, while remaining in a heated body, adds to its
bulk, but does not increase its weight. Fire may be recognised by certain effects, notably heat, light, colour,
expansion, and changes in bodies due to burning or fusion.
Boerhaave finds the most reliable criterion in its expansive
power: it dilates water, but it dilates the lighter spirit of
wine 'more nimbly' and to a greater extent.

So he leads on to a description of Drebbel's air-
thermometer, and shows for the first time the great value of
thermometers in chemistry. He solicited 'that industrious
artist, *Dan. Gab. Fahrenheit*', to furnish him with two
thermometers: 'one made of the densest fluid, *viz*. mercury;
the other of the rarest, *viz*. spirit of wine'. Boerhaave's
own thermometric observations on mixtures of liquids, and
other experiments which Fahrenheit made at his request,
led Joseph Black in 1760 to the idea of specific heats.
Boerhaave's own interpretations of such experiments, and
of many others dealing with the evolution of heat on mixing
various liquids, are very confused. Much of his account of

fire is devoted to his views on combustion, an important subject which calls for separate treatment in this review.

Boerhaave regards Air as 'a fluid scarcely perceivable by our senses, and which only discovers itself by the resistance it makes to the velocity of moving bodies; or by its own vehement motion against other bodies, called wind'. It is concerned in most operations, both of nature and art; is necessary to support life; and also animates fire. Boerhaave refers to the formation of 'air' in fermentation and putrefaction, and by the admixture of various substances; but he draws no distinction between different kinds of 'air'. Nor does he attribute any chemical character to the air, beyond regarding it as an 'element'. In discussing its properties, he confines himself to physical phenomena, arising chiefly from the weight of the atmosphere and the elasticity of air.

Coming to its composition, Boerhaave is evidently considering the atmosphere as contaminated air, when he states that air contains elastic parts, fire, and water, with 'extremely numerous other substances' which 'continually float therein', including exhalations from plants and animals, smoke, fumes, salts, and sulphur from burning bodies. Moreover, there is a 'latent virtue' in the atmosphere, 'whereby the life of animals and vegetables is supported; and tho' this cannot be understood from any other property of the air, yet it may be discovered by diligent search'.

As regards the third 'instrument', Water is 'a very fluid, scentless, tasteless, transparent, colourless liquor, which turns to ice with a certain degree of cold'. Boerhaave considers that 'to obtain water pure, is impossible; for, so long as the form of water remains, it always contains fire'— and, of course, water that contains fire is not pure, or 'homogeneal', as le Febure would have said. Ice, although perhaps devoid of fire, is evidently not regarded as pure water, because it is no longer fluid. Furthermore, since water freezes at thirty-two degrees, much more easily than alcohol or quicksilver, Boerhaave infers 'that a large quantity of fire is requisite to keep water fluid'. Another way of regarding water is as 'a certain species of glass, which melts with thirty-three degrees of heat', but which cannot be heated 'above two hundred and fourteen degrees'. Ice floats upon water, 'the specific gravity of ice being to that of water as eight to nine'.

Boerhaave was impressed with the universal occurrence of water, as disclosed by the combustion of the most diverse substances, and also with its solvent property. He noticed that a saturated aqueous solution of one substance could still dissolve another; but that water 'perfectly saturated with dissolved salts cannot be mixed with alcohol'. However, he observed that 'if water be saturated with a salt that easily separates from it, alcohol will dissolve the water, and the salt fall to the bottom', Epsom salt being given as an example. Although 'it would scarce be suspected', water dissolves air. Pure distilled water does not cause fine soap to curdle, like less pure water; also it gives no turbidity with a solution of pure silver in aqua fortis.

After repeatedly distilling water, Boerhaave found himself unable to verify Boyle's finding that some of the water was transmuted into earth in this operation.

Little is said about Earth, which Boerhaave defines as 'a fossil, simple, hard, brittle body, that remains fix'd, without melting, in the fire; and neither dissolves in water, alcohol, oil, or air'. It is obtained in the calcination of vegetable or animal matter, and is present in 'fossil salts', such as nitre, sea-salt, 'or any other pure native mineral salts'. Moreover, 'the liquid fossil sulphurs', such as bitumen and petroleum, yield pure earth when the residue from the burning is calcined. Boerhaave is dubious whether the metals contain earth.

A consideration of the fifth instrument, comprehended under the term Menstruums, leads to an exposition of Boerhaave's ideas on chemical combination, an extensive subject which it is convenient to examine under a separate head.

BOERHAAVE ON CHEMICAL CHANGE

Under the head of Menstruums, Boerhaave sets out his ideas on what came later to be called chemical change and chemical affinity. He acknowledges the word menstruum to be 'a barbarous term', derived from the alchemists' practice of heating their mixtures for a philosophical month of forty days.[1]   He defines it as 'a body, which, when artificially applied to another, divides it subtily; so that the particles of the solvent remain thoroughly intermixed with those of the solvend'; and he adds that it is 'the property of a menstruum, to be it self equally dissolved, at the time it dissolves the solvend'.

In discussing this so-called instrument, 'wherein chemists place their chiefest excellence; and whereunto they ascribe the greatest effects of their art', Boerhaave distinguishes between chemical union and mechanical admixture.

'The particles of a menstruum,' he says, 'after by their action they have dissolved the solvend, presently join with the particles thereof, so as to produce a new compound, often very different from the nature of the simple resolved body. We must, however, allow, that the parts of the solvent, after its concretion, no longer touch one another; but are separated by the interposition of the particles of the matter dissolved. Again, the separating particles, which before constituted the solvend, are now separated from each other, by the interposition of the particles of the solvent every where between them. From this division, separation and new concretion of ·heterogeneous parts, there arises a great number of new bodies by means of menstruums.'

The particles of solvent and solvend prefer heterogeneous union to homogeneous union. 'Thus, whilst *aqua-regia* dissolves thrice its weight of gold into a yellow liquor, the parts of the dissolved gold remain united with those of the *aqua-regia;* so that the particles of gold, tho' eighteen times heavier than *aqua-regia*, remain suspended therein: whence there must evidently be a certain mutual corresponding power between each particle of the gold and *aqua-regia*, whereby they mutually act upon, embrace, and detain each other; otherwise the particles of the dissolved gold would fall to the bottom, the saline particles rest thereon distinct, and the water float separate over them both: whereas they all three, tho' so different, unite together in the form of one simple uniform liquor.'

[1] *Prelude,* 153.

Although the action 'excites itself', it is 'increased by fire'. Boerhaave contrasts such actions with 'the other solutions of bodies, which chiefly happen in a mechanical manner; when the solvent recedes from the solvend, and is not reciprocally dissolved thereby: so that, after the solution, they separate from each other, according to their different specific gravities'. Here he refers to a physical solution, from which solvent and solute may be directly separated.

Even in the first kind of action, Boerhaave considers that the 'solvent' and 'solvend' maintain their separate identities in the union. 'The changes wrought upon bodies by the dissolving power of menstruums, seem greatly to depend upon the minute particles of the menstruum now cohering with the particles of the solvend; and can scarcely be attributed to a true and proper alteration introduced by the menstruum into the dissolved particles. . . . For, tho' pure metals, such as gold, silver, and mercury, thoroughly dissolved by their acid solvents, at first appear changed in all their parts; yet they may easily be separated from their menstruums, in the form of a calx, which being fused in the fire, we thus recover the metal again unchanged.'

In another place, Boerhaave states that if a drachm of dry *lapis infernalis* (silver nitrate) be placed in a cavity made in an ignited piece of Dutch turf, after it ceases to smoke, it will immediately melt, glow, and inflame, like nitre. Afterwards, 'pure silver will be found in the hollow, as much in quantity as was dissolved in making of the *lapis infernalis*'. He then points out that 'this excellent experiment shews the physical manner wherein acids do but superficially adhere to silver'; and, in a sentence reminiscent of Lemery (p. 119), he adds that 'whilst surrounding their metallic mass,' these acids 'arm the ponderous principles thereof with *spiculæ*'.

The two kinds of particles are pictured as undergoing a mutual attraction in 'the action of dissolution'. Their coherence is attributed to 'an appetite of union', rather than to 'a mechanical union, or an unfriendly commotion'.

In reviewing the different kinds of menstruums, Boerhaave mentions water, aqueous liquors, oils, alcohol,

alkalies, acids, and neutral salts. Thus, red-lead dissolves
in heated oil-olive to yield 'a metallic balsam, or an excellent
cement'; strong distilled vinegar dissolves shells, chalk and
stony matters, forming a hard and dry mass; and sulphur
and mercury, when ground together and heated, yield
cinnabar. The acids mentioned are acetous, oil of vitriol,
the acid of nitre, the acid of sea-salt, and aqua regia. Natural
salts include sal-ammoniac, sea-salt, nitre, borax, and others.

The discussion of menstruums ends with an account of
the Alcahest, or universal menstruum, of Paracelsus and
van Helmont. Boerhaave was more than doubtful about
the existence of a solvent which was reputed to be 'immut-
able and immortal', remaining 'numerically the same in
weight and virtue; as well after being a thousand times
employed, as after being but once used'.

'It may be expected', concludes Boerhaave, 'I should
declare my sentiments, whether any chemist was ever in
possession of the alcahest. I answer frankly: that *Helmont*
complains the phial of it, once given to him, was taken from
him; whence it is certain, he could not have made many
experiments with that liquor.' Boerhaave overcame the
temptation to speculate upon the nature of a phial that
would resist the action of a universal solvent! He was always
cautious, and chary of committing himself; so that he
leaves the intelligent reader to add *verb. sap.* to his statement.

BOERHAAVE ON COMBUSTION

Like all chemists up to the late eighteenth century,
Boerhaave found the irresistible problem of combustion full
of apparent contradictions, for which no satisfying explanation seemed possible. Combustion, or burning, the most
familiar, spectacular, and fundamental of all chemical
processes, found a place in the earliest theories of physical
science. From the Sun-God of the ancient civilisations, fire
descended as an element into the Aristotelian scheme, and
as a sulphureous principle into the sulphur-mercury theory
of metals and the later *tria prima* of Paracelsus.[1] 'What
flames and is burnt is Sulphur', wrote Paracelsus. The

[1] *Prelude, 25.*

burning of wood, or the calcination of a metal, was regarded by the mediaeval alchemists and also by Paracelsus as due to the escape of an inflammable principle which they called 'sulphur'. Thus, in burning, a substance decomposed into its constituent principles, one of which was liberated as fire, heat, light, or sometimes in the form of sulphureous fumes. This inflammable principle was pictured as an unctuous or oily constituent, with a general resemblance to molten sulphur; the other constituents, in the Paracelsian scheme, were a mercurial or metalline principle, and a principle of fixity known as salt, or sometimes as the earthy principle. Hence when a metal was calcined, the sulphureous principle escaped, leaving the mercurial principle and earthy material behind in the form of a calx.

Sometimes the earthy or saline residue was lacking. Thus, Basil Valentine wrote: 'If a rectified *Aqua vitae* be lighted, then Mercury and the vegetable Sulphur separateth, that Sulphur burns bright, being a meer fire, the tender Mercury betakes himself to his wings and flieth to his *Chaos*'.[1]

In this way, the theory recognised unconsciously a distinction between inorganic and organic materials.

Logically, this explanation of combustion ought to have been abandoned if the new conception of an element advanced in Boyle's *Sceptical Chymist* had been accepted. Curiously enough, however, only eight years after Boyle's publication, Becher advanced in 1669 a reactionary theory according to which bodies were composed of the Aristotelian air and water, associated with a modified *tria prima*, consisting of three earths. These were called *terra pinguis* (fatty, or inflammable earth), *terra mercurialis* (mercurial earth), and *terra lapida* (vitreous earth), corresponding closely to the Paracelsian sulphur, mercury, and salt. On combustion, the fatty earth was supposed to burn away, leaving the remainder of the body to disintegrate. It seems likely that Becher's ideas were coloured by his observations on the burning of coal and its destructive distillation.

At the beginning of the eighteenth century, while

---

[1] *Prelude*, 27.

Boerhaave was still a young man, Becher's pupil, Stahl, remodelled this theory into the celebrated Theory of Phlogiston. Becher's *terra pinguis*, or fatty earth, was renamed *phlogiston*.[1] Stahl depicted this *materia ignis*, or material of fire, as the essential constituent of all combustible bodies: when they burnt, the phlogiston was liberated, passing into the air as an impalpable entity, accompanied by light and heat. Combustible bodies were thus composed of phlogiston and the palpable products of combustion: metals consisted of phlogiston plus an earthy residue, or calx; and sulphur was composed of phlogiston plus an acid.

To the organic chemist, the Theory of Phlogiston bears the clear fire-mark of the age of iatro-chemistry which gave it birth. It accounted well enough for the burning of organic material or of sulphur, but came to grief when applied to the calcination of metals. The obvious *loss* of material streaming into the air from the fiery jets of burning wood or coal[2] has no parallel in the calcination of metals: wood and coal dwindle to a light ash, but metals *gain* weight in the process. The phlogistians, mistaking a property for a material substance, and gain of oxygen for loss of phlogiston, were led into the morasses of a negative world, in which they floundered until the day of Lavoisier.

Boerhaave, living in the heyday of the Theory of Phlogiston, made no reference to it!

This astonishing fact may perhaps be ascribed to his independent outlook, and to his habit of avoiding criticism of contemporary writers. Boerhaave's own view is disclosed in a section of his treatise on Fire, bearing the title 'Of Fewel, or the Pabulum of Fire'. Like his predecessors and contemporaries, he took the negative view. He regarded combustible bodies as containing a combustible and an incombustible ingredient, the former being eliminated in

---

[1] Gr. *phlegein*, to burn; *cf.* the plant-name, phlox.

[2] The Rev. John Clayton, D.D., in a letter written to Robert Boyle (d. 1691), but not published until 1744, actually described the collection of coal-gas in bladders (p. 199). It is interesting to speculate whether Stahl would have identified Clayton's inflammable 'Spirit' with phlogiston, had he known of this astonishing experiment.

the burning; but he was more closely akin in thought to the alchemists than to Stahl. Metal calces, he held, are not the earthy elements of metals; they differ only in form from the metals themselves. The combustible ingredient, or *pabulum ignis*, is not always the same: sulphur, for example, consists of a combustible oily ingredient, or *oleum*, together with an acid.

To the word pabulum he attached 'the precise idea of a matter feeding fire, and converted by the same into the very substance of elementary fire'. He concluded from his own experiments that in vegetables, 'oil, in whatever form it existed, whether thick, or thin like a spirit, is the only pabulum of fire'. Thinking that he had obtained this pabulum in its most concentrated form in alcohol, he turned his attention to this spirit of vegetable origin. 'Knowing by experiments', he wrote, 'that other bodies only become inflammable, as they contain some proportion of this alcohol, or at least of something exceeding like it in point of tenuity; since the other grosser parts remaining after the separation of this subtile one are no longer inflammable; so I promised myself, if I could once discover this in alcohol, it would be easy to find the manner wherein fire is maintain'd by fewel in all other combustible bodies.'

Accordingly, he distilled some alcohol with 'dried fixed alcaline salt of tartar' (ignited potassium carbonate), so that it was 'impossible by any further art to procure the least drop more' of water from it. Next, he ignited some of the pure distillate in a brass vessel, which he then covered with a bell jar of glass, having a small hole at the top. He observed that the thin fume ascending through the orifice extinguished the flame of a candle, 'much the same as the vapour of water would do'. He also observed signs of water within the vessel.

'How great was my disappointment', exclaimed Boerhaave, 'upon finding that alcohol, by passing through the fire, becomes a vapour, which no longer retains the nature of alcohol, nor seems to be any thing more than pure water. This shews us some fix'd limits of science. The pabulum of fire, consumed by it, leaves water; and itself becomes so

A first View of Practical Chymistry begun in the Univerfal Magazine in December 1747.

Printed for J. Hinton at ÿ Kings Arms in S.t Pauls Church Yard London. 1747.

39. A First View of Practical Chymistry, in 1747.

(See p. 155.)

Defign'd & Engrav'd for the Univerfal. Magazine 1748. for J. Hinton at the Kings Arms, in S.t Pauls Church Yard, London

40. A Second View of Practical Chymistry, in 1747.
(See p. 156.)

light, as to dissipate into the chaos of air, and thus eludes all further pursuit.'.

Lacking the technique of handling gases, devoid of any idea of the chemical nature of air and water, and ignorant of the existence of 'fixed air', could Lavoisier himself have done more?

Here is what Richard Watson wrote of the same process, in the first volume of his *Chemical Essays*, published at Cambridge some fifty years later (1781): 'If you set *spirits of wine* on fire, they will, if pure, burn intirely away . . . you may by proper vessels collect the vapour of burning spirits, and you will find it to be an insipid water, incapable of combustion. The principle effecting the combustion of the spirits of wine, and dispersed by the act of combustion, is the phlogiston.'

Turning from organic to inorganic bodies, Boerhaave was faced with the problem of the increase of weight of metals upon calcination. Here he referred to Boyle's 'treatise of *the ponderability of flame*', and Homberg's observations on the gain in weight of antimony when submitted to solar calcination (p. 107). Although these experiments indicated 'that elementary fire is capable of concreting instantaneously with bodies and considerably augmenting their weight', and although he was 'convinced of the ability of those great men for making experiments, and their candour in relating them', yet Boerhaave observed that he had himself found that a piece of iron, of eight pounds, weighed the same whether hot or cold. Here again, he asserted his independent outlook. According to Boerhaave's experiment, fire was 'void of gravity'; but his attempts to account for Homberg's results were unconvincing.

Such, in brief, were Boerhaave's views on combustion. Before we dismiss his idea of a *pabulum ignis*, or self-contained source of fire or energy, as a mere ingenious conceit, we shall do well to reflect upon modern ideas concerning the internal burning of explosives, the disintegration of radium and uranium, and the annihilation of matter, with a progressive release of energy. 'The bodies themselves', wrote Boerhaave, 'are consumed and dissipated by the action

M

thereof, so as almost to disappear from our notice; for the fire once collected in them usually continues, and retains its active nature, till those parts of the bodies, wherein it was before supported, be dissipated by the fire.'

CHEMICAL PRISONERS OF TIME

The most striking feature of the era of phlogiston was its air of chemical stagnation. From the days of Hooke and Mayow till those of Black and Priestley, chemistry languished like a sleeping beauty, in a state of suspended animation. The question inevitably arises whether the work of Hooke and Mayow, in the absence of the obsessive and negative Theory of Phlogiston, could have led during the lifetime of Boerhaave to an anticipation of the positive views of Lavoisier. One who looks back into the *New Method of Chemistry*, through a pair of eighteenth-century spectacles, will see clearly that such an advance could not have been achieved by a generation which had no knowledge of different kinds of 'airs' or of the technique of handling them—and which, indeed, had only rudimentary ideas on the nature of chemical change. Lavoisier himself would have been as powerless as Boerhaave to bridge this great chemical gulf without the pioneering work of Black, Priestley, and Cavendish.

As the history of flying demonstrated anew in a later age, it takes time to leap away from *terra firma* and establish oneself in a gaseous medium. We are all children of our own age; and, in that sense, prisoners of time. As a chemist, Lavoisier could not have been born into a better age; nor, as a man of affairs, into a worse. He reaped both the reward and the penalty.

Who that knows his *Micrographia*, published in 1665, can doubt that Robert Hooke (1635–1703) would have reaped that reward had his age but fallen a hundred years later? Here are some of his statements, amazing in their prescience and clarity: 'Air is the *menstruum* or universal dissolvent of all *sulphureous* bodies. . . . *The dissolution* of sulphureous bodies is made by a substance inherent, and mixt with the Air, that is like, if not the very same, with that

which is fixt in *Salt-peter*. . . . *In this dissolution* of bodies
by the Air, a certain part is united and mixt, or dissolv'd
and turn'd into the Air, and made to fly up and down with
it. . . . The dissolving parts of the Air are but few . .
and therefore a small parcel of it is quickly glutted, and will
dissolve no more. . . . There is no such thing as an
Element of Fire. . . . That shining transient body which
we call *Flame*, is nothing else but a mixture of Air, and
volatil sulphureous parts of dissoluble or combustible bodies.'

Boerhaave, like Hooke, knew nothing of the methods of
isolating and handling gases, and held no clues to the composition of air, fixed air, or water; and, while air is the food
of fire, fixed air and water are the products of combustion of
all organic materials.

Air is the food of fire, the 'universal dissolvent' of
combustible bodies, the true *pabulum ignis*. 'They are
but sparks', said Boerhaave philosophically, referring to
calumny and detraction, 'which if you do not blow them,
will go out of themselves.' A world of 'still more surprizing
things' lay hidden in that remark!

THE CHANGING LABORATORY

The revolutionary nature of Boerhaave's *Elementa
Chemiae*, notably his treatment of chemical theory and his
conception of chemistry as an independent science, marked
the coming of the real chemistry to the text-books. A
parallel change was taking place in the laboratories, which
gradually turned from the prosecution of alchemy and iatro-
chemistry to that of chemistry. The first volume of Boerhaave's comprehensive work ends with an illustrated
description of the chemical apparatus, vessels, lutes, and
furnaces of his day; while the second volume, with further
appropriate copperplate illustrations, is essentially a complete text-book of practical chemistry.

This second volume, indeed, contains no fewer than 227
'Processes, or Operations of the Art'. These chemical and
pharmaceutical preparations are described in detail under
the familiar heads of Chemical Operations upon Vegetables
(1 to 88), Animals (89 to 127), and Minerals (128 to 227).

The properties and uses of the preparations are also given. That Boerhaave was a skilled and fastidious practical chemist is evident from the character of his directions; and some examples of his laboratory technique are well worthy of study.

'Glauber's *spirit of nitre*' was prepared as follows:

'Put eighteen ounces of pure dry nitre, reduced to an impalpable powder, into a clean glass retort, and pour thereon six ounces of pure, and highly rectified oil of vitriol: immediately place the retort in a sand-furnace, and apply a large glass receiver; luting the juncture with a mixture of lime-clay and a little sand. There will presently arise a heat, and a red fume; apply a moderate fire, and the receiver will soon be full of red fumes, and a liquor begin to drop gradually. Increase the fire to the utmost that sand will give; and then let all spontaneously cool. As soon as the neck of the retort is a little cold, separate the receiver, and have at hand a strong dry glass, with a narrow neck, fitted with a slender funnel; pour the liquor into a bottle, thro' the funnel, under a chimney, to prevent the red fume from any way coming to the lungs, for it is sharp, fiery, incredibly volatile and diffusive; as soon as the spirit is in, exactly stop the mouth of the containing glass with a glass-stopper: in like manner, stop the receiver, and set it by for the same use; it will remain for many weeks filled, with a red vapour, in continual motion. The liquor, in the glass will appear of a gold-colour, with a red vapour always appearing in the empty part above, even for years, as I have found by experience: and if at any time opened, a volatile, copious, red vapour immediately flies out. The operation is best performed in the cold winter season.'

It is noticeable that excess of nitre was used in this operation. Boerhaave described the more difficult preparation of dehydrated alcohol in an equally precise and workmanlike way:

'A kind of furnace was made for a bath-heat, that could not admit a greater heat than of 214 degrees; and herein a large still was placed, and common spirit of wine poured into it, so as to fill two thirds thereof; the still was now fitted with a head rising in a tall, upright, slender pipe, which, bending at the top, came down and fitted into the worm. The distillation, here, is so performed, that the water of the bath coming to boil, makes the spirit of wine boil stronger. . . .

'Yet upon carefully examining the matter, I find that even thus a little water will still remain mixed with the alcohol, being in the distillation raised therewith. Hence I have repeated the operation. . . .

'I conceive, that the spirit, by this method, can never be perfectly separated from the phlegm, tho' it is but a very small quantity that is here left behind. After this therefore I took the alcohol prepared by distillation in this furnace, and half filled the still therewith; then adding half a pound of pure decrepitated, hot and dry salt, I put on the head, carefully closed the junctures, and left them thus together for twelve hours, in a heat so small, as by no means to make the alcohol boil. Then I distill'd off the spirit, and kept the first two ounces apart, because some little aqueous vapour might happen to lodge in the pipe of the still or worm; and this alcohol of the first running will easily wash it off. I afterwards received two thirds of the following alcohol in a pure dry glass vessel, and kept it perfectly well stopped . . . and by this means I can in this furnace readily prepare a perfectly pure alcohol for all chemical uses.'

That the laboratory of Boerhaave's day was greatly different from the picturesque alchemical dens painted by Brueghel, Teniers, and their contemporaries is evident from various eighteenth-century engravings. Two very instructive representations of the kind were published in the *Universal Magazine* (London) in 1747. The first of these (Fig. **39**) depicts the laboratory as a rectangular chamber, spacious and lofty, with a neat arrangement of apparatus, together with large laboratory units set up for specific kinds of operations. The adjoining pharmacy, or apothecary's shop, and the pharmacopoeia lying on the shelf, are tokens of the iatro-chemical influence; moreover, two of the other titled books bear the names of Paracelsus and Lemery. The other visible title is Boerhaave.

The vessels in the foreground comprise (from left to right): a glass pipe or funnel; retort standing on a roundle; pelican or circulatory vessel; receiver with glass pipe (tube) for digestion processes; another retort; receiver; and subliming furnace with aludels. The chemist is shown at work, down on his knees in front of a furnace in which a copper still, tinned within, is being heated; the still is fitted with a Moor or Death's Head, the beak or pipe of which passes through a barrel containing cooling water and delivers the distillate into a receiver. On the chemist's right is another still; this is flanked by a so-called Serpentine for obtaining spirit of wine from brandy and the like, a process accomplished by fractional distillation from a tinned copper still through a zigzag fractionating column made of tin. Behind this unit is a so-called 'matrass of rencounter', beside which stands 'a Labourer beating Drugs in a Mortar'. The only identifiable reagent is aqua fortis, contained in a squat stoppered bottle, standing on a shelf next to the books.

The second 'View of Practical Chymistry' (Fig. 40) also depicts a spacious and orderly laboratory, opening this time into another of the same general type. Once again, distillation units form the most prominent part of the equipment. Picturesque exhibits inherited from the bygone era of alchemy hang from the ceiling. On the floor, in the foreground, are shown several kinds of tongs, a black-lead crucible, and 'iron rings to break glasses with'.

The laborant is receiving instructions from his chief; these seem to be concerned with material undergoing fusion in the 'melting furnace' which the chief is regarding so intently. To the right of this furnace is a *Balneum Mariae*, or water-bath, from which distillations are being made. The unit in the corner is used for subliming flowers of sulphur; adjoining it, on the left, is 'a furnace for distilling hartshorn in quantity'. The apparatus standing on the floor, on the extreme left, is the celebrated 'glass bell for making spirit of sulphur' (p. 106); beside it is a 'more commodious apparatus' for the same purpose. The subsidiary room contains a digesting furnace, with another water-bath, on the right.

The ventilation of these eighteenth-century laboratories seems to have depended upon the opening of doors and windows. The absence of tables or benches also seems strange to the modern chemist; but beakers, test-tubes, and other small pieces of apparatus requiring such fittings found no place in the large-scale preparative work which formed the chief activity of the chemists of that age.

REFERENCES

Boerhaave, H., *Elementa Chemiae*, 2 vols., Lugduni Batavorum, 1732.

Bugge, G. (ed.), *Das Buch der grossen Chemiker*, 2 vols., Berlin, 1929–1930.

Burton, W., *An Account of the Life and Writings of Herman Boerhaave*, London, 1743.

Dallowe, T., *Elements of Chemistry:* Being the Annual Lectures of Herman Boerhaave, M.D. Formerly Professor of Chemistry and Botany, And at present, Professor of Physick in the University of Leyden. Translated from the Original Latin, by Timothy Dallowe, M.D., 2 vols., London, 1735.

Davis, T. L., 'The Vicissitudes of Boerhaave's Textbook of Chemistry', *Isis*, 1928, **10**, 33.

Hill, G. B. (ed.), *Boswell's Life of Johnson*, 6 vols., Oxford, 1887.

Hooke, R., *Micrographia*, London, 1665; *Extracts from Micrographia*, Alembic Club Reprints, No. 5, Edinburgh, 1902.

Johnson, S., 'The Life of Dr. Herman Boerhaave, late Professor of Physick in the University of Leyden in Holland', *Gentleman's Magazine and Historical Chronicle*, London, 1739, **9**, 37, 72, 114, 172.

Kopp, H., *Geschichte der Chemie*, 4 vols., Braunschweig, 1843–1847.

Lysaght, D. J., 'Hooke's Theory of Combustion', *Ambix*, 1937, **1**, 93.

Mayow, J., *Medico-Physical Works*, being a Translation of *Tractatus Quinque Medico-Physici*, Alembic Club Reprints, No. 17, Edinburgh, 1907.

McKie, D., 'Some Early Work on Combustion, Respiration and Calcination', *Ambix*, 1938, **1**, 144.

Shaw, P., *A New Method of Chemistry* . . . Translated from the Original Latin of Dr. *Boerhaave's Elementa Chemiæ*, as Published by Himself, 2 vols., London, 1741.

Shaw, P., and Chambers, E., *A New Method of Chemistry* . . . Written by the very Learned H. Boerhaave, London, 1727.

Thomson, T., *The History of Chemistry*, 2 vols., London, 1830–1831.

Watson, R., *Chemical Essays*, 5 vols., Cambridge and London, 1781–1789.

CHAPTER VIII

CHEMISTRY GROWS BRIGHTER

ENTER JOSEPH BLACK

FROM Boerhaave's time onwards, chemistry won increasing recognition as an independent branch of science. As it grew in importance, students of the subject multiplied, and methods of teaching it became more efficient. One of the most celebrated teachers of chemistry in the second half of the eighteenth century was Joseph Black (1728–1799). To most chemists of the present day Black is deservedly known as the founder of the doctrines of latent heat and specific heat, as the discoverer of 'fixed air', now known as carbon dioxide, and as the first to weigh a gas in combination.

Black's discovery that an 'air', with properties quite distinct from those of ordinary air, could be 'fixed' by a solid alkali or alkaline earth, and released from its solid combination at will, came as a revolutionary idea to the fixed minds of the chemists of 1755. It disclosed a new world. It opened the way to the 'pneumatic chemistry' of Priestley and his contemporaries, and this led in turn to Lavoisier's foundation of the new chemistry.

'He had discovered', wrote Robison in 1803, 'that a cubic inch of marble consisted of about half its weight of pure lime, and as much air as would fill a vessel holding six wine gallons. . . . What could be more singular than to find so subtile a substance as air existing in the form of a hard stone, and its presence accompanied by such a change in the properties of that stone?'

If anything could be more singular, it is perhaps the fact that the process of lime-burning had been a familiar practice for thousands of years.

Joseph Black, known only to most modern chemists as a brilliant investigator in chemistry, was equally famous in his own day as a teacher of that expanding science. In 1756 he was appointed to the dual post of professor of anatomy and lecturer on chemistry in the University of Glasgow, of which he was an alumnus. Later, he exchanged chairs with the professor of medicine. In 1766, William Cullen, professor of chemistry in the University of Edinburgh, having migrated to a medical chair, Black entered upon his long tenure (1766–1799) of the Edinburgh chair of chemistry. It was in Edinburgh that he achieved his reputation as one of the greatest teachers that chemistry had yet seen.

JOSEPH BLACK, THE LECTURER

Most of Black's pupils at Edinburgh were students of medicine; but some came from the factory and workshop. Although students of this second type had often received little or no preparation suitable for such a course, Black realised their importance in the industrial and economic order of the days to come. It was largely on their account that he took so much care to expound chemistry with the utmost clarity and simplicity at his command, and to this end he made full use of experiments and exhibits in his lectures.

Black is the first great teacher of chemistry whose methods and idiosyncrasies can be reconstructed in satisfying detail. This interesting possibility arises from the existence of contemporary descriptions of the manner of his lectures, together with manuscript and printed versions of their matter.

His colleague, John Robison, editor of the printed version of Black's lectures, tells his readers in the preface that Black's 'personal appearance and manner were those of a gentleman, and peculiarly pleasing. His voice in lecturing was low, but fine; and his articulation so distinct that he was perfectly well heard by an audience consisting of several hundreds.'

Referring to his experimental illustrations, Robison

describes them as 'ingeniously and judiciously contrived, clearly establishing the point in view, and never more than sufficed for this purpose. While he scorned the quackery of a showman the simplicity, neatness, and elegance, with which they were performed, were truly admirable.' His lectures provided 'such a treat to his scholars' that the enthusiasm spread to others, and in Black's hands chemistry became a cultural instrument.

A particularly vivid description of Black as a lecturer was written many years later by Lord Brougham and included in his memoirs. 'The gratification of attending one of Black's last lecture courses exceeded all I have ever enjoyed,' he wrote. 'I have heard the greatest understandings of the age giving forth their efforts in their most eloquent tongues—have heard the commanding periods of Pitt's majestic oratory—the vehemence of Fox's burning declamation . . . but I would without hesitation prefer, for mere intellectual gratification . . . to be once more allowed the privilege . . . of being present, while the first philosopher of his age was the historian of his own discoveries, and be an eyewitness of those experiments by which he had formerly made them, once more performed by his own hands.'

A remark curiously complementary in tone was made in 1878 to Sir Henry Roscoe by the illustrious French chemist, J. B. A. Dumas, then in his seventy-ninth year: 'I have seen many phases of life; I have moved in Imperial circles, I have been Minister of State; but if I had to live my life again, I would always remain in my laboratory, for the greatest joy of my life has been to accomplish original scientific work, and, next to that, to lecture to a set of intelligent students'.[1]

Of Black's experiments, Brougham said that they 'were often like Franklin's, performed with the simplest apparatus

---

[1] Among these was Louis Pasteur, who, as a young student of twenty, wrote on 9 December 1842: 'I attend at the Sorbonne the lectures of M. Dumas, a celebrated chemist. You cannot imagine what a crowd of people come to these lectures. The room is immense, and always quite full. We have to be there half an hour before the time to get a good place, as you would in a theatre . . . there are always six or seven hundred people.'

—indeed with nothing that could be called apparatus at all.
. . . I remember his pouring fixed air from a vessel in
which sulphuric acid had been poured upon chalk, and
showing us how this air poured on a candle extinguished the
light. He never failed to remark on the great use of simple
experiments within every one's reach; and liked to dwell on
the manner in which discoveries are made, and the practical
effect resulting from them in changing the condition of men
and things.'

Brougham described his features as 'singularly graceful,
full of intelligence, but calm, as suited his manner and
speech. His high forehead and sharp temples were slightly
covered, when I knew him, with hair of a snow-white hue,
and his mouth gave a kindly as well as a most intelligent
expression to his whole features.'

In Kay's caricature of Black at the lecture-table (Fig.
41), drawn in 1787, one can perceive, lurking around the
mouth, the pleasing smile, mentioned by Robison, 'which
began to form on his countenance, when he was about to
exhibit or relate anything that he considered as peculiarly
interesting'.

Black was an excessively skilled and neat manipulator.
Brougham describes how he poured 'boiling water or
boiling acid from a vessel that had no spout, into a tube,
holding it at such a distance as made the stream's diameter
small, and so vertical that not a drop was spilt. . . . The
long table on which the different processes had been carried
on was as clean at the end of the lecture as it had been before
the apparatus was planted upon it. Not a drop of liquid, not
a grain of dust remained.'

Black took meticulous care in his lectures, as also in his
conversation, to assign to every investigator his proper share
in the discoveries under discussion. 'I have heard him with
astonishment,' wrote Brougham, 'in bearing testimony to
the great merits of Lavoisier . . . and bestowing praise
unstinted upon his works, without even making the least
allusion to the entire suppression in them of all references
to his name as founder of the new school of chemistry, by
the discovery of latent heat and permanently elastic fluids.'

In order to stimulate still further the interest of his students in chemistry, Black established a chemical society consisting of members of his class who found a special appeal in the subject. In 1785 this society, which appears to have been the earliest of all chemical societies, consisted of fifty-nine members. It was possibly through the influence of Benjamin Rush, one of Black's earliest pupils at Edinburgh (1766–1768), that James Woodhouse founded the first chemical society in the New World—the Chemical Society of Philadelphia—in 1792. Benjamin Rush is still more noteworthy as the original incumbent of the first American chair of chemistry, which was established in the Medical School of the University of Pennsylvania, in 1769.

THE SUBSTANCE OF BLACK'S LECTURES

Black's lectures were not published during his lifetime: according to Robison, 'Dr. Black peculiarly disliked appearing as an author'. However, his students, like Boerhaave's earlier in the century, made exhaustive notes from which manuscript copies of the lectures were written and circulated. Complete versions of this kind, bound in several volumes, could be bought in Black's day for four or five guineas. Two examples, in the St. Andrews collection, may be used to convey an idea of their nature.

The first set comprises 106 lectures in six volumes, bound handsomely in tree-calf, with gilt edges, and written beautifully, in the same hand throughout. Lecture 1 is dated 'Octr. 29th, 1771' (Fig. 42), and the fly-leaf of the first volume bears a pencilled note by H. B. F. Beaufoy: 'This is a Copy of the Lectures of the Celebrated Chemical Lecturer at Edinboro Dr. Black. Copies of his Lectures were obtained by paying for permission to copy them. This Copy was made by Henry Beauf[o]y Esq. M.P. for Great Yarmouth, Norfolk, & Secretary to the Board of Control, during the time he was a student at the above University, after Quitting the Dissenting Academy at Warrington in Lancashire, where he studied under Dr. Priestley, Aikin, &c.' This set follows closely the plan of the printed work, except that in Vol. VI the only metals included are mercury, antimony, bismuth, zinc, lead, and tin; but probably there were eight volumes originally. On an average, about 15 leaves of manuscript are devoted to each lecture.

Lecture 1, Oct.ʳ 29.1771.

The purpose of our Meeting is to open a course of Lectures on Chemistry. I shall at present make some remarks on the Nature of Chemistry with the Changes it has undergone in the different periods of its history; next I shall take Notice of the plan we are to pursue in this Course, And Lastly mention such Books as are proper for your perusal. With regard to the General Nature of Chemistry, we may Observe that Chemistry is an Experimental science Discovering many Active principles in the different kinds of matter; no science was ever more properly called Experimental, for from Experiments alone the conclusions

42. A page from H. Beaufoy's MS. version of Black's Lectures (1771).

As compared with the lecture notes of a modern student, the absence of tables and diagrams (and, of course, of formulae and equations) is noteworthy. However, as an indication of Black's interest in heat and thermometry, the first volume contains a printed diagram of various thermometric scales; besides this, at the end of the same

volume there is a folding inset, seven feet long, with a
carefully lettered drawing of a Brobdingnagian Fahrenheit

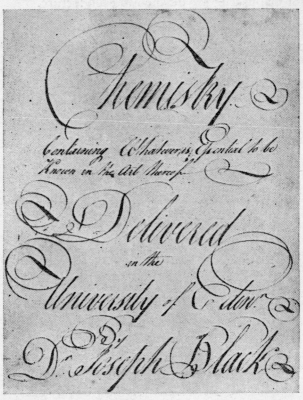

43. Title-page of another MS. version of Black's Lectures
(*c.* 1775)

thermometer, numbered from 1100 above zero to 450
below. Some of the entries on various levels read: 'Iron red
hot from 1050; Iron shines in the twilight 884; Iron shines
briskly in the dark 750; Quicksilver boils 600; Human
blood 97 to 100; Frost 32; Greatest cold Ob. in England
4; Brandy freeses 33; Siberian cold 120; Quicksilver
freeses 350'.

The second set, confined to two volumes, covers only
the first 44 lectures, ending with the discussion of Salts.

The manuscript is written in several hands on 586 quarto leaves, and the first volume (Fig. 43) bears the bookplate of William Herbert, the bibliographer. The date of this set is probably about 1775. It is closely similar to the first two volumes (containing 42 lectures) of the Beaufoy set; but it differs from this set, and from the printed version, by giving Black's introductory lecture. This was mostly in the nature of a general moral exhortation, and a few extracts from it will serve to illustrate Black's style and the fidelity of his reporter. The lecture begins as follows:

'Gentlemen, As Established Custom forbids us to enter upon any Essential part of our Course, I hope you will forgive me, if from zeal to your Improvement, not only in this study but in the other branches of your Education, I offer you a few general Cautions & remarks with regard to this subject. . . .

'I first address myself to the modest & diffident, who are commonly endued with ingenuity and parts, but are in danger of allowing them to remain inactive. They commonly set out with ardour, and have a high relish for the enjoyment which knowledge affords to the mind, but by the multiplicity and extent of the Science to which they aspire, they are discharged, their ardour cools, and they seek relief from the disagreeable object which the loss of their time occasions, in amusement and dissipation. . . . Imagining that their own Capacity is inferior to the ordinary rate, they suffer themselves to sink into a dispirited inactivity. But did they know the difficulties and labours the greatest men have struggled thro' in their first advances, they would find their own case to be no ways particular.

'That difficulty at first, and seeming want of Success, has its foundation in the nature and constitution of the human mind, which is more or less slow in the apprehension of Ideas and things, and requires a repetition of them to fix them in the memory. . . .'

After much more encouragement of this kind, Black comes at last to some general observations on chemistry. He begins by remarking that less than a century ago 'it wore a garb which rendered it disgustful'. He emphasises its nature as an experimental science rather than an art, and refers in a general way to its interest and applications.

Coming finally to books, he is unable to recommend any one which is 'sufficiently extensive'. He adds: 'I use an arrangement of my own which I hope will be easily carried along'. The books he mentions as 'most necessary' are Macquer's *Elements of the Theory and Practice of Chymistry* (London, 1758), 'particularly the Theory for the Elementary part, & Lewis' New Dispensatory for the application of it to farmacy. The first of these contains a Clear and Concise account of most of the facts relating to Chemistry, and Lewis' book contains fully & distinctly that part of our Science that is applied to the purpose of Medicine, but I would have those who want to inform themselves more fully to read Dr. Boerhaave's treatise on fire in the first part of his Chemistry, & Martin's Essay on Heat & Thermometers. These have the greatest connection with the first part of our course.'

For the later lectures he recommends Neumann's *Chemical Works* (London, 1759), 'published and abridged by Lewis, & the Diction. Chemie, in which McQuer is supposed to have had the principal hand, particularly the translation of it which is correct and elegant, & enriched with many new observations which were not known to McQuer'. Black refers here to the *Dictionary of Chemistry*, translated from the French by James Keir, and published at London in 1771.

Black gave his last course of lectures in the winter of 1796–1797; but the printed version of his *Lectures on the Elements of Chemistry* was not issued until 1803, nearly four years after his death. This edition was undertaken in order to forestall a proposed unauthorised publication from sets of students' notes. The work, in two large quarto volumes, was prepared for publication from Black's manuscripts by John Robison, who dedicated it to James Watt, 'Dr. Black's most illustrious Pupil'. Apart from the omission of the first three or four lectures, comprising the introductory discourse and a short historical survey, the arrangement of the printed version is similar to that of the manuscript copies which have been mentioned.

41. Joseph Black Lecturing.

From an etching by John Kay, Edinburgh, 1787. (See p. 161.)

44. Dr. Black taking gentle exercise.
(Kay, 1787.)   (See p. 175.)

PHILOSOPHERS

45. Dr. Hutton and Dr. Black.
(Kay, 1787.)   (See p. 175.)

During his tenure of the Edinburgh chair, Black witnessed the approach and arrival of modern chemistry. The eventful discoveries of that period must have kept his lectures in a state of continual flux, and there are naturally considerable differences between the final printed version and the manuscript copies written in the closing years of the era of phlogiston. The rapid changes in Black's later period are reflected in Robison's editorial comment: 'I am not certain that he has been fully decided as to the way in which he should introduce the new doctrines of combustion and acidification'. The printed version affords an illuminating picture of chemistry in the period between the death of phlogiston and the birth of the Atomic Theory, and throws much light upon the difficulties of the chemical interregnum between the publication of Lavoisier's *Traité Elémentaire de Chimie* in 1789 and Dalton's *New System of Chemical Philosophy* in 1808.

The eighteenth-century chemists were very expansive in their writings. Black's two volumes, covering only a small fraction of the work included in a modern elementary text-book of inorganic chemistry, weigh more than eight pounds, and Boerhaave's *Elementa Chemiae* tips the scale only a little short of this. The manuscript versions imposed a still greater burden upon the early students of chemistry: each of the numerous Beaufoy volumes exceeds three pounds in weight. No wonder that some of Black's pupils suffered themselves 'to sink into a dispirited inactivity' at the mere sight of these monumental tomes!

In the first of Black's printed volumes, about twenty pages are devoted to a 'Definition of Chemistry', and more than two hundred to the succeeding account of the 'General Effects of Heat'. This part of the course occupied about twenty lectures. Most of it deals with physical aspects of heat.

Chemically, the most important problem here discussed is that of combustion. In the second of the manuscript versions mentioned above, Black puts forward, with some reserve, 'an opinion or Theory in Chemistry' according to which 'the quality of Inflammability depends upon the

N

presence of a particular principle or Ingredient abounding in Inflammable substances to which they give a name of Phlogiston'. After reviewing the evidence usually adduced in favour of the theory, he adds that the increase of weight observed in the burning of phosphorus and other bodies 'will probably make many of you reject the whole opinion of the existence of a Common principle of Inflammability'.

At the corresponding point in his printed lectures he states that 'another theory . . . which . . . is the opposite or contrary to this, has lately been formed, and is fast gaining ground, especially on the continent'. He then mentions 'the fundamental experiments', following his discovery of fixed air, which were made 'on the nature and qualities of atmospherical air, and of a number of other elastic fluids'. These were first made, says Black, 'and the leading inferences were first drawn in this country, by Dr. Priestley, the Honourable Mr. Cavendish, and my friend Mr. Watt. But it was chiefly in France that they were repeated, with proper attention to all the circumstances that would affect the result, and this result was made the foundation of a new theory of combustion. . . . The unfortunate Lavoisier, who fell a sacrifice to the ambition of his philosophical associates, and whose unjust and cruel fate, and the loss which science has suffered by it, cannot be too much deplored . . . was the principal author of the new theory.'

Through these later French experiments, 'it has become clear and evident', continues Black, 'that a considerable quantity of the air is really absorbed, and combined with the matter of the burning body, so as to form, in many cases, a dense compound, in which the air so absorbed is totally deprived of its usual form of an elastic fluid: And the additional weight which the matter of the burning body acquires, has been found to correspond exactly to the weight of the air which has been absorbed by it'.

This quotation throws into sharp relief the significance of Black's initiating discovery that an 'air' could be 'fixed' and weighed in a solid combination. The astounding new idea had come to stay.

Following the lengthy discussion of the 'General Effects

of Heat', a short section of about thirty-five printed pages, or four lectures, is sufficient to cover the 'General Effects of Mixture', including 'theories of chemical mixture and combination' and 'elective attractions'. By this last term Black designates 'those numerous cases, in which a third body frequently acts on a compound of two ingredients, so as to separate these from one another, and join itself to one of the two'.

After this, a description of 'Chemical Apparatus' fills more than fifty printed pages, and from the manuscript copies it is seen that Black spent about eight lectures on this work.

In view of modern methods of producing high temperatures, much interest attaches to Black's reference to concave mirrors and convex lenses as instruments 'which produced effects that appeared astonishing when they were new; such as melting in a moment many earths and stones, which were reckoned before perfectly unfusible'. He mentions a speculum, made by the Viletti, of Lyons: 'the diameter of the speculum is 43 inches, the diameter of the focus half an inch, the distance three feet'. A lens used by Homberg and Geoffroy had a diameter of 33 inches, with a focal length of 12 feet. Few chemists realise nowadays the once important consideration that although the speculum is the more powerful, the lens is the more convenient, 'because the speculum directs the rays upwards towards the sun. The object cannot be so conveniently exposed to them in that situation, and it interrupts light.' It may be recalled that the burning-glass with the aid of which Priestley discovered oxygen on 1 August 1774 had a diameter of only a foot.

The descriptive account of the various substances, which comes next, is entitled 'The Chemical History of Bodies'. This fills the remainder of the first and the whole of the second printed volume, and takes up nearly nine hundred pages, and all the other lectures, amounting probably to more than a hundred in a full course.

Since earth, air, fire, and water had at last made their final exit from the chemical stage and the elements of modern chemistry still hesitated on tiptoe in the wings, Black naturally found it difficult to devise a satisfactory classification of his substances. As he was unable 'to determine what are the ultimate elements of bodies', he arranged them arbitrarily in a number of classes suggested by their properties. These classes, which the Beaufoy manuscript attributes to Cullen, were 'Salts, Earths, Inflammable Substances, Metals, and Waters'.

The briefest survey of this descriptive section in the printed lectures is sufficient to indicate the striking advances that had been made in chemistry since Boerhaave's time, the most revolutionary innovation of all being the accounts of various gases. Alkalies, acids, and compound or neutral salts are all included under the general head of salts. After giving full descriptions of three alkalies (vegetable, fossil, and volatile) and six acids (sulphuric, nitric, muriatic, acetous, acid of tartar, and acid of borax), Black proceeds 'to explain how these nine salts, or saline substances, unite with one another to form the compound salts'.

Under nitre, Black refers to 'the escape of the oxygenous gas' from the heated salt, and to the considerations which 'have induced Mr. Lavoisier to consider vital air as the cause of acidity, and to call it *oxygen* gas'. At the end of the account of salts, closing the first volume, there is an interesting mention of the new French system of chemical nomenclature drawn up at Paris in 1787 by 'Messrs. Lavoisier, De Morveau, Berthollet, and Fourcroy'. Black admits the necessity of reform, but points out that by using the 'latinised French words' of these chemists, which appeared to him 'at first very harsh and disagreeable', it would in future 'scarcely be possible to think on chemical subjects in a way different from their theories'.

Black's account of fixed air falls under the heading of alkaline earths. Here he remarks: 'I fully intended to make this air, and some other elastic fluids which frequently occur, the subject of serious study. But my attention was then forcibly turned to other objects. A load of new official duties was then laid upon me.' He refers here to his dual appointment at Glasgow in 1756. 'We know not how many different airs may be thus contained in our atmosphere, nor what may be their separate properties', he observes.

A historic interest attaches to the account of fixed air which Black gave in his early lecture courses at Edinburgh. In Lecture 62 of the Beaufoy manuscript of 1771–1772 he remarked that others have used the name mephitic air, 'but I thought it better to use a word already familiar in philosophy, than to invent a new one, before we were fully acquainted with the nature and properties of this substance'.

Fixed air, he said, 'is plainly an Elastic fluid like air, but entirely different in its properties . . . it seems to be produced from common air by the respiration of animals and by burning fuel . . . of the same kind is that elastic matter which arises from vegetables during Fermentation'. He found that when chalk was burnt to quicklime it lost 40 parts in the 100.

Here are some experiments described in Lecture 63: 'Into this Glass Syphon, I shall pour a quantity of Lime Water. . . . I now apply my mouth to the pipe, and suck in the common air through it; The fluid bubbles a little, but is not altered in its transparency. . . . But I now blow through it, and it becomes instantly muddy, the fixed air from the Lungs being attracted by the Lime, it loses its solubility and is precipitated.' He used the same test to show the presence of fixed air in 'air which has passed through burning Charcoal'.

'Mr. Cavendish', he said, 'has published some Experiments, very lately in the Philosophical Transactions, he has made Experiments on other kinds of Elastic fluids . . . as the inflammable Elastic fluid which is produced from Metals in their dissolution in acids. . . . He was the first that observed that fixed air was capable of mixing with Water. . . . He found the specifick Weight of it to common air in the proportion of one to one and half,[1] and that 1 part Mephitic to 9 parts of Common air extinguished the flame of a small wax candle.'

'That it is heavier than common air', Black continued,

---

[1] Black's reporter has here reversed the relationship.

'will appear by the following experiment. Into this vessel I shall put a quantity of Chalk, and having poured a little water into it I shall expel the air by means of the diluted vitriolic acid. I cover the vessel slightly, that the common air may have liberty to come out, while the Mephitic air is detached from the Chalk. The fixed air cannot be distinguished by its appearance from common air. If I now hold a candle below the Lip of this Glass, you see it immediately extinguished. The air will remain in the vessel a very considerable time though I take off the cover, and if I now incline the vessel to one side, we perceive the Mephitic air running out by its extinguishing the flame of a candle at some distance, and this in consequence of its being a fluid heavier than the surrounding atmosphere.'

In this contemporary account, Black makes it clear that Cavendish was chiefly responsible for the early study of the properties of fixed air.

Returning now to the printed version of Black's lectures, the list of 'Inflammable Substances' contains some strange bedfellows, including 'inflammable air', phosphorus, sulphur, charcoal, Bolognan phosphorus, and a variety of organic materials ranging from spirit of wine, sulphuric æther and sugar, through oils, soot and 'cahoutchouc', to soap, tar and pit-coal.

The fifteen metals are arranged in the order: arsenic, magnesium (*i.e.* manganese), iron, mercury, antimony, zinc or spelter, bismuth or tinglass, cobalt, nickel, lead, tin, copper, silver, gold, and platina or platinum. Iron takes up most space of all, followed by mercury. Under iron are discussed such subjects as Prussian blue, writing ink, green vitriol, cast iron, steel, and the medicinal virtues of iron; and under mercury are found 'nitrous air', 'eudiometry', and 'various oxyds of azote'.

In this curious classification, the description of chlorine falls under the head of manganese: 'Mr. Scheele called this vapour or gas the *dephlogisticated muriatic acid*', says Black, who considers it 'one of the most remarkable objects in chemistry'. In defending Scheele's interpretation of his new gas in terms of phlogiston, Black holds it 'to be unpardonable arrogance in the French chemists to say that no man can entertain the belief of the existence of phlogiston who has a grain of common sense'. He points out that Scheele, for whom he cherished the warmest admiration, was 'the first that expressed any dissatisfaction with the simple form in which this theory was delivered by Dr. Stahl', and that 'Scheele's dissertations, of every kind, will ever stand in the very first rank of chemical writings'.

'Since the time of Dr. Scheele,' adds Black, with unconscious irony, in view of later developments (p. 187), 'all these phenomena of the muriatic acid and manganese have been maturely considered, and carefully investigated, and clearly explained, principally by the chemists of France. We now hold that the change of appearance and properties which the muriatic acid suffers depends on the addition to it of a great quantity of oxygen which it acquires from the manganese. For this reason, the muriatic vapour which I am now considering has got the name of Oxygenated Muriatic Acid. Mr. Kirwan calls it the Oxymuriatic Acid.'

Under his final head of 'Waters', Black gives a brief review 'of the variety of waters found in nature', together with an account of the dissolved matter, and some rudimentary remarks on water analysis. It is noteworthy that he discusses seriously the question of 'the convertibility of water into earth' before coming to the 'lately formed' opinion 'that water is not a single elementary substance but a compound'. He adds that 'this idea of the nature of water was suggested by Mr. Watt (Phil. Trans. 1784). Mr. Cavendish, however, was the first who gave it solid foundation and credibility.'

JOSEPH BLACK, THE MAN

Black's contemporaries made many references to his distinctive personality and the charm of his character. Robison comments upon 'his sweetness of manner', which with other attributes made him 'a most welcome visitor in every family'. First and foremost a man of science, 'he was a stranger to none of the elegant accomplishments of life. . . . He had a fine or accurate musical ear . . . he sung, and performed on the flute, with great taste and feeling; and could sing a plain air at sight.' Robison adds, without the explanation that the statement seems to demand: 'I speak of Dr. Black as I knew him at Glasgow: After his coming to Edinburgh, he gave up most of these amusements'.

Attractive of countenance, engaging in manners, of calm and unruffled temperament, 'he was of most easy approach, affable, and readily entered into conversation, whether serious or trivial'. Lord Brougham described him as 'a person whose opinions on every subject were marked by calmness and sagacity, wholly free from both passion and prejudice, while affectation was only known to him from the comedies he might have read'.

Black was interested in art as well as in music. Robison has left it on record that figure, of every kind, attracted his attention. 'Even a retort, or a crucible, was to his eye an example of beauty or deformity. . . . Naturally, therefore, the young ladies were proud of Dr. Black's approbation of their taste in matters of ornament. These are not indifferent things; they are features of an elegant mind.'

Although a confirmed bachelor, Black 'was in particular a favourite with the ladies. I could not but remark', says Robison, 'that they regarded themselves as honoured by the attentions of Dr. Black; for these were not indiscriminately bestowed, but exclusively paid to those who evinced a superiority in mental accomplishments, or propriety of demeanour, and in grace and elegance of manners.'

Love of propriety and of order, and a passion for neatness and precision, were among Black's dominant characteristics. 'His chambers', wrote Dr. Adam Ferguson, 'were never seen lumbered with books and papers, or specimens of mineralogy, &c. or the apparatus of experiments. . . . Every thing being done in its proper season and place, he seemed to have leisure in store.'

Black was of a very sociable disposition, although in later life his activities of this kind were restricted by delicate health. He welcomed the visits of friends and relatives, and was both hospitable and generous. 'His table', says

Ferguson, 'was plentiful and elegant. . . . His contributions for all public purposes were liberal, and like a gentleman; and his purse was open to assist his friend.'

His calm air, correct attire, and orderly habits are all brought out in a caricature drawn by John Kay in 1787 (Fig. 44), which shows him indulging in one of 'those hours of walking and gentle exercise' necessary, as Robison says, 'for Dr. Black's ease'. Another caricature (Fig. 45) of the same date, in Kay's unique and fascinating record of 'the golden age of Edinburgh society', shows Black conversing with Dr. James Hutton, a versatile and erratic genius who was for many years his closest friend.

It is said of Black and Hutton in Kay's *Portraits* that 'they were remarkable for their simplicity of character, and almost total ignorance of what was daily passing around them in the world'. On one occasion, the two philosophers innocently arranged a weekly meeting of a club of 'highly respectable literary gentlemen', of which they were members, in a house afterwards found to possess a very dubious reputation. On another, they carried out a practical experiment designed to overcome the popular prejudice, which they had argued to be absurd, against stewed snails as an article of diet. Unfortunately, the experiment came to an early and abrupt end, as Dr. Hutton cast a look of aversion upon the smoking dish, and started up from the table, vociferating 'Tak' them awa'! Tak' them awa'!', and 'giving full vent to his feelings of abhorrence'.

This brief sketch may well end with an original description of a student making Black's acquaintance, in the days when a professor's stipend was derived largely from fees paid to him by the members of his class. 'I remember the first time I ever was in his society', writes Lord Brougham. 'When I went to take a ticket for his class, there stood upon his table a small brass instrument for weighing the guineas given. On learning who I was, he entered into conversation in a most kind manner. . . . When I was going away he said: "You must have been surprised at my using this instrument to weigh your guineas, but it was before I knew who you were. I am obliged to weigh them when strange students come, there being a very large number who bring light guineas; so that I should be defrauded of many pounds every year if I did not act in self-defence against that class of students." '

As we may surmise, Black weighed the light guineas with much less satisfaction than he weighed fixed air in combination; but, as Brougham remarks, 'there was certainly no reason why he should pay a sum of forty or fifty pounds yearly out of his income on this account'. Neither Boerhaave's nor Black's students seem to have conformed to a very high standard of morality.

ENTER MRS. MARCET

Very few chemists could mention off-hand the most popular book on chemistry in the first half of the nineteenth century, and still fewer could say who wrote it. The book was called *Conversations on Chemistry; in which the Elements of that Science are familiarly explained and illustrated by Experiments.* It was first published in 1805, in London, two years after Black's *Lectures* and three years before Dalton's *New System*. The author was not Dalton, nor Davy, nor Gay-Lussac, nor Berzelius: the book was written by a woman, Mrs. Jane Marcet.

Through the phenomenal success of this work, which appeared in two modest little volumes, 'price 14s. in Boards', Mrs. Marcet became the first great populariser of chemistry. No fewer than sixteen English editions were published between 1805 and 1846; more remarkable still, about the same number of American editions appeared in the same period, and it is stated that by 1853 more than 160,000 copies had been sold in the United States. The book was also translated into French. The earlier editions were published anonymously, but in the English edition of 1837 (Fig. 46) Jane Marcet's name appeared on the title-page.

In 1769 Jane Haldimand was born in London of Swiss parentage. Reared in the age of phlogiston, she was twenty when Lavoisier published his *Traité*, thirty-nine when Dalton's *New System* appeared, and eighty-nine when she died, in the year that witnessed the birth of the theory of

molecular structure (1858). In 1799 she married Alexander
Marcet, an eminent physician and chemist, of Swiss national-
ity, who lived in London and was elected into the Royal

CONVERSATIONS

ON

C H E M I S T R Y;

IN WHICH

THE ELEMENTS OF THAT SCIENCE

ARE

FAMILIARLY EXPLAINED

AND

ILLUSTRATED BY EXPERIMENTS.

IN TWO VOLUMES.

BY JANE MARCET.

The Thirteenth Edition, enlarged and corrected.

VOL. I.

ON SIMPLE BODIES.

LONDON:

PRINTED FOR

LONGMAN, ORME, BROWN, GREEN, & LONGMANS,
PATERNOSTER-ROW.

1837.

46. Title-page of *Conversations on Chemistry*,
by Jane Marcet (1837)

Society in 1808. She was an intelligent woman, with
personality, distinction, and charm. Her social background
enabled her to make the acquaintance of many of the
leading figures in the world of science and literature, among
them Wollaston, de la Rive, Davy, Faraday, Lord Brougham,

Sydney Smith, Hallam, Harriet Martineau, and Maria Edgeworth. Naturally, she attended Davy's lectures at the Royal Institution; here, to quote her own words, 'the numerous and elegant illustrations, for which that school is so much distinguished, seldom failed to produce on her mind the effect for which they were intended'.

Her exposition of chemistry is cast in the form of a dialogue, interspersed with questions, between a teacher, Mrs. B., and two pupils, Caroline and Emily. Probably her adoption of this model was influenced by an acquaintance with Richmal Mangnall's *Historical and Miscellaneous Questions, for the Use of Young People*, first published in 1800. This masterpiece of the celebrated schoolmistress of Crofton Hall became an important factor in the education of English girls in the first half of the nineteenth century: no ladies' seminary of the period could possibly have done without it. Somewhat surprisingly, it contained the elements of astronomy, and was dedicated to the Astronomer Royal, Neville Maskelyne. These early works were succeeded later in the century by a flood of 'simple catechisms', on every conceivable subject, by the redoubtable Mrs. Gibbon and others. Mrs. Marcet herself produced other 'conversations'[1] on natural philosophy, vegetable physiology, and political economy, the last of which won the warm praise of Lord Macaulay.

Mrs. Marcet (Fig. 47) was keenly interested in young folk, and she had a talent for clear exposition and dramatic presentation, even when dealing with a subject so recondite as chemistry. Her characterisation in *Conversations on Chemistry* is both consistent and convincing.

Mrs. B.—her full name seems to have been Mrs. Bryan—is the earnest teacher, whose primary aim is to impart solid and lasting instruction. Her conversation is prim and somewhat stilted; at times she becomes rhetorical; and she drives her tandem on a fairly tight rein. Her science includes prunes as well as prisms.

---

[1] Her attractive little volume, *Conversations on Botany* (between 'Mother' and 'Edward'), embellished with 20 coloured plates, was published anonymously at London in 1817.

Emily is the equally serious pupil. She can always be relied upon to follow where Mrs. B. leads, and to ask the right question and supply the right answer. In later life she will display no evidences of a misspent youth behind her façade of spectacles and blue stockings.

Caroline, on the other hand, although her father has a lead-mine in Yorkshire, shows a somewhat perfunctory interest in chemistry, except at exciting moments. She is fond of spectacular experiments, and hails explosions with unladylike ejaculations. Girl-like, she values 'the giddy pleasure of the eyes'. She is always ready to take a risk in the interests of science—and has to be restrained by Mrs. B. from inhaling laughing-gas and liberating the 'extremely fetid' phosphoretted hydrogen gas in the house. Sad to say, she is also inclined to be careless. She burns a hole in her gown and damages her finger with sulphuric acid. In trying to blow a bulb at the end of a glass tube, which she has closed in the alcohol blowpipe, she causes Emily to exclaim reproachfully: 'You blew too hard; for the ball suddenly dilated to a great size, and then burst in pieces'. Caroline is the kind of girl that would cheerfully faint in the H_2S-room, or use her gown as a chymical artist's palette, or jerk her neighbour's most prized preparation on to the floor and step on it to make sure. At the same time, she is very critical, and never loses a chance of scoring off Mrs. B. Fortunately, in the interests of humanism, there are still many Carolines in chemistry classes.

Mrs. Marcet shows great skill in sustaining the illusion that the experiments she describes in detail, with the aid of her own admirable drawings, are actually in progress. The demonstration of the collection and properties of oxygen is vividly portrayed; then, coming to hydrogen, one seems to see the iridescent bubbles rising through the air and bursting against the ceiling. In this way Mrs. Marcet emphasised, in those early days, the great importance of experimental demonstrations in the teaching of science.

She took great pains to maintain an accurate and up-to-date text, with the result that her *Conversations* give a picture of contemporary chemistry at once reliable and interesting. Thus, in the third English edition (1809) she refers to fundamental changes made necessary 'by the brilliant discoveries in electro-chemical science'; in the fifth edition (1817) she introduces 'various important applications, such as the gas-lights, and the miner's-lamp'; and in the tenth edition (1825) she includes a new Conversation on the steam-engine. Even at the age of seventy-six she wrote to Faraday for details of his latest discovery, for mention in the new edition of her book.

In the original preface Mrs. Marcet conceives 'that some explanation may be required' from a woman having the temerity 'to offer to the public, and more particularly to the female sex, an Introduction to Chemistry'; but she points out that 'the general opinion no longer excludes women from an acquaintance with the elements of science'. She has a strong claim to rank as a pioneer in the movement for the emancipation of women, although she made no such claim.

In considering *Conversations on Chemistry*, the tenth English edition, published in 1825, is an appropriate version to select. The two neat duodecimo volumes contain twenty-five Conversations, covering nearly seven hundred pages; they deal with simple and compound bodies respectively. The first volume has three Conversations on light and heat and one on the steam-engine, and the last part of the second volume has a good deal to say about plant and animal physiology; so that, according to modern views, the work is not solely chemical. At the outset, the elementary substances recognised at the time are arranged in three classes. The details of the classification embody some interesting peculiarities; but the fundamental scheme, when contrasted with Black's, shows that nothing less than a chemical earthquake has taken place in the interim.

Class I includes the 'imponderable agents': heat or caloric, light, and electricity. Caloric, a kind of ghostly phlogiston, together with light, headed the list of elements in Lavoisier's *Traité*; electricity was added to these 'imponderable elements' by Berzelius. Class II includes agents capable of uniting with inflammable bodies: oxygen, chlorine, iodine, and fluorine. Class III has five divisions, including (1) hydrogen, forming water; (2) bodies forming acids: nitrogen, sulphur, phosphorus, carbon, boracium, fluorium; (3) metallic bodies forming alkalies: potassium, sodium, ammonium, lithium; (4) metallic bodies forming earths: calcium, magnium, barium, strontium, silicium, alumium, yttrium, glucium, zirconium, thorinum; (5) readily reducible metals, subdivided into (i) malleable: gold, platina, palladium, silver, mercury, tin, copper, iron, lead, nickel, zinc, and cadmium, and (ii) brittle: arsenic, bismuth, selenium, tellurium, cobalt, tungsten, molybdenum, titanium, chrome, antimony, manganese, uranium, columbium or tantalium, iridium, osmium, rhodium, and cerium.

ENTER MRS. B., CAROLINE, AND EMILY

Mrs. B. As you have now acquired some elementary notions of Natural Philosophy, I am going to propose to you another branch of science . . . this is Chemistry. . . .

Caroline. To confess the truth, Mrs. B., I am not disposed to form a very favourable idea of chemistry, nor do I expect to derive much entertainment from it. . . . I grant, however, there may be entertaining experiments in chemistry, and should not dislike to try some of them: the distilling, for instance, of lavender or rose water.

In this way Mrs. B. opens the bowling, and Caroline plays forward to the first ball, with a characteristic stroke. Mrs. B. then tells her that she takes a very narrow view of chemistry, and in order to open her eyes adds that the universe itself is Nature's laboratory, 'and there she is incessantly employed in chemical operations'. In her succeeding remarks Mrs. B. mentions that in the last thirty years chemistry has experienced an entire revolution, and that 'instead of four, chemists now reckon no less than fifty-six elementary substances'. The conversation following the announcement of the detailed list is again characteristic:

Caroline. Well, it must be confessed that this is rather a formidable list: you will have much to do to explain it, Mrs. B.

Mrs. B. A chemical division being necessarily founded on properties with which you are almost wholly unacquainted, it is impossible that you should at once be able to understand its meaning or appreciate its utility.

Emily. It does not appear to me so difficult; allow me to look at it. Here are first the three imponderable agents; then the all potent oxygen, with its insignificant associates; next follow the bodies which oxygen metamorphoses, converting one of them into water, seven into acids, four into alkalies, and ten into earths. Finally, there are six malleable, and nine brittle metals, upon which oxygen operates a double transformation, converting them either into oxides or acids, according as it more or less predominates.

Although Emily's arithmetic is scarcely 'according to Cocker', her meaning is clear: the scheme pivots on oxygen. The treatment throughout is mainly descriptive and qualitative, and theory is reduced to a minimum. At this stage the chief theoretical idea advanced is that of *Chemical Attraction*, which 'consists in the peculiar tendency which bodies of a different nature have to unite with each other. It is by this force that all compositions and decompositions are effected.' Mrs. B. illustrates this statement by dissolving copper in nitric acid and exhibiting a specimen of copper nitrate crystals.

Caroline. How very beautiful they are, in colour, form, and transparency! Nothing can be more striking than this example of chemical attraction.

Mrs. B. goes on to explain that 'oxygen is always found united with the negative electricity, and the variety of bodies with which it so readily combines are all united with the positive electricity, so that if Sir H. Davy's hypothesis be correct, their mutual attraction is thus explained'.

Caroline. Most clearly; oh! I am sure, Mrs. B., it must be so.

In the course of her expositions, Mrs. Marcet touches upon the discoveries and views of Black, Priestley, Cavendish, Scheele, Lavoisier, Berthollet, Volta, Franklin, Berzelius, Wollaston, and other recent and contemporary masters; but it is evident that her particular hero is Sir Humphry Davy, whose lectures at the Royal Institution made so deep and lasting an impression upon her.

The description of the preparation of oxygen (Fig. 48) and the demonstration of its properties provides a good

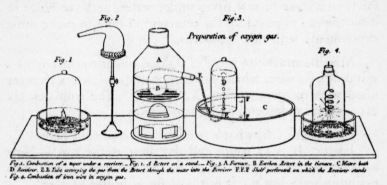

48. Preparation of Oxygen Gas.   After a drawing by J. Marcet

example of her skill in imparting an air of reality to accounts of practical operations:

Mrs. B. I have put some oxide of manganese into a retort, which is an earthen vessel with a bent neck, such as you see here. (Plate X, Fig. 2.)—The retort containing the manganese you cannot see, as I have enclosed it in this furnace, where it is now red-hot. But, in order to make you sensible of the escape of the gas, which is itself invisible, I have connected the neck of the retort with this bent tube, the extremity of which is immersed in this vessel of water. (Plate X, Fig. 3.)—Do you see the bubbles of air rise through the water?

Caroline. This, then, is pure oxygen gas; what a pity it should be lost!   Could you not preserve it?

Mrs. B. We shall collect it in this receiver . . . the bubbles which issue from the retort . . . rise through the water to the upper part of the receiver.

Emily. The bubbles of oxygen gas rise, I suppose, from their specific levity?

Mrs. B. Yes; for though oxygen forms rather a heavy gas, it is light compared to water . . . the receiver . . . is now full of gas, and I may leave it inverted in water on this shelf . . . for future experiments. . . .

Caroline. It is a very clever contrivance, indeed; equally simple and useful. How convenient the shelf is for the receiver to rest upon under water, and the holes in it for the gas to pass into the receiver! I long to make some experiments with this apparatus.

Mrs. B. attaches a piece of lighted tinder to the end of a spiral of iron wire, which she then introduces into a receiver filled with oxygen. (Plate X, Fig. 4.) The iron quickly becomes incandescent, and burns vividly.

Caroline. Oh, what a brilliant and beautiful flame!

Emily. It is as white and dazzling as the sun!—Now a piece of melted iron drops to the bottom: I fear it is extinguished; but no, it burns again as bright as ever.

Mrs. B. It will burn till the wire is entirely consumed, provided the oxygen be not first expended. . . .

Caroline. I never saw a more beautiful light. My eyes can hardly bear it! How astonishing to think that all this caloric was contained in the small quantity of gas and iron inclosed in the receiver; and without producing any visible heat! . . .

Mrs. B. You are not quite correct . . . in saying the caloric dazzled you; for caloric is invisible; it affects only the sense of feeling; it was the light which dazzled you.

Caroline. True; but light and caloric are such constant companions, that it is difficult to separate them, even in idea.

Mrs. B. The easier it is to confound them, the more careful you should be to preserve the distinction.

Caroline. But why has the water now risen, and filled part of the receiver?

Mrs. B. Indeed, Caroline, I did not suppose you would have asked me such a question! I dare say, Emily, you can answer it.

Emily. Let me reflect.—The oxygen has combined

with the wire; the caloric has escaped; consequently nothing can remain in the receiver, and the water will rise to fill the vacuum.

CAROLINE. I wonder that did not occur to me.

In the experiments with hydrogen, Mrs. B. blows some soap-bubbles with the gas and releases them into the air. .

CAROLINE. Now a bubble ascends; it moves with the rapidity of a balloon. How beautifully it refracts the light!

EMILY. It has burst against the ceiling—you succeed now wonderfully.

Encouraged by this outburst of enthusiasm from her pupils, Mrs. B. is spurred on to further efforts. She blows more bubbles, this time with 'a mixture of hydrogen and oxygen gases, in the proportions which form water'. Caroline immediately becomes alert.

CAROLINE. Here is a fine large bubble rising—shall I set fire to it with a candle?

MRS. B. If you please——

CAROLINE. What an explosion!—It was like the report of a gun: I confess it frightened me much.

It throws light on the proprieties of the day that in earlier editions Caroline opened her rapturous exclamation with the word 'Heavens'; but this was now expunged as an unbecoming word for a young lady to use in 1825. Later in the Conversations, however, Caroline managed to get the offending ejaculation past the censor, doubtless much to the shocked delight of ladies' seminaries all over the country.

On passing to a study of compound bodies, Mrs. B. outlines 'the principal laws by which chemical combinations are governed'. These are not, as might be expected, the now familiar laws of Dalton. Chemical attraction, says Mrs. B., produced by the attraction of the opposite electricities, takes place only between bodies of a different nature, for example, an acid and an alkali, or oxygen and a metal; it can take place between two, three, four, or even more bodies (elements); combination is attended by a change of temperature, arising 'from the extrication of the

two electricities in the form of caloric'; the properties
which characterise bodies, when separate, are altered or
destroyed by their combination; the force of chemical
affinity between the constituents of a body is estimated by
that which is required for their separation.

Mrs. B. also explains the 'law of definite proportions',
referring accurately to the composition of water by volume
and by weight, in illustration. She then makes her sole
reference to the atom, but does not mention Dalton, the
atomic theory, atomic weights, or atomic symbols. This
most striking omission is probably a reflection of Davy's
reluctance to accept Dalton's views: 'Mr. Dalton is too
much of an Atomic Philosopher', wrote Davy. With this
introduction to the second volume, we may again listen in
to Mrs. B. and her two pupils:

EMILY. And pray what can be the cause of this singular
uniformity in the law of combination?

MRS. B. Philosophers have not yet been able to give us
any decisive information upon this point; but they have
attempted to explain it in the following manner: since
chemical combination takes place between the most minute
particles of bodies, may we not suppose that the smallest
particles or portions in which bodies combine, (and which
we may call *chemical atoms,*) are capable of uniting together
one to one, or sometimes one to two, or one to three, &c.,
but that they cannot combine in any intermediate proportion?

One of the few references to quantitative composition
falls under the heading of ammonia, known as the volatile
alkali, and also as hartshorn, because 'the horns of cattle,
especially those of deer, yield it in abundance'.

EMILY. I long to hear something of this alkali; is it not
of the same nature as hartshorn?

MRS. B. Yes . . . this alkali . . . is most commonly extracted from a compound salt, called *sal ammoniac* . . . which
consists of a combination of ammonia and muriatic acid.

CAROLINE. Then it should be called *muriat of ammonia.*
. . . I am surprised to see sal ammoniac inscribed on the
label.

Mrs. B. That is the name by which it has been so long known, that modern chemists have not yet succeeded in banishing it altogether. . . .

Caroline. You said that ammonia was more complicated in its composition than the other alkalies; pray of what principles does it consist?

Mrs. B. A few years since, Berthollet . . . having heated ammoniacal gas under a receiver, by causing the electrical spark to pass repeatedly through it, he found that it increased considerably in bulk, lost all its alkaline properties, and was actually converted into hydrogen and nitrogen gases . . . the proportions appear to be, one volume of nitrogen gas to three of hydrogen gas.

In the discussion of acids, Mrs. B.'s keen eye detects a stain on Emily's gown, when they reach 'sulphureous acid'. Probably the stain would have been attributed to Caroline, rather than to the impeccable Emily, but for Caroline's earlier adventures with sulphuric acid. Listen to Mrs. B. as she enlarges upon the bleaching properties of the junior acid:

Mrs. B. I can show you its effect in destroying colours, by taking out vegetable stains—I think I see a spot on your gown, Emily, on which we may try the experiment.

Emily. It is the stain of mulberries: but I shall be almost afraid of exposing my gown to the experiment, after seeing the effect which the sulphuric acid produced on that of Caroline——

Mrs. B. There is no such danger from the sulphureous . . . we must first wet the stain with water, and now hold it in this way, at a little distance, over a lighted match: the vapour that arises from it is sulphureous acid, and the stain, you see, gradually disappears.

Finally, we may listen in once more, this time to a part of Conversation XX, which tells of the development of views concerning Scheele's dephlogisticated muriatic acid, since we last encountered it in the guise of Mr. Kirwan's oxy-muriatic acid (p. 173):

Emily. And how do you obtain the oxy-muriatic acid?

MRS. B. It may be most conveniently obtained by distilling muriatic acid over oxide of manganese, which supplies the acid with the additional oxygen . . . I have collected some in this jar——

CAROLINE. It is not invisible, like the generality of gases; for it is of a yellowish colour. . . .

MRS. B. You had better keep your handkerchief to your nose when I open it.—Now let us drop in this little piece of phosphorus——

CAROLINE. It burns really; and almost as brilliantly as in oxygen gas! . . .

MRS. B. All these curious effects are owing to the very great facility with which this acid yields oxygen to such bodies as are strongly disposed to combine with it. . . . Let us collect some vegetable substances to put into this glass, which is full of gas.

EMILY. Here is a sprig of myrtle——

CAROLINE. And here some coloured paper——

MRS. B. We shall also put in this piece of scarlet riband and a rose.

EMILY. Their colours begin to fade immediately. But how does the gas produce this effect?

MRS. B. The oxygen combines with the colouring matter of these substances, and destroys it. . . .

CAROLINE. You have not told us yet what is Sir H. Davy's new opinion respecting the nature of muriatic acid, to which you alluded a few minutes ago?

MRS. B. True: I avoided noticing it then, because you could not have understood it without some previous knowledge of the oxy-muriatic acid, which I have just introduced to your acquaintance.

Sir H. Davy's idea is, that muriatic acid, instead of being a compound, consisting of an unknown basis and oxygen, is formed by the union of oxy-muriatic gas with hydrogen. . . . According to this view of the subject, the name of *oxy-muriatic acid* can no longer be proper, and therefore Sir H. Davy has adopted that of *chlorine*, or *chlorine gas*, a name which is simply expressive of its greenish colour; and in compliance with that philosopher's theory, we have placed chlorine in our table among the simple bodies.

CAROLINE. But what was Sir H. Davy's reason for adopting an opinion so contrary to that which had hitherto prevailed?

MRS. B. There are many circumstances which are favourable to the new doctrine; but the clearest and simplest fact in its support is, that if hydrogen gas and oxy-muriatic gas be mixed together, both these gases disappear, and muriatic acid gas is formed.

Jane Marcet's phraseology often illustrates the faith of her age in a wholly beneficent Providence. Even in the processes of fermentation and decay she discerns 'the beautiful economy of Nature, which, whether she creates, or whether she destroys, directs all her operations to some useful and benevolent purpose'; and she infuses something of the religious fervour of a Jean Beguin into her valedictory sentence: 'In contemplating the works of the creation, or studying the inventions of art, let us, therefore, never forget the Divine Source from which they all proceed; and thus every acquisition of knowledge will prove a lesson of piety and virtue'.

FARADAY'S TRIBUTE

From this brief survey it is evident that Mrs. Marcet's modest work exercised a widespread influence on the early teaching of chemistry in Great Britain and the United States. That influence was not limited to the Carolines and Emilys and their brothers, sisters, and cousins. One of the greatest men of science of the nineteenth century owed his introduction to chemistry to Mrs. Marcet. Michael Faraday, during his period of apprenticeship to Mr. Riebau, the bookseller of Blandford Street, London, began to explore the ocean of knowledge that lay around him. Faraday has left it on record that he loved to read the scientific books which came under his hand, and that he delighted particularly in the electrical treatises of the *Encyclopædia Britannica* and in Mrs. Marcet's *Conversations on Chemistry*. He supplemented his reading of the doings of Mrs. B., Caroline, and Emily by making 'such simple experiments in chemistry as could be defrayed in their expense by a few pence per week'.

Soon after Mrs. Marcet's death, in 1858, Faraday wrote to Auguste de la Rive a letter which will remain as a warm and eloquent tribute to the memory of this benefactress of chemistry:

'Mrs. Marcet was a good friend to me, as she must have been to many of the human race. I entered the shop of a bookseller and bookbinder at the age of 13, in the year 1804, remained there eight years, and during the chief part of the time bound books. Now it was in those books, in the hours after work, that I found the beginning of my philosophy. . . . Mrs. Marcet's *Conversations on Chemistry* . . . gave me my foundation in that science. . . .

'I was a very lively, imaginative person . . . but facts were important to me, and saved me. I could trust a fact, and always cross-examined an assertion. So when I questioned Mrs. Marcet's book by such little experiments as I could find means to perform, and found it true to the facts as I could understand them, I felt that I had got hold of an anchor in chemical knowledge, and clung fast to it. Thence my deep veneration for Mrs. Marcet: first, as one who had conferred great personal good and pleasure on me, and then as one able to convey the truth and principle of those boundless fields of knowledge which concern natural things, to the young, untaught, and inquiring mind.

'You may imagine my delight when I came to know Mrs. Marcet personally ; how often I cast my thoughts backwards, delighting to connect the past and the present; how often, when sending a paper to her as a thank-offering, I thought of my first instructress, and such like thoughts will remain with me.'

REFERENCES

Armstrong, E. V., 'Jane Marcet and her *Conversations on Chemistry*', *J. Chem. Education*, 1938, **15**, 53.

Black, J., *Lectures on the Elements of Chemistry*, delivered in the University of Edinburgh . . . now published from his Manuscripts by John

47. Mrs. Jane Marcet, 1769–1858.
(See p. 178.)

49. One of the Advantages of GAS over OIL.
Rich^d. Dighton Inv^t. et Sculp. 1824.   (See p. 203.)

Robison, LLD., Professor of Natural Philosophy in the University of Edinburgh, 2 vols., Edinburgh, 1803.

Brougham, Henry (Lord), *Lives of Men of Letters and Science, who flourished in the time of George III*, 2 vols., London, 1845–1846.

Idem. *The Life and Times of Henry Lord Brougham*, 3 vols., Edinburgh and London, 1871.

Jones, Bence, *The Life and Letters of Faraday*, 2 vols., London, 1870.

Kay, J., *A Series of Original Portraits and Caricature Etchings*, 2 vols., Edinburgh (2nd edn.), 1877.

Kendall, J., 'Some Eighteenth-century Chemical Societies', *Endeavour*, 1942, 1, 106.

Mackenzie, J. E., 'The Chair of Chemistry in the University of Edinburgh in the XVIIIth and XIXth Centuries', *J. Chem. Education*, 1935, 12, 503.

[Marcet, J.], *Conversations on Chemistry*, 2 vols., London (3rd edn.), 1809; (5th edn.), 1817; (10th edn.), 1825; (13th edn.), 1837.

Smith, E. F., *Old Chemistries*, New York, 1927.

Thorpe, Sir [T.] E., *Essays in Historical Chemistry*, London, 1923.

CHAPTER IX

CHEMISTRY BECOMES EXHILARATING

THE EARLY HISTORY OF GASES

THE study of gases, without which modern chemistry would have been impossible, may be said to have begun with van Helmont (1577–1644), who introduced the word 'gas' about 1630. He applied this new term, derived probably from the Greek word *chaos*, to certain invisible 'spirits', which could neither be kept in vessels nor reduced to a visible form. He discriminated between different kinds of gases, such as *gas carbonum*, from burning charcoal; *gas sylvester*, from fermentation and other sources; and an inflammable *gas pingue*, formed in the putrefaction and distillation of plant and animal matter.

Boyle, in 1660, showed that van Helmont was wrong in supposing that a gas could not be confined in a vessel, as he succeeded in collecting a 'factitious air' (hydrogen) in a bottle containing iron nails and filled with and inverted over dilute oil of vitriol. Boyle was probably the first to collect a gas, and in his simple apparatus the inverted bottle served both as generator and receiver. He showed that the gas was inflammable, by igniting it at the flame of a candle.

The next marked advance in the preparation and collection of gases is usually ascribed to the Rev. Stephen Hales, Minister of Teddington, in Middlesex. In his *Vegetable Staticks* (1727) he described the destructive distillation of various materials in an iron retort, made of a musket barrel, which was heated at a smith's forge. The liberated 'air' was passed into a water-filled receiver, inverted in a vessel of water, and thus, in Hales' own words, 'a good part of the acid spirit and sulphureous fumes were by this means interrupted and retained in the water'. Among twenty-three bodies distilled in this particular way were horn, oystershell, oak, wheat, tobacco, sugar, coal, salt-petre, *sal tartar*, and minium. In this and other forms of apparatus Hales prepared and collected impure specimens of carbon dioxide, coal gas, oxygen, hydrogen, and nitric oxide. He regarded them all as 'true air, and not a mere flatulent vapour', because he could find no difference in specific gravity or elasticity between 'air of tartar' and common air; nevertheless, he recorded that a live sparrow died instantly when put into the 'air' from oak shavings. Hales' experiments were thus purely quantitative, and he considered them to 'shew in how great a proportion Air is wrought into the composition of animal, vegetable, and mineral Substances, and withal how readily it resumes its former elastick state'. One of the most lavish sources of such an 'air' was coal: according to Hales, 'half a cubick inch, or 158 grains of *Newcastle coal*, yielded 180 cubick inches of air, which rose very fast from the coal'.

In the second half of the eighteenth century, the knowledge of different kinds of 'airs'—as gases were still generally called—progressed apace. Black rediscovered carbon dioxide, under the name of 'fixed air', in 1754; Cavendish characterised 'fixed air' and 'inflammable air' (hydrogen) in 1766; Priestley discovered many new gases, and introduced improved methods of manipulating them, from 1770 onwards; and at about the same time Scheele used collapsed bladders for the collection of his 'fire air' (oxygen).

Such, in its main lines, is the summary of the early history of gases to be found in many accounts of the subject. Too often an exceptional investigation of the first importance, falling between the observations of Boyle and Hales, is inaccurately reported, or even omitted altogether. It is in this period, at a date which has been the subject of many conjectures, that an isolated experiment of the Rev. John Clayton flashes like a meteor across the chemical skies. The story of Clayton's discovery of coal gas, apart from its intrinsic appeal to chemists, is one of general interest and unusual fascination. Accordingly, it is well worth while in this place to attempt to give a more complete and accurate outline of the story than has hitherto proved possible.

THE BURNING FOUNTAIN OF WIGAN

From remote times, in various parts of the world, 'burning fountains' have been the objects of intense interest, often merging into veneration and worship. Such freaks of nature have been caused by the accidental ignition of inflammable gases escaping through fissures in the earth. It was an inflammable exhalation of this kind, in Lancashire, which led indirectly to the discovery of coal gas in the second half of the seventeenth century.

A short communication published in the *Philosophical Transactions* of the Royal Society for 1667 gives an account of this natural phenomenon in the following words:

'*The Description of a Well, and Earth in* Lanchashire, *taking Fire by a Candle approached to it.*

'*This was imparted by that Ingenious and Worthy Gentleman,* Thomas Shirley *Esq; an Eye-witness of the thing, now to be related in his own words;* viz.

'About the later end of *February* 1659, returning from a Journey to my house in *Wigan,* I was entertained with the relation of an odd Spring, situated in one Mr. *Hawkley's* Ground (if I mistake not) about a mile from the Town, in that Road which leads to *Warrington* and *Chester.*

'The people of this Town did confidently affirm, that the Water of this Spring did burn like Oyle; into which Error they suffered themselves to fall for want of a due examination of the following particulars.

'For when we came to the said Spring (being five or six in company together) and applyed a lighted Candle to the surface of the Water; 'tis true, there was suddenly a large flame produced, which burnt vigorously; at the sight of which they all began to laugh at me for denying, what they had positively asserted: But I, who did not think my self confuted by a laughter grounded upon inadvertency, began to examine what I saw; and observing, that this Spring had its eruption at the foot of a Tree, growing on the top of a neighbouring Bank, the Water of which Spring fill'd a Ditch that was there, and covered the burning place lately mention'd; I then applyed the lighted Candle to divers parts of the Water, contained in the said Ditch, and found as I expected, that upon the touch of the Candle and the Water, the Flame was extinct.

'Again, having taken up a dishful of Water at the flaming place, and held the lighted Candle to it, it went out. Yet I observed that the Water at the burning place did boyle, and heave like Water in a Pot upon the Fire, though my hand put into it perceived it not so much as warm.

'This boyling I conceived to proceed from the Eruption of some bituminous or sulphureous Fumes; considering, this place was not above 30 or 40 yards distant from the mouth of a Coal-pit there. And indeed *Wigan*, *Ashton*, and the whole Country, for many miles compass, is underlaid with Coal. Then applying my hand to the surface of the Burning place of the Water, I found a strong breath, as it were a Wind, to bear against my hand.

'Then I caused a *Dam* to be made, and thereby hindering the recourse of fresh water to the Burning place; I caused that, which was already there, to be drained away; and then applying the burning Candle to the surface of the dry Earth at the same point, where the Water burned before; the Fumes took fire, and burn'd very bright and vigorous. The Cone of the Flame ascended a foot and a half from the Superficies of the Earth. The Basis of it was of the Compass of a Mans hat about the brims. I then caused a Bucket-full of Water to be poured on the fire, by which it was presently quenched, as well as my companions laughter was stopped, who then began to think, the Water did not burn.

'I did not perceive the Flame to be discolour'd, like that of sulphureous Bodies, nor to have any manifest *scent* with it. The Fumes, when they broke out of the Earth, and prest against my hand, were not, to my best remembrance, at all hot.'

This early and very interesting communication to the *Philosophical Transactions* suggests that the burning fountain of Wigan was due to an escape of firedamp from an adjacent deposit of coal, the phenomenon being rendered all the more spectacular by the presence of water around the blow-hole. Of all the contemporary Fellows of the Royal Society who must have read Shirley's account, Robert Boyle was probably the one to whom it made the greatest appeal. At this time Boyle was particularly interested in the character of various exhalations making their way into the atmosphere. In 1674 he published an account of his observations of this kind in *An Experimental Discourse of some unheeded Causes of the Insalubrity and Salubrity of the Air*, in the course of which he referred to 'a place upon the borders of Lanca-shire, where the water and mud of a ditch is so copiously impregnated with subterraneal exhalations (whether they be bituminous, sulphureous, or of some unknown kind), that they may easily be fired at the surface of the water, or earth, and made to burn like a candle, as an ingenious man did, at my request, successfully try'.

THE DISCOVERY OF COAL GAS

It is at this point that the Rev. John Clayton, later Dean of Kildare, comes into the story. Until the appearance of an admirable biographical research by Layton (p. 232) in 1926, the published references to Clayton had been very scanty and inaccurate. In particular, Dean Clayton had been con-fused with two other John Claytons: one of these was elected into the Royal Society in 1663, when the future Dean Clayton was but six years old; the other, a Virginian botanist, was born in 1693, some years after Dean Clayton's historic experiment.

Layton's researches show that the Rev. Dr. John Clayton was a scion of an historic and distinguished Lanca-shire family, the Claytons of Fulwood. He was born in 1657, took his B.A. degree from Merton College, Oxford, in 1677, and graduated M.A. in 1682. He visited Virginia before 1686, and was inducted as Rector of Crofton, near Wakefield, in 1687. Leaving Crofton in 1698, he was Rector of St. Michan's Church, Dublin, from 1698 to 1725, and Dean of Kildare from 1708 until his death at Dublin on 23 September 1725. To these details may be added his election as F.R.S. on 30 November 1688.[1]

Coming now to the important matter of Clayton's scientific publications, the *Philosophical Transactions* for 1693 contain in the first place (p. 781) 'A Letter from Mr. John Clayton, Rector of Crofton, at Wakefield, in Yorkshire, to the Royal Society, May 12, 1688, giving an Account of several Observables in Virginia, and in his Voyage thither, most particularly concerning the Air.' The account is continued in further letters (pp. 790, 941) dealing with the soil and other 'observables' of Virginia, and the last of these (p. 978) mentions the writer's 'return home for England, May 1686'. Still another paper on Virginia appears in the *Philosophical Transactions* for 1694 (p. 121).

The first letter is particularly important, because Clayton refers in it to 'some sulphureous Spirits which I have drawn from Coals, that I could no way condense, yet were inflammable, nay *would burn* after they had passed through Water, and that seemingly fiercer, if they were not overpowered therewith. I have kept of this Spirit a considerable time in bladders, and tho' it appeared as if they were only blown with the Air, yet if I let it forth and *fired it* with a Match or Candle, it would continue burning till all was spent.'

This is the sole published reference to Clayton's distillation of coal which appeared in his lifetime, and it was not until 1744 that a detailed account of the investigation appeared in the *Philosophical Transactions* for 1739 (p. 59), in the form of an undated letter which Clayton had written to Robert Boyle, who died in 1691. A copy of the letter was forwarded in 1740 to the Royal Society by Clayton's eldest son, Dr. Robert Clayton, at that time Bishop of Cork, who had found the original among his father's papers in his own handwriting. The publication is described as '*An Experiment concerning the* Spirit of Coals, *being part of a Letter to the Hon.* Rob. Boyle, *Esq; from the late Rev.* John Clayton, *D.D.*' It begins as follows:

[1] *The Record of The Royal Society of London*, 4th edn., London, 1940. The dubiety about Clayton's election is due to the fact that, like five other Fellows out of the seven elected on that date, he did not sign the Charter-Book.

'Having seen a Ditch within two Miles from *Wigan* in *Lancashire*, wherein the Water would seemingly burn like Brandy, the Flame of which was so fierce, that several Strangers have boiled Eggs over it; the People thereabouts indeed affirm, that about 30 Years ago it would have boiled a Piece of Beef; and that whereas much Rain formerly made it burn much fiercer, now after Rain it would scarce burn at all. It was after a long-continued Season of Rain that I came to see the Place and make some Experiments, and found accordingly, that a lighted Paper, though it were waved all over the Ditch, the Water would not take Fire. I then hired a Person to make a Dam in the Ditch, and fling out the Water, in order to try whether the Steam which arose from the Ditch would then take Fire, but found it would not. I still, however, pursued my Experiment, and made him dig deeper; and when he had dug about the Depth of half a Yard, we found a shelly Coal, and the Candle being then put down into the Hole, the Air catched Fire, and continued burning.'

There is little doubt that Clayton visited the site that Shirley had examined in 1659, and that in the meantime the force of gas had greatly abated. The reference to the burning of brandy suggests the pale and almost invisible flame of methane, or firedamp. Clayton took the matter much further than Shirley had done, by preparing artificially an inflammable spirit from a sample of coal obtained near the site. His description of the destructive distillation and its result is given in graphic language:

'I observed that there had formerly been Coal-pits in the same Close of Ground; and I then got some Coal from one of the Pits nearest thereunto, which I distilled in a Retort in an open Fire. At first there came over only *Phlegm*, afterwards a black *Oil*, and then likewise a *Spirit* arose, which I could noways condense, but it forced my Lute, or broke my Glasses. Once, when it had forced the Lute, coming close thereto, in order to try to repair it, I observed that the Spirit which issued out caught Fire at the Flame of the Candle, and continued burning with Violence as it issued out, in a Stream, which I blew out, and lighted again, alternately, for several times. I then had a Mind to try if I could save any of this Spirit, in order to which I took a turbinated Receiver, and putting a Candle to the Pipe of the Receiver whilst the Spirit arose, I observed that it catched Flame, and continued burning at the End of the Pipe, though you could not discern what fed the Flame: I then blew it out, and lighted it again several times; after which I fixed a Bladder, squeezed and void of Air, to the Pipe of the Receiver. The *Oil* and *Phlegm* descended into the Receiver, but the Spirit, still ascending, blew up the Bladder. I then filled a good many Bladders therewith, and might have filled an inconceiveable Number more; for the Spirit continued to rise for several Hours, and filled the Bladders almost as fast as a Man could have blown them with his Mouth; and yet the Quantity of Coals I distilled were inconsiderable.

'I kept this Spirit in the Bladders a considerable time, and endeavour'd several ways to condense it, but in vain. And when I had a Mind to divert Strangers or Friends, I have frequently taken one of these Bladders, and pricking a Hole therein with a Pin, and compressing gently the Bladder near the Flame of a Candle till it once took Fire, it would then continue flaming till all the Spirit was compressed out of the Bladder; which was the more surprising, because no one could discern any Difference in the Appearance between these Bladders and those which are filled with common Air.

'But then I found, that this Spirit must be kept in good thick Bladders, as in those of an Ox, or the like; for if I filled Calves Bladders therewith, it would lose its Inflammability in 24 Hours, though the Bladder became not relax at all.'

This astonishing experiment, carried out by an amateur of chemistry, offers a striking contrast to the earlier distillation of coal by the skilled and experienced Glauber (p. 98), who missed the inflammable spirit completely. Clayton at a stroke had discovered coal gas, had invented a new technique for collecting and storing a gas in a separate receiver, had shown how to use it as an illuminant, and had

P

demonstrated that it could even be passed through water—
that ancient enemy of fire—without losing its inflammability.
His only other investigations in physical science appear to
have been experiments on nitrous particles in the air, and
on the elastic force of steam, which, with another paper on
the natives of Virginia, were published in the *Philosophical
Transactions* for 1739.[1] Logical in reasoning, skilful in
experimentation, John Clayton was also a keen observer of
nature. In the early history of gases he deserves a place of
honour beside his fellow divine, Stephen Hales.

WHEN WAS COAL GAS DISCOVERED?

Various writers have assigned different dates to Clayton's
discovery of coal gas: these range from 1664, when Clayton
was seven years old, to 1739, fourteen years after his death.[2]

From the reference in Clayton's first paper on Virginia,
the investigation must have been carried out before 12 May
1688. Layton, inclining to the opinion that it took place
between 1680 and 1685, before Clayton's visit to Virginia,
suggested 1684 as a 'likely date'. This suggestion, however,
is rendered untenable by a further piece of evidence which
appears to have been generally overlooked. In the fifth
volume of Birch's edition of Boyle's works (London, 1744,
p. 646) there is a particularly interesting and illuminating
letter meriting quotation in full. It runs as follows:

Mr. John Clayton *to Mr*. Robert Boyle.

Virginia, James-City, June 23, 1684.

Honoured and worthy Sir,

IN *England*, having perused, among the rest of your admirable
treatises, that ingenious discourse of the Noctiluca, wherein, as I
remember, you gave an account of several nocturnal irradiations;
having therefore met with the relation of a strange incident in that

---

[1] These papers also were forwarded to the Royal Society by Dr. Robert Clayton,
Bishop of Cork. The final communication on Virginia was a letter in answer to
queries sent to John Clayton in 1687 by Dr. Grew. In the *Dictionary of National
Biography* all the papers by Dean Clayton in the *Phil. Trans.* are attributed to John
Clayton the botanist (1693–1773), although most, or all, of them were written
before his birth.

[2] Thus, Muspratt (1860) and the *Encyclopædia Britannica* (1929) quote 1664,
and Gray (in *The Operative Chemist*, London, 1828), and others, give 1739 as the
date of Clayton's original distillation.

nature, from very good hands, I presumed this might not prove unwelcome; for the fuller confirmation of which, I have enclosed the very paper colonel *Diggs* gave me thereof, under his own hand and name to attest the truth, the same being likewise asserted to me by madam *Diggs* his lady, sister to the said *Susanna Sewall*, daughter to the lord *Baltimore*, lately gone for *England*, who I suppose may give you fuller satisfaction of such particulars, as you may be desirous to be informed of. I cannot but admire the strangeness of such a complicated spirit of a volatile salt and exalted oil, as I deem it to be, from its crepitation and shining flame: how it should transpire through the pores, and not be inflamed by the joint motion and heat of the body, and afterwards so suddenly to be actuated into sparks by the shaking or brushing of her coats, raises much my wonder.

ANOTHER thing I am confident your honour would be much pleased at the sight of, a fly we have here, called, the fire-fly, about the bigness of the cantharides; its body of a dark colour, the tail of it a deep yellow by day, which by night shines brighter than the glow-worm; which bright shining ebbs and flows, as if the fly breathed with a shining spirit. I pulled the tail of the fly into several pieces, and every part thereof would shine for several hours after, and cast a light round it. Be pleased favourably to interpret this fond impertinency of a stranger. All your works have to the world evidenced your goodness, which has encouraged the presumption, and it is that, which bids me hope its pardon. If there be any thing in this country I may please you in, be pleased to command; it will be my ambition to serve you, nor shall I scruple to ride two or three hundred miles to satisfy any query you shall propound. If you honour me with your commands, you may direct your letter to Mr. *John Clayton*, parson of *James* city, *Virginia*.

Your humble servant, and,
though unknown, your friend,
JOHN CLAYTON.

This letter throws a good deal of fresh light on Clayton's career. It shows that soon after his ordination, probably in 1683, he went out to Virginia, to enter upon his first clerical appointment. He could not have discovered coal gas in 1684, as he was then in Virginia. If he had discovered it before sailing for Virginia, it seems very unlikely that he would have omitted to play such a high trump card in his first letter to the great Robert Boyle, whom he was so anxious to impress favourably and to serve. He was familiar with Boyle's publications, and it is hard to imagine that he would have been content to contribute his ninepence to the Noctiluca if he had been able at that time to offer his noble to the subterraneal exhalation upon the borders of Lancashire, in which Boyle had shown so great an interest in an earlier publication.

The letter also brings out Clayton's lively interest in natural phenomena, especially in relation to light, flame, and phosphorescence. At that time phosphorescence, in particular, was attracting much attention (p. 118), and Boyle had published tracts on the 'Aerial Noctiluca' in 1680 and the 'Icy Noctiluca' in 1682. Clayton's examination of Virginian fireflies falls into line with this current interest; but his letter does not make it clear whether the admirable Susanna Sewall was charged with nocturnal irradiations or her coats with static electricity.

Clayton returned to England in May 1686, was inducted to the Rectory of Crofton in July 1687, and mentioned his distillation of coal in a letter to the Royal Society dated 12 May 1688. The most likely conclusion is that in this period, stimulated by further correspondence with Boyle, Clayton went to Wigan, and made his investigation. There are several subsidiary circumstances supporting this conclusion. Clayton had a connection with Wigan through an uncle, who owned the adjacent manor of Adlington at that time. In his account he refers to a time 'about 30 Years ago', when the flame 'would have boiled a Piece of Beef': this agrees with Shirley's observation, made in 1659. Finally, it is evident that after Clayton's initial letter of 1684 a correspondence developed between him and Boyle; for in the *Philosophical Transactions* for 1739 (p. 63), Clayton's son, then Bishop of Cork, refers to a letter in which Boyle had put seventeen queries to Clayton. These facts point to the conclusion that Clayton discovered coal gas between May 1686 and May 1688, the most likely year being 1687.

GAS AND GAITERS

With Boyle's death in 1691, and his own translation to Ireland in 1698, it is regrettable that Clayton's scientific work came to an early end. Some sixty years elapsed before his discovery of coal gas became generally known. Richard Watson, indeed, repeated some of Clayton's work so late as 1767. It was not until 1792 that William Murdoch began to use coal gas on a substantial scale as an illuminant, in place of candles and lamps. Murdoch was a friend of James Watt, junior, son of the celebrated James Watt, the pupil of Joseph Black; and as early as 1798 Murdoch introduced gas-lighting into part of the premises of Boulton and Watt at Soho, Birmingham. In 1804, Winsor demonstrated the new system of lighting at the Lyceum Theatre, in London; in 1807, Pall Mall was lighted with gas; and in 1810, the first gas company was incorporated in London. From that time gas-lighting spread apace, and coal gas became an essential factor in the social and economic developments of the Victorian era.

This revolutionary transition from rushlights, tallow candles, and oil-lamps to coal gas was not accomplished without much opposition, distrust, and ill-will, particularly from those with vested interests in tallow and whale-oil. The objections were based mainly upon the alleged dangers of fire and explosion, which were seized upon and distorted by the virile caricaturists of the day. 'Arrah, honey, if this man bring fire thro' water we shall soon have the Thames and the Liffey burnt down—and all the pretty little Herrings & Whales burnt to cinders', is the legend attached to one of the figures in Rowlandson's caricature (1809) entitled 'A Peep at the Gas Lights in Pall-Mall'.[1] Another striking caricature of the period, by Dighton, shows 'One of the Advantages of Gas over Oil' (Fig. 49). Some opponents deplored the approaching extinction of the whale fisheries and the consequent loss of British naval supremacy; others objected to the use of gas because it burnt without a wick, and was therefore held to be uncanny!

Nevertheless, gas-lighting had come to stay, and in the end the new illumination seems to have captivated all beholders. It is difficult for a generation accustomed to

---

[1] For a reproduction of a somewhat similar caricature, by Cruikshank (1815), see A. Findlay, *The Spirit of Chemistry*, London, 1930.

modern standards of illumination to enter into the ecstasies of writers who declared that 'where gas-light exists there is no night; where gas-light is there is continuous day', and who waxed eloquent over the entrancing beauty of ladies viewed in a primitive form of gas-light now considered very dim and murky. 'Near the termination of each tube', wrote Accum in 1820, 'there is a stopcock, or valve, upon turning which when light is required, the gas instantly flows out in an equable stream. There is no noise at the opening of the valve, no disturbance in the transparency of the atmosphere; the gas instantly bursts on the approach of a lighted taper into a peculiarly brilliant, soft and beautiful flame; it requires no trimming or snuffing to keep the flame of an equal brightness. Like the light of the Sun itself, it only makes itself known by the benefit and pleasure it affords.'

Sam Weller paid a tribute to a vogue of the age when he talked of 'a pair o' patent double million magnifyin' gas microscopes of hextra power'; but the old gentleman in the small clothes was still more apposite when he exclaimed to Miss La Creevy: 'She is come at last—at last—and all is gas and gaiters!' The expression may have had a strange ring to many; but, after all, coal gas was discovered by one who later became a Dean, and thus went from gas to gaiters.

HILARIOUS DAYS

In the very infancy of gas-lighting, Humphry Davy, a young Cornishman born at Penzance on 17 December 1778, was being wafted to fame by gusts of gas of a widely different nature. Ostwald[1] divided men of genius into two types, the romantic and the classical. Humphry Davy carried out his dramatic experiments on the inhalation of nitrous oxide at the age of twenty; at twenty-two he took London by storm through his brilliant lectures at the Royal Institution; at twenty-four he was elected to the Royal Society; at twenty-eight he discovered potassium. Here, then, is a perfect example of the romantic genius in chemistry.

At the age of thirty-four Davy made his still greater

[1] In G. Bugge's *Das Buch der grossen Chemiker*, Berlin, 1929, 1, 405.

discovery of Faraday, and there followed that wonderful example of the age-old story of the master and the apprentice, provided by the interwoven careers and contrasting personalities of the romantic Davy and the classical Faraday. However, like van 't Hoff, who also leaped to fame at the age of twenty-two, Davy had burnt himself out at fifty. If the romantic type be symbolised by Davy's flaming globule of potassium, the classical type may be likened to the candle, about which Faraday lectured so aptly and charmingly to his juvenile auditory at the Royal Institution. Faraday's first important discovery was made when he was about thirty, and the flame of his genius shone clear and steady until he entered into the twilight of a long and fruitful life.

Returning now to our youthful romantic, Davy was not quite out of his teens when, in 1798, he obtained an appointment in Dr. Thomas Beddoes' Pneumatic Institution at Bristol, which had been founded by this former student of Joseph Black for studying the medicinal effects of gases. The breathing of ordinary air being a vital necessity, it was naturally of peculiar interest to investigate the effects of breathing the new 'factitious airs' discovered in this period. The so-called 'medicated airs' used in the experiments were popularly supposed to be explosive, and the Institution was therefore regarded with some suspicion; but Davy burst into 'tumultuous delight' when he first entered its well-appointed laboratory.[1]

Davy was fortunate in turning his attention to nitrous oxide, a gas which Priestley had discovered in 1772. In 1799, he breathed, 'in the presence of Dr. Beddoes and some others, sixteen quarts of it for near seven minutes'. In a letter written at the time Davy stated: 'It appears to support life longer than even oxygen gas, and absolutely intoxicated me. Pure oxygen gas produced no alteration in my pulse, nor any other material effect; whereas this gas raised my pulse upwards of twenty strokes, made me dance about the

---

[1] On his way to Bristol, on 4 October 1798, Davy met at Okehampton the public coach, bedecked with laurels and ribbons, which was bearing westwards the tidings of Nelson's great victory in the Battle of the Nile.

laboratory as a madman, and has kept my spirits in a glow ever since.'

Such spectacular happenings, coming at a time when gases were a fashionable novelty, speedily created a furore, which was by no means limited to the world of science. An interesting passage in Cottle's *Early Recollections of Coleridge* (1837) contains a graphic account of one of the many ludicrous incidents of the time:

'Mr. Southey, Mr. Clayfield, Mr. Tobin and others inhaled the new air. One, it made dance, another laugh, while a third, in his state of excitement, being pugnaciously inclined, struck Mr. Davy rather violently with his fist. It now became an object . . . to witness the effect this potent gas might produce on one of the softer sex, and he prevailed on a courageous young lady, (Miss ———), to breathe out of his pretty green bag, this delightful nitrous oxide. After a few inspirations, to the astonishment of everybody, the young lady dashed out of the house, when, racing down the square, she leaped over a great dog in her way; but being hotly pursued by the fleetest of her friends, the fair fugitive . . . was at length overtaken and secured, without further damage.'

It was through Mrs. Beddoes, a sister of Maria Edgeworth, that Davy, on the very threshold of his meteoric career, became acquainted with Coleridge, Southey, and the Tobins, besides Maria Edgeworth herself. Maria, who witnessed some of the experiments, wrote that 'a young man, a Mr. Davy, at Dr. Beddoes', who has applied himself much to chemistry, has made some discoveries of importance, and enthusiastically expects wonders will be performed by the use of certain gases, which inebriate in the most delightful manner'. To this statement, however, she appended a word of caution: 'I have seen some of the adventurous philosophers who sought in vain for satisfaction in the bag of *Gaseous Oxyd*, and found nothing but a sick stomach and a giddy head'.

Robison struck a note of disapproval at the end of Black's *Lectures* (1803), by remarking of 'nitrous oxyd' that 'its effects, when breathed for some time, are very wonderful, and were first discovered, I believe, by Mr. Davy.

To those who are not hurt by the sight of folly, they are also very amusing.' Judging from the contemporary writer, Fiévée, the inhalation of 'exhilarating' or 'laughing' gas became a vogue at the time; for in his *Lettres sur l'Angleterre* he condemned the practice as a national vice of the English! So far as Davy was concerned, however, Brougham commended his boldness and courage in exposing himself to serious hazard 'in breathing some most deleterious gases', and added that 'both in his trials of gaseous mixtures, and in his galvanic processes, he had made many narrow escapes from the danger of violent explosions'.

The caricaturists were not slow to exploit the new craze. Of their productions, Gillray's coloured caricature (1802) of a lecture at the Royal Institution is the best known; although it reflects perhaps too faithfully the coarse and boisterous humour of the day, this representation has a historic interest in chemistry.[1] It depicts Dr. Thomas Garnett lecturing to a fashionable audience, with Humphry Davy acting as lecture assistant. Garnett is administering the exhilarating air—with unfortunate results—to Sir John Hippesley, whose nostrils he pinches between finger and thumb. Davy stands by with a pair of bellows, belching forth gas. On the lecture bench, among other things, are bottles of oxygen and hydrogen and a collapsed bladder. Count Rumford stands at one side, and the audience also includes Isaac Disraeli, Lord Stanhope, Earl Pomfret, and Sir H. Englefield. An open book belonging to one of the audience is inscribed, 'Hints on the nature of Air requir'd for the new French Diving Boat'. The drawing is entitled *'Scientific Researches!—New Discoveries in PNEUMATICKS! —or—an Experimental Lecture on the Powers of Air'*.

'CHEMISTRY NO MYSTERY'

Even George Cruikshank was attracted by the hilarious aspects of chemistry, and two of his drawings lend distinc-

---

[1] Original impressions of this famous caricature are very rare. A carefully censored part of it was reproduced in T. E. Thorpe's *Humphry Davy* (London, 1901). There is a complete but somewhat dim reproduction in black-and-white in Sir W. A. Tilden's *Famous Chemists* (London, 1921), and a very clear one in colour in E. Cohen's *Das Lachgas* (Leipzig, 1907).

tion to a modest little volume issued in London, in 1839, under the title *Chemistry No Mystery*. This easy and racy account of chemistry was written by John Scoffern, surgeon, and sometime assistant chemist at the London Hospital, who also held private classes and gave a course of practical chemistry at No. 18, Barbican. It purports to be a shorthand record of a course of lectures delivered by an enthusiastic Old Philosopher to a literary and scientific institution in a village of South Devon, 'after the manner of that at Arcueil, in France'.

The Old Philosopher (hereinafter designated by the letters O.P.) opens the first of his course of twenty-one lectures in a style that would have horrified Joseph Black and staggered his hearers. 'My dear young Friends,' he starts: 'If I were to present myself before you with an offer to teach you some new game:—if I were to tell you an improved plan of throwing a ball, of flying a kite, or of playing at leapfrog, oh, with what attention you would listen to me. Well, I am going to teach you many new games. I intend to instruct you in a science full of interest, wonder, and beauty; a science that will afford you amusement in your youth, and riches in your more mature years. In short, I am going to teach you the science of chemistry.'

This gambit shows that the O.P.'s style is much less formal than Mrs. B.'s; moreover, he is fond of relating chemical stories and jokes that would have shocked Mrs. B., although they would have delighted Caroline. At the same time, his treatment of the subject is sound and instructive. He makes good way through the 'imponderables'— light, heat, and electricity—to oxygen, nitrogen, hydrogen, chlorine, carbon, and other non-metallic elements. Altogether, he reckons fifty-five elements, besides the 'imponderables'.

After discussing the non-metals, the O.P. begins in Lecture IX to tell his audience about compounds of these elements with each other, beginning with those of oxygen and nitrogen. At this point he outstrips Mrs. B. by boldly introducing the Atomic Theory. Besides the atmosphere, which, however, 'is regarded by most persons to be a mechanical mixture', nitrogen, he says, combines with oxygen in the proportion of 14 parts of nitrogen to 8, 16, 24, 32, and 40 parts of oxygen. He then develops the ideas of atoms and relative atomic weights. 'As the atomic or equivalent weight of nitrogen is fourteen, and that of oxygen is eight,' he continues, 'we may state the five compounds of nitrogen, and oxygen as is done in this diagram:

Nitrogen.	Oxygen.	
1	1	Protoxide of Nitrogen.
1	2	Binoxide of Nitrogen.
1	3	Hyponitrous Acid.
1	4	Nitrous Acid.
1	5	Nitric Acid.

According to which statement it appears, that the smallest possible quantity of protoxide of nitrogen, commonly

50. Apparatus for preparing and collecting Laughing Gas. After J. Scoffern, 1839

called laughing-gas, is composed of one atom, or equivalent of nitrogen in union with one of oxygen.'

In accordance with current ideas, the O.P. took the atomic weight of oxygen as 8 (instead of 16), and made no distinction in nomenclature between atoms and molecules, the first of these terms being used exclusively. His apparatus for preparing and collecting laughing gas is shown in Fig. 50. He heated 'nitrate of ammonia' in a half-pint glass retort, so that it simmered without violently boiling.

The heating was done with a spirit-lamp. To collect the gas he used a pneumatic trough and a glass receiver fitted with a brass cap and stopcock. He dipped a bladder into water, to make it supple, squeezed the air out of it, and screwed it on to the receiver by means of a brass tube tied into its mouth. When he opened the stopcock and pressed the receiver well down under the water, the gas distended the bladder and filled it.

The O.P. explained to his young friends that 'if one atom of nitrate of ammonia be employed, then we shall get three atoms of water and two of laughing-gas' (which were regarded as HO and NO respectively). He expressed the reaction, not by an equation, but by the scheme below:

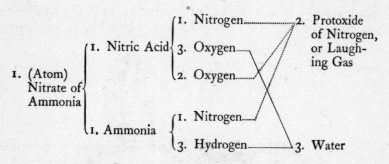

'Those diagrams for expressing chemical changes are just getting into fashion,' remarks the O.P., 'and they are certainly far more convenient than mere words.' To the modern chemist they appear very cumbrous; but such representations were the precursors of the marvellously compact equations of the present day. The above diagram, for example, falls easily into the following form:

$$NO_5 . NH_3 = NO_5 + NH_3 = 2NO + 3HO$$

A GAS ESCAP(AD)E

Having proceeded thus far with his lecture, the O.P. was unwise enough to hand round among his audience a large number of bladders filled with the gas. He instructed the recipients to hold the nostrils firmly between fingers and thumb, to expel as much air as possible from the lungs, and to breathe out of and into the bladders for about half a minute.

'Oh, how shall I describe the scene which followed?' runs the account of the ensuing episode, which formed the subject of Cruikshank's frontispiece (Fig. **51**). 'For one instant, the silence of our Lecture-room was only broken by the deep-drawn inspirations of those who were breathing the gas: all seemed to be enjoying the extreme of happiness, they puffed and pulled as if they could not get enough. It was, indeed, irresistibly ridiculous to see a large room filled with persons, each of whom was sucking from a bladder, and this alone made me laugh right well; but in another instant began their ecstacies, some cast their bladders from them with a jerk, and, forgetting the ridiculous figures they made, kept breathing laboriously; their mouths thrown wide open, and their noses still tightly clenched: some jumped over the tables and chairs; some were bent upon making speeches; some were very much inclined to fight; and one young gentleman persisted in attempting to kiss the ladies. I have heard it insinuated that he breathed very little of the gas, and that he knew very well what he was doing. . . . As our instructor had predicted, we did not after this exhibition feel very much inclined to study philosophy, and therefore the Lecture, although short, was brought to a conclusion.'

A DAMSEL IN DISTRESS

Having by this time warmed to his work, the O.P. passed a little later in the course to another dramatic scene, in which sulphuretted hydrogen came forward to play a leading rôle.

'Hydrosulphuric acid gas', begins this gentle and joyous narration, 'enters into the composition of certain mineral waters; Harrowgate water, for instance, contains a large quantity of it; and connected with this subject, I have an anecdote to relate to you.

'It *was* a practice with those ladies who were particularly ambitious of possessing a white skin, to daub themselves with a preparation of the metal bismuth, which is one of these that sulphuretted hydrogen blackens. Now it is represented on creditable authority, that a lady made beautifully white by this preparation, took a bath in the Harrowgate waters, when her fair skin changed in an instant to the most jetty black. You may judge how much was her surprise at this unlooked-for change; uttering a shriek, she is reported to have swooned; and her attendants, on viewing the extraordinary change, almost swooned too, but their fears in some measure subsided on observing that the blackness of the skin could be removed by soap and water.'

A chemist was once defined as a poet who has taken the wrong turning. Of Sir Humphry Davy, indeed, Coleridge remarked that 'if Davy had not been the first Chemist, he would have been the first Poet of his age'. It is fitting, therefore, that a chemist should endeavour to pay a tribute in verse to this fair victim of a lack of chemical knowledge:

The Surpris'd Lady

'You may judge how much was her surprise
at this unlooked-for change'

We do not share her great surprise;
We know the law that underlies
This lady's change of hue:
For what she thought was H_2O
Contained some H_2S, and so
She came down in Group II.

The lamentable incident finds a concise interpretation in the following scheme, which for once literally deserves to be called a personal equation:

$$2\,Bi(OH)_2NO_3 + 3H_2S = Bi_2S_3 + 2HNO_3 + 4H_2O$$

Pearl-white   Black ppt.
                               (Group II)

A MENACING MAGISTERY

Pearl-white—the 'packhorse in this great affair'—in its original form, was discovered by Libavius about 1600; and Lemery is said to have introduced it as a cosmetic. Many names, and still more formulae, have been assigned to it, by dozens of investigators who have fallen victims to its charms.[1] Among its names are magistery of bismuth, blanc d'Espagne, Spanish white, white cosmetic, and bismuth subnitrate. The horrid dangers that environ the milk-white bismuth-using siren (as a poet who has taken the wrong turning might fitly observe) are so varied, unsuspected, and insidious, as to suggest that the use of this cosmetic should be limited by law to Honours graduates in chemistry. For observe: if the user bathes in the waters of Harrowgate, she turns black, in accordance with the requirements of the above equation; if she sits too close to a coal-fire in the gloaming, a similar fate may overtake her at a critical moment; if she uses the preparation too often, her skin will become rough and red; if she leaves it on too long, she will slowly turn yellow; and if she swallows it by accident, she will develop methaemoglobinura. The replacement of this menace by such innocuous materials as zinc white and starch takes not the least place among the services which chemistry has rendered to mankind.

A VIOLENT REACTION

Cruikshank, being understandably at a loss to do justice to the story of the damsel in distress, was constrained to dedicate the illustrated title-page to a minor episode of a professional giant whom the O.P. had once, in his boyhood, expelled from a show-caravan, at the height of a performance, by liberating the noxious stench of 'this disgusting sulphuretted hydrogen' beneath the flooring of the stage. Cruikshank's illustration (Fig. 52) shows the giant 'bursting from the caravan with the dwarf clinging tightly round his neck'. 'I am sorry to own', confessed the O.P., 'that when young I employed my little stock of scientific knowledge chiefly in playing practical jokes, and this propensity did not entirely leave me until the fair-day.' It left him then because of the giant's reaction to H_2S—but this time it was the O.P. who turned black (and blue). 'I found myself two days afterwards in bed, surrounded by two doctors and

---

[1] See, for example, J. W. Mellor, *Comprehensive Treatise on Inorganic and Theoretical Chemistry*, London, 1929, 9, 706-711.

a nurse', concluded the O.P.; 'and I have many times since then been thankful that my fondness for practical joking experienced such a timely and salutary check.'

GAIETY IN THE 'ANNALEN'

During the period through which we are now passing in imagination, a fundamental theory of molecular structure was slowly taking shape. In 1832, Wöhler and Liebig had published their classical paper on the radical of benzoic acid, leading up to the Radical Theory and to Liebig's definition of organic chemistry as 'the chemistry of compound radicals'. A few years later, in 1840, the French chemist, Dumas, based his Theory of Types largely upon his study of the chlorination of acetic acid. Taking the view that the fundamental chemical nature of an organic compound often persisted through a series of substitution processes, he was sometimes tempted to push his theory to inordinate lengths. Dominated by an idea, he exposed himself to criticism which reached a spectacular climax in a most unusual type of paper to be found on pp. 308-310 of *Liebigs Annalen der Chemie und Pharmacie* for 1840 (Fig. 53).

This delightful satire, penned by Wöhler and published lightheartedly by Liebig, took the ostensible form of a serious contribution to Substitution and the Theory of Types. To heighten the illusion, it was dated from Paris, and written in French; it bore the significant signature, S. C. H. Windler (otherwise 'Swindler'). In it, with much circumstantial detail, the writer describes how he had substituted atom after atom of manganous acetate, MnO, $C_4H_6O_3$, by chlorine, until at last he obtained a yellow crystalline mass containing nothing beyond chlorine and water. The vapour density showed that its formula had to be expressed by $Cl_2Cl_2 + Cl_8Cl_6Cl_6 + aq$. 'Voilà donc la substitution la plus parfaite de tous les élémens de l'acétate de manganèse', exclaims the writer dramatically at this point. The refreshing *jeu d'esprit* ends by pointing out that bleaching with chlorine in England is now carried out according to the laws of substitution, and that the bleached goods preserve their types. A jaunty footnote adds that

Laughing Gas.

51. Laughing Gas.

G. Cruickshank del.   E. Evans sc.   From *Chemistry No Mystery*,
J. Scoffern, London, 1839.   (See p. 211.)

52. Title-page of *Chemistry No Mystery*, by John Scoffern,
London, 1839.
G. Cruikshank del.   E. Evans sc.   (See p. 213.)

308

Ueber das Substitutionsgesetz und die Theorie der Typen *).

Monsieur !   Paris le **1. Mars 1840.**

Je m'empresse de vous communiquer un des faits les plus
eclatants de la chimie organique. J'ai vérifié la théorie des
substitutions d'une manière extrêmement remarquable et
parfaitement inattendue. C'est seulement dès àprésent qu'on
pourra apprécier la haute valeur de cette théorie ingénieuse
et qu'on pourra entrevoir les decouvertes immenses, qu'elle
nous promet de réaliser. La découverte de l'acide chloracétique et la constance des types dans les composés chlorés,
derivés de l'éther et du chlorure d'éthyle m'ont conduit aux
expériences que je vais maintenant décrire. J'ai fait passer
un courant de chlore à travers une dissolution d'acétate de
manganèse, sous l'influence directe de la lumière solaire.
Après 24 heures j'ai trouvé dans le liquide une superbe cri-
stallisation d'un sel jaune violacé. La dissolution ne conte-
nait que le même sel et de l'acide. hydrochlorique. J'ai ana-
lysé ce sel: c'etait du chloracétate de protoxide de manganèse.
Jusqu'ici rien d'extraordinaire, simple substitution de l'hy-
drogène de l'acide acétique par un nombre d'equivalens egaux
de chlore, déjà connu par les belles recherches sur l'acide
chloracétique. Ce sel chauffé à 110° dans un courant de
chlore sec fut converti avec dégagement de gas d'oxigène
en un nouveau composé jaune d'or, dont l'analyse conduisait
pour sa composition à la formule $Mn\ Cl_2 + C_4\ Cl_6\ O_3$.
Il y avait donc substitution de l'oxigène de la base par du
chlore, ce qu'on à observé dans une foule de circonstances.
La nouvelle matière se dissolvait dans du chloral bien pur

---

*) Briefliche Mittheilung an J. L.

53. S. C. H. Windler makes Chemical History

the London shops are supplying fabrics of spun chlorine (evidently consisting of bleached goods true to type), which are in great demand for night-caps, drawers, etc.[1]

FUN IN THE 'BERICHTE'

In 1886 a still more remarkable comet appeared in the chemical firmament, in the form of a special issue of the *Berichte der Deutschen Chemischen Gesellschaft*, dated 20 September. This had all the outward indications of an ordinary issue: the printed cover (Fig. 54) consisted of the familiar drab paper; the type and arrangement of the contents appeared equally normal to the casual observer; and, in fact, the issue was printed and published through the channels used by the genuine *Berichte*. So skilful, indeed, was the camouflage that the editor of one of the leading chemical journals in London—whose mind was evidently soaring above the sordid details of life at the moment— is said to have automatically torn the issue apart into sections and dispatched them to his abstractors according to his usual custom.

A more discerning eye would have noticed at least two apparent misprints on the drab cover, which bore the intriguing inscription, in the usual type: 'Berichte der Durstigen[2] Chemischen Gesellschaft. Unerhörter[3] Jahrgang'. Inside, the list of contents appeared as usual; but the titles and authors' names were reminiscent of *Alice in Wonderland*. The first communication, by two collaborators named Tea and Totalor, dealt with the significance of the

---

[1] Liebig's decision to publish this jesting allusion to a subject which at the time was causing him much concern came as a surprise to Wöhler, who, moreover, wished to change the pseudonym from 'Schwindler' to a gallic form, such as 'Professor Ch. Arlatan'. Wöhler made these points clear in an intimate letter to Liebig, dated from Osnabrück, 29 March 1840: 'Mein Herz hat nicht daran gedacht, dass Du den Spass von der Substitutionstheorie solltest drucken lassen. Auch wird die Sache sehr verlieren, wenn sie nicht französisch gelesen wird. Auch müsstest Du für den Verfasser einen französischen Namen, und nicht Schwindler, wählen, welche Bezeichnung mir überhaupt nicht ganz die richtige zu sein scheint. . . . Mann könnte den Verfasser eher z.B. Charlatan, also Professor Ch. Arlatan, nennen, aber es ist zu plump und grob. Jedenfalls müsste es aber ein Franzose sein.'

[2] 'Reports of the *Thirsty* (instead of German, or *Deutschen*) Chemical Society.'

[3] '*Unheard of* (instead of Nineteenth, or *Neunzehnter*) Annual Issue.'

removal of alcohol, and another was concerned with the synthesis of cognac. The names of authors appearing in the abstracts and patent list were equally worthy of inclusion

BERICHTE

DER

DURSTIGEN

CHEMISCHEN GESELLSCHAFT.

UNERHÖRTER JAHRGANG.

No. 20.

(Ausgegeben um 20. September.)

BERLIN.

EIGENTHUM DER DURSTIGEN CHEMISCHEN GESELLSCHAFT

COMMISSIONSVERLAG von R. FRIEDLÄNDER & SOHN

N.W. CARLSTRASSE 11

1886.

54. Front cover of *Berichte der Durstigen Chemischen Gesellschaft*, Berlin, 1886

in the schoolboy's list of the things which are 'probable but not possible': among them were Heuschrecker, R.; Bierfreund, C.; Alicke, A.; Belicke, B.; Celicke, C.; Delicke, D.; Kari-Hiri; Sloper, Ally, in Philadelphia; Moses, Iky, in Eatanswill (England); and Porkins, James W.,

in Chicago.   The name of the chairman of the imaginary
meeting of this peculiar Society, on 20 September—Aujust

3536

reichen, so erhält man ein höchst vollkommenes Analogon des
Kekulé'schen Benzolsechsecks:

Fig. 1.

Nun aber besitzt der genannte Macacus cynocephalus ausser
seinen eigentlichen vier Händen noch ein fünftes Greifwerkzeug in Form
eines caudalen Appendix.   Zieht man diesen mit in Betracht, dann
gelingt es, die 6 Individuen des gezeichneten Ringes auch noch in
anderer Weise mit einander zu verbinden.   So entsteht das nach-
folgende Bild:

Fig. 2.

Es erscheint mir nun höchst wahrscheinlich, dass die Analogie
zwischen Macacus cynocepbalus und dem Kohlenstoffatom eine voll-

55. A page from *Berichte der Durstigen Chemischen
Gesellschaft*, Berlin, 1886

Kuleké—bore a curious resemblance to that of the President
of the German Chemical Society for that year—August Kekulé.
Two of the sixteen communications appearing in this
unique journal may be given in order to illustrate in more

detail the character of these contributions to chemical science and entertainment. The normal *Berichte* for 1886 comprised 3347 numbered pages, and the special issue[1] is numbered from 3517 to 3568. On page 3531 appears a communication entitled 'Vorlesungsversuch', which may be translated as follows:

1135.   E. Schläuling: Lecture Experiment.

It is well known that one may demonstrate the blue colour of water in deep layers by means of a glass tube, 50 metres long, filled with water, and closed at both ends with parallel plates. This method is capable of improvement, owing to the unwieldy nature of the tube. In my own lecture-room, for example, members of the class are obliged to jump over the apparatus, already in position, in order to gain access to their seats. Added to this, there are certain students who are unable to detect the blue colour without long practice in tube-gazing.

All such drawbacks can be completely overcome, simply by adding, before the start of the lecture, a suitable amount of methylene blue to the water. This little dodge enables one to reduce the length of the apparatus considerably: indeed, I have found it remarkably easy to demonstrate the required colour * even in a simple test-tube. I can thus warmly recommend this form of the lecture experiment to all colleagues.

University Laboratory,
Cloud Cuckooland.

* S. Radde, Colour Scale, Table XIII, 37.

Another communication (Fig. 55), bearing the entirely plausible heading 'Zur Constitution des Benzols,' professes to illuminate the fundamental problem of the structure of the benzene molecule and the nature of tautomerism, matters which were exciting a lively interest at the time. As will be seen from the appended translation, even the sternest critic of this contribution could hardly accuse it of a lack of vivacity or imagination:

1138.   F. W. Findig: On the Constitution of Benzene.
(Received on 31 June; communicated to the Meeting.)

For some time the constitution of benzene has engaged the attention of the greatest living chemists. In these circumstances I cannot

[1] Unfortunately, this issue is seldom found in bound sets of the *Berichte*, and is therefore exceedingly rare: copies bought originally for 1 mark were sold fifty years later in Germany for eighty times this sum.

refrain from joining in the discussion of the problem. It is clear that the viewpoint from which the constitution of benzene has been regarded hitherto is short-sighted and unsatisfactory. I have made a fresh start, setting out from the principle that the sciences are ordained to render each other mutual help. I have discovered that zoology is capable of rendering the greatest service in clearing up the behaviour of the carbon atom. I am going to try to make this clear to the reader, although I doubt whether he will be able to grasp the idea.

Just as the carbon atom has 4 affinities, so the members of the family of four-handed animals possess four hands, with which they seize other objects and cling to them. If we now think of a group of six members of this family, e.g. *Macacus cynocephalus*, forming a ring by offering each other alternately one and two hands, we reach a complete analogy with Kekulé's benzene-hexagon: (Fig. 1).

Now, however, the aforesaid *Macacus cynocephalus*, besides its own four hands, possesses also a fifth gripping organ in the shape of a caudal appendix. By taking this into account, it becomes possible to link the 6 individuals of the ring together in another manner. In this way, one arrives at the following representation: (Fig. 2).

It appears to me highly probable that a complete analogy exists between *Macacus cynocephalus* and the carbon atom. In this case, each C-atom also possesses a caudal appendix, which, however, cannot be included among the normal affinities, although it takes part in the linking. Immediately this appendix, which I call the 'caudal residual affinity', comes into play, a second form of Kekulé's hexagon is produced; this, being obviously different from the first, must behave differently.

Thus, depending upon conditions, a benzene ring will assume one or other of these two forms, and will correspondingly possess a constantly changing constitution.

It is impossible to conceive of a more beautiful example of tautomerism * than the one facing us here. The hypothesis that a molecule is able to change its constitution, and rearrange itself comfortably, in accordance with the needs of the experimenter, belongs to the most magnificent conquests of the searching and critical spirit of man; this achievement, applied to the benzene theory, stands out as a brilliant guiding star to future research!

Private Laboratory,
Schnurrenburg-Mixpickel.   May 1886.

---

* 'Tautomerie' is the correct way of writing this new word, which I have introduced into science. The rendering 'Traute Marie' [Sweet Marie] belongs to the province of malicious inventions, and so does its derivation as a caressing name which I am said to have bestowed upon my pet theory.—F.

This unorthodox issue of the *Berichte* ends with a poetic supplement of light verse, consisting of eleven items contributed wholly by Emil Jacobsen and Otto N. Witt. An entertaining satire from Jacobsen's facile pen, entitled 'Thiophen', is evidently aimed at Victor Meyer and the contemporary 'thiophene school' of chemists. In the course of a lecture experiment at Zürich (p. 265; Fig. **63**), in 1882, Meyer's assistant, Sandmeyer, handed him by chance, instead of the usual coal-tar benzene, a specimen which had been prepared in the lecture course by heating benzoic acid with lime: this failed to give Baeyer's indophenin colour-reaction, which had hitherto been regarded as a characteristic test for benzene. Following up this clue, Meyer eventually showed that the production of the deep-blue colour was due to the presence in coal-tar benzene of about 0·5 per cent. of a sulphur-containing impurity, which he isolated in 1883 and named thiophene. This dramatic discovery created a sensation at the time, which was even enhanced when Meyer found that the new substance bore a startling similarity to benzene, chemically as well as physically. During the next five years, Meyer and numerous collaborators devoted themselves to an intensive study of thiophene and its derivatives, chronicled in no fewer than 106 original papers. The contemporary literature of chemistry testifies to the strenuous exertions of this enthusiastic band of workers on the sulphureous stranger, and the crest of the thiophene wave happened to coincide with the publication of the *Berichte der Durstigen Chemischen Gesellschaft* in 1886. Jacobsen's poem runs as follows, in free translation:[1]

---

[1] The original opens as below:

> *Ward einst ein Studio in Jene*
> *Von einem Examen beschwert,*
> *Der hatte vom Thiophene*
> *Sein Lebtag noch nichts gehört.*

> *Und als der Professor ihn fragte,*
> *Was er hielte vom Thiophen,*
> *Der Studio nichts wusste und sagte*
> *Als: 'ein Körper wär es und schön'.*

Thiophene

(*From the German of Emil Jacobsen*)

There once was a student of Jene
To whom his exam. was no game:
Of thiophene—naught could be plainer—
He'd never heard even the name.

So, when the Professor invited
His views on the said thiophene,
The student dismissed it—quite blighted—
As 'merely a compound, and clean.'

Upon his head then the Professor
Laid hands that both blessed and approved:
'May God keep thee fresh—and still fresher—
A long time,' he prayed, deeply moved.

'For he who remains unaffected
By the sulphur-soaked air all around
Must be a born chemist, selected
By the good God on that very ground.'

Following the elder Perkin's preparation of mauveine
from coal-tar aniline (1856), and Kekulé's fundamental
theories (p. 341) of molecular structure (1858) and the
benzene ring (1865), organic chemical research in the last
half of the nineteenth century was concerned mainly with
the rich field of coal-tar chemistry. One of the many landmarks in this work was Skraup's synthesis of quinoline, in
1880. The great interest which this outstanding achievement aroused among contemporary chemists is commemorated in a fanciful poem by Otto N. Witt—himself
an eminent worker in organic chemistry—entitled 'Das
wehmüthige Chinolinmolecul':

The Melancholy Quinoline Molecule

(*From the German of Otto N. Witt*)

Once I was young and was Benzene,
Ah, those were joyous days, I ween;
A tiny trace of Thiophene
Was aye with me, and aye unseen.

But then, alas, there came a man
Who forthwith took me and began
To separate with acids keen
My life-long comrade Thiophene.

Surrounded now with salt and ice,
Tormented in this freezing vice,
With none at hand to heed my cries,
I had at last to crystallise.

And then they pressed me—'twas no fun—
Until my tear-drops ceased to run,
And sobbingly arose my call:
'Farewell, last drop of Toluol!'

Away I flowed, but—God be kind!—
Naught but nitration could I find,
Which made of me another creature,
And left me no redeeming feature.

My molecule was full of style,
Gracious, symmetric, volatile:
Now, NO_2's my one fallal—
An inorganic radical!

Mixed with acids and with turnings
Made of iron, all my yearnings
Count for naught, and presently I'm seen
Metamorphosed into Aniline.

And now, according to the mode,
I'm treated after Skraup's methōd:
So all this pother's ended in
My rise to rank as Quinoline.

And yet, as I so often say,
I think with longing of the day
When I, a youthful innocent,
As Benzene on life's journey went.

THE LITERATURE RELAPSES

This most vivacious of all issues of the *Berichte* was the
last expiring flash of that genial flame of chemical humour
and entertainment which lit up the gas-bladders of John
Clayton and diffused so generously from those of Humphry

Davy. The exhilarating effects of these gases, and of the lively mood that such pioneering work engendered, had persisted for a long time; but at last a period of relapse set in, and gradually the invigorating influence of humour and humanism evaporated almost entirely from the literature of chemistry.

As Scoffern remarked at the end of his sprightly book: 'We entered upon the study of our science with sportiveness and mirth; but towards the conclusion of our labours we have been compelled to become more serious, and to use language more in accordance with the nature of our subject. As a young lion torn from the forest is tame and playful, allowing caresses, and joining in every frolic, so we found chemistry; but as it grew to its full size and formidable strength,—it became a thing no longer to be played with;— demanding all care, attention, and respect.'

It is impossible to imagine the appearance of the light-hearted effusions of Wöhler, Jacobsen, or Otto Witt in any similar chemical journals of the first half of the twentieth century. With ever-increasing specialisation, the chemist has been forced in a large degree to get to know 'more and more about less and less'; to lose his sense of chemical perspective; and to neglect the historic and humanistic appeal of chemistry. The staid, formal, and highly regimented journals which he has to read, do little to widen his chemical horizon. Twentieth-century chemistry has seemed to be in danger of relapsing into a jargon-laden esotericism reminiscent of alchemy.

Yet there are signs on that horizon of a new chemical dawn. The constantly increasing importance of chemistry in the activities of everyday life and the service of the community has led in turn to a growing demand for a simple presentation of chemical facts and principles. Chemistry, for so long interested in 'airs', has now 'gone on the air' in a new sense.

In order to give an idea of the way in which even a specialised and technical field of chemistry may be expounded in simple terms, designed to interest and instruct the vast heterogeneous audiences of the wireless world, this chapter may fitly close with an example of the new 'radiochemistry',[1] illustrating at the same time another aspect of the chemistry of gases, with which the chapter began.

A BROADCAST ON EXPLOSIVES

Years ago, as a boy in a Somerset village, I sometimes amused myself and impressed my friends by filling a jam-jar with water, turning it upside down in the village horse-pond, and poking the mud beneath it with a stick. Bubbles of marsh-gas, released from the bed of the pond, rose through the water and soon filled the jar. When I held a lighted match near the mouth of the inverted jar, the gas took fire and burnt quietly with an almost invisible flame. Occasionally, however, when a good deal of air had got into the jar, the mixture exploded with a very pleasing pop.

It's a long way from my village horsepond to Hamburg and Berlin, and still further, you may think, from marsh-gas to 'block-busters'; but the links in the chain are clearly traceable, so why not let's see how they run?

Marsh-gas, which arises from sodden and decaying vegetation, is the simplest of hundreds of thousands of organic compounds. Organic compounds are substances containing carbon. Marsh-gas, also known as methane, is a hydrocarbon, or compound containing carbon and hydrogen only. It's the same as fire-damp of coal mines. Its molecule, or ultimate chemical particle, is written CH_4, because it's formed by the combination of one carbon atom, C, with four hydrogen atoms, H_4. These molecules are excessively minute. A hollow pin's-head would hold enough of them to provide several million each for every man, woman and child in the world.

When marsh-gas burns, it undergoes a chemical change known as oxidation. Through reaction with oxygen, which forms about one-fifth of the surrounding air, the carbon of the marsh-gas is burnt to carbon dioxide and the hydrogen is burnt to water vapour. So there are two oxidation processes going on together: the burning of carbon and the

[1] The fifth broadcast in the B.B.C. series 'Science at your Service', given by the author on 29 October 1943 (7.40-8 P.M.), and published in *The Listener*, 4 November 1943.

burning of hydrogen. We know from common experience that each of these processes liberates energy in the form of heat: consider a glowing brazier of charcoal, on the one hand, and an oxy-hydrogen blowpipe, on the other. These tell of the enormous stores of heat evolved in the burning of carbon in the brazier and of hydrogen in the blowpipe. So it isn't surprising that marsh-gas, which contains carbon and hydrogen in combination, should burn with a hot flame; or that coal-gas, which is mainly a mixture of hydrogen and marsh-gas, should do the same.

When marsh-gas is burnt in a jar, or from a gas-jet, the heat is quickly dissipated through the surrounding air; moreover, the burning takes place quite slowly. The molecules of marsh-gas have to queue in the tube behind the jet, and wait for their ration of atmospheric oxygen until they quit the tube and get out into the air.

We reach a very different result when we mix marsh-gas, in a closed space, with twice its volume of oxygen and spark it. There's no queueing of molecules now. Each marsh-gas molecule has next to it the two oxygen molecules it needs. The reaction, started by the hot spark, spreads fiercely through the mixture. The equally sudden liberation of heat makes the mixed gaseous products so hot that in their efforts to expand they may shatter the confining vessel with a loud report. In common speech, the mixture explodes.

And now for a word of warning to any unskilled person who may think of trying experiments with explosives: it's the same as Mr. Punch's advice to those about to get married—Don't! With explosives, the consequences may be even more serious. The French scientist, Dulong, lost an eye and three fingers in explosives research—and, remember, *he* was a skilled and experienced chemist:

> The many perils that environ
> The man who meddles with a siren
> Are naught beside the ones that he
> Invites, who flirts with TNT.

An explosion is usually an exceedingly rapid oxidation, or burning. An explosive is a material capable of developing a sudden high pressure by the rapid formation of large volumes of gas. The explosive power of marsh-gas mixed with oxygen is relatively feeble, because the expansion is due entirely to the heat effect: except for the heat set free in the process, the volume of gas in this example would be the same before and after the burning. Enormously more powerful effects are produced in the explosion of suitable liquids or solids. A given space will accommodate a much greater weight of an explosive in the liquid or solid form than as a gas. This economy of packing in liquid and solid explosives is one of the leading factors in producing great pressure when the explosive suddenly gasifies. The second factor is the simultaneous liberation of vast stores of heat, leading to a further expansion.

When solid gunpowder explodes, it produces 500 times its own volume of gases, measured at the ordinary temperature; but the liberated heat causes a further eightfold expansion to 4000 volumes. Nitroglycerine is still more powerful: 1 volume of this oily liquid gives rise on exploding to 1200 volumes of gas, expanding again about eightfold through the action of the generated heat to 10,000 volumes. That is to say, a thimbleful of liquid nitroglycerine is transformed in the twinkling of an eye into 60 pints of gas at a fierce heat exceeding 5000° Fahrenheit. On the same scale, a foot-rule would leap out to a length of two miles. Once started, nothing can stop or moderate this sudden burning and release of energy.

Why is nitroglycerine so much more powerful than gunpowder? Briefly, because in gunpowder the fuel and the oxygen are done up in separate packets, or molecules; whereas in nitroglycerine both the fuel and the necessary oxygen are packed together in the same molecule. In gunpowder, the fuel *specks* of carbon and sulphur lie side by side with the oxygen supply, contained in separate *specks* of nitre. In nitroglycerine, the fuel *atoms* of carbon and hydrogen are arranged in the same molecule with a sufficient number of oxygen *atoms* for their complete burning. The mixing here is done inside each infinitesimal molecule: it is of the most intimate nature we can imagine. Most modern explosives are of this kind: nitroglycerine, guncotton, cordite, trinitrotoluene, all contain the fuel atoms and the oxygen atoms arranged within the same molecule.

The molecules of such explosives are very delicately poised. The fuel atoms are temporarily held apart from the oxygen atoms by molecular policemen, consisting of atoms of nitrogen. Their lot is not a happy one; for they must always be on duty. The moment these pillars of molecular law and order relax their vigilance there's a molecular dog-fight, virulent and contagious, and the countless legions of molecules collapse, with spectacular unanimity.

There are several ways of distracting the attention of these molecular policemen, so that explosion may occur. Sometimes heat does it, sometimes friction, sometimes concussion. Explosives are very temperamental. For instance, trinitrotoluene or cordite will suffer the impact of a bullet without exploding; but mercury fulminate explodes when struck by a hammer, and nitrogen iodide is so very touchy that one would hesitate to sneeze near it, and a fly using a crystal of it as a landing-ground might no longer interest a spider. Again, cordite and trinitrotoluene burn without exploding when ignited in the open air, but mercury fulminate and lead azide explode with great violence when ignited under any conditions.

Many of the powerful modern explosives can only be roused to full explosion by means of detonation. In this process, discovered by Nobel in 1864, the explosion of a small charge of an initiatory explosive or detonant, such as mercury fulminate, sets off the main explosive lying near it. These detonants, which may be exploded by percussion or a spark, set up violent shock waves. So, when trinitrotoluene is fired by a suitable detonator, instead of burning quietly it undergoes an instantaneous collapse, caused by an explosive wave: this originates in the detonator, and moves through the TNT at a speed of more than 4 miles a second. This is what happens when a bomb or shell explodes.

Explosives such as gunpowder and cordite, which always burn comparatively slowly, without detonating, may be used as propellants. It's gunpowder that sends the shot after the rabbit, and cordite that sends the bullet after the foeman. Other explosives, such as TNT, lyddite, and gun-cotton, burn rapidly to detonation when confined. These are known as high explosives. They cannot be used as propel-lants, because they would detonate and shatter the weapon. High explosives are used for filling shells (Fig. 56), bombs, torpedoes, and mines, and also for demolition work.

A few miles from the fine horsepond I mentioned just now, there's a grey old town called Ilchester. It stands at the junction of the Fosseway with the Roman road to Dorchester; but Ilchester is older even than the Roman roads. Here, in 1214, was born Roger Bacon, the earliest of the great scientists of England. It was in a Latin text, written in 1242, that Bacon first made known the composi-tion of gunpowder, the oldest explosive. This Franciscan monk was perhaps the first to make gunpowder explode and to realise its power. According to a mediaeval legend, another monk, the mysterious Berthold Schwarz (Fig. 57) of the Black Forest in Germany, first used it as a propellant.

The introduction of modern explosives, beginning about 1850, was due largely to the Swedish chemical engineer, Nobel, who invented dynamite, blasting gelatine and ballistite, and founded the Nobel Prizes—including the Peace Prize.

Modern organic explosives are made chiefly from fats, cotton, and coal, all of which are natural sources of energy, containing the fuel atoms, carbon and hydrogen. In the manufacture of these explosives, the glycerine from fats, the cellulose of cotton, and the benzene and toluene of coal-tar, are treated with nitric acid, under special conditions, in order to introduce the necessary oxygen and nitrogen atoms into the molecules. The nitric acid, formerly obtained from Chili saltpetre, is now prepared chiefly from atmospheric nitrogen. Indeed, to the Germans—because of British sea-power blocking the importation of Chilean nitrate—the manufacture of nitric acid from the air was essential before the war of 1914–1918 could be undertaken. So they made sure of it before committing themselves.

Through the intervention of plant life, fats, cellulose, and coal also originate from the air, this time from gaseous carbon dioxide and water vapour. Nitric acid, fats, cellulose, and coal—they all come ultimately from the air. Explosives are thus slowly woven from atmospheric gases, unto which, in the moment of explosion, they return, shedding suddenly their fabulous stores of strangely acquired energy, caught up mainly from solar radiation by the living plant.

How does all this that I've been talking about affect you? Economically and industrially the manufacture of explosives is closely linked with the production of such familiar commodities as fats, glycerine, soap, cotton, coal, dyes, drugs, petroleum, and fertilisers. In the great chemical industries depending upon coal-tar, for example, explosives form one of many groups of fine chemicals, including dyes and drugs. These are so closely interlocked that a member of one group is often a by-product in the preparation of a member of another group. So, in the war of 1914–1918, Great Britain was sorely handicapped in producing explosives because of the lack of a strong organic chemical industry, and a corresponding dearth of skilled organic chemists. After the war, the position was safeguarded by a Dyestuffs Act, which prevented Germany from resuming her old practice of dominating the British fine chemical market by underselling. It says little for the public appreciation of scientific problems in Great Britain that the renewal of this Act hung by a thread in 1937—a little more than two years before the start of a new war by Germany.

In the popular mind, explosives mean solely the propulsion of missiles, the bursting of bombs and shells, and destructive activities in general. Let us remember, however, that besides their destructive abuses in war, explosives have constructive uses of the highest value in peace. Many vital industrial and engineering operations would be impossible without their aid. In peace-time such civil activities as quarrying, mining, tunnelling, and the construction of roads and railways utilise explosives in hundreds of thousands of tons every year. Under proper control, explosives have an unrivalled capacity for doing useful work, as we may see in such wonderful constructions as the Simplon Tunnel

56. Fitting Shells with Exploders.
British official photograph, 1942. (See p. 229.)

Des Ehrwürdigen und Sinnreichẽ Vatters Bertold Schwartz genandt, Fran-
ciscaner Ordens, Doctor, Alchimist und Erfinder der freyen kunst des Buchsenschiessens
im Jar 1380.

Sechi da was thüet die Zeit, und die Natur darneben
durch Scharffsinnige leüht, offtmals an den Tag geben
Des Buchsenschiessens kunst Erzeügt durch Fewres art
und aus der Natur dünst. du mal geboren wardt

57. Berthold Schwarz in his Laboratory.
From a copper engraving by R. Custos, 1643. (See p. 229.)

and the Panama Canal. Economic, political, and even geographical considerations are clearly bound up with such achievements.

Think of the revolution accomplished in the excavation and removal of rock through the use of blasting explosives! Formerly this was done painfully by hand, with hammer and chisel, supplemented by 'fire-setting', or splitting and flaking the rock by means of fire and cold water. Think again of the impossibility of mining coal for modern needs without the help of explosives! Consider, too, the incessant research providing ever safer explosives for this purpose.

It has sometimes been urged that we should abandon explosives and explosives research, because man has mis-applied the discoveries. This position is untenable. Apart from the difficulty of securing international agreement in such a matter, there's an inherent urge in the human mind 'to follow knowledge like a sinking star'. It's no more possible to ban scientific research than to forbid exploration, mountaineering, or crossword puzzles. Remember also the interrelations of explosives: coal-tar constituents are the common parents of TNT, lyddite, saccharin, synthetic indigo, salvarsan, and M & B 693.

Even a controlled production of 'key' chemicals—such as ammonia, nitric acid, and sulphuric acid—used in making explosives, is complicated by their position as 'key' chemicals in numerous essential industries, including agriculture.

Scientists naturally deplore, even more than others, the perversion of their own discoveries and the debasement of their work and genius. Listen to the eighteenth-century Dutch scientist, Boerhaave, the most famous physician, the foremost chemist, and the most erudite scholar of his day. The art of war, he observed in 1732, has turned entirely upon the one chemical invention of gunpowder. 'God grant', he added, 'that mortal men may not be so ingenious at their own art, as to pervert a profitable science any longer to such horrible uses.'

When man discovered fire, he took into his keeping an instrument with unbounded possibilities for good, or evil. Fire, says the old proverb, is a good servant but a bad

R

master. But we haven't banned the use of fire because a cigarette-end thrown carelessly into a rickyard may destroy a whole harvest. Explosives are a refined form of fire.

Let us end where we began, at that instructive horse-pond. Beside it stood the village smithy. 'Your fire's out!' I said one day to my friend the smith. He stroked the long bellows-handle caressingly, and a glow soon appeared in the embers. 'Out, is ur?' said the smith. 'Why, zonny, there's vire enough in he vur to burn down all London!' Whereupon he thrust an unfinished horse-shoe into the midst of the glow.

'The fault, dear Brutus, is not in our stars, but in our-selves.' This being so, may we not look forward to an enlightened age in which the discoveries of science will be used entirely for the benefit of mankind? What practical measures can we take to realise this ideal? I won't attempt to answer that question; but it's one which you might profitably think about and discuss.

References

Accum, F., *Description of the Process of Manufacturing Coal Gas*, with 7 coloured Ackermann plates, 2nd edn., London, 1820.
Berichte der Durstigen Chemischen Gesellschaft. Unerhörter Jahrgang. Ausgegeben am 20. September. Berlin, 1886.
Birch, T., *The Life of the Honourable Robert Boyle*, London, 1744.
Boyle, R., *Works* (ed. Birch, T.), 5 vols., London, 1744.
Hales, S., *Vegetable Staticks* . . . By Steph. Hales, B.D., F.R.S., Rector of Farringdon, Hampshire, and Minister of Teddington, Middlesex. London, 1727.
Hughes, S., *The Construction of Gas-Works and the Manufacture and Distribution of Coal Gas*, 6th edn., revised by W. Richards, London, 1880.
Layton, W. T., *The Discoverer of Gas Lighting: Notes on the Life and Work of the Rev. John Clayton, D.D., 1657–1725*, London, 1926.
Masson, I., *Three Centuries of Chemistry*, London, 1925.
Partington, J. R., *A Short History of Chemistry*, London, 1937.
Read, J., *Explosives* (Pelican Books, A100), London, 1942.
Scoffern, J., *Chemistry No Mystery; or, A Lecturer's Bequest.* Being the subject-matter of a course of lectures, delivered by an Old Philosopher, and taken in short-hand by one of the audience, whose name is not known. Arranged from the Original Manuscript, and Revised, by John Scoffern. London, 1839.
Thorpe, T. E., *Humphry Davy, Poet and Philosopher*, London, 1901.

CHAPTER X

HUMOUR AND HUMANISM IN MODERN LABORATORIES

WÖHLER VISITS BERZELIUS

P RESENT-DAY students of chemistry look upon the existence of laboratory accommodation as a *sine quâ non*, and
do not realise that the experimental facilities they take
for granted were generally unknown, even in a rudimentary
form, until about the middle of the nineteenth century. In
Great Britain, it was not until 1845 that the first public
provision for the practice of experimental chemistry became
available with the opening in London of the Royal College
of Chemistry. It may indeed be said that Thomas Thomson
had admitted students into his laboratory at Edinburgh for
practical instruction in chemistry in the first decade of the
nineteenth century, and that soon afterwards Stromeyer had
done likewise at Göttingen; but these and a few other
enlightened men were in advance of their times, and such
provision was not effectively developed in any country until
the stimulating influence of Liebig's celebrated laboratory
at Giessen came in due course to make itself felt in the
outside world. At the Hofmann Memorial Lecture, in
1893, Lord Playfair remarked that in Graham's time, about
1840, organic chemistry was little known or studied in
Great Britain and that all aspiring chemists who had the
necessary means 'used to flock either to the laboratory of
Liebig at Giessen or to that of Wöhler at Göttingen'.[1]

---

[1] The following interesting letter, in the St. Andrews collection, from Professor
G. D. Liveing (*cf.* p. 284) to T. E. [later Sir Edward] Thorpe, illustrates this
matter further:

'Cambridge 3 Feb 1897. My dear Thorpe, I am sending you a copy of my
predecessor's [Cumming's] syllabus of lectures, issued in 1834. It was probably
in use in 1837. You will find no organic chemistry in it, but later, when I attended

Wöhler and Liebig, two of the greatest figures in modern chemistry, were born at the dawn of the nineteenth century, within three years of each other. Both of them had an innate enthusiasm for chemistry, and as students they encountered the difficulties of that age in obtaining access to any form of practical training in chemistry apart from the simulacrum afforded by working with an apothecary. There is much interest, both human and historical, in the difficulties of these two typical young chemists of the opening decades of the nineteenth century; indeed, it is justifiable to claim that the early struggles and experiences of Wöhler and Liebig led to the birth of chemical laboratories thrown open to students for instruction and research.

Friedrich Wöhler (1800–1882) was born at Eschersheim, near Frankfurt. At the age of nineteen he entered somewhat reluctantly upon the study of medicine in the University of Marburg. He devoted his spare time to practical experiments upon cyanogen compounds in his private room, in the course of which he made the discovery of the curious formations known as 'Pharaoh's serpents', arising djinn-like from ignited pills of mercuric thiocyanate. The repugnant odours of cyanogen compounds filled the house, and it was a relief to Wöhler's landlady when he left Marburg for Heidelberg, attracted by Leopold Gmelin. At Heidelberg he continued his medicinal studies, but his passion for chemistry induced him to work at the same time in Gmelin's makeshift laboratory. Here, in the romantic

his lectures, towards the end of the forties, organic chemistry took its place in the course displacing some of the lectures on metals. The lectures were always experimentally illustrated. But there was absolutely no opportunity for any one who studied the subject here to show his knowledge except by publishing some research, and no opportunity of making any research unless the man found his own laboratory & apparatus.

'I started the first laboratory for students here in 1852 at my own expence, hiring a cottage in the town which I converted into a laboratory.

'But Cumming was always at work himself, but it was chiefly at electricity. In his time & in the earlier time of my tenure of the professorship, such subjects as Heat and Electricity were considered as part of Chemistry. The difference which I made was to separate the lectures on physics entirely from those on Chemistry, but I continued to lecture on physics until a new chair of physics was founded & filled by Clerk-Maxwell. Now I feel how purely artificial the distinction between the different departments of molecular physics is. Most truly yours, G. D. Liveing.'

surroundings of the old cloisters, to which Bunsen succeeded later in the century, Wöhler began the researches on cyanic acid which led up a few years afterwards to the twofold discovery of artificial urea and isomerism.

Wöhler graduated in medicine at Heidelberg in 1823; but he had already decided to abandon medicine for chemistry. Of all the chemists of that day the most famous was Berzelius (1779–1848), and it was to Berzelius at Stockholm that Wöhler now turned his eyes. Acting on Gmelin's advice, he wrote to ask for a place in Berzelius' private laboratory. Berzelius replied: 'One who has studied chemistry under Leopold Gmelin will certainly find little to learn from me. Nevertheless, I cannot neglect this happy opportunity of making your acquaintance, and will therefore welcome you heartily as my collaborator in practical work.'

Accordingly, in the autumn of 1823 Wöhler left Heidelberg for Stockholm. Many years later, in 1875, he wrote an account of his experiences and travels with Berzelius for the German Chemical Society, from which the details now given are taken. He had to wait at Lübeck for six weeks before the small sailing-ship in which he had taken passage was ready to leave; but he made full use of his time in scientific work of one kind and another. With the help of a local apothecary, Kindt, he prepared a considerable quantity of metallic potassium in a home-made apparatus which they operated in Kindt's wash-house; Wöhler took this as a present to Berzelius, who used it in experiments on the isolation of silicon, boron, and zirconium. At Lübeck, Wöhler met Mitscherlich, who was returning from a sojourn with Berzelius.

Wöhler sailed from Lübeck on 25 October 1823. On reaching Stockholm he stayed overnight in a rude tavern. Here he made the acquaintance of a medical student who spoke neither German nor French, so they got on as well as they could in Latin. On the next morning this student showed Wöhler the way to the dwelling of the great Swedish chemist, then at the height of his fame, recently ennobled by Charles XIV, and supreme among the chemists of the day.

'My heart beating rapidly,' runs Wöhler's account, 'I stood before Berzelius's door and rang the bell. The door was opened by a man of distinguished appearance, neatly clad, and in the prime of life. It was Berzelius himself. He welcomed me most cordially, said that he had been expecting me for some time past, and enquired about my journey; he spoke in German, with which he was thoroughly conversant, as also with French and English. I followed him into his laboratory like one in a dream, doubting whether I could really be in this classical place which was the goal of my desires. . . .

'On the very next day I began working. For my personal use I was given a platinum crucible, a balance with weights, and a wash-bottle. Before all, I was expected to provide myself with a blowpipe, to the use of which Berzelius attached great importance. Beside this, one had to find spirit for the spirit-lamps and oil for the table blowpipe: ordinary reagents were provided; although I had to get prussiate of potash, for example, from Lübeck, because it was unprocurable in Stockholm.

'At that time I was the only one in the laboratory; before me came Mitscherlich and H. and G. Rose, and I was followed by Magnus. The laboratory comprised two ordinary rooms fitted in the simplest way; there were no furnaces or ventilating hoods; no service of water or gas. In one room stood two common long tables, made of deal; Berzelius worked at one of these, I at the other. On the walls there were some cupboards with the reagents; in the middle stood the mercury-trough and the table blowpipe, the latter under an oilskin hood communicating with a flue. Besides this, there was the washing-up place, consisting of a stoneware cistern with a tap, standing over a tub. Here the severe Anna, Berzelius's cook, used to clean the apparatus every day. The other room housed the balances and some cupboards containing instruments and apparatus; in an adjoining small workshop there was a lathe. Close by, in the kitchen where Anna cooked the meals, stood a small furnace, seldom used, and a sand-bath, always kept hot.'

Wöhler began his work by undertaking a course of

mineral analysis under Berzelius' close supervision. Sometimes he worked too rapidly, with the consequence that his
results were discordant. 'Doctor,' Berzelius would exclaim
reprovingly, 'das war geschwind, aber schlecht' ('Doctor,
that was fast but faulty'). His analytical work on wolfram
led Wöhler to the discovery of several new compounds of
tungsten; but Berzelius's deepest interest was reserved for
Wöhler's resumed investigations on cyanic acid, which
appeared to have an important bearing upon Davy's revolutionary ideas, put before the Royal Society on 12 July 1810,
concerning the nature of oxymuriatic acid. Berzelius, for
a long time a doubting Thomas and staunch upholder of
the old views, surprised Wöhler by his repeated use of the
name 'chlorine'. One day Anna Sundström, who was clean-
ing a vessel at the tub, remarked that it smelt strongly of
oxymuriatic acid. Wöhler's earlier surprise sublimed into
astonishment when he heard Berzelius correct her, in words
that have since become historic: 'Hark thou, Anna, thou
mayest now speak no more of oxymuriatic acid; but must
say chlorine: that is better'.[1] These words, issuing from the
mouth of the great chemical lawgiver of the age, sealed the
fate of oxymuriatic acid.

In talking to Wöhler of his visits to England and France,
Berzelius gave him some vivid character sketches of Gay-
Lussac, Thenard, Dulong, Wollaston, Davy, and other
eminent scientists of the day. Among them, Gay-Lussac
and Davy took the first place in his esteem. Berzelius kept
up a correspondence with many of them, and allowed
Wöhler to look through his portfolios of letters. It can be
imagined with what awe Wöhler met Davy, in the course of a
journey across southern Sweden, undertaken in July 1824,
towards the close of his stay with Berzelius. At Hälsing-
borg, where Berzelius was awaiting him, Davy arrived
several days late, having been unable to tear himself away
earlier from some absorbing salmon-fishing at Halmstad.
Berzelius introduced Wöhler, and Davy addressed a few
polite words of encouragement to the unknown young

[1] In Wöhler's German rendering: 'Hör' Anna, Du darfst nun nicht mehr sagen
oxydirte Salzsäure, sondern musst sagen Chlor, das ist besser'.

chemist; he then fell into an animated conversation with Berzelius, conducted alternately in English and French. After half an hour of this, Davy left hurriedly for Copenhagen—'as we found later,' adds Wöhler somewhat dryly, 'not to bother himself with chemistry or physics, but to set out on a snipe-shooting expedition with Forchhammer'.[1]

Wöhler left Berzelius on 17 September 1824, having established with him the foundation of a great and lasting friendship. In the following year he was elected to a post as teacher of chemistry in the new Gewerbeschule, or technical school, in Berlin, where he remained until 1831. Meanwhile, in 1829, he had begun his classical collaboration with Liebig.

LIEBIG WALTZES WITH GAY-LUSSAC

Justus Liebig (1803–1873) was born at Darmstadt. While still a schoolboy he excited the merriment of his master and schoolfellows by declaring to them in public his ambition of becoming a chemist: that the idea of chemistry as an independent subject of study, leading to a career, should have seemed ludicrous in those days is not surprising when one recalls that little less than a hundred years later chemistry was still generally confused with pharmacy in Great Britain. Upon leaving school, Liebig gained some experience of chemistry in an apothecary's shop at Heppen-

---

[1] 'I was informed at Copenhagen, that the jack-snipe certainly breeds in Zeeland, and I saw a nest with its eggs, said to be from the island of Sandholm, opposite Copenhagen', wrote Davy in *Salmonia: or Days of Fly Fishing* (2nd edn., London, 1829, 335). This anonymous work, consisting of 'a series of conversations' held between four fly fishers, in settings including London, Denham (May 1810), Loch Maree (time—middle of July), Leintwardine, near Ludlow (time—beginning of October), Downton, and the Fall of the Traun, Upper Austria (time—July), deserves a much wider reputation than it has achieved. It displays Davy's intimate knowledge of the habits and natural history of fishes, insects, and birds, his expert acquaintance with the technicalities of fly fishing and the diverse types of European fishing waters, his general love of nature, and his poetic imagination. *Salmonia* was largely composed during Davy's last visit to Nether Stowey in 1827.

A holograph letter in the St. Andrews collection, dated 'Tuesday' (5 March 1816), and addressed to 'Rich[d] Horsman Solly Esqre., Great Ormond Street', testifies to Davy's passion for the sport which detained him at Halmstad: 'I hope you recollect that our engagement holds for the 10 or 11, i.e. Sunday or Monday. I have therefore refused all invitations beyond that time. Lord Somerville has written to his fisherman & the middle of March is the right time. The Salmon will be out of the river [Tweed] by the end of the month.' (*Cf. op. cit.* 331.)

heim. Not content with pounding drugs and compounding pills, he began to carry out chemical experiments in the attic in which the apothecary had lodged him. Apparently he was already investigating fulminates, for the attic window suffered severely in an explosion. The apothecary thereupon sent Liebig back to his father.

Liebig's interest in fulminates may be traced back to a certain day of his boyhood when he stood in the marketplace at Darmstadt and watched a pedlar using silver fulminate for charging toy crackers. This chance occurrence originated a series of events leading to the recognition of isomerism, one of the fundamental phenomena of physical science; from the same incident sprang also the collaboration between Liebig and Wöhler, one of the most celebrated associations in the history of science:

> Think nought a trifle, though it small appear;
> Small sands the mountain, moments make the year,
> And trifles life.[1]

Soon after leaving the apothecary, Liebig persuaded his father to send him to the University of Bonn, then recently founded. From Bonn he followed his professor, Kastner, to Erlangen, where in 1822, at the age of nineteen, he took the degree of Doctor of Philosophy. He had sustained his interest in fulminates, and at about the time of his graduation he published a paper on fulminating mercury. Liebig found that neither Bonn nor Erlangen offered encouragement or facilities to the would-be chemist. In Liebig's own words, 'it was then a wretched time for chemistry' in Germany. Young chemists with enthusiasm and ambition had to go either to Paris or Stockholm. The accommodation available at Stockholm in 1823 has already been seen through the eyes of Wöhler. Even in France, distinguished at that time by such brilliant experimenters as Gay-Lussac, Thenard, Dulong, Vauquelin, Chevreul, and Arago, there was no public laboratory for instruction in analytical or experimental chemistry. There were some good courses of lectures, but the aspiring practical chemist had to seek

---

[1] Edward Young (b. 1681).

admission to a private laboratory or workroom and to content himself with facilities of a very modest kind.

It was a prepossessing young man that arrived in Paris in 1823. 'Liebig', wrote Platen, 'was never more beautiful', and described him as 'of slender form, a friendly earnestness in his regular features, great brown eyes with dark shady eyebrows, which attracted one instantly'. In that summer Liebig gave an account to the Academy of Sciences of his earlier work on fulminating silver. Among the audience was the great Alexander von Humboldt, who was so much impressed by the young chemist that he introduced him to Gay-Lussac.

Joseph Louis Gay-Lussac (1778–1850), one of the most illustrious of France's many great men of science, was at the same time a romantic figure, adventurous and unconventional. In his earlier years, during the turmoil following the French Revolution, he had occasion one day to enter a draper's shop in Paris. Behind the counter sat a charming girl of seventeen, whom he observed to be reading a book in the intervals between serving customers. Closer observation of a spectacle so pleasing disclosed that the young lady was studying intently a treatise on chemistry. This volume played the part of a catalyst, and sealed the young man's fate. Finding that her formal education had been abandoned as a result of the Revolution, Gay-Lussac packed the captivating Josephine back to school at his own expense: their marriage, which followed in 1808, was remarkably happy and successful. Later in his career, Gay-Lussac rose to be a peer of France.

In Gay-Lussac's private laboratory, to which von Humboldt's introduction gained him speedy admittance, Liebig collaborated with the French savant in a further research on the salts of fulminic acid. The manipulation of these dangerously explosive substances demanded courage, as well as skill and perseverance; but in the end the composition of fulminic acid was established. Gay-Lussac was wont to justify his first name by indulging in a frisky waltz around his laboratory to mark any outstanding success achieved within its walls, and the young Liebig was astonished to find himself called upon to celebrate the outcome of the research on the fulminates in this way with his chief.

The successful work culminating in the Waltz of the Fulminates led to Liebig's appointment in 1824 to the chair of chemistry in the University of Giessen, where he remained for twenty-eight years. When appointed he was only twenty-one, and it is said that his youthfulness gave offence to the more venerable among the professors; time, however, came to his rescue in this matter.

THE DAWN OF A NEW DAY

It was a curious coincidence that the years 1823 and 1824 witnessed the elucidation of the composition of cyanic acid and also of fulminic acid, the first problem being solved by Wöhler in Stockholm and the second by Liebig in Paris. The astonishing conclusion was reached that these two distinct substances have the same ultimate chemical composition: they possess the same elements (carbon, hydrogen, oxygen, and nitrogen) combined together in the same proportions, and yet they exhibit widely different properties. This revolutionary idea was unpalatable to the somewhat rigid Berzelius, until four years later—in 1828—Wöhler showed that a similar relationship exists between ammonium cyanate and urea, and that the first of these substances can actually be transformed into the second. Convinced at last, Berzelius in 1830 coined the word 'isomerism' to denote the new phenomenon. Wöhler's work on urea had an even greater significance, for he had now prepared artificially for the first time one of the most typical products of animal metabolism, thus striking the first blow at the prevailing theory of the operation of an imagined 'vital force' in the production of organic substances.

Meanwhile, Wöhler and Liebig had come so closely together in their work that they began a correspondence in the winter of 1828; then they met at Frankfurt. Collaboration soon followed. In a letter to Liebig, dated 8 June 1829, Wöhler wrote: 'It must surely be some wicked demon that again and again imperceptibly brings us into collision by means of our work, and tries to make the chemical public believe that we purposely seek these apples of discord as opponents. But I think he is not going to succeed. If you are so minded, we might, for the humour of it, undertake some chemical work together, in order that the result might be made known under our joint names. Of course, you would work in Giessen, and I in Berlin, when we are agreed upon the plan, and we could communicate with each other from time to time as to its progress.'

It was in this way that Wöhler became Liebig's lifelong friend and his close collaborator in one of the most significant and harmonious associations to be found in the annals of chemistry. From 1831 until 1836 Wöhler held a teaching post in the Gewerbeschule at Cassel, and it was during this period that Wöhler and Liebig's most important joint publication appeared. Their classical paper entitled 'Untersuchungen über das Radikal der Benzoesäure' ('Researches on the Radical of Benzoic Acid'), which appeared in Liebig's *Annalen der Pharmacie* in 1832, threw the first gleam of light on the puzzling but fundamental problem of organic molecular structure.[1] Berzelius rightly hailed it as the dawn of a new day for organic chemistry, and its opening sentence is equally felicitous: 'When one succeeds in discerning a ray of light shining upon the dark domain of organic nature and possibly marking the entrance to a path of future knowledge, one has reason to take courage, although conscious of the immensity of the field which awaits exploration'.

Altogether, Wöhler and Liebig published fifteen papers in collaboration. The last one of note, dealing with uric acid and a rich array of derived substances, appeared in 1838, following close on the heels of their important work on amygdalin. Thereafter, although they remained on terms of intimate friendship, their chemical interests diverged: Wöhler devoted himself mainly to inorganic chemistry, and Liebig turned to the chemistry of agriculture and physiology.

[1] A review of early work on organic molecular structure is given *e.g.*, in the author's *Text-Book of Organic Chemistry*, London, 1946, p. 40 *et seq.*

Liebig's brilliant researches contributed greatly to the advance of chemical science; but his influence on the development of the whole vast field of chemical endeavour rested to an even greater degree upon his eminence as a teacher. His methods heralded the dawn of yet another new day in chemistry. Unlike Berzelius, Gay-Lussac, and other eminent chemists of their generation, Liebig did not confine his attention to students who had already gained experience. He took in hand also the novices, and taught them systematically in the laboratory as well as in the lecture-room. At Giessen, he provided the first public laboratory for the teaching of experimental chemistry. In the course of a few years the Giessen laboratory became famous; a few years more, and it began to serve as a model for new chemical institutes in Germany and other lands. At Giessen, Liebig had conceived a new system of teaching. He had founded the first real school of chemistry.

In Liebig's own words: 'Actual teaching in the laboratory, of which practical assistants took charge, was only for the beginners; the progress of my special students depended on themselves. I gave the task and supervised its carrying out. There was no actual instruction. Every morning I received from each individual a report on what he had done the previous day, as well as his views about what he was engaged on. I approved or criticised. Everyone was obliged to follow his own course. In the association and constant intercourse with each other, and by each participating in the work of all, everyone learned from the others. Twice a week in winter I gave a sort of review of the more important questions of the day. We worked from break of day till nightfall. Dissipation and amusements were not to be had at Giessen. The only complaint which was continually repeated was that of the attendant [Aubel], who could not get the workers out of the laboratory in the evening when he wanted to clean it.'

The massive influence on nineteenth-century chemistry which Liebig exerted through his pupils may be gauged from a contemplation of such familiar names as Fehling, Frankland, Fresenius, Gerhardt, A. W. Hofmann, Kopp,

Playfair, Regnault, Stenhouse, Strecker, Varrentrapp, Volhard, Will, Williamson, and Wurtz, all of whom passed through the Giessen laboratory and took its inspiration and methods with them into the wider world of chemistry. Moreover, it was through attending Liebig's lectures at Giessen that Kekulé, who had entered the University as a student of architecture, turned from the macroscopic to the molecular aspect of his chosen art.[1]

A drawing made by Trautschold in 1842 (Fig. 58) depicts the Giessen laboratory in full operation. The print was originally entitled 'Life and labour in Justus Liebig's first chemical laboratory at Giessen. Students in the main working-room. After the sketch by Trautschold 1842.' A list of the workers was then given in the following terms: 'No. 1. Ortigosa (Mexican). Nos. 2 and 3. Names unknown. No. 4. Keller. No. 5. Dr. Will, assistant to Liebig, later professor of chemistry and successor to Liebig at Giessen. No. 6. Adolf Strecker, assistant to Liebig, 1860 professor of chemistry at Tübingen and 1870 at Würzburg. No. 7. Aubel, attendant. No. 8. Wydler from Aarau. No. 9. Varrentrapp. No. 10. Scherer, professor. No. 11. Name unknown. No. 12. Emil Böckmann. No. 13. A. W. Hofmann, assistant to Liebig until 1845, later professor of chemistry in Berlin, founder of the German Chemical Society.'[2]

The likeness to a modern laboratory is evident at a glance, perhaps the most striking feature being the appearance at last of benches provided with cupboards, drawers, and shelves for reagent bottles. There is, however, no evidence of heating, or even lighting, by gas. The Bunsen burner had not yet been invented, and the main heating operations were accomplished by using charcoal; this often had to be fanned to promote combustion, and the resulting dust must have been a great handicap in the laboratory.

---

[1] Kekulé's lecture notes, entitled 'Experimentalchemie vorgetragen von Prof. Dr. v. Liebig. 1848 ', and bearing the flyleaf inscription 'A. Kekulé stud. chem.', were reproduced in facsimile many years afterwards (c. 1937). They cover 346 pages, written in a close and beautiful script, with many neat little sketches.

[2] Other notes on the workers shown here are given in F. Ferchl's *Von Libau bis Liebig Chemikerköpfe und -Laboratorien*, Mittenwald, 1930.

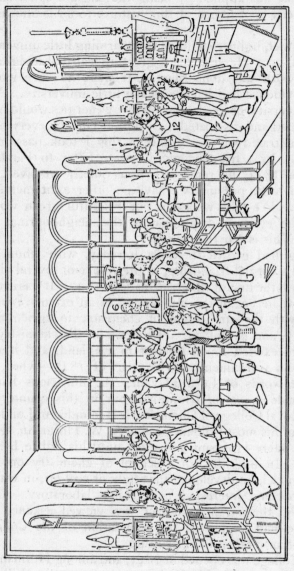

58. Liebig's Laboratory at Giessen, in 1842. Redrawn from the contemporary drawing by Trautschold

Gentle heat was applied by using the Argand spirit lamp. The modern appearance of this historic room is shown in Fig. **59**.

The quiet, unhurried life of the charming little university town in Upper Hesse made a great appeal to Liebig, and his best work was done there. 'It was', he once wrote, 'as if Providence had led me to the little university. At a larger university, or in a larger town, my energies would have been divided and dissipated . . . but at Giessen everything was concentrated on work, and in this I took passionate pleasure.' In a friendly and intimate letter to Faraday, written in 1844, he remarked 'how quietly we live . . . except scientific pursuits we have no other excitements of the mind. We take walks in our beautiful green woods and in the evening drink tea at the neighbouring old castles. This is our recreation.'

Liebig had grown to know Faraday, with whom he cultivated a cordial friendship, in the course of several visits to England, the first of which he made in 1837. It was in this period that he began the publication of an extensive work dealing with the application of chemistry to agriculture, physiology, and pathology. His views on the chemistry of agriculture excited much interest in England, and it was largely as a consequence of his visit of 1842—when, to quote the words of Lord Playfair, 'the illustrious Baron Liebig made a sort of triumphal tour in this country'— that the Royal College of Chemistry was founded in London, with one of his most brilliant pupils, A. W. Hofmann, as its director. Here Hofmann remained until his call to Berlin in 1864. In building up a school of chemistry on the Giessen model, he developed the study of coal tar, in which he had become interested in Liebig's laboratory. Unfortunately, this strange subject was viewed askance by those who had supported the foundation of the College because of an interest in agriculture.

The College was opened in 1845, and among Hofmann's later pupils was W. H. Perkin, sen. (later Sir William Perkin), who entered the College in his fifteenth year. Hofmann had struck a very rich vein. New compounds

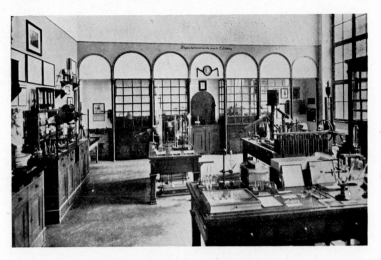

59. Liebig's Laboratory at Giessen, *c.* 1930.

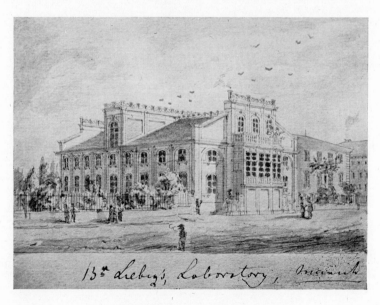

13ᵉ Liebig's Laboratory, Munich

60. Liebig's Laboratory at Munich, in 1855.
From an original drawing, with an inscription by Liebig. (See p. 248.)

R.W.Bunsen, G.Kirchhoff, and H.E.Roscoe
1862

61. Bunsen, Kirchhoff, and Roscoe, 1862.

From *The Life and Experiences of Sir Henry Enfield Roscoe*, London, 1906.
(See p. 252.)

simply tumbled out of the test-tubes and beakers. Almost every experiment led to something fresh. Perkin records that one day Hofmann came to look at a steam distillate which one of the students had obtained from nitrated phenol. 'Taking a little of the substance in a watch glass, he treated it with caustic alkali, and at once obtained a beautiful scarlet salt of what we now know to be ortho-nitrophenol. Several of us were standing by at the time, and, looking at us in his characteristic and enthusiastic way, he at once exclaimed, "Gentlemen, new bodies are *floating* in the air".'

It was soon after this, in the Easter vacation of 1856, that Perkin, then a lad of eighteen, discovered 'aniline purple', or 'mauve', working as he said 'in my rough laboratory at home'. This was the genesis of the great coal-tar dye industry. Still another new day had dawned in chemistry.

Meanwhile, in 1836, Wöhler had moved from Cassel to Göttingen, where he succeeded Stromeyer in the chair of chemistry; here, in the famous University founded by George II, he remained until his death nearly fifty years later, in 1882. At Göttingen, Wöhler developed a school of chemistry second only in renown to that of Liebig at Giessen. Like Liebig, he afforded his pupils a thorough training in all branches of the science; by his own teaching and through his many eminent pupils he exerted a great influence on the progress of chemistry. It is said that in his first twenty-one years at Göttingen more than eight thousand students attended Wöhler's lectures or worked in his laboratory.

One of the most distinguished of his later students, Otto Wallach (who succeeded Victor Meyer in the Göttingen chair in 1889), entered Wöhler's laboratory in 1867. Life was then very strenuous, for the laboratory hours lasted from seven o'clock in the morning until five o'clock in the afternoon; and although the gas was then turned off, 'after that hour, in winter, many operations had to be finished by the scanty light of candles which the students had brought with them'. Wallach records also that 'in Wöhler's laboratory indolence was not tolerated: anyone

s

who did not occupy his working place regularly must expect to receive from the *Hofrat* a letter summoning him to vacate it'.

Liebig's activities at Giessen and Wöhler's at Göttingen coincided in time over a period of sixteen years, until Liebig's translation to Munich in 1852 (Fig. **60**). The close friendship of these two paladins of chemistry flourished without interruption until Justus von Liebig's death in 1873. In a celebrated passage dealing with that friendship, Hofmann contrasted the fiery and impetuous temperament of Liebig, 'seizing a new thought with enthusiasm', with the calm deliberation and immovable equanimity of Wöhler, 'entering upon a fresh problem after full reflection'. Both of them followed the path of enquiry in their several ways, remarked Hofmann, and both were animated by the same intense love of truth. 'Can we marvel', he concluded, 'that between two such natures, so differently ordered, and yet so complementary, there should ripen a friendship which both should reckon as the greatest gain of their lives?'

A GOLDEN AGE AT HEIDELBERG

When Wöhler left the Gewerbeschule of Cassel for Göttingen, in 1836, he was succeeded at Cassel by a young man named Robert Wilhelm Bunsen (1811–1899), who was destined to achieve a reputation exceeding even that of his illustrious predecessor. 'The value of a life devoted to original scientific work is measured by the new paths and new fields which such work opens out', wrote Roscoe. 'In this respect, the labours of Robert Wilhelm Bunsen stand second to those of no chemist of his time.' This great figure in nineteenth-century chemistry enjoyed the friendship of such seniors and contemporaries as Berzelius, Gay-Lussac, Dumas, Wöhler, and Liebig; he linked the past with the future through becoming the master of a galaxy of eminent pupils, among whom are reckoned men like Baeyer, Beilstein, Bernthsen, Carius, Curtius, Erlenmeyer, Friedländer, Graebe, Ladenburg, Victor Meyer, Roscoe, Sprengel, T. E. Thorpe, Treadwell, Wanklyn, and dozens of other chemists of high distinction. His active labours in the cause of chemistry extended over a period of nearly sixty years: 'living to the ripe age of 88', says Roscoe, 'in his later years, Bunsen stood alone in his glory'.

After graduating in 1830 at Göttingen, his birthplace, Bunsen visited Paris, Berlin, and Vienna, making the acquaintance of men of science in these three capitals, and then returned to Göttingen as a *Privatdozent*[1] in 1834. Two years later he succeeded Wöhler at Cassel; from 1839 to 1851 he occupied the chair of chemistry at Marburg; finally, after a short time at Breslau, he was invited to succeed Gmelin at Heidelberg, at that time the Mecca of German studentry:

> *Alt Heidelberg, du feine,*
> *Du Stadt an Ehren reich,*
> *Am Neckar und am Rheine*
> *Kein' and're kommt dir gleich.*[2]

Here, in the ancient and renowned Ruperto-Carola Universität, Bunsen remained in active work for a period of almost forty years, from 1852 until his retirement in 1889.

Much of our knowledge of Bunsen as a man is due to the celebrated English chemist, Sir Henry Roscoe, who passed from the status of a pupil to that of an intimate friend, and maintained a close and cordial relationship with his former master over a space of nearly fifty years. Roscoe has left a description of his first meeting with Bunsen, in 1853, at Heidelberg: 'I shall never forget the first sight of the man who afterwards became one of my most intimate and valued friends, and to whom I owe more than I can tell. At that time, Bunsen was at the height of his powers, physical and mental; he stood fully six feet high, his figure was well knit and powerful, his manner was one of suave dignity, whilst his expression was that of great kindliness

---

[1] An unsalaried member of the teaching staff, receiving certain fees from students.

[2] In free translation, this opening verse of the famous student-song may be rendered as follows:

> Old Heidelberg so fine,
> Dear city, honour'd name,
> On Neckar and on Rhine
> None other hath like fame.

and of rare intelligence.' Roscoe summed up some of Bunsen's other leading characteristics in the words: 'His was a heart free from guile, guiding a temper equable and amiable. . . . Simple and straightforward, he disliked assumption and hated duplicity; single-minded and wholly devoted to his science, he abhorred vanity and despised popularity-hunting. . . . Another and a remarkable trait in his character was his keen sense of humour.' Anything in the nature of ostentation was foreign to his temperament, and he was rarely to be seen at public functions, even academic ones.

Heinrich Debus, writing of Bunsen's earlier period at Marburg, described him as a man of abstemious habits, who seldom drank wine but rarely allowed his cigar to go out. He took his *Mittagessen* at the sign of 'The Knight' (*Gasthaus Zum Ritter*), where this midday meal of three courses and dessert cost only 70 pfennig. Here, according to the old German custom, Robert Schwaner, the Falstaffian host, presided at a long table, with his regular professors, lecturers, and assistants arranged to right and left in strict order of precedence, these being followed by other guests. At this picturesque table Debus records that he met many famous men, including Mitscherlich, Graham, and Hofmann.

It was a strange laboratory to which Bunsen succeeded at Heidelberg. Occupying remnants of the buildings of an ancient monastery, it brought back faint memories of Roger Bacon, Berthold Schwarz, Basil Valentine, and other monkish labourers—real or imaginary—in the cause of alchemy. 'The old refectory was the main laboratory, the chapel was divided into two, one half became the lecture-room and the other a storehouse and museum', wrote Roscoe. 'The cloisters were enclosed by windows and working benches placed below them. Beneath the stone floor at our feet slept the dead monks, and on their tomb-stones we threw our waste precipitates! There was no gas in Heidelberg in those days; nor any town's water supply. We worked with Berzelius' spirit-lamps, made our combustions with charcoal, boiled down our wash-waters from our silicate analyses in large glass globes over charcoal fires, and went for water to the pump in the yard. Nevertheless, with all these so-called drawbacks, we were able to work easily and accurately.'

Roscoe was among the last to work in this picturesque and romantic laboratory, for in 1855 a new laboratory built for Bunsen by the government of Baden was opened in the Plöck Strasse. Gas-lighting had now reached Heidelberg, and this innovation led to Bunsen's invention of the 'Bunsen burner' for his new building. Bunsen's inventive mind and manipulative skill found its most useful expression in this indispensable adjunct of modern civilisation. His practical ingenuity may also be discerned in his elegant gasometric methods (1838–1845), the carbon-zinc cell (1841), the grease-spot photometer (1844), and the water filter-pump (1868). Even so late as 1887, Bunsen devised a new vapour calorimeter, so original in conception and accurate in performance as to constitute a remarkable achievement for a man of seventy-six. 'Before Bunsen gave a piece of apparatus to the chemical world,' wrote Sir Edward Thorpe, 'he left it practically perfect; the striving after perfection was a veritable passion with him.'

Roscoe has expressed the pleasure experienced by those who worked with Bunsen in the laboratory: 'Entirely devoted to his students, as they were to him, he spent all day in the laboratory, showing them with his own hands how best to carry out the various operations in which they were engaged. . . . Often you would find him seated at the table blow-pipe [with foot-bellows]—the flame in those days was fed with oil—making some new piece of glass apparatus, for he was an expert glass blower, and enjoyed showing the men how to seal platinum wires into the eudiometers, or to blow bulb-tubes for his iodometric analyses.' In the laboratory, wrote Debus, Bunsen was always accessible to any of his students, and he devoted himself particularly to the weak and backward ones.

Bunsen's first serious research was the classical one on the cacodyl compounds, begun at Cassel in 1837 and lasting for some six years. Berzelius—who had now risen to the dignity of a baron—characterised this work 'at once so important and so dangerous', as 'a foundation stone of the theory of compound radicals': it supported Liebig in his definition of organic chemistry, in 1843, as the chemistry of compound radicals, and brought Bunsen into the front rank of experimentalists.

Roscoe's own work with Bunsen, extending from 1855 to 1863, consisted of a series of studies on the chemical action of light. In 1857 Roscoe was appointed to succeed Frankland in the chair of chemistry at Owens College, Manchester; but at that time he used to spend his summers in Heidelberg, where there was always a bed at his disposal in Bunsen's bachelor establishment. A period of intensive work was then usually followed in the autumn by an excursion with Bunsen, together with Kirchhoff (Fig. 61) or Häuser, the historian, into the Bavarian highlands, Switzerland, or Tyrol; for Bunsen was a good walker, with a keen appreciation of nature; travel was his chief relaxation.

The first place among Bunsen's many and diverse researches is taken by his work on spectrum analysis. In a letter dated 15 November 1859, he told Roscoe of 'a most beautiful and most unexpected discovery' made by his colleague and collaborator, Kirchhoff: 'He has found out the cause of the dark lines in the solar spectrum, and has been able both to strengthen these lines artificially in the solar spectrum, and to cause their appearance in a continuous spectrum of a flame, their position being identical with those of the Fraunhofer's lines. Thus the way is pointed out by which the material composition of the sun and fixed stars can be ascertained. . . . By this method, too, the composition of terrestrial matter can be ascertained, and the component parts distinguished. . . . Thus, if you have a mixture of Li, Ka, Na, Ba, Sr, Ca, all you need to do is to bring a milligram of the mixture in our apparatus in order to be able to ascertain the presence of all the above substances by mere observation . . . it is possible to detect 5/1000 of a milligram of lithium with the greatest ease and certainty, and I have discovered the presence of this metal in almost every sample of potashes.'

Soon afterwards Bunsen discovered two new alkali metals, caesium (1860) and rubidium (1861). On 6 November 1860 he wrote to Roscoe: 'I am calling the new metal "cæsium", from "cæsius" blue, on account of the splendid blue line in its spectrum. Next Sunday I hope to find time to make the first determination of the atomic weight.'

Bunsen's strong sense of practical values was also evident in his lectures on general chemistry, which he delivered every weekday, at 8 A.M. in the summer and 9 A.M. in the winter. He performed all the lecture experiments himself, and paid much attention to preliminary rehearsals. Although his own work played a great part in the development of chemical theory, Bunsen devoted little time in his lectures to the discussion of theoretical questions. 'His mind', said Roscoe, 'was eminently practical; he often used to say that one chemical fact properly established was worth more than all the theories one could invent.' He did not lean upon the work of others. On one occasion, at Marburg, Debus was about to undertake a research on the colouring matter of the madder root, when Dr. Genth, an assistant in the laboratory, advised him to read through all the publications on the subject before beginning work at the bench. 'Nein,' interjected Bunsen, 'lesen Sie Nichts!' ('No, read nothing!') Debus comments that it was some time before he learnt to appreciate the true inwardness of this illuminating remark.

This great chemist, 'so kindly modest, all accomplished, wise', was also a man of wit and humour, endowed with a rich humanity; so that it is fitting to end our glance at the golden age of Bunsen in Heidelberg with a characteristic anecdote bearing upon his lectures and bringing back a vision of the chapel of the ancient monastery. Although attendance at such lectures was not compulsory, the lecturer was often called upon to append his signature to certificates of attendance needed by students for formal purposes. Considerable latitude was shown in this matter, and Bunsen was wont to sign the proffered card with the good-natured endorsement, 'mit ausgezeichnetem Fleiss' ('with marked industry').

At the end of one of his courses, however, as Roscoe relates, a certain applicant impressed Bunsen by his completely unfamiliar appearance. 'Aber, Herr Dingskirch,' expostulated Bunsen, glancing from the familiar card to the unfamiliar applicant, 'ich habe Sie in der Vorlesung gar nicht gesehen' ('But, Mr. Dingskirch, I've never seen you at a lecture'). 'Ja, Herr Geheimerath,' came the plausible reply, 'ich sitze aber immer hinter dem Pfeiler' ('Quite so, Herr Geheimerath; but, you see, I always sit behind the pillar'). Bunsen shook his head sadly, as he remarked: 'Ach, da sitzen so viele' ('Ah, what a lot of you sit there!'). So saying, he signed the certificate, and endorsed it—'mit ausgezeichnetem Fleiss'.

BAEYER AND MUNICH

When Liebig migrated from Giessen to Munich in 1852, the Giessen laboratory lost its fame as a centre of research. However, it could not have been said that what was Giessen's loss was Munich's gain; for at Munich Liebig's interest in experimental research evaporated, and he made no effort to cultivate the Giessen tradition on Bavarian soil. It was as if in this larger university and town he could no longer concentrate his energies (p. 246). The pre-eminence hitherto enjoyed by Giessen now passed to Heidelberg, and so Bunsen's laboratory became the Mecca of aspiring young chemists from all over the world.

One of the early arrivals in the new Heidelberg laboratory, opened in 1855, was a young man from Berlin named Adolf Baeyer (1835–1917). Here, among others, he met Roscoe, Lothar Meyer, Lieben, and Beilstein. To begin with, Baeyer helped Bunsen and Roscoe in some of their experiments on the combination of chlorine and hydrogen in sunlight. Being, however, attracted to organic chemistry, which had now become of subsidiary interest to Bunsen, the young Baeyer attached himself to Kekulé, then a *Privatdozent* at Heidelberg. In a way reminiscent of Berzelius, Kekulé had created a makeshift laboratory in a room and kitchen of a rented house, and it was here that Baeyer worked for about two years and discovered arsenic methyl chloride, in an investigation which gained him the Berlin doctorate in 1858.

After spending some years as a teacher of organic chemistry at the Gewerbe-Institut in Berlin, Baeyer was called to the Strassburg chair in 1872, and three years later he succeeded Liebig at Munich. Here his first task was to provide the adequate laboratory accommodation that Liebig had so strangely neglected, and the fine building opened in 1877 served for a long time as a model for other laboratories.

Baeyer's exceptional talent as an investigator in organic chemistry now became apparent, and Munich rose to the premier position as a school of organic chemical research. His work on phthaleins was succeeded by the classical researches on indigo and its derivatives, which W. H. Perkin, jun., characterised as 'among the most brilliant in the whole range of organic analysis and synthesis'. The ensuing work on polyacetylene derivatives led to the development of the famous 'Spannungs Theorie', or 'Strain Theory', of cyclic compounds. Between 1884 and 1893 Baeyer's researches on aromatic and hydroaromatic compounds, bound up in turn with his sustained interest in succinylsuccinic ester, led to a development of new views on aromatic characteristics and to the centric formula for benzene, also advanced by H. E. Armstrong. In this way Baeyer was moved to undertake a systematic reduction of the phthalic acids, investigations which Perkin later considered 'so masterly in all their details that they must always remain as a monument to Baeyer's experimental skill and theoretical ability'.

From the work on succinylsuccinic ester sprang also the first synthesis of a terpene, dihydrocymene, $C_{10}H_{16}$. With this achievement, Baeyer entered 'fresh Woods, and Pastures new', and between 1893 and 1899 he published a pioneering series of investigations on the terpenes, recorded in twenty-five papers in the *Berichte*. Then, at the age of sixty-five, in 1900, he opened yet another new and fruitful field of researches on peroxides and oxonium salts.

Baeyer, like Bunsen, was a striking example of the classical genius in chemistry. He continued his original work to a ripe old age: his first paper was published in Liebig's *Annalen* of 1857 and his last, at the age of eighty, in the *Annalen* of 1915. His final paper, in Perkin's words, 'contains the first description of the oxonium colouring matters . . . and this brilliant piece of theoretical and experimental work shows that Baeyer retained his great powers as a thinker and investigator to the last'.

Baeyer's enormous influence on the development of organic chemistry was not limited to the results of his own investigations, great as these were. A still wider effect of this eminent investigator and teacher was exerted through the constant stream of distinguished young chemists passing from his laboratories to the outer world. British chemistry, for example, owes a considerable indirect debt to Baeyer through his illustrious pupil, W. H. Perkin, jun.

After obtaining his doctorate under Johannes Wislicenus at Würzburg in 1882, Perkin spent about four years at Munich, where he qualified as a *Privatdozent*. Among his contemporaries with Baeyer were Otto Fischer, Königs, Friedländer, Bamberger, Curtius, and von Pechmann. Perkin, to whom Baeyer became 'the object of a lifelong intellectual devotion', regarded him as the founder of modern structural organic chemistry.

Perkin has left it on record that Baeyer's real joy was in his laboratory, that he deplored any outside work which took him away from his bench, and that 'he would have been horrified at the waste of time and energy, due to attendance at committees and other meetings, which would seem to be an essential part of the routine of heads of Chemical Departments in this country'. In spite of his vast output of original work, Baeyer's collaborators were by no means numerous; as a rule he delegated the supervision of *Doktoranden*, and the suggestion of their research topics, to his *Privatdozenten*. Nevertheless he made a daily round of the research laboratories, chatting with the workers, criticising their results, admiring their new compounds, and making it 'out of the question for any one to forget for a moment that research was the only thing that really mattered'.

HUMOUR AND HUMANISM IN BAEYER'S LABORATORY

To Professor Hans Rupe, of the University of Basel, in Switzerland, who entered the private laboratory at Munich as assistant to Baeyer in 1891, we owe some intimate glimpses of contemporary life in that famous centre of chemical research, and of the Master who was its dominating figure.

At that time the great indigo problem had been solved, but the classical work on the reduction of the phthalic acids was in full swing. These investigations, so well known in the abstract because of their bearing upon the constitution of benzene, take on at once a rich vesture of human interest to the reader of Rupe's delightful reminiscences. The work was beset with difficulties. At one time, for example, during the intensive search for dihydrophthalic acids, gigantic quantities of sodium amalgam, up to forty kilograms a week, were prepared and used in vain. Rupe remarks with feeling that the situation became very disagreeable to the assistants. It must have been, indeed, a 'schwere, scheussliche und gefährliche Arbeit' ('heavy, hideous and hazardous task'); but no labour was too tedious for the Master and his band of devoted helpers. There was, as Rupe says, something of the magnificent in this prolonged contest with matter.

Eventually, however, even Baeyer was supersaturated with these hydrogenations ('übersättigt von diesen Hydrierungsarbeiten'), and the sorely tried assistants hailed with deep relief the transference of his interest to succinylsuccinic ester and diketocyclohexane. By means of a dodge ('Kunstgriff') of which Baeyer was very proud (treatment with sodium amalgam in presence of sodium bicarbonate), the diketone was reduced to quinitol. At the first glimpse of the crystals of the new substance Baeyer ceremoniously raised his hat!

It must be explained here that the Master's famous greenish-black hat plays the part of a perpetual epithet in

Rupe's narrative. As the celebrated sword-pommel to Paracelsus, so this romantic hard-hitter or 'alte Melone' to Baeyer: the former was said to contain the vital mercury of the mediaeval philosophers; the latter certainly enshrined one of the keenest chemical intellects of the modern world. Hats are not associated as a rule with chemical research, although it is true that Trautschold's illustration (Fig. 58) shows the striking variety of headgear which was to be seen in Liebig's laboratory at Giessen in 1842: these choice pieces, although perhaps not including an 'alte Melone', ranged from the postman's cap of Ortigosa the Mexican through the tam-o'-shanter of his unnamed neighbour to the stylish topper favoured by A. W. Hofmann. Two wearers of toppers are also shown on a balcony in a drawing of Liebig's laboratory at Munich in 1855 (Fig. 60). So perhaps the tradition of laboratory hats descended from Liebig to Baeyer. However that may be, Baeyer's head was normally covered. Only in moments of unusual excitement or elation did 'the Chef' remove his hat: apart from such occasions his shiny pate remained in permanent eclipse.

When, for example, the analysis of the important diacetylquinitol was found to be correct, Baeyer raised his hat in silent exultation. Soon afterwards the first specimen of dihydrobenzene was prepared, by heating dibromohexamethylene with quinoline: Baeyer ran excitedly to and fro in the laboratory, flourishing the 'alte Melone' and exclaiming: 'Jetzt haben wir das erste Terpen, die Stammsubstanz der Terpene!' ('Here we have the first terpene, the root-substance of the terpene series!'). Such is the glimpse from behind the scenes of the dramatic way in which the Master entered upon his famous investigations on terpenes.

Incidents of this kind may appear to be slight, and yet cumulatively they throw a stream of light upon the personality of this great chemist. There is no doubt, for example, that at times 'the Chef' was unduly impulsive. One morning he burst into the private laboratory and, without having lit his cigar (an indication in itself of unusual emotional disturbance), raised the ancient 'Melone' twice, and exclaimed: 'Gentlemen [the audience was composed

of Claisen and Brüning], I have just had word from Emil
Fischer that he has brought off the complete synthesis of
glucose. This heralds the end of organic chemistry: let's
finish off the terpenes, and only the smears ['Schmieren']
will be left!' Rupe's reminiscences are rich in snapshots of
this kind, which are often more revealing than pages of
formal description could be.

Baeyer's customary tools were test-tubes, watch-glasses,
and glass rods. As an example of his endless patience,
Willstätter relates having seen him keep a test-tube in
gentle play over a flame for three-quarters of an hour when
activating magnesium with iodine. He valued at least three
things which were deemed of fundamental importance by
the alchemists: for he impressed upon his students that the
essential requirements of the chemist are patience, money,
and reticence.

Since Baeyer favoured the use of simple apparatus, the
introduction into his laboratory of any device savouring of
complexity had to be undertaken with great tact. The first
mechanical stirrers, worked by water-turbines, were
smuggled in one evening. On the following morning, 'der
Alte' ('the Old Man') beheld them in full working order.
For a time he affected to ignore them; then he contemplated
them unwillingly, with an air of challenge; next came the
first remark, so anxiously awaited: 'Geht denn das?'
'Jawohl, Herr Professor, ausgezeichnet, die Reduktionen
sind schon bald fertig' ('Is it working then?' 'Oh yes, Herr
Professor, splendidly—the reductions are already about
finished').

The Herr Professor was finally so greatly impressed that
he took the exceptional step of summoning the Frau
Professor from the adjoining residence. 'Die Lydia' ('The
Lydia'), as she was known informally in the laboratory, stood
by the merrily clattering apparatus for a while, lost in silent
admiration. Then she uttered these unforgettable words:
'Damit müsste man gut Mayonnaise machen können!'
('What a lovely idea for making mayonnaise!'). Truly a
great deal depends upon one's point of view!

Rupe's charming account affords glimpses also of the

personnel surrounding 'the Chef'. Among them, Herr Leonhard, the old Bavarian factotum inherited by Baeyer from Liebig, stands out by reason of his liberal attitude towards the ethics of lecture demonstrations. Upon occasion he triumphed over his scruples to 'help' his experiments in their constant fight against the malignity of matter ('Tücke des Objektes')—that bane of the whole tribe of lecture-assistants—as witness his dry reply to a remark upon the difficulty of making chloroform from alcohol and bleaching powder: 'Wissens Herr Doktor, dös Chloroform, dös is schon do herinnen, do feit si nix'. In other words, there was no need for the Herr Doktor to anticipate failure, as Herr Leonhard had already staved off that possibility by calmly putting some ready-made chloroform into the generating flask!

There was also the old *Laboratoriumdiener*, or laboratory assistant, whom Baeyer had brought with him from Strassburg. Carl Gimmig, a veteran zouave of the war of 1870, who had been captured by the Germans at Metz, was known in particular for his compelling six-o'clock cry: 'Ihr Herre, s'isch Zeit!' ('Time, gentlemen!'). If the workers lingered, Carl remorselessly turned off the gas at the main and became 'terribly evident'. Sometimes it fell to Carl to clean a hundred test-tubes at the end of a morning's activity in the private laboratory, but he consoled himself by referring in his Alsatian dialect to the days of the researches on indigo, when the number had often mounted to four hundred.

There is, too, in Rupe's memoir, an instantaneous snapshot of a 'filia hospitalis' of the laboratory, the fair daughter of Herr Inspektor Fehl, who as chief of the laboratory staff lived in the chemical institute; but of her it may be said, as of her prototype in the song so beloved of the old-time German studentry, that 'die Füsschen laufen wie der Wind' ('her little feet run like the wind') off these attractive pages.

Baeyer's lectures, in which he took great pleasure, were mostly elementary courses, and were marked by clearness and simplicity of diction, with occasional delicate touches of

North German humour or sarcasm. He urged his listeners to think in terms of phenomena; and, like Kekulé, he emphasised the importance of giving occasional rein to the imagination: 'so viele Chemiker haben nicht genügend Phantasie' ('so many chemists are lacking in imagination'), he used to say.

Rupe relates that Baeyer was not often seen at that time in the teaching laboratories. Sometimes, however, hat on head and wearing his long indigo-blue 'cutaway', he would stride through the rooms, holding himself erect with a set look on his face, 'every inch a king'. Then, conversation was suddenly stilled, and everybody busied himself behind his bench. But although 'the Chef' was often regarded as the 'stiff Prussian', unapproachable and severe, he was in reality a kindly man who did much good by stealth. He was free from vanity; and, unlike many men of learning, he was always ready to acknowledge ungrudgingly the merits of others.

Baeyer was often represented as a stern and forbidding examiner, but this impression seems to have been based largely upon his uncomfortable mannerisms: he invariably turned his back upon the candidate, and if the answer lingered he would begin to tap impatiently upon the table with his pencil.

On one occasion, as Rupe relates, a pharmaceutical candidate appeared in the private laboratory, known to such victims as the 'lead chamber', for his oral examination in inorganic and analytical chemistry. He had already failed twice, and this was his last chance. He was very poor, very industrious, and had a good practical record; but he was a martyr to examination fright ('Examensangst') and completely devoid of self-confidence. When Baeyer heard of this his heart was touched, and he said that he would do what he could. The candidate came in, pale and trembling, and after a friendly greeting 'der Alte' took his seat with him at the table and promptly turned his back upon him.

The candidate survived the first few questions. Then followed a stereotyped question on the analysis of ferrous compounds, which everybody had to answer. 'What do you need for it?' 'Potassium permanganate, Herr Professor,' came after a little hesitation. 'Good, what else?' A pause. The Professor began to get impatient, the candidate looked round in despair, and the ominous tapping of the pencil began. A couple of moments more, and the aspirant's name would be lost to the list of Bavarian apothecaries for ever.

'Then', proceeds Rupe's narrative, 'I took the large stock-bottle bearing the label SULPHURIC ACID from its place, and held it towards the poor culprit. Baeyer had his back to me also, and I sent up an urgent prayer to Heaven that "the Chef" would not turn round and that the candidate might not be so demoralised as to make this help come too late.

'Suddenly a gleam of understanding appeared on his face, and at the very last moment he came out with : "Sulphuric acid, Herr Professor." "Ah, yes, you know it well enough," and since the candidate was now able to write out the equation correctly—he had suddenly acquired confidence —he was allowed to depart in peace; and soon afterwards he completed his qualification. But it was evident that he had not guarded his tongue, for from that time onwards I stood in the highest regard of the whole pharmaceutical brotherhood of Munich. I intended later to confess to Baeyer, but no opportunity occurred. He never learned of this incident.'

May those who hold the mistaken view that chemistry is a subject utterly devoid of human interest seek a truer orientation in this matter from such writings as Rupe's sparkling reminiscences of life and labour in the laboratory of Adolf von Baeyer.

WERNER AND ZÜRICH

The research schools founded in the nineteenth century by such eminent chemists as Liebig, Wöhler, Bunsen, and Baeyer attracted enthusiastic students from many countries. This state of affairs continued into the early years of the twentieth century, and up to the outbreak of the war of 1914–1918 it was a common practice for ambitious young British and American chemists to undertake post-graduate

62. Alfred Werner, 1866–1919 (c. 1907).
(See p. 264.)

Das alte chemische Laboratorium an der Rämistrasse.

63. University Chemical Laboratory, Zürich, *c.* 1907.
(See p. 265.)

64. 'The Catacombs' at Zürich.
(See p. 266.)

work in one of the Continental laboratories, under a recognised master of the branch of chemistry in which they were particularly interested. Many of the most popular schools were in Germany, but there were others in France, Switzerland, Austria, Sweden, Denmark, Holland, and Belgium, in which English-speaking students were to be found. The choice of a place of study and research was determined by the attraction of the master rather than by other circumstances, such as the situation of the school or the character of the laboratory accommodation.

Soon after leaving the Finsbury Technical College, London, I found myself, in October 1905, at Zürich, in Switzerland, working as a *Doktorand*, or student for the degree of Doctor of Philosophy, under Alfred Werner (1866–1919). This great chemical genius and inspiring teacher was then in the plenitude of his power, although he had not as yet reached the height of his fame. Born in a humble environment at Mulhouse in Alsace, Werner evinced from an early age a natural and instinctive aptitude for chemistry. After surmounting initial difficulties he succeeded, in 1886, in entering the Eidgenössisches Polytechnikum[1] at Zürich, an educational institution of great fame, in which he studied under Hantzsch and Lunge. In 1889, at the age of twenty-three, he suggested to Hantzsch a tetrahedral configuration for the nitrogen atom in oximes, thus opening his epoch-making contributions to stereochemistry, or space chemistry, a growing science owing its inception to Pasteur some forty years earlier and by this time firmly established upon Le Bel and van 't Hoff's theory of molecular configuration (1874).

After spending a year in Paris as a student under Marcelin Berthelot, Werner returned to Zürich, and in 1893 entered upon a meteoric career of the romantic type with the publication entitled *Beiträge zur Konstitution anorganischer Verbindungen* ('Contributions to the Constitution of

---

[1] The English rendering, 'Federal Polytechnic', does scant justice to the adjective, which refers to the 'comrades of the oath' of confederation: a romantic account of the swearing of the original oath by representatives of the cantons of Schwyz, Uri, and Unterwalden, at night on the Rütli, overlooking the Vierwaldstättersee (Lake of Lucerne), is given in Schiller's beautiful play, *Wilhelm Tell*.

T

Inorganic Compounds'): in this historic paper he laid the foundations of his celebrated Coordination Theory of valency and chemical constitution. In the same year he succeeded Victor Merz in the chair of chemistry at the University of Zürich.

Werner (Fig. **62**) was thus enabled during the next twenty-five years, with the aid of a host of practical collaborators, to work out the details of his new theory, the wide scope of which he indicated in a work published in 1905 under the title *Neuere Anschauungen auf dem Gebiete der anorganischen Chemie* ('Newer Views in the Field of Inorganic Chemistry'). These views had a profound effect upon the development of chemical systemisation, besides foreshadowing the electronic theory of valency.

The climax of Werner's work came in 1911, when— after many abortive attempts—he succeeded at last in resolving a coordinated cobaltic compound, $\left[\begin{array}{c} Cl \\ NH_3 \end{array} Co \ en_2 \right] X_2$, into optically active components. This was a stereochemical achievement of the first order, confirming the octahedral environment of the central metallic atom. Many other optical resolutions of a great variety of coordination compounds followed; so that Morgan was able to write, in 1920: 'the spatial configuration of the co-ordination complex with six associating units is now as firmly established as that of the asymmetric tetrahedral carbon atom'.

Werner's position as a great creative genius in chemistry was recognised by the award to him, in 1913, of the Nobel Prize for Chemistry. Altogether he published 169 research papers, the first with Hantzsch in 1890 and the last with Karrer in 1917. Besides special articles and publications, he wrote two authoritative books (*Lehrbuch der Stereochemie* 1904, and *Neuere Anschauungen* 1905). To complete the tale of his enormous output of work, it must be added that no fewer than two hundred *Doktoranden* published dissertations for the doctorate, embodying work conducted under his immediate supervision.

With its two institutions of higher learning, the University and the Eidgenössisches Polytechnikum, Zürich has a deserved reputation as a great educational centre. In the first decade of the twentieth century a veritable constellation of chemists of high standing engaged the attention of the student choosing Zürich as his centre of activity. In the University were to be found Werner, Pfeiffer, Abeljanz, and Grün, and in the handsome modern chemical laboratories of the Polytechnikum the greater variety of teachers included Lunge, Treadwell, Bamberger, Gnehm, Willstätter, Grand-mougin, Constam, Berl, Schmidlin, and Kaufler. Werner had succeeded Merz in the old laboratory on the Rämistrasse (Fig. **63**), which had been used until 1887 as the chemical institute of the Polytechnikum; and here, amidst the most unpromising surroundings, he carried out the greater part of the work which made him famous.

This old building, although sadly lacking in accommodation and equipment, was already rich in chemical achievement; for it was within its walls that the brilliant and ill-fated Victor Meyer (1848–1897) had spent his most productive years. Meyer, one of Bunsen's most distinguished pupils, had left Heidelberg in 1868 to work at organic chemistry in Baeyer's small but famous laboratory in the Gewerbe-Institut at Berlin. Later, in 1872, he was called in his twenty-fourth year from a post on Fehling's staff at the Stuttgart Polytechnic to succeed Johannes Wislicenus at Zürich, as Professor Ordinarius and Director of the Chemical Laboratory of the Eidgenössisches Polytechnikum. Between 1872 and 1885, in the laboratory on the Rämistrasse, he conducted his classical researches on nitroparaffins, discovered ketoximes and aldoximes, and devised his method of determining vapour density; here, too, he made what was perhaps his most spectacular discovery—that of thiophen (p. 221). Even in those days, the laboratory facilities were inadequate, and in Meyer's celebrated pyrochemical investigations on the halogens and various gaseous compounds the only room available was so small that the temperature frequently rose to 50° (122° F.).[1]

---

[1] According to a Zürich tradition, Victor Meyer used to keep on his desk a specimen of diphenylmethane: this hydrocarbon, melting at 26·5° C. (80° F.), marked the transition temperature between work in the laboratory and recreation in the Lake, if it became liquid on a summer morning by ten o'clock!

In 1885, Meyer followed Hübner at Göttingen, and finally, in 1889, succeeded his old chief, Bunsen, at Heidelberg. During Meyer's thirteen years at Zürich, about 130 original papers and memoirs had found their way into chemical literature from the little low building on the Rämistrasse.

In spite of the historical associations of this laboratory (with which, moreover, most of those who worked in it were probably unacquainted), the first sight of its gloomy and untidy interior was enough to strike dismay into the heart of the most enthusiastic *Doktorand*. The best accommodation in the building was reserved for students undergoing training in medicine and teaching, and in analytical work. The *Doktoranden* were housed in sunless cellars and basements which needed artificial light even at midday in the bright Swiss summer. These quarters reeked of pyridine. Arrangements for heating and ventilating were rudimentary. All chemicals, reagents, and solvents, with the exception of washing-soda, commercial acids, and distilled water (sometimes of dubious antecedents), had to be bought at the basement store or from a Kahlbaum agency in the city; even common apparatus could often be borrowed only with difficulty from the gruff Swiss storekeeper and laboratory attendant, the Herr Widmer, owing to the limited stock available.

The basement rooms used as research laboratories were known familiarly among the *Doktoranden* as 'Die Katakomben' ('The Catacombs'). It was in the largest of these underground cellars (Fig. **64**) that a would-be *Doktorand* was usually given some practical exercises to perform, in order to afford Werner an opportunity of assessing his ability.[1] Later, the fortunate *Doktorand* was promoted to one of the smaller rooms opening off the central passage of this subterranean microcosm, and generally accommodating four or five workers (Fig. **65**).

Continental students in those days, particularly in Germany and Austria, were traditionally attracted to teachers

---

[1] The author's initial working-place was at the bench with the worker's back to the window on the right (Fig. **64**).

rather than to teaching institutions; owing to this circumstance, and to freedom of migration from one university to another, the *Doktoranden* in Werner's school came from a great diversity of countries and academic centres. Many of them, in their tales of peregrinations, reminded one of the wandering students of mediaeval times. To rub shoulders with men of such diverse origins and experiences was an education in itself.

In person, Werner was a man of heavy build, broad-shouldered and somewhat stocky. His head was massive and well-formed, with a great width from eye to ear. His features were rather stern, sometimes even grim, in repose; but when he was in the right mood, responding perhaps to a new result at the bench, a singularly charming smile would sometimes irradiate his face and light up his eyes, like a gleam of sunshine dispelling a cloud-shadow from an alpine meadow. It has been said that he was temperamental and subject to sudden changes of mood: for my part, I came to this great man as a stranger, and received from him nothing but kindness from first to last. 'Bei Ihnen,' my colleagues used to say, 'ist der Alte immer in guter Laune' ('With you, the Old Man is always in a good humour'), as if this were an exceptional circumstance. It is certain that as he passed along the corridor from one *Doktoranden-raum* to another his mood sometimes changed from sunshine to storm; but there was usually a reason to be found in the unintelligent action of an unfortunate *Doktorand*, and Werner did not suffer fools gladly.

As a rule, Werner made the rounds of his research men twice a day, and he seemed to expect something new on each occasion: it was well, therefore, to hold something in reserve. A common greeting was 'Nun, was gibt's Neues?' ('Well, anything fresh?'). As the time approached for his morning or afternoon visit, passers-by in the corridor were often greeted with the query 'Ist der Alte schon unterwegs?' ('Is the Old Man already on the way?'). An affirmative answer led to an assiduous attention to work in progress on the benches. A *Doktorand* was held to be particularly favoured if Werner showed sufficient interest in the work to place his large cigar down on the edge of the bench, lighted end outwards, and handle an exhibit. Occasionally Dr. Paul Pfeiffer, his chief of staff,[1] was present in the large room of the Catacombs (Fig. **64**) when Werner appeared; and then a lengthy discussion was apt to ensue upon some point of interest in the current researches. I was greatly flattered one day when Werner brought Pfeiffer up to my bench in this room to show him the latest result.

Werner had an astonishing capacity for work. Often he maintained more than twenty research students working simultaneously under his immediate direction; but he had no difficulty in carrying the details of each investigation clearly in his mind. He delivered also at least eight lectures weekly throughout the University session. Reaching the laboratory at 8 A.M., he was often the last to leave. His lecture-room was designed for about 130 students; but usually almost double this number crowded in to hear him. The gangway and even the window-ledges carried their quotas of attentive listeners, and others had to stand at the sides of the lecture-bench. On a hot summer day students sometimes fainted in this room. Zürich is a cosmopolitan city, and Werner lectured to a cosmopolitan audience: the feminine part, for instance, ranged from a pair of elegantly gowned American girls, wearing very ornamental hats, to bareheaded Russians and Poles with short hair and severe attire, of which a buckled leather belt usually formed the central ingredient.

In his lectures, as in conversation, Werner spoke with great deliberation. His German had a characteristic native accent—quite distinct from the broad Swiss speech of Kleiner, his colleague in physics—and was very easy for a foreigner to follow. The bulk of his lectures were general courses, richly illustrated with experiments. His lecture assistant was a *Doktorand*. In the winter semester he gave 5 lectures weekly on elementary inorganic chemistry, 2 on the second part of an introductory course of organic chemistry, dealing with aromatic compounds, and 1 on advanced stereochemistry; in the summer semester he gave 5 lectures

---

[1] Afterwards professor of chemistry at Bonn.

weekly on an introductory course of organic chemistry, 2 on advanced inorganic chemistry, treated from the viewpoint of the Co-ordination Theory, and 1 on introductory stereochemistry. Even his elementary lectures were characterised by a novelty of presentation, and his more specialised courses could not fail to stimulate and inspire.

In the 'gemüthlich' company of kindred souls, Werner was of a convivial disposition, and in a congenial circle his robust sense of humour came into full play. His crowded hours had little relief beyond an evening visit to the 'Pfauen' or the 'Seehof', where he would play chess—of which he was inordinately fond—or indulge in a game of billiards with Kleiner; sometimes also he would take a hand at Jass, a popular Swiss card game of those days.

An anecdote related to me many years later by a former member of his staff throws an interesting sidelight on this phase of Werner's character. The new colleague had found it difficult to get on terms with his chief, whom, so far, he had met only at the laboratory. One evening, however, Werner came across him in a less conventional environment, seated at a table with a newly-filled *Bierkrug* before him. As Werner approached, his colleague greeted him with the customary 'Prosit!' and tossed off the jorum with polished skill at a single draught—'in einem kräftigen Schluck', as he expressed it. Werner regarded him steadily. 'Come. There's more in you than I thought!' said 'der Alte'; and after this chance encounter Werner's gruffness was replaced by complete amiability.

Werner was a French national by birth, and he looked towards Paris rather than Berlin. In the war of 1914–1918, his sympathies lay with France and the allied nations. Above all, he had a great and wholly understandable affection for Zürich and Switzerland, and in 1895 he became a naturalised Swiss citizen. His fame was such that he received several calls to other universities, among them Vienna (1899), Basel (1902), and Würzburg (1910); but he declined them all. He went so far as to visit the Würzburg laboratories: in the preceding year he had at last moved into a fine new laboratory at Zürich, and his stereotyped comment, as the Würzburgers showed him one treasured asset after another, was a laconic, 'Ja. Was haben Sie sonst?' ('Yes. What else have you got?'). On his return to Zürich, after he had rejected this last invitation, the students organised a torch-light procession (*Fackelzug*) in his honour.

DIVERSIONS OF A 'DOKTORAND'

At the far end of the Pestalozzistrasse lies the tiny Fehrenstrasse, and here in 1905–1907 was to be found the modest Pension Frischknecht. Across the way an orchard stretched up a sunny slope of the Zürichberg towards the great dome of the Kreuzkirche with its massive and melodious bells. Efficient, frugal, honest, and an avowed admirer of the English, Frau Frischknecht was a buxom Hamburgerin with a Swiss husband. It was no empty phrase to say that she took a personal interest in her cosmopolitan collection of guests.

Through the window of my *Studentenbude*, or student bed-sitting-room, on the parterre, strange sights could be seen. Large St. Bernard dogs, harnessed to little carts, went by with the morning milk; black-avised chimney-sweeps, laden with the paraphernalia of their profession, strode down the middle of the road, wearing tall box-hats and smoking large cigars; and small children would perch up on the window-sill and chatter away in the broad *Zürcherdeutsch* dialect through the open window. In the winter this last attraction was lacking, owing to the installation of double windows. The room was then heated by a closed stove burning briquettes. Here, too, the industrious student literally burnt the midnight oil, since light was provided by a standard kerosene lamp with a glass chimney, above which the shaving-water was heated in the morning.

The normal breakfast of a student, served in his room at about 7.30 A.M., consisted of a cup of coffee, a roll, and a pat of butter. The other two meals were communal and of a substantial kind: they were *Mittagessen* at 12.15 P.M. and *Abendessen* at 6.45 P.M. The total cost per month of board

65. A *Doktorandenraum* at Zürich.
(See p. 266.)

66. A Swiss *Studentenbude*, *c.* 1907.
(See p. 275.)

67. Zürich students in the Pragel Pass, 1906.
(See p. 275.)

68. A View of Zürich.
("Photoglob Zürich." (See p. 279.)

and lodging, including laundry and mending, never exceeded 110 francs[1] in this Pension.

A *Doktorand* working at chemistry under Werner had little spare time. The first lecture began at 8.15 A.M., even in the winter when the sides of the pavements were banked high with snow; apart from the break for *Mittagessen*, work in the Catacombs went on until 6 P.M. The doctorate was a difficult degree in the University of Zürich, as many wandering students from less exacting German and Swiss universities found to their cost. Besides conducting his research work (*Doktorarbeit*) in the laboratory, the student had to prepare himself simultaneously for the crucial examinations for the doctorate at the end of his period. In the University of Zürich these examinations embraced a chief subject (*Hauptfach*) and three subsidiary subjects (*Nebenfächer*). In my own case the chief subject was chemistry, with physics, crystallography-mineralogy, and stereochemistry as subsidiary subjects. In addition, it was compulsory to attend a course of lectures on the calculus, although fortunately there was no examination in this subject. These last lectures were very difficult to assimilate, besides falling at a time which severely handicapped laboratory operations. The result may be guessed; but the professor of mathematics—a very eminent man in his subject—was abnormally short-sighted, and although there was no pillar in his lecture-room, as in Bunsen's at Heidelberg, he made no difficulty about signing my attendance card at the end of the course.

In chemistry, it seemed advisable for a foreign *Doktorand*, having little initial knowledge of German beyond the meaning of 'Ja' and 'Nein', to attend most of Werner's lectures—partly to gain an acquaintance with chemical terms and phraseology, but also to get a new outlook upon familiar material. Werner's eight weekly lectures were supplemented by five or six from Pfeiffer, who dealt with specialised fields including advanced aromatic chemistry, terpenes,

---

[1] About £4 : 8s. In order to preserve a sense of proportion it may be recalled that in England at that time a young graduate in chemistry could hardly expect a salary of more than £75 per annum at the outset of his career.

heterocyclic compounds, alkaloids, proteins, dyestuffs, and an introduction to physical chemistry. In my first two semesters I attended all of the chemistry lectures, apart from Werner's advanced inorganic chemistry and Pfeiffer's heterocyclic chemistry, thus leaving the second-year lecture-hours almost free for physics (with Kleiner) and crystallo-graphy-mineralogy (with Grubenmann). Unfortunately, all this left little time to attend special lectures by Willstätter and other stars at the Polytechnikum.

The workers in the Catacombs formed a little com-munity of their own, and in spite of disabilities life in these gloomy cells was full of interest and incident. At midday, when a student left his bench for *Mittagessen*, he would call out 'Mahlzeit!' upon leaving the room, this picturesque salutation being short for 'ich wünsche Ihnen eine gesegnete Mahlzeit!' ('May your meal be blessed!'). Finding it difficult to work from *Mittagessen* to *Abendessen* without a break, I began to brew a cup of tea at about 4 P.M. At first, my colleagues in the *Doktorandenraum* viewed this unprecedented practice with amusement; but soon the large and genial Austrian, Herr *stud. chem.* Nicolay, followed my example, and eventually all my colleagues in this room succumbed to the insidious habit: workers in other rooms would then come along to ours, in order to joke at the 'Engländer' and his friends partaking of 'fife-o'clock tay', as it was called.

Students had, of course, to carry out their own com-bustions and other analytical determinations. The com-bustion-room was a tiny cell which was called upon to accommodate half a dozen of the old-fashioned furnaces, and the temperature of the room rose to giddy heights when several furnaces were in operation at once, especially in the hot summer months. In my first summer semester I was still working in the large room of the Catacombs (Fig. **64**). The bench facing mine was occupied at that time by Alfred Schaarschmidt,[1] a brilliant young student from Jahnsbach in Saxony, who had previously worked under Hantzsch at Leipzig. One day, early in July, Schaar-

---

[1] Afterwards professor of chemistry at Charlottenburg.

schmidt was excited about a new substance he had synthesised, and early in the morning he announced his intention
of submitting it to combustion analysis. I found out later
that the sweltering heat in the combustion-room had
daunted even the enthusiastic Schaarschmidt and induced
him to postpone the operation. Innocent of this, however,
when I returned from *Mittagessen* I looked over at Schaarschmidt and enquired: 'Ist Ihre Verbrennung schon
fertig?' ('Have you already finished your combustion?').
Schaarschmidt decided that here was a grand opportunity of
airing his command of colloquial English; so he leaned over
his bench towards me and replied: 'No, Meestaire Reet.
Z' ghost is veeling—but z' meat is veak!' ('The ghost is
willing—but the meat is weak!').

In the early days I had my own lingual difficulties, and
it was not until the lapse of two or three months that I found
it possible to think in German. When one begins to speak
German in one's dreams, real progress has been made, and
it is curious that the dream-German is much more fluent
than the waking-German. Beautiful walks abounded in the
neighbourhood of Zürich, and a favourite excursion on a
Saturday afternoon or Sunday was to the summit of the
Uetliberg—or 'Uetli', as the Zürchers called it affectionately
—a hill rising some 1200 feet above the level of the Lake of
Zürich, which it overlooks. Often at about Christmas-tide
when Zürich lay shrouded in thick fog, notices were to be
seen in the streets reading 'Uetliberg hell!', and on such
days the ascent was doubly agreeable, for it took one up
out of the fog into bright sunshine, with a wide view of
the distant Alps across the 'Nebelmeer', or sea of fog, lying
over the city and lake. Moreover, there was a restaurant
on the summit which provided a remarkably good *café
complet*.

One fine Saturday afternoon, soon after reaching
Zürich, I was making the ascent in the company of my
friend, Watson Smith, jun.,[1] and J. V. Dubský (later
professor of chemistry at Brno in Czechoslovakia). Lagging

---

[1] Watson Smith, sen., had worked under Victor Meyer at Zürich, and was later
a member of Roscoe's staff at Manchester.

somewhat behind, I revolved in my mind certain German phrases from Werner's lecture that morning, and unconsciously ejaculated 'Eine ganz merkwürdige Erscheinung!' ('A very remarkable phenomenon!'). This aroused Dubský's eager attention. He looked intently away across the lake, danced about on the steep slope, and demanded anxiously: 'Wo—wo—wo?' ('Where—where—where?'). It was some little time before I was able to compose the ludicrous situation by explaining to him, through the fluent German of the forbearing Watson Smith, that I was merely rehearsing some expressions from Werner's lecture, in order to fix them in my memory.

Here is another incident. Scene: the *papeterie* shop of Denzler in the Plattenstrasse. Time: autumn, 1905. Enter a *stud. phil.* newly arrived from England, with a knowledge of German derived almost wholly from a small and misleading pocket-dictionary which brings him into one embarrassing situation after another. The student needs a pen-nib (still a common article of purchase in those days).

Stud. phil.: 'Guten Morgen, Fräulein: ich brauche einen Schnabel' ('Good morning, Fräulein: I need a Schnabel'). The Fräulein registers intense consternation, raises her hands, and protests that such a thing as a Schnabel has never been stocked by the house of Denzler, and never will be. The student finds this incredible, and remarks laboriously that in his country every stationer's shop has many Schnäbel.

The Fräulein again raises her hands heavenwards, and asks the student from what country he comes hither. When he replies 'Aus England', her excitement subsides somewhat, for at this time the tastes and actions of Englishmen are widely held on the Continent to be quite unpredictable.

The Swiss lose no opportunity of acquiring English. The quick-witted Fräulein invites the student to explore the shop for a Schnabel, offering at the same time to tell him the German name for each article he encounters, in return for the English equivalent from him. The student lights upon a rich variety of objects. The Fräulein follows him round. Two vocabularies begin to grow rapidly. Interest is well maintained. The search prolongs itself. At intervals the Fräulein ejaculates teasingly, 'Es gibt aber kei'Schnabel!' ('But there's no Schnabel!').

But every good thing comes to an end. All too soon, the explorer begins to rummage in a drawer at the back of one of the counters. It is filled with small boxes. Upon opening one of these he sees before him an assorted set of the long-sought pen-nibs. 'Ah—Schnabel—Schnabel!' he exclaims in triumph, extracting one of the nibs and flourishing it before the astonished eyes of the Fräulein. 'Ach wo!—Kei' Schnabel!' protests the Fräulein indignantly. . . . 'Feder! Feder!'

And upon reaching home and consulting a large and reliable dictionary, the student finds that 'Schnabel' means 'nib' only in the sense of a bird's beak, and that vulgarly it is used to denote the mouth.[1]

The *stud. phil.* ought to have said 'Feder' or 'Spitze'; but a vocabulary acquired in this way is never forgotten.

Studentenbuden, or students' lodgings, to suit the resources of every type of student could be found in Zürich in those days, and the student arranged for his own accommodation, often in a Pension (Fig. **66**). There was no lack of recreations and amusements in and around Zürich. Music and the drama flourished, and the official student-card conferred many privileges upon the holder, including cheap admission to concerts and theatrical performances. In the summer there was swimming, also rowing, tennis, and even golf; in the winter, ski-ing, skating, and sledging —there was also the 'Young Fellows' Fussball Klub; and for the greater part of the year excursions could be undertaken into the mountains when time allowed (Fig. **67**).

The Swiss children took to ski-ing soon after they could walk. In the winter it was a common pastime to shoot down the ice-bound roads of the Zürichberg on sledges or the larger bob-sleighs. These sometimes came through into the heart of the city across the Plattenstrasse, preceded by loud

---

[1] Thus, in the Somerset dialect, *snabble* means to *snap* up in eating (like a bird); it is interesting that there are many other similarities, such as *lear* (Som.), *leer* (Ger.), meaning empty.

warning cries of 'Obach!' from the occupants. Upsets were frequent, but all students paid a small compulsory insurance entitling them to free hospital treatment in case of accident or illness.

The student-body, both in the University and Polytechnikum, was of a cosmopolitan nature. Most of the European countries were represented, and there was also a sprinkling of students from the New World. Many of them belonged to student corporations, or *Verbindungen*, of which there were more than a dozen, including among them the Corps Tigurinia, Utonia, Zofingia, Teutonia, Turicia, and Helvetia. The distinctive caps of these student associations formed a common and very picturesque feature of the streets of Zürich, and upon occasion the members were to be seen in many-coloured mediaeval costumes, jack-booted, and carrying rapiers and brilliant banners.

The winter semester lasted from about 24 October to the end of February, with a break of three weeks at Christmas and the New Year; the summer semester began about 20 April and went on for three months, with a short break at Easter. The outstanding student function of the year was the *Weihnachtskommers*, a kind of combined Christmas party, smoking-concert, and variety performance, held just before the Christmas recess. The preparations were inaugurated some weeks in advance at a meeting of the students of the Faculty or subject concerned: a committee was elected, subscriptions were taken, and moving spirits then went ahead with the plans. . . .

At last the great day comes, and towards 8 P.M. all roads lead to the Casino Hottingen. The transverse table at the top of the capacious room is reserved for the Rector, Dean, professors, and other men of note; and from it several other long tables extend to the footlights and orchestra at the opposite end. Above is a gallery for the accommodation of lady visitors, who take no active part in the proceedings. A *Festzeitung* is provided in the form of an alleged 'Biertechnischer' Edition, issued by the Zürich Chemical Society, and containing the 'Proceedings of the

Meeting held on 14 December 1906 in the lecture-room of the Casino Hottingen'. Among many witty and topical items it contains a *Fest-Cantus* ingeniously connecting the pursuit of science with beer-drinking, and ending:

> *D'rum ruft mit voller Lungenkraft:*
> '*Es lebe hoch die Wissenschaft!*'
> *Und schreit mit aller Energie:*
> '*Hoch lebe die Chemie!*' [1]

A skit on the distilled water prepared by the much-abused Herr Widmer begins: 'The raw material, *aqua destillata purissima laboratorii chemici Almae Matris Turicensis*, consists of a thick dark liquid with a repulsive odour, which raises blisters when placed upon the tongue, and gives rise to nausea and tears'. The complicated method of preparing pure water is then given, a yield of 0·5 per cent. being obtained.

The proceedings open by a sudden report resembling the crack of a rifle and caused by the *Vorsitzender* (chairman) at the head of the room, and his vice at the bottom, simultaneously slapping their swords of office with great force upon the table in front of them. 'Si-len-ti-um!' roars the former, and forthwith announces a song. Everyone instantly finds his seat, song-books are opened, the orchestra strikes up, and three hundred voices start 'mit voller Lungenkraft' upon the well-known opening song 'Hier sind wir versammelt zu löblichem Tun, d'rum Brüderchen! *Ergo bibamus!*' The recurrent theme, *ergo bibamus*, is suitably honoured at the end of the last verse. 'Colloquium!' yells the *Vorsitzender*, and the animated buzz of conversation pervades the great room until again quelled by the vicious crack of the swords and another stentorian 'Silentium!'

After delivering a short speech of welcome the *Vorsitzender* again announces 'Colloquium!' Gradually things liven up. Amid the ever-increasing hum of voices the

---

[1] In free translation:

> Then shout with voices in alliance:
> 'Prosperity and growth to Science!'
> And cry with all your energy:
> 'Long life to Chemistry!'

punctuating 'Prosit' makes itself evident. You catch the
eye of an acquaintance: 'Prosit!' he shouts, holding his
Bierkrug in the air, from whence it descends to the appointed
place; 'Prosit!' you reply, following his example; and
immediately two empty vessels are snatched up by an alert
Fräulein, to reappear replenished in a few seconds. Every
Doktorand of course cherishes the hope of catching the eye
of his Professor. So the reign of the first *Vorsitzender*—a
Doktorand—draws to an end, and finishes in a great blaze
of enthusiasm, as the company after singing the song of the
evening—'Stosst an! Zürich soll leben! Hurrah hoch!'—
proceeds to 'rub a Salamander'.

'*Ad exercitium Salamandris!*' shouts the *Vorsitzender*,
assuming the rôle of toastmaster. The company rises.
'*Eins! Zwei! Drei!*'—the charged mugs are raised in
readiness. '*Eins!*'—quick action is needed; for '*Zwei!
Drei!*' follow rapidly, and the empty mugs are lowered upon
the table. '*Eins! Zwei! Drei!*'—the mugs are rubbed to and
fro upon the table. '*Eins!*'—mugs are raised about a foot
above the table. '*Zwei!*'—steady. '*Drei!*'—crash! Three
hundred mugs are simultaneously brought down with full
force upon the table, and the Salamander is *fertig*.

And now the *Vorsitzender* takes up his *Bierkrug*, song-
book, and *Festzeitung*, and vacates the chair. The lion of
the assembly, the Professor Ordinarius of Chemistry in the
University, a mighty man of valour in the chemical world,
takes up his *Bierkrug*, song-book, and *Festzeitung*, and
occupies the chair. Right nobly does Alfred Werner, in
this most congenial of all environments, uphold his reputation as a speaker of the first order—a reputation won in
many a crowded lecture-room. He tells us of the wonders
of the new University Chemical Institute, now being planned.
It will have water laid on, of course; it will have gas and
electricity laid on, *ganz bestimmt*: it will have air and also
steam laid on, *selbstverständlich*: it will have vacuum laid on,
natürlich; and one more thing will be laid on in this wonderful laboratory, *unbedingt*—and that will be—beer! He sits
down amidst a storm of applause, and we rub a Salamander
in his honour.

Speech, song, colloquium—how the time flies! The room takes on a misty tint, in spite of its size. The orchestra beats all previous records. The 'Pros't'-storm increases in intensity. And the songs are rendered more vociferously than ever. Zürich (Fig. **68**), the Athens of the Limmat, has been described as the intellectual centre of Switzerland, and on this evening one might with equal truth describe the Casino Hottingen as the intellectual centre of Zürich. What a galaxy of talent graces the high table! In the chair is one of the foremost scientists of the day. On either hand sit the second chemistry professor and the mathematics professor—twin thunderbolts of war. Flanking them are the Rector, the Dean, and many other professors; and 'doctors in their nobby hats are plentiful as tabby cats'.

But again 'Silentium!' 'Meine Damen und Herren,'[1] announces the chairman, 'the next item is *Tempora Mutantur!*, a comic opera without music, in two isomers, by Siegfried Wagner.' Werner resumes his seat with eyes fixed upon the curtain, for he is as fully interested as anyone present, and seeing that he is world-famous as a stereo-chemist, he is naturally interested in these isomers.

The first 'isomer' is a telling skit upon the conditions prevailing in the old chemical laboratory on the Rämistrasse, the members of the staff being cleverly caricatured. As one amusing incident succeeds another, Werner becomes completely absorbed. The scene terminates by the gruff, roughly clad and over-punctilious Herr Widmer walking in with his eternal cigar, turning off the gas in spite of all protests, and clearing the laboratory about an hour before time.

The second 'isomer' illustrates the coming state of affairs in the wonderful new laboratory of which Werner has told us in his speech. An immaculately dressed *Doktorand* is discovered sitting at a dainty table with two very lively and fashionable young ladies. Anon he calls for the Herr Widmer. A smart liveried person in tails, knee-breeches, and bright-yellow stockings enters briskly, lays

---

[1] Werner always opened his lectures with 'Meine Herren und Damen', except the one following the *Weihnachtskommers,* when with a broad smile he affected to forget himself and began with 'Meine Damen und Herren'.

U

the table noiselessly and dexterously, and starts to draw corks and hand round refreshments in the most professional manner. Professors and students alike roar with delight.

Presently the *Doktorand* asks his lady friends to excuse him for a moment, as he has to analyse a new substance. He then proceeds to carry out a nitrogen determination—which he explains used to take a whole morning in the old laboratory. Placing some of the substance in an opening of a most complicated piece of apparatus, he intimates to the Fräuleins that this awfully improved method of analysis is due to Herrn Professor Werner, whom no doubt they have encountered in the course of their optical activities. At that moment the said professor rings up, and asks when it would be convenient for him to call at the laboratory. 'In a couple of minutes,' answers the *Doktorand*, returning to finish his glass of champagne.

A motor-horn sounds, and the begoggled professor enters, attended by certain members of his staff, all bearing a life-like resemblance to their originals although clad in the cumbrous motoring attire of the day. The *Doktorand* walks across to the apparatus, inserts a ten-centime piece and touches a spring, whereupon a gramophonious voice ejaculates: 'One hundred and twelve point six five two per cent. nitrogen . . . gurr-r-r.' The counterfeit present-ments of Werner, Pfeiffer, and other eager onlookers then quaff one another's healths in champagne; and the curtain falls upon the intriguing spectacle of the pseudo-Werner and the pseudo-Pfeiffer dancing with the two fascinating Fräuleins, to the new and ravishing strains of 'The Merry Widow'.

One of the doctors now takes the chair, and the in-numerable candles on the *Christbaum* herald the appearance of the *Weihnachtsmann*, as the curtain rises for the last time. This venerable personage, white with the snows of Time and holding a shepherd's crook in one hand, proceeds to distribute gifts among the professors, doctors, and students. For the students these gifts have little intrinsic value, being designed to emphasise some eccentricity rather than to fill a long-felt want. The sly humour running through the

Weihnachtsmann's accompanying remarks is appreciated by all—with the possible exception of the recipient.

Time flies: and now the speeches have all been made, the songs all sung; the last *Bierkrug* has been tilted skywards; the candles on the *Christbaum* have died down and guttered out. Professors, doctors, and students make their way homewards. Silence descends upon the Casino Hottingen.

FROM 'DOKTORAND' TO 'DOKTOR'

With Werner's *Doktoranden*, the *Doktorarbeit* seemed usually to yield results suitable for an 'Inaugural-Dissertation' for the degree of Doctor of Philosophy by the end of the third or fourth semester. I was Werner's 101st *Doktorand*, and my thesis, entitled *Untersuchungen in der Cumar- und Cumarinsäurereihe* ('Researches in the Coumaric and Coumarinic Acid Series'), was one of an organic-stereo-chemical nature, without any bearing on the Co-ordination Theory. A fee of 375 francs was payable upon handing in the thesis, and the printing of the prescribed 200 copies before the degree diploma was issued cost about the same amount. Occasionally, an indigent student was obliged to postpone taking his degree until he had obtained an appointment and saved the necessary sum of about £30.

What most candidates regarded as the real ordeal came after the thesis had been accepted. First came the essay. The candidate was handed a sealed envelope and locked up alone in a room. There he found writing materials, also a bell, which he could ring if he needed refreshments, and when he had finished. The envelope contained a single sheet of paper bearing three titles—such as 'Nitroverbindungen', 'Die Riechstoffe', 'Intramolekulare Umlagerungen' —upon one of which the candidate was allowed to write for as long as he wished.

If the essay were satisfactory, the candidate was admitted to the final and most formidable stage—the oral examinations. For these, an hour was allowed in the *Hauptfach* and half an hour in each of the three *Nebenfächer*. The candidates— many of whom wore evening dress—were admitted one by one into a room at which the examiner and sundry officials sat at a table: the candidate bowed and took a seat, and the ordeal was upon him. Werner had a reputation as a very difficult examiner, probably because he had an unusually comprehensive knowledge of so many fields of chemistry. When I left the room, after an interview which was both interesting and pleasant, I found Herr *cand. chem.* P—— outside the door, clad in evening dress and shaking in his shoes. 'Ist der Alte in guter Laune?' he whispered hoarsely. 'Grossartig!' I replied encouragingly; and Herr *cand. chem.* P——, plucking up heart, went in and pulled it off.

In mineralogy, Grubenmann produced various crystal-models for discussion, and a specimen of apatite for identification: as I left him he remarked slyly in English (it was time for *Mittagessen*), 'Good *appetite!*' Kleiner, in physics, was the last and most difficult examiner. It was not altogether easy to follow questions on specific inductive capacity and such-like propounded in broad Swiss speech; moreover, Kleiner deliberately laid his watch down upon the table at the start of the questioning, and made one feel like a last-wicket batsman having to keep up his end till close of play.

On the day following the last examination I had not yet heard the result when I met Werner and Pfeiffer coming along the Rämistrasse in company. As I drew level with them their hats came off in a sweeping synchronised motion, and two voices rang out in unison: 'Guten Morgen, Herr *Doktor!*' Then I knew.

RETURN OF AN ALUMNUS

On 29 April 1933, as delegate[1] of the University of St. Andrews to the centenary celebrations of the University of

---

[1] Charged with the presentation of the following: 'Address of the University of St. Andrews to the University of Zürich: We, the Senatus Academicus of the University of St. Andrews, send our cordial greetings to the Senate of the University of Zürich upon the occasion of the centenary celebrations. We take a particular pleasure in so doing, for we feel that our two foundations are bound by ties stronger than those of formal academic kinship. Our land of lochs, muirs, and bens has much in common with your beautiful country of lakes, alps, and mountains; and our ideals of freedom are personified in the heroic figure of Wallace even as yours find a local habitation and a name in that of Tell.

'Throughout the five centuries during which our University has existed, its teachers and students have followed with sympathy and admiration the struggles for freedom and progress of such of your reformers as Zwingli, in the cause of

Zürich, I stood once more in the Rämistrasse, facing the site of the old laboratory. In its place rose one of the magnificent academic buildings of a later age. I was invited to admire this; but as my mouth framed the words of congratulation my eyes seemed to behold a flaming 'Ichabod!' above the handsome doorway. Even the pyridine odour had vanished. . . .

Memories . . . bitter-sweet memories . . . those walks of auld lang syne through the beautiful green woods of the Dolder and Elefantenbach when all the world was young . . . the flowery meads and sunlit snows of lovely canton Glarus . . . alpenglow at eventide on the noble Urirotstock . . . ascents of the Uetliberg ending in the social *café complet* . . . the Christmas view of the Alps from that friendly summit, with sunshine sparkling on the snow, and Zürich enshrouded in a *Nebelmeer* far down below . . . the melodious bell-music from the Kreuzkirche at nightfall . . . the cheery cosmopolitan life of the Pension within and the city without . . . *Mittagessen* with fellow-students of many nations at the Hotel Metropole . . . multilingual musical evenings at 'Sonnenbühl' with the hospitable Knecht family . . . 'der Alte' on his round of the Catacombs . . . the *Weihnachtskommers* in the Casino Hottingen . . . and that prophetic student-song:[1]

religion, Paracelsus, in the cause of science, and Pestalozzi, in the cause of education. Your city, your canton, and your country may well take pride in the achievements, during the first century of its existence, of a renowned University which has maintained in full measure the traditions of these and others of your compatriots who have laboured so diligently and successfully in the service of humanity.

'We congratulate you upon the past, and send you our sincere good wishes for the future; and we are glad to nominate as our representative at your celebrations our colleague Dr. John Read, Professor of Chemistry in this University, and at the same time a graduate of your University who had the privilege of studying under the illustrious Alfred Werner.

'In token whereof we affix hereunto our Seal, this Nineteenth day of December, in the Year of our Lord, 1932.

'J. C. IRVINE, *Vice-Chancellor and Principal.*'

[1] In free translation:

The pride of student life and ways
   Has gone beyond recapture.
Farewell for ever, golden days,
   So free and full of rapture.
In vain I cast my gaze around,
Thy trace can nevermore be found.
   O jerum, jerum, jerum,
   O quae mutatio rerum!

O alte Burschenherrlichkeit,
Wohin bist du verschwunden?
Nie kehrst du wieder, goldne Zeit,
So froh und ungebunden.
Vergebens spähe ich umher,
Ich finde deine Spur nicht mehr.
O jerum, jerum, jerum,
O quae mutatio rerum!

POPE AND CAMBRIDGE

William Jackson Pope (1870–1939), with whom I was closely associated for eight years after leaving Werner, provided a marked contrast to my former chief. Each was a great stereochemist, but they had little else in common; even as stereochemists they were divergent, Werner's genius being of the romantic type, Pope's of the classical. Born, bred, and educated in London, Pope had attracted the attention of H. E. Armstrong while still a student at the Finsbury Technical College, and he followed Armstrong to the Central Technical College at South Kensington. When I first made his acquaintance in the autumn of 1907 he was Professor of Chemistry in the Municipal School of Technology at Manchester, a post which he had held since 1901. At that time he still bore a look of youthfulness, and mentally and physically he was at the height of his powers. His mental alertness, originality of outlook, and intellectual capacity were impressive from the outset. When he had shaken hands he asked: 'Well, and what do you think of Werner's Co-ordination Theory?' Evidently he was unable at that time to share to the full the opinion of an ardent disciple; but British chemists in general were not disposed to regard Werner's views with the attention they deserved until he achieved the first optical resolution of a co-ordination compound in 1911.

In the summer of 1908 Pope was elected to succeed G. D. Liveing as Professor of Chemistry in the University of Cambridge. At that time, relics of an earlier rigidity of thought still lingered on at Cambridge. Pope's two immediate predecessors, Liveing and Cumming, had occupied the chair between them for ninety-three years.

Hence it fell to Pope to introduce a series of reforms, a process naturally calling for much tact, particularly as his appointment was in some ways revolutionary and such as to cause a flutter among the parochially minded in Cambridge. Pope was not a Cambridge man, and, in fact, all of the numerous degrees which he eventually accumulated, including his M.A. Cantab., were honorary. He used to say jestingly that it seemed to him a waste of time and effort to take degrees by examination. One of his first objectives at Cambridge was the centralisation of the chemistry teaching in the University Chemical Laboratory, and this led to the abolition of various college laboratories and to the provision of efficient courses in fields of work which had been covered hitherto only by private tuition.

In build, Pope was tall and rather spare. In disposition, he was essentially very English. He did not wear his heart on his sleeve, and it was only after continued acquaintance that his shell of reserve wore through and revealed the shy and attractive humanity of his character. One of the outstanding features of his personality was his refined and permeating sense of humour. He had a fund of witty and whimsical stories, which he told upon occasion with great effect. He had a special feeling for Cockney character and wit.

Pope's own humour had a delicate quality as difficult to pin down as a floating strand of gossamer, and his anecdotes were often flavoured with an aromatic quality incapable of condensation into cold print. I recall one day describing to him the cramped accommodation of the Thames Conservancy Laboratory at Kennington Green, as I knew it early in 1905. This laboratory, in which we analysed some two dozen samples of waters and effluents daily, consisted of a *ci-devant* greenhouse in the garden of the chief chemist, C. E. Groves, F.R.S. 'It was so small,' I concluded, 'that one could hardly swing a cat in it.' 'Ah, Groves had such a long reach,' remarked Pope, opening his large cigarette-case reflectively. The picture called up in these few words, so spoken, of the veteran chemist, very tall and most sedate, baulked in his attempts to swing a cat in a greenhouse, like a bowler trying in vain to find his length, was irresistibly ludicrous, and typically Popeian.

On another occasion, many years later, at a Chemical Society Dinner held in Glasgow, H. E. Armstrong was entrusted with the toast of the city fathers. Rapidly losing sight of his text, 'H. E. A.' was soon knee-deep in lush meadows, discoursing at great length on the merits of grass, milk, and manures—a field in which he was apt at that time to wander at large on divers occasions, appropriate and inappropriate. Pope, who followed his old chief in proposing the next toast, began by remarking blandly that it was clear from Professor Armstrong's interesting researches that Nebuchadnezzar was a Glasgow man!

Pope was a man of deep culture, with wide interests, ranging from his beloved stereochemistry and crystallography to photography, literature, languages, art, music, and the drama. In his earlier years he sought recreation in the violin. He had also the tastes of a connoisseur, particularly in alchemical paintings and engravings, apothecaries' jars and mortars, and choice editions and bindings of English and foreign literary classics. He was fond of travel and of congenial company, and in his later years he became an international figure in chemistry. Of the many eminent chemists who visited him at Cambridge, perhaps Meldola (under whom I had studied at the Finsbury Technical College) came most frequently. Armstrong, too, with whom Pope kept up a lifelong friendship, was occasionally to be seen, and so was Barlow, his mathematical collaborator in the valency-volume theory. Among visitors from overseas, Paternò, Walden, and P. C. Ray left lasting impressions.

The most prominent members of the chemistry staff in Pope's early days at Cambridge were Sir James Dewar, H. J. H. Fenton, W. J. Sell, C. T. Heycock, H. O. Jones, S. Ruhemann, J. E. Purvis, and F. W. Dootson. A great character, held in high esteem by all of us, was F. J. Stoakley, head of the extensive laboratory staff: an East Anglian racy of the soil, massive and reliable, he commanded great respect in his own sphere. He became deeply attached to

Pope, whom he helped much in expert photography and other highly skilled work.

Stoakley, like Herr Inspektor Fehl at Munich, had quarters in the chemistry block.[1] Adorning the window of his parlour, on the ground floor, and very evident to the passer-by in Pembroke Street, stood a fine aspidistra in a pot—the pride of the feminine side of his household. Late one night, on his way home from Sidney Sussex College, Pope came upon Stoakley, pacing the pavement of Pembroke Street, and drawing mechanically at a pipe which had long since gone cold. An exchange of remarks showed Stoakley to be in an unusually subdued mood, and in response to Pope's sympathetic enquiries the secret came out. 'We'd settled down comfortably after supper,' said Stoakley, 'when the cat came in, jumped suddenly into the window, and curled up bang on top of the aspidistra . . . *and I laughed!*'

This story, which became known under the title of 'The Cat and the Aspidistra', delighted Pope. The incongruity of the plant and animal actors, the dominating human note, the dramatic climax expressed so simply and unexpectedly in three words, all found responsive vibrations in a sense of humour the main chords of which were refinement, artistry, and humanity.

Pope was distinguished as a lecturer by the attractive quality of his voice and speech, the clarity of his statements, and an easy command of his subject. With his research men he was always resourceful when help was called for; but after a topic had been decided upon and fully discussed he encouraged his junior collaborators to cultivate self-reliance. He always listened attentively to their ideas and suggestions, and never paraded his own great knowledge and experience: indeed, in all such relationships he was one of the most modest and considerate of men. It has been well said of him that he wore his 'weight of learning lightly like a flower'.

In his chemical work Pope was a true artist, in whom a delicate intuition was blended with a bold originality of

[1] On the extreme left in Fig. **69**.

conception. In the apt words of W. H. Mills, himself a master worker in stereochemistry, Pope's main achievements were 'concerned in one way or another with molecular configuration, opening up new fields of stereochemistry and enriching others. His discovery of optically active compounds of nitrogen, sulphur, selenium and tin, and his pioneer work on centroasymmetric substances will always remain landmarks in the history of the science.' These landmarks are more familiar in the stereochemical landscape than in their humanistic environment, to which we may now devote some attention.

'SCIENCE THE SINNER'

One of my first investigations with Pope at Cambridge arose logically from some of his earlier work on the stereochemistry of organic derivatives of sulphur and selenium. In 1900, Pope and Peachey obtained optically active methylethylthetine bromide, [MeEtS·CH$_2$·COOH]Br, and two years later Pope and Neville resolved methylphenylselenetine bromide, [MePhSe·CH$_2$·COOH]Br. It was now hoped to prepare the selenium analogue of the first of these substances, namely, methylethylselenetine bromide, [MeEtSe·CH$_2$·COOH]Br, and thus to determine the effect produced upon the optical rotatory power of an asymmetric molecule by changing its central asymmetric atom from sulphur to selenium.

Pope and Neville had wisely avoided preparing the necessary methylethyl selenide, a volatile and revolting liquid; the methylphenyl selenide of their choice proved to be a yellow oil, boiling at 200°, 'with a not unpleasant aromatic, garlic-like odour'.

In our Cambridge investigation, which has not hitherto been described, a stick of selenium, contained in a long test-tube of hard glass, was heated in a current of hydrogen with a vigorous Bunsen flame. The selenium slowly disappeared, through conversion into hydrogen selenide, and the issuing mixture of that gas with hydrogen was passed into alcoholic sodium hydroxide. The resulting solution of sodium hydrogen selenide was warmed firstly with an equivalent of ethyl iodide, and secondly with equivalents of methyl iodide and sodium ethoxide. The methylethyl selenide had then to be isolated and warmed with bromo-acetic acid, in order to yield the desired and inoffensive methylethylselenetine bromide.

The initial operation was comfortably accomplished in the private laboratory; but for the succeeding stages, on account of the sensational odour, it was found necessary to work on the open roof of the building (Fig. **69**), with the wind behind the operator. The selenide was used only in small quantities of a few grams, with strict precautions against its escape into the air; but nevertheless the incidents that followed were worthy of the imaginative powers of a Wells and the graphic pen of a Defoe. It is said of some perfumes that their full strength becomes apparent only at great dilutions. The same rule seemed to apply to these alkyl selenides; the odour grew increasingly unbearable with dispersion; indeed, it seemed to pass out of the realm of odours into that of the creepy sensations of a nightmare. Defying the restraining action of alkaline permanganate traps, the demoralising whiffs of vapour swept down upon defenceless Cambridge.

It was particularly unfortunate that the roof-experiments chanced to coincide with the Darwin Centenary celebrations, held at Cambridge in June 1909. Open-air tea-parties in the gardens of houses bordering the distant Parker's Piece were interrupted, and when the guests retired indoors the objectionable odour pursued them and haunted their tea-cups. On the following afternoon a garden party at Christ's College unhappily lay also to leeward, and similar discom-forts ensued. At street corners, in college combination rooms, in taverns and barbers' shops, in the old horse-trams —wherever men gathered in Cambridge the dominant subject of conversation and debate was The Smell.

Vigorous protests poured in to the local authorities, letters from indignant ratepayers appeared in the press, business men in Petty Cury and elsewhere to leeward closed their offices and sent their staffs away on hurried holidays, until the discomfiture should be overpast: in brief, a general unease sat in the usually serene air of Cambridge. At last, the seat of disturbance was traced to the University Chemical Laboratory, and the *Cambridge Daily News* came out with the clarifying headlines: 'WHAT WAS IT? SUSPECTED DRAINS EXONERATED. SCIENCE THE SINNER.'

At this juncture it was decided to continue the work in the open country of the fens. Permission had to be secured, and one evening I found myself with Stoakley on the doorstep of a farmer near Waterbeach. Stoakley knocked, and the farmer himself appeared. It was not in Stoakley's nature to dissemble, nor was he mealy mouthed. 'Good evening,' he began, in his strong and clear East Anglian voice: 'we've come down here to make a thundering big stink!' The farmer stood up well to this opening, and began to show a kind of professional interest as Stoakley proceeded to describe the wondrous works in Cambridge—this modern land of Ham. 'Come on out and smell my muckheap,' said the farmer, at the end of a most impressive narration. The specimen in his yard was exceptionally large and odoriferous; but Stoakley dashed his hopes of successful competition by the verdict that, after recent experiences, it seemed to us a bed of roses! In the end, after assuring the farmer that The Smell would not (*a*) damage his butter, (*b*) injure his herd of cows, (*c*) affect their milk yield, or (*d*) stop his grass from growing, we obtained permission to operate in a large field on the banks of the Cam, well removed to leeward from the farmhouse.

So it came about that, early one morning in July 1909, Pope, Stoakley, and I boarded a motor-boat at Chesterton Bridge and set off down the Cam with two large packing-cases containing the necessary apparatus and materials for continuing the research. We landed on the right bank of the river, the incomparable Stoakley having thoughtfully arranged the site so that certain supplies could be readily obtained from a riverside hostelry: this was situated to windward and had a reputation for its fine 'nutty' ale. It was a sunny day, with a light breeze blowing downstream, so that in every way the conditions were excellent.

Our two packing-cases served the same purpose as the deal tables of Berzelius, and, like him, we used spirit-lamps (reinforced, however, with a primus stove) for heating our flasks. As the work progressed, it was interesting to notice the effect of the odour on animal life in the neighbourhood. The farmer joined us at an early stage, but his stay was short: a hasty visit to leeward convinced him that Stoakley's opening assertion had been amply fulfilled. A large herd of his cows formed into a semicircle to leeward and provided a silent but appreciative audience. A few hundred yards downstream, the river took a bend to the right, and it was just before reaching this point that boats and barges, coming upstream from the direction of Ely, entered the odoriferous belt: the confusion among the occupants of these craft, as the strange invisible perfume hit them one after another, was most entertaining. Soon we began to experience the reaction of the smaller fauna: creeping and flying insects of many kinds swarmed over the apparatus, some of them even making determined attempts to force a way past the stoppers into the flasks. Their whole behaviour indicated that they felt they were missing something really good.

We finished our operations in the midst of one of the gorgeous sunsets for which the fens are famous. Altogether it was a memorable day; but the scientific results were not sufficiently definite to lead to any publication. At this point the research was abandoned, partly on account of its unpleasant nature, but perhaps mainly because another investigation of far greater importance now began to monopolise our attention—and this time, in alchemical phraseology, we 'hitt the *Marke*'.

These 'gentle and joyous' experiences can have had few parallels in the history of chemistry, and it is well that they should be placed on record. It is interesting to reflect, in conclusion, that had the victims of the episode been conversant with the history of chemistry they might have found some consolation in the thought that *plus ça change, plus c'est la même chose;* for Leo Africanus wrote, about 1500, that 'chemists are a most stupid set of men, who contaminate themselves with sulphur and other horrible stinks', and Chaucer had conveyed the same idea more than a century earlier still, when he wrote:

> And evermore, wher ever that they gon,
> Men may them knowe by smellyng of bremstoon;
> For al the world thay stynken as a goat,
> Their savour is so rammysh and so hot,
> That though a man from them a mylè be,
> The savour wil infect him, trustè me.

CENTROASYMMETRY

The brilliant idea of producing a centroasymmetric compound came to Pope while he was in Manchester, and in 1906 he published a joint paper with W. H. Perkin, jun., describing the synthesis of a suitable substance for the purpose. The molecule of this substance, 1-methyl-cyclo-hexylidene-4-acetic acid, according to the theory of the tetrahedral arrangement of carbon valencies, should give a non-superposable mirror-image, although it contains no formally asymmetric atom. Such substances, which Pope termed centroasymmetric, should presumably be capable of existing in right- and left-handed forms, displaying optical activity. Perkin and Pope's synthesis was a difficult process, but soon after Pope's translation to Cambridge a simpler preparative method was devised by Wallach, in Göttingen. The position of the problem at the end of 1908 may be seen from the following letter (Fig. 70):

The University, Manchester.
Dec. 18, 08.

My dear Pope,

Wallach's acid arrived on Monday & I began experimenting with it at once. I should have finished before but I had to spend Thursday in London. There can be no doubt as to the constitution of the acid because, when oxidised by permanganate, it is quantitatively converted into 1:4-methylcyclohexanone & oxalic acid.

I took 6 grams of the acid dissolved it in dil. Na_2CO_3 (2·4 grams) and then mixed the solution with 6 grams acid and 13 grams of cinchonine both dissolved in alcohol. On evaporating somewhat a salt began to separate in a semi-solid condition, & after waiting over night I collected the rather gummy salt, decomposed it with sodium carbonate & obtained an acid which was *absolutely inactive*. This I have sent you labelled 'acid from sparingly soluble cinch^{n} salt.' The original sod. carb. sol. from which the salt had sepd. was acidified & the acid found to be *inactive*. This is labelled, I think, 'readily soluble cinchonine salt', or words to that effect.

I next took 6 grams acid, 2·4 grams Na_2CO_3, & mixed with alcoholic solution of 6 grams acid & 20 grams brucine. When this was evaporated to a thin syrup nothing separated for many hours, but after about 30 hours round balls had begun to form & on vigorously stirring the whole became semi-solid. When once separated this salt is beautifully crystalline & very sparingly soluble, but the acid from it was again *inactive*: (labelled sparingly soluble brucine salt) & the acid from the sodium carbonate filtrate was also inactive. I then tried the melting points of the various specimens but they are practically the same, & the acids seem to have the same physical properties generally.

The whole of the acid (now about 25 grams, originally 30 grams) I have sent on to you for you to see whether you can get anything optically active out of it. If not the question arises, What other differences may the two enantiomorphous modifications possibly exhibit & how can we prove these experimentally?

The problem must surely be a very interesting one whichever way it goes, & you may be more fortunate than I have been. When I have worked up my residues I shall probably have another 4 grams which I will send on, &, although I have no idea how the acid is made, Wallach made it in little more than a week so it should be possible to get a considerable amount if necessary, which I hope will not be the case.

Kind regards,
Yours sincerely,
W. H. PERKIN.

Fortunately, it proved possible to accomplish the resolution and to complete the whole investigation without further calls upon Wallach. The problem was rendered difficult, however, initially by the reluctance of the acid to yield a crystalline salt with an optically active base, and thereafter by the mutual solubility of the brucine salts of the *l*- and *d*-acid in the solid state. The account of the resolution, the accomplishment of which followed closely upon the heels of the spectacular but unprofitable work on the organic selenides, was published towards the end of 1909, simultaneously in the *Journal of the Chemical Society* and the *Annalen*. It appeared under the names of Perkin,

Pope, and Wallach; but the immediate credit for the successful issue of the work is due to one who has hitherto

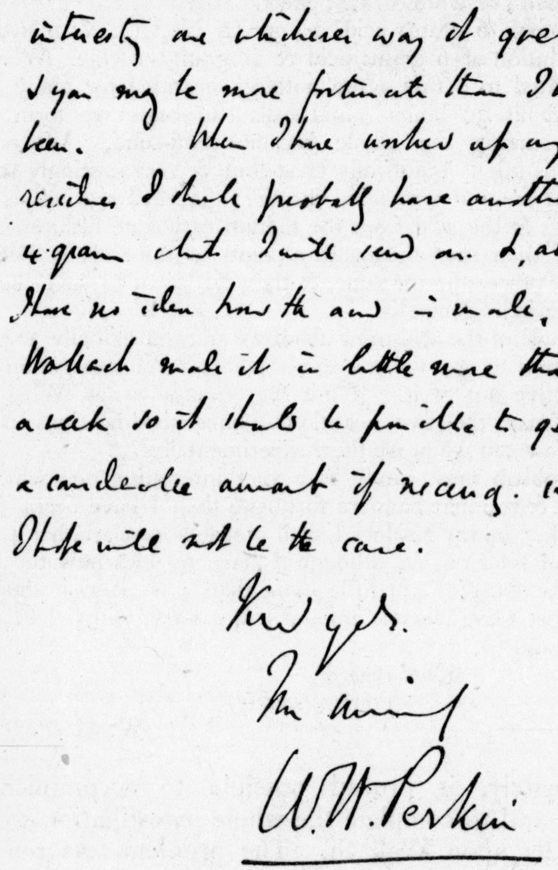

interesting one whichever way it goes.
& you may be more fortunate than I have
been. When I have worked up my
residues I shall probably have another
4-gram which I will send on &, although
I have no idea how the acid is made,
Wallach made it in little more than
a week so it should be possible to get
a considerable amount of racemic. which
I hope will not be the case.

Yrs ysd.

Yours sincerely

W. H. Perkin

70. Part of a holograph letter from W. H. Perkin, jun., to W. J. Pope, 18 December 1908

remained 'unwept, unhonoured and unsung' in chemical history—to wit, a dilatory laboratory boy.

This anonymous hero neglected to clean up a forbidding accumulation of watch-glasses, test-tubes, and the like, in the private laboratory when told to do so. Each of these contained a syrupy or glassy film of a salt of the cyclo-

69. University Chemical Laboratory, Cambridge, *c.* 1912.
(See p. 289.)

72. J. E. F. de Kok, W. J. Pope, and W. H. Mills,
(Cambridge, 1915.)
(See p. 297.)

73. The Author (Cambridge, 1913).

hexylidene acid with an alkaloid or other optically active base, such as menthylamine or bornylamine. These specimens had adorned the laboratory for many weeks, but no sign of crystallisation was evident in any of them, in spite of assiduous scratching and treatment with solvents.

Three days after the errant laboratory boy had been told to clean the apparatus I sent for him. While awaiting his arrival (fortunately he was a dilatory boy, as aforesaid), I happened to notice a tiny white speck in one of the watch-glasses, containing a specimen of the brucine salt. Under a lens this speck proved to be crystalline. It was used as a seed, and the resolution followed in due course.

Pope was of a phlegmatic temperament, but when the time came at last for the crucial polarimetric test he was noticeably excited, and he even accompanied me to the polarimeter, at that time installed in a little alcove overlooking the attendants' laboratory on the first floor. The instrument was lying at zero, and a mere glance into the eyepiece showed that the solution of the ammonium salt was strongly laevo-rotatory. Pope did not hesitate to show his delight. It was a moment to bring visions of Cortez and Pasteur (p. 341). In that rare moment the long labour of a tedious research met with its full reward. A new landmark had been set up in the expanding domain of chemistry in space. 'This resolution', wrote Gibson in 1940, 'constituted the greatest advance in stereochemistry since Pope's own classical discoveries of the synthesis and resolution of compounds containing asymmetric atoms other than carbon. It may be described as the basis of all modern stereochemical investigation.'

In a second paper on centroasymmetry, published in 1911, an observation I had made at Zürich proved of great value in studying the way in which the optical activity is affected when a centroasymmetric substance is converted into one containing an asymmetric carbon atom, or *vice versâ*: for in my *Doktorarbeit* I had shown that whereas 50 per cent. aqueous potash usually effects the change $R \cdot CHBr \cdot CHBr \cdot COOH \longrightarrow R \cdot CH:CBr \cdot COOH$, dilute

x

sodium carbonate (or dilute potash) converts the dibromo-acid quantitatively into $R \cdot CH:CHBr$. The work did not pass unheeded in Zürich, and a congratulatory message arriving from Werner (Fig. 71) soon after the publication

PROF. DR. A. WERNER

Freie Strasse 111
ZÜRICH

Zürich 13ten Mai 1910

Sehr geehrter Herr Doktor!

Ich habe mit Freuden gesehen, dass Sie an der interessanten Arbeit über die optisch-activen Methyl cyklohexyliden essigsäure reges mitgeholfen haben und gratuliere Ihnen herzu besten.

Mit herzlichen Grüssen,
Ihr J. A. Werner

71. Holograph letter from A. Werner to the Author, 13 May 1910

of the first paper testified to the interest he maintained in his former *Doktoranden*.

Early in 1914 we at last solved another fundamental stereochemical problem upon which we had been engaged intermittently since 1908, namely, the production of an optically active compound owing its asymmetry to the only carbon atom in its molecule. This substance, chloro-iodomethane sulphonic acid, $CHClI \cdot SO_3H$, contains less than 5 per cent. of carbon, and its optically active anion is composed of 8 atoms, only 3 more than the minimum number required for a lone asymmetric carbon atom linked to four different single atoms, $Cabcd$.

THE SUSCEPTIBLE CHYMIST

After the outbreak of war, later in 1914, the petroleum resources of the Royal Dutch Shell Group were placed at the disposal of Great Britain and her allies. Not least among the many technical problems of great importance in the prosecution of the war came the elaboration of a successful production of high explosives from East Indian petroleum. A team of Dutch chemists, headed by J. E. F. de Kok, manager of the great experimental laboratories of the Royal Dutch Shell Group at Amsterdam, came to Cambridge to collaborate with Pope and certain members of his staff in an investigation of this difficult problem (Figs. **72, 73**).

Those were strenuous days. The work, which had a very successful outcome, was conducted under the pressure of momentous happenings. There was little time for relaxation: 'the Germans are not standing still', as one of the Dutchmen remarked. Nevertheless, even these feverish activities had their human and humorous side.

Certain nitrating operations, carried out in a small pilot plant, led to the liberation of considerable volumes of nitrous fumes, the inhalation of which sometimes brought on cyanosis. One day, Mijnheer B——, a young member of the Dutch research team, had fallen a victim to such an attack, and I was delegated to take him out into the fresh air. We went for a gentle cycle ride, along the road to Wimpole. It was high summer, in 1915. The sun shone; yellow-hammers sang in the dusty hedgerows; larks sped upwards, showering down a rain of liquid song which changed to mist and vanished into cloudless blue; from the meadows all around came the click of busy mowing-machines. 'This is good!' I called to B——, as we rode along in company. His reply was not unduly enthusiastic. 'Yes—that—can—be', he said. . . . 'But—as for me—I like better to cycle with my zveetheart in Holland.'

Later experience showed, as I chanced to mention to Pope one morning, that nine times out of ten, in replying to a remark upon any lay activity in which he was engaged, B—— would manage to achieve a mental encompassment of his 'zveetheart in Holland'. Pope evidently thought my statement was exaggerated, and resolved to put it to the test of experiment. That evening a party of us, including B——, dined at his house in Brooklands Avenue. We came to the walnuts and wine, and B—— began to blow some remarkably fine smoke-rings. Pope seized the opportunity. Cocking me one of his droll glances, he turned to B—— and observed blandly: 'You seem to be quite an expert at blowing smoke-rings, B.——' B—— hesitated momentarily. Then a gleam came into his eye, and to the exceeding great joy of at least one of his auditors he replied: 'Yes—that—can—be. . . . But—as for me—I like better to see—as we sit out on his flat roof at nightfall—the smoke-rings that are blew by the father of my zveetheart in Holland!'

ENVOI

As the war developed, Pope undertook the investigation of other chemical problems of great national importance. Notable among these were the highly successful work on the large-scale production of mustard gas from ethylene (with C. S. Gibson), providing effective retaliation to the German introduction of noxious gases in warfare, and the preparation of new sensitisers for use in aerial photography (with W. H. Mills). For such eminent contributions to national security in times of stress, Pope received a knighthood at the end of the war. Then the maestro, Cincinnatus-like, returned to his beloved stereochemistry.

'ARS LONGA, VITA BREVIS'

John Ferguson, in the introduction to his *magnum opus*, the *Bibliotheca Chemica*, takes the long view of the historian, and in so doing strikes the melancholic note of chemistry's predecessor, alchemy. 'The chemistry of the moment', he writes, 'is also merely a phase, and by its more rapid development is so much less stable than that of three hundred years ago, when discovery made slower advance. . . . Let not the modern student of science imagine that he and his work will escape the universal doom. His discoveries, his theories, the most recent, the most comprehensive and progressive,

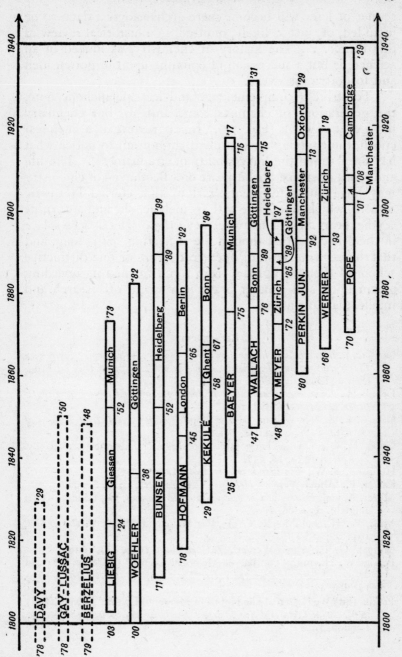

74. Chronology of some Modern Schools of Chemistry. Illustrating Chapter X

sooner or later will become mere archaeological data, to be included, or, just as likely, omitted, in a historical review of this time. . . . The history of chemistry, as indeed of all science, is but a succession of epitaphs upon forgotten men and forgotten discovery.'

To strike a complementary and less melancholic note, the generations of chemists come and go, but chemistry flows ever onwards (Fig. 74). In any review of a chemical epoch, the contemplative student cannot fail to notice what has been called the 'inevitability of gradualness'. The life and work of even a Shakespeare or a Beethoven of chemistry may form but a transient swirl in that eternal Hermetic Stream, which, like Time with its melancholic and Saturnine scythe, bears all its sons away; nevertheless, let us seek solace in the reflection that though life is fleeting, art is long, and that the expiring flash of one great figure or one distinctive school of thought lights a fresh torch to shed its revealing gleam upon still another brave new world of research and intellectual adventure.

REFERENCES

Carrière, J., *Berzelius und Liebig, ihre Briefe von 1831–1845, mit erläuternden Einschaltungen aus gleichzeitigen Briefen von Liebig und Wöhler*, München und Leipzig, 1893.

Debus, H., *Erinnerungen an Robert Wilhelm Bunsen und seine wissenschaftlichen Leistungen*, Cassel, 1901.

Gibson, C. S., 'Sir William Jackson Pope', *Obituary Notices of Fellows of the Royal Society*, 1941, **3**, 291.

Good, H. G., 'On the Early History of Liebig's Laboratory', *J. Chem. Education*, 1936, **13**, 557.

Hofmann, A. W., *The Life-Work of Liebig*, London, 1876.

Karrer, P., 'Alfred Werner', *Helvetica Chimica Acta*, 1920, **3**, 196.

Meyer, E. von, *History of Chemistry*, trans. M'Gowan, G., London, 1891; 2nd edn., London, 1898.

Mills, W. H., and Moody, G. T., 'Sir William J. Pope', *J. Chem. Soc.*, 1941, 697.

Morgan, G. T., 'Alfred Werner', *J. Chem. Soc.*, 1920, **117**, 1639.

Perkin, W. H., jun., 'The Baeyer Memorial Lecture' (10 May 1923), in *Memorial Lectures delivered before The Chemical Society, 1914–1932*, London, 1933.

Perkin, (Sir) W. H., sen., 'The Hofmann Memorial Lecture' (5 May 1893), in *Memorial Lectures delivered before The Chemical Society, 1893–1900*, London, 1901.

Roscoe, Sir H. E., 'The Bunsen Memorial Lecture' (29 March 1900), in *Memorial Lectures delivered before The Chemical Society, 1893–1900*, London, 1901.

Idem.   *The Life and Experiences of Sir Henry Enfield Roscoe*, London, 1906.

Rupe, H., 'Adolf von Baeyer als Lehrer und Forscher: Erinnerungen aus seinem Privatlaboratorium', *Sammlung chemischer und chemisch-technischer Vorträge*, Stuttgart, 1932.

Ruzicka, L., 'The Otto Wallach Memorial Lecture' (10 March 1932), in *Memorial Lectures delivered before The Chemical Society, 1914–1932*, London, 1933.

Shenstone, W. A., *Justus von Liebig: his Life and Work*, London, 1895.

Thorpe, Sir [T.] E., *Essays in Historical Chemistry*, London, 1923.

Idem.   'The Victor Meyer Memorial Lecture' (8 February 1900), in *Memorial Lectures delivered before The Chemical Society, 1893–1900*, London, 1901.

Tilden, Sir W. A., *Famous Chemists: the Men and their Work*, London, 1921.

Wöhler, E., and Hofmann, A. W., *Aus Justus Liebigs und Friedrich Wöhlers Briefwechsel*, 2 vols., Braunschweig, 1888.

Wöhler, F., 'Jugend-Erinnerungen eines Chemikers', *Berichte der deutschen chemischen Gesellschaft*, 1875, **8**, 838.

Anon.   *75 Jahre chemischer Forschung an der Universität Zürich* [Zürich, n.d. (1909)].

75. Justus Liebig, 1803–1873.
From the relief by David,
Paris, 1837

CHAPTER XI

CHEMISTRY REACHES THE
AUSTRALIAN BUSH

EUCALYPT AND KANGAROO

'I SHALL remember you when I get a kangaroo,' wrote Sir Joseph Banks from Soho Square to M. Broussonet in Paris, on May Day 1789; 'the ship which carries the curiosities destined for me is not yet arrived, but if it does it will bring one which is yours.'

The Australian flora and fauna are full of surprises for Europeans.

Some years ago, on a remote Tasmanian sheep station near Hamilton, an English visitor had the good fortune to attract the favourable attention of a small daughter of his host—a winsome blue-eyed lassie of some eleven summers. They took frequent walks together among the eucalypts, and held communion on divers matters of high import as they wandered around the paddocks under the blue Tasmanian skies. The visitor was a professor from the University of Sydney. One morning, on the way to school, the Tasmanian lassie suddenly asked him:

'Does the University of Sydney *belong* to you?'

'Oh *no*,' said the professor decidedly.

'Are you *head* of it, then?' asked the lassie.

'Not at *all*, my dear,' said the professor, even more firmly; 'I'm only a *professor* in it.'

'Then who *is* the head?' she demanded.

'The *Chancellor*,' said the professor.

His small companion suddenly drew closer and displayed a wide-eyed interest.

'Oh, *we've* got one of *them* too, at *our* school,' she said, shaking her fair curls with a suggestion of disdain. 'He crawls over the *walls*,' she added unexpectedly.

'He catches *flies*,' she went on, dancing lightly towards the school. 'And his *antics!* You ought to have *seen* him in our geography lesson yesterday! . . . Does *yours* catch flies, in Sydney?'

'I hardly *think* so,' said the professor. 'At least,' he continued, with scientific caution, 'I've never caught him *at* it.'

'*Ours* catches *mosquitoes* too,' said Daisy proudly. 'And *eats* them!'

She hurried along the pathway to the entrance of the little stone building, dragging the professor by the hand like a reluctant scholar.

'If we're *quick* we shall be able to see him before school begins, and then you can tell me if he *looks* like yours.'

'I don't think he can either *look* or *behave* very much like ours,' said the professor dubiously, as they went forward to the schoolroom door: 'his interests seem to be *quite* different.'

They peeped into the schoolroom; then entered silently. It was a quaint chamber, with an old-world flavour, and as dusty and full of oddly assorted properties as an alchemical laboratory. A cheerful wood-fire crackled in the grate on that chilly August morning; but the room seemed to be unoccupied.

'But where *is* your Chancellor?' asked the professor. 'I don't *see* him!'

The Tasmanian lassie gave a little ecstatic wriggle, and pointed triumphantly to a spot upon one of the walls. There, in languorous nonchalance, sprawled an enormous spidery insect—the school tarantula, otherwise the Chancellor of Hollow Tree School!

Australia, the land of the eucalypt and the kangaroo, is full of surprises for the European.

BOTANY BAY

At dawn on 20 April 1770, Lieutenant Hicks, on board Captain Cook's ship *Endeavour*, obtained the first glimpse on record of the eastern coast of Australia. Cook named the land Point Hicks. Sailing northwards, Cook landed in

Australia on 29 April 1770. Under date Sunday, May 6th, his journal (now in the Mitchell Library, Sydney) contains the entry (Fig. 76): 'The great quantity of this sort of fish found in this place occasioned my giving it the name of

76. 'The name of *Botany Bay*.'   An entry in Captain Cook's Journal for 6 May 1770

Stingray Harbour'.   Before reaching Batavia, he changed the entry to: 'The great quantity of New Plants, etc., Mr. Banks and Dr. Solander collected in this place occasioned my giving it the name of [*Botanist* corrected to] *Botany Bay*'.

Mr. Banks (later Sir Joseph Banks) recorded (3 May) how he carried ashore at Botany Bay 'all the drying paper, nearly 200 quires, of which the largest part was full, and spreading them upon a sail in the sun, kept them in this manner exposed the whole day, often turning them, and sometimes turning the quires in which were plants inside out'.   In the following month his specimens were soaked with sea-water as a result of the historic accident near the Endeavour River; but they are still extant in good condition—many of them were presented by the Trustees of the British Museum to the National Herbarium at Sydney in 1904, so that they are now preserved within a few miles of the spot at Kurnell where Banks and Solander gathered them in 1770.

The name Botany Bay enshrines for all time the striking impression which the strange trees, shrubs, and flowers of the eastern seaboard made upon these early visitors to Australia. From its discovery onwards, Australia has appeared to the outside world as the habitat of a strange flora and fauna. Multitudes who have never been remotely 'within coo-ee' of the great southern continent picture it to themselves as the land of the eucalypt and the kangaroo. A great deal lies behind this popular conception of Australia. The eucalypt and the kangaroo are vivid symbols of a unique flora and fauna; more than that, in some degree they are typical survivals into the present age of an order of living things inherited from a remote epoch, and elsewhere obsolete or non-existent. This ancient order, seemingly unchangeable or developing in a unique manner in its isolated Australian environment, has stamped its impress as deeply upon the indigenous plant products of Australia as upon the visible characteristics of the parent flora.

The interest in the flora and fauna of Australia is maintained in the *Journal* of Dr. John White, published twenty years after Cook's landing at Botany Bay. White was surgeon-general to the First Settlement, under Governor Phillip. The *Journal* opens with a record of Commodore Phillip's voyage from England, by way of Rio de Janeiro and the Cape of Good Hope, to Botany Bay, which he reached on 20 January 1788, with his fleet of marines, officials, and convicts. The momentous voyage, lasting more than eight months, led to the First Settlement in Australia and the founding of New South Wales. White's account of this Odyssey is a lively document of historic value; besides being a mine of information, the *Journal* reveals its author as an observant student of humanity as well as of nature.

The chronicle of winds and weather, of hardships, delinquencies, and punishments, is relieved by a romantic episode at Rio, where White and 'two other gentlemen belonging to the fleet' discovered a convent-school containing about seventy young ladies who were not 'suffered to quit the con-

vent on any other terms than that of marriage'. Those who
failed to get a husband early in life had to take the veil; a
hard fate for the owners of 'most lively, piercing, dark eyes;
in the captivating use of which they are by no means unskilled', as White recorded from first-hand observations.

'Many of these young ladies', he wrote, 'were very
agreeable both in person and disposition; and by frequently
conversing with them at the grate, we formed as tender an
intercourse with them as the bolts and bars between us
would admit of.' During a stay of a month at Rio, White
and his two friends, to use his quaint expression, attached
themselves to 'three of those who appeared to be the most
free and lively', making them presents, 'and receiving more
valuable ones in return'. However, even the combined
efforts of these three gentlemen of the fleet were unequal to
banishing the veil, as apparently they were unable to secure
the necessary 'approbation of the bishop'. 'When we took
a last farewel,' ends the narration, sorrowfully, 'they gave
us many evident proofs of their concern and regret.'

On 26 January 1788, Phillip removed the incipient
settlement from Botany Bay to Port Jackson (now known as
Sydney Harbour). 'Port Jackson', wrote White, 'I believe
to be, without exception, the finest and most extensive
harbour in the universe, and at the same time the most
secure; being safe from all the winds that blow. It is
divided into a great number of coves, to which his excellency
has given different names. That on which the town is to be
built, is called Sydney Cove.'

Soon after the removal from Botany Bay to Port Jackson,
White ran out of oil of peppermint, which was much prized
in those days as a specific for 'gouty and cholicky pains' and
'disorders arising from wind'. The surgeon-general and
his first assistant, Dennis Considen,[1] found an efficient
substitute in the oil distilled from the leaves of a tree growing
on the shores of Port Jackson. The relevant statement,
in an Appendix to White's *Journal*, runs as follows: 'The
name of Peppermint Tree has been given to this plant by

[1] See J. H. Maiden, *Sir Joseph Banks*, Sydney, 1909, 155. In the Appendix
to White's *Journal* the name is given as D. Considor.

Mr. WHITE on account of the very great resemblance between the essential oil drawn from its leaves and that obtained from the Peppermint (*Mentha piperita*) which grows in England. This oil was found by Mr. WHITE to be much more efficacious in removing all cholicky complaints than that of the English Peppermint, which he attributes to its being less pungent and more aromatic.' This is the first reference to an Australian essential oil.

This Appendix contains an account of the flora and fauna of the new land, with many fine illustrations, among them a drawing entitled 'The Peppermint Tree'. Further, it is stated that this tree undoubtedly belongs to 'the same genus with that cultivated in some greenhouses in England, which MR. L'HERITIER has described in his *Sertum Anglicum* by the name of *Eucalyptus obliqua* . . . but we dare not assert it to be the same species'. White's Peppermint Tree was, indeed, a species of *Eucalyptus*; it is now known as *E. piperita*, or the Sydney Peppermint, and is common around Sydney and in the Blue Mountains of New South Wales. *E. obliqua*, of which the original specimens came from Tasmania, was the first species named, and the one upon which L'Héritier founded the genus in 1788.

In 1771, the year after Cook's landing at Botany Bay, the Dutch botanist Gaubius made the first recorded mention of crystalline menthol, or 'mint camphor', the solid substance which forms the chief constituent of the *Mentha* peppermint oils. For more than a hundred years after the publication of White's *Journal* it seems to have been taken for granted that the 'peppermint' oils from *Mentha* and *Eucalyptus* contained a common odoriferous constituent; at one time this was supposed to be menthone, a ketone which accompanies menthol in the *Mentha* oils. In 1900, however, the peppermint odour in the genus *Eucalyptus* was shown by the Australian chemist, H. G. Smith, to be due to a distinct ketone which he isolated and named piperitone.

AMONG THE EUCALYPTS

The strangeness of the indigenous flora of Australia to the European visitor arises from the fact that so much of this vegetation belongs to the *Myrtaceae*, a large family of which Europe claims only a single species in the sweet-scented myrtle of the poets (*Myrtus communis*). In Australia there are more than eight hundred species of *Myrtaceae*, a number exceeded only by the much less conspicuous *Leguminosae*, with some thirteen hundred species. Of the forty-five genera of *Myrtaceae* represented in Australia, the most important is *Eucalyptus*, the predominant genus of the Australian flora. This genus is a highly specialised form of myrtaceous plants, developed in great profusion probably after the separation of Australia from the great tropical lands and adapted to its xerophilous and more barren environment. Among other myrtaceous genera occurring in Australia are *Myrtus*, *Eugenia*, *Angophora*, *Backhousia*, *Melaleuca*, *Leptospermum*, and *Darwinia*. The last three of these genera are shrubby, the others, like *Eucalyptus*, mainly trees. All of them except *Myrtus* and *Eugenia*, which bear fleshy berries, have dry fruits. Myrtaceous genera with dry fruits are chiefly Australian, but a few representatives are found in New Guinea, Celebes, New Caledonia, with neighbouring islands, and New Zealand. The shape and size of the fruits are important in the identification of *Eucalyptus* species.

The indigenous occurrence of the genus *Eucalyptus* is mainly confined to Australia, New Guinea, and Celebes, but suitable species are now cultivated extensively in many other countries, ranging from New Zealand to California, India, South Africa, and the Mediterranean region, mainly as timber trees of exceptionally rapid growth and for their beneficial effect when planted on marshy land. For example, near Rotorua, New Zealand, *E. oreades* readily grows in thirty years to a height of 120 feet, with a diameter at breast-height of 3 feet. The harder kinds of eucalyptus, such as the Ironbarks, are of much slower growth.

Suitable species have been cultivated in sheltered sites even so far north as Kinlochourn, in north-west Scotland: of some fifty species originally planted out (about 1895), the hardiest were *E. coccifera*, *E. gunnii*, and *E. urnigera*, all of which occur in Tasmania. At Kinlochourn, *E. coccifera* reached a height of 30 to 65 feet in thirty years: this is an endemic Tasmanian eucalypt, growing on or near the snow-line. *E. gunnii*, which grows well in the open in mixed plantations at St. Andrews, on the exposed east coast of Scotland, is the so-called 'Cider Tree' of Tasmania, of which Baron F. von Mueller wrote in his *Eucalyptographia*: 'The sap of at least the alpine *variety* has not an unpleasant taste, and bush people have converted it into a kind of cider'. The exudation, or 'cider', is also very popular among opossums and wattle-birds.

In travelling along an Australian bush track one may often traverse a natural forest of eucalypts of many species. In age, these may range from seedlings a few inches high and a few months old to monarchs of the forest originating before the days of Captain Cook and the First Settlement. Among them, in a particular district of New South Wales, may be seen gigantic Bloodwoods (*E. corymbosa*), distinguished by their rough scaly bark, of warm red hue, and long dark dribbles of exudation; clean-limbed Peppermints (*E. phellandra*), with narrow leaves and delicately latticed bark; lofty White Stringybarks (*E. eugenioides*), with the characteristic ridged bark, fibrous and intertwining; graceful Gully Ashes (*E. smithii*), grey-limbed with long pendulous leaves; and many others.

Such *Eucalyptus* species are strongly individualistic in appearance. They may be trim eucalypts, with bark persistent on trunk and branch; unkempt eucalypts, with bark partly adherent and partly shed; dishevelled eucalypts, waving long barky tresses in the breeze; stark eucalypts, spreading white arms wide against the cloudless blue of an Australian sky; spotted eucalypts; sombre eucalypts; silvery eucalypts; and eucalypts of still other types, in bewildering variety. Between their boles, in this district of New South Wales, a luxuriant scrub grows in profusion: many species of leptospermum, with small sweet-scented leaves; feathery, dark-green wattles; stiff-leaved banksias; slender-stemmed waratahs; soft-petalled flannel flowers, reminiscent of edelweiss: new species at every turn, illustrating the richness and strangeness of the bush vegetation in this region of Australia.

The ecology of the eucalypts is of great interest. The species differ greatly in kind according to soil, altitude, climate, and other environmental conditions, as Leichhardt noticed for the Australian flora generally during his historic overland expedition from Moreton Bay to Port Essington in 1844–1845. Some *Eucalyptus* species grow on a siliceous granite or sandstone formation; others require a basic type of rock, such as basalt, furnishing a clay soil. As the climate becomes colder, specific eucalypts are found at lower levels: thus, *E. delegatensis* descends from about four thousand feet above sea-level in Victoria and New South Wales to between two and three thousand feet in Tasmania. In the natural distribution of the genus, each region accordingly possesses a characteristic selection of species adapted to the locality in which they grow. In general, it is unusual to find a eucalyptus forest composed exclusively of one species; for, with the exception of *E. phellandra* and a few other species, the gregariousness of the eucalypt is generic rather than specific.

Soil, altitude, and climate must be taken particularly into account in selecting species of *Eucalyptus* for successful cultivation, whether in Australia or in other countries. Thus, in Northern Rhodesia, in a latitude of only about 10° S., and at some six thousand feet above sea-level, it has been found possible to cultivate without difficulty a number of species growing naturally at lower altitudes and in more southern latitudes in Australia: these include *E. globulus*, *E. saligna*, *E. rostrata*, *E. botryoides*, *E. teretecornis*, *E. macarthuri*, *E. staigeriana*, and *E. citriodora*. At Abbotsbury,[1] in Dorset, the rare Tasmanian species, *E. unilata*, has been observed to grow to an even larger size than in its native habitat.

Eucalypts vary in size from small shrubby 'mallees' to giant forms like the noble *E. regnans*, which, in Gippsland, has been known to exceed 300 feet in height, with a girth of nearly 70 feet.[2] The large trees occur chiefly in

---

[1] Many species were planted out at Abbotsbury in the same period (about 1895) as those at Kinlochourn, mentioned above.

[2] Anthony Trollope quoted the following particulars in support of the statement that the genus *Eucalyptus* has produced the tallest of all trees. In a letter

77. Oil-Glands and Venation in a Leaf of *E. smithii*.
Enlarged 4.5 diameters, from a direct sun-print. (See p. 312.)

78. Cutting Mallee (*E. cneorifolia*), in Kangaroo Island,
South Australia.

(See p. 315.)

79. A three-tank Bush Still at Wingello, New South Wales, (1920).

(See p. 315.)

regions having a sandy soil poor in mineral constituents, of which they store only a minute amount (0·025 to 0·05 per cent.) in their timber: this peculiarity has been advanced as a prime factor affecting their growth to such great dimensions.

THE EUCALYPTUS OIL INDUSTRY

Although the biochemical features of living organisms are much less obvious than their morphology, yet the earliest settlers in Australia quickly became aware of the richness of the trees and shrubs of the 'bush' in fragrant oils and also in resinous exudations. So long ago as 1845, the indomitable Leichhardt, lost a while to civilisation in unknown northern Australia, wrote in his journal of 'that sweet breath of vegetation, which is so remarkably experienced in Australia, where the numerous Myrtle family, and even their dead leaves, contribute so largely to the general fragrance'.

The astringent exudations, so common among eucalypts, were mistakenly called 'gums', and the name was transferred to the trees themselves, originally by Banks in 1770. Banks, like William Dampier long before him, likened eucalyptus exudations to the famous Dragon's Blood which had excited the imagination of the alchemists. 'Upon the sides of the hills', runs an entry made by Banks on 23 May 1770, 'were many of the trees yielding a gum like *Sanguis draconis.*' The Somerset man, indeed, actually bestowed the name of Dragon-trees upon the eucalypts of the north-western coast of Australia, in 1688, at the same time likening them to trees which furnished a source of the *quinta essencia*, or *pabulum ignis*, in his own homeland. 'Most of the Trees that we saw are Dragon-trees, as we supposed,' he wrote, in what is probably the first precise reference to

---

dated 'Melbourne Botanic Garden, 21st February, 1872', W. Ferguson, Inspector of State Forests, mentioned some gigantic eucalypts, found in the Watts River district of Victoria, which he identified as *E. obliqua, E. amygdalina*, and *E. goniocalyx*. One fallen specimen he found to be '435 ft. from its roots to the top of the trunk. At 5 ft. from the ground it measures 18 ft. in diameter, and at the extreme end where it has broken in its fall, it is 3 ft. in diameter. This tree has been much burnt by fire, and I fully believe that before it fell it must have been more than 500 ft. high.'—A. Trollope, *Australia and New Zealand*, 2 vols., London, 1873, **1**, 527.

eucalypts; 'and these too are the largest Trees of any there. They are about the bigness of our large Apple-trees, and about the same heighth: and the Rind is blackish, and somewhat rough. The Leaves are of a dark colour; the Gum distils out of the Knots or Cracks that are in the Bodies of the Trees. We compared it with some Gum Dragon, or Dragon's Blood, that was aboard, and it was of the same colour and taste.'

Far more important than their spectacular exudations are the timbers of the eucalypts. Many of them are economic assets of very great value to Australia. Chemically, however, the greatest interest of this premier genus of Australia lies in its essential oils. These oils are secreted in minute, semi-transparent leaf-glands, which may be seen when a leaf is held up to the light; sometimes, too, a similar oil is found in the bark and wood. By using sensitised paper, with the leaves as negatives, direct sun-prints may be obtained in which the oil-glands appear as tiny black dots and the veins as fine black lines. The number of these glands is astonishing. Under a magnification of 4·5 diameters, a leaf of *E. smithii*, only 10 cm. long, was found to contain about 900 oil glands per sq. cm. of actual surface, corresponding to more than 10,000 in the whole leaf (Fig. **77**).[1]

Essential, or essence-like, oils possess fragrant odours, as the name indicates. They are more mobile and more volatile than the 'fixed' plant oils, such as linseed, cotton-seed, coconut, and olive oils; unlike these oils, they are not of a fatty nature, and are unassimilable. Their high inflammability is largely responsible for the fierceness of Australian bush fires. Besides *Eucalyptus*, the other myrtaceous genera mentioned above are also lavish sources of essential oils, and so are many other native Australian plants belonging to the *Coniferae*, *Rutaceae*, *Labiatae*, and other families. Hence the essential-oil industry, which grew up in Australia around the eucalypts, has gradually extended to

---

[1] The average yield of oil in this species is about 1·8 per cent., based on the weight of the leaves and twigs. The black bands bounding the two leaf-margins in Fig. **77** represent parts of the sensitised paper not covered by the leaf.

embrace many species in other genera and families of indigenous plants. Of all such oils, those of the eucalypts are by far the commonest and the most important, and it was an oil of this type that Dr. John White first distilled in 1788 at Sydney Cove.

It is often supposed that 'eucalyptus oil' is a standard material consisting mainly or wholly of eucalyptole, otherwise known as cineole, the odour of which is disseminated so freely from handkerchiefs during epidemics of colds or influenza. The term 'eucalyptus oil', however, is a vague one with no precise meaning. In fact, each species of *Eucalyptus*—of which several hundred[1] are known—has its own distinctive oil, and each oil is a complex mixture of constituents. White's original eucalyptus oil, as we have seen, had an odour of peppermint, and not of eucalyptole. The odours of eucalyptus oils range indeed over a wide gamut, including turpentine, eucalyptole, peppermint, lemon, and geranium among its dominant notes.

These oils and their numerous ingredients have been applied in many ways. The original uses of eucalyptus oils were medicinal. For such purposes the oil of *E. globulus*, or Blue Gum, formerly took first place; but eventually this was replaced by cineole oils of the same general character obtained from species producing higher yields of oil. Thus, the leaves and twigs of *E. globulus* furnish less than one per cent. of oil, a yield which is doubled in *E. polybractea* and nearly quadrupled in *E. australiana*. These three oils are rich in cineole, and are used mainly as mild disinfectants or germicides. This useful property is exhibited in different degrees by many other eucalyptus oils, and is not peculiar (as was formerly supposed) to those containing cineole. The first factory for the extraction of eucalyptus oils was started in Victoria by Bosisto in 1854. As the oils from various species became better known, some were found to be of value for perfumery, some for use in special processes

[1] The numbers of *Eucalyptus* species recognised by different investigators vary over a wide range, up to a maximum of some five hundred. There are also considerable variations in the nomenclature of the genus: for the purposes of this account it has proved simplest to adopt the nomenclature of Baker and Smith.

such as the 'flotation' process for concentrating ore, and some for the manufacture of fine organic chemicals. Eventually therefore the distillation of eucalyptus oils grew into an important Australian industry.

This industry literally has its roots in the Australian bush, and in favourable localities the oil distillers' camps with their batteries of crude stills are a familiar sight. The suitability of a species as a commercial source of oil depends upon the composition and yield of the oil; also, for naturally growing trees, upon the accessibility of the species. The average yield of oil furnished by the mature leaves and terminal branchlets ranges from about 3·5 per cent. in *E. australiana* and *E. phellandra* to 0·06 per cent. in *E. corymbosa*, and dwindles to mere traces in still poorer species.

In the harvesting of eucalyptus leaves for distillation, the trees may either be lopped or felled; although felling may appear extravagant, it is often favoured by experienced distillers. When the tree is cut down within a foot or two of the ground, a strongly foliaceous 'sucker growth' soon appears, and this may be harvested again and again without destroying the reproductive capacity of the tree. The phoenix-like eucalypt conforms to the general motto of the Australian flora, which is '*Resurgam!*' It combines amazing vitality with unusual rapidity of growth in favourable conditions; thus, after the lapse of a couple of years, the decapitated stump may have surpassed the ideal of Dean Swift by producing not merely two, but three, or even four, sturdy stems where only one grew before.

The scrub of Blue Mallee (*E. polybractea*) in the Wyalong district of New South Wales is sometimes treated still more severely. Mallees are dwarf eucalypts having a bunchy growth of small stems springing from an expanded root-stock. In western New South Wales, and also in South Australia and other regions, mallee eucalypts cover large areas. One of them, *E. oleosa*, stores water in its roots, a beneficent provision that was appreciated by the Australian aborigines. Three mallees, in particular, yield excellent cineole oils: besides the Blue Mallee of New South Wales, these are *E. odorata* and *E. cneorifolia*, from which the bulk of South Australian eucalyptus oil is distilled; the last-named species occurs chiefly in Kangaroo Island.

In dealing with the Blue Mallee, the distiller sometimes flattens and partly uproots the scrub by driving a heavy roller over it; and after the hardly used vegetation has dried in the strong sun he completes its seeming destruction by burning it off. The bare waste which repels the eye at this juncture seems to lack any germ of life. But, *resurgam!* In a short time the irrepressible eucalypt reappears; a pleasing dull-blue mantle of *E. polybractea* clothes the landscape; and after a twelvemonth the distiller's faith is justified by the sight of a luxuriant growth of mallee rising waist-high.

The harvesting of the leaf is simpler from mallees than from trees, but the remaining operations are the same for material from either source. In Kangaroo Island the native mallee (*E. cneorifolia*) is cut by hand, using a sickle (Fig. **78**). The regrowth continues indefinitely if the cutting is limited to alternate years; but too frequent cutting causes the leaf to die out. Apart from the native material, mallees may be successfully cultivated in plantations for the commercial production of their essential oils.

In order to liberate the oil, the harvested leaves and twigs are brought into contact with steam: this bursts the oil glands and causes a slow vaporisation of their contents. The old-fashioned field-still usually consisted of a cubical iron tank with a capacity of 400 gallons corresponding to about 800 pounds of material, when fitted for direct firing. In apparatus of this type, the tightly packed leaves and twigs rest upon a grating, below which water is boiled by means of a wood-fire beneath the tank. As the steam forces its way up through the mass of leaves it becomes charged with the vaporised oil, and the mixed vapours are condensed during their passage through a water-cooled exit-tube. The liquid mixture of water and oil runs down into a receiver which is so constructed as to allow the relatively small layer of oil to be drawn away from the water on which it floats.

In the old type of apparatus shown in Fig. **79**, three such tanks are linked together by an iron pipe; this forms a T-joint with an exit-pipe passing through a fourth condensing tank at the rear, into which water is pumped from a creek below the *E. macarthuri* tree on the left.

In another type of distilling plant, steam is passed into digesters from an independent boiler. Sometimes the digesters are sunk into the ground in order to facilitate the handling of the fresh and spent leaf.

A newer type of still is shown in Fig. **80**: the 1000-gallon pot is fitted with an inside grating or grid-bottom for direct firing; the lid is removable, and there is an exit-tube leading to a condenser. Steam is raised by boiling water in the bottom of the pot, spent leaf being used as fuel. Such stills are usually built on sloping ground, so as to permit of easy charging and firing at the different levels.[1]

The procedure now outlined is not restricted to the winning of eucalyptus oils: it may be applied generally in the separation of essential oils from plant materials, provided that the chemical constituents are not damaged by steam.

There are many cineole-bearing species of *Eucalyptus*, and the reputation of the cineole oils has suffered in the past, owing to occasional confusion in the field. A vernacular name, such as Messmate, Mahogany, Blue Gum, White Gum, and so forth, may be interpreted in various ways, according to local opinion. For this reason, many years ago, reliable distillers began to adopt the systematic latinised names. The use of scientific nomenclature 'out back' in the Australian bush may cause surprise; yet—as a 'bush-whacker' once remarked, in somewhat different words—there is nothing inherently difficult in the pronunciation of '*Eucalyptus macarthuri*', and the name is decidedly more euphonious than the synonymic 'Camden Woollybutt' or 'Paddy's River Box'.

In this and many other ways the bush distiller is eminently adaptable and full of resource. Let us take a backward glance at him in a primitive gunyah near Wingello. He is sitting on a kerosene tin before a packing-case, making

---

[1] The charge of spent leaf from the last operation, drawn from the still by means of chains hooked to a crane, is seen behind the operator in Fig. **80**, together with a heap of ash from the burning of superfluous spent leaf not required for firing the still. The exit-pipe is visible on the right of the pot.

shift to answer a business letter. He dips his quill into home-made charcoal ink, and writes in the dim light of a primitive lamp: this, too, has been made on the premises, and it burns the home-distilled oil of *E. macarthuri.* 'Greenhide and stringybark are the backbone of Australia!' he murmurs, gazing at his humble bark roof, as he quotes a saying familiar to the early pioneers to whom he is so closely akin in spirit. He is indeed a virile and picturesque Australian type, full of first-hand knowledge mingled with the lore of the bush. Some day perhaps an Australian master will arise to do by him as Thomas Hardy has done by the tranter and the reddleman of Wessex.

CHEMICAL CHARACTERISTICS OF EUCALYPTS

It is now time to sketch in the scientific background of the eucalyptus oil industry. The first chemical investigation of such an oil was carried out by Cloëz in 1870: this French chemist obtained an impure specimen of cineole by fractionally distilling the oil of *E. globulus.* Since that time numerous investigators in Australia and elsewhere have gradually unfolded the fascinating chemistry of the Australian flora. At the present day, in the genus *Eucalyptus* alone, the essential oils of some two hundred species have been examined chemically.

So interwoven are the relationships in this genus, so refined the specific distinctions, that effective studies could be prosecuted only through the combined efforts of the botanist and the organic chemist. Happily, such a collaboration was forthcoming. In 1895, H. G. Smith (1852–1924) published, in collaboration with J. H. Maiden, the distinguished Australian botanist, his first original contribution to organic chemistry, in the form of a paper dealing with the kinos, or resinous exudations, of eucalypts. In the same year, R. T. Baker (1854–1941) became Curator of the Sydney Technological Museum, where he acted also as Economic Botanist; and in 1899 Smith was appointed Assistant Curator and Economic Chemist at the Museum. The two colleagues entered into an enthusiastic collaboration, and from that time until their retirement in 1921 carried out at the Museum a classical series of botanico-chemical investigations on the Australian flora.

Baker and Smith were both born in Kent, and made their ways separately to Sydney in the early 'eighties; they were pioneers of scientific investigation in a new country, and it is remarkable that both of them were largely self-educated for their main life-work. Handicapped in various ways, and receiving less scientific recognition and material reward than could have been desired, they were animated by the spirit that inspired Scheele, of whose life and work Smith was a great admirer: 'The elucidation of new phenomena is my sole concern,' wrote Scheele to Gahn in 1774, 'and how happy. is the investigator when the final success of his struggles brings joy to his heart.'

The researches of Baker and Smith on the genus *Eucalyptus* were published at Sydney in 1902, with a revision in 1920. These researches on the essential oils of numerous species, representative of the Australian mainland and of Tasmania, showed that altogether the genus elaborates more than forty[1] distinct chemical constituents of such oils, of which about half owed their first recognition in eucalyptus oils to Smith. Most of these substances are hydrocarbons or oxygenated derivatives belonging to the terpene series, such as pinene, phellandrene, limonene, cineole, piperitone, eudesmol, geraniol, citral, and citronellal; in addition, there are aliphatic and aromatic constituents. Some of them are peculiar to the Australian flora, which also provides the most abundant source of some of the others.

Each oil contains a certain selection of these constituents in definite proportions, and is thus distinctive for the species. The composition of the leaf-oils appears to remain sensibly unchanged in eucalypts cultivated outside their natural Australian habitat; this has been shown, for example, for *E. macarthuri*, *E. citriodora*, and *E. globulus* grown in Northern Rhodesia. The yields of oil may sometimes be increased by cultivation. Baker and Smith concluded that *Eucalyptus* species may be characterised chemically as well as morphologically. More remarkable still, they were sometimes

[1] Later, still more constituents were isolated by other investigators.

80. Distilling *E. cneorifolia*, in Kangaroo Island (1944).
(See p. 316.)

81. Types of *Eucalyptus* Leaf-venation.
E. corymbosa (Group I), *E. smithii* (Group II), *E. radiata* (Group III).

(See p. 320.)

82. Bush-Sprite and Scribbly Gum.
After May Gibbs. (See p. 321.)

able to discern a chemical distinction between closely related species, or varieties, when no decisive morphological distinction was apparent. For example, they founded the species *E. phellandra* almost wholly on chemical evidence: 'the economic importance of separating this species from *E. australiana*', they wrote in 1920, 'can be judged from the fact that at the present time the value of the oil of the latter species is more than double that of *E. phellandra*'.

This quotation illustrates the dual significance of Baker and Smith's collaborative researches, in which the latent economic possibilities were no less important than the immediate scientific advances. The full value of *Eucalyptus* oils as sources on a vast scale of many fine organic chemicals gradually became evident. The crude oil of a good cineole-bearing species, such as *E. polybractea* or *E. smithii*, may contain more than 80 per cent. of cineole, which separates readily (especially from the 'first-hour oil' of the distillation) as a glacial crystalline mass when the oil is cooled in an ammonia refrigerator. *E. dives* oil, when fractionally distilled, may yield about 50 per cent. of piperitone and 40 per cent. of phellandrene: hence it becomes a potential source of such related substances as thymol and menthol. The oil of *E. macarthuri*, containing some 75 per cent. of geranyl acetate, together with a little free geraniol, offers an abundant source of this valuable ingredient of perfumes; this oil contains in addition the much rarer eudesmol, a crystalline sesquiterpene alcohol. In New Zealand, where this species is valued also for general and farming purposes, it is grown in extensive plantations around Rotorua.

The crude oil of *E. citriodora*, the Citron-scented Gum of North Queensland, consists almost wholly of citronellal (90 per cent.); and another Queensland species, *E. staigeriana*, yields a lemon-scented oil containing about 16 per cent. of citral. This oil played a part in one of H. G. Smith's most spectacular demonstrations of the value of Australian plant products for everyday purposes. On the occasion of a formal dinner famous in the annals of the Royal Society of New South Wales, Smith smuggled into the menu an alleged sago pudding flavoured with lemon,

which, during his after-dinner speech, he divulged to have
been made under his supervision from the starch of the
Burrawang 'Palm' (*Macrozamia spiralis*), flavoured with
the leaf-oil of the Lemon-scented Ironbark (*E. staigeriana*).
Fortunately, the effect of this *tour de force* upon the Fellows
was more agreeable than the sequel to Basil Valentine's much
earlier but fundamentally similar experiment with an
antimonial preparation upon the monks of St. Peter of
Erfurt![1]

Baker and Smith's generalisations from this joint work
are remarkably interesting. They concluded that the oil
from any *Eucalyptus* species growing under natural conditions maintains a comparatively constant composition; that
each chemical constituent increases in amount through a
sequence of species until it reaches a maximum in one or
more of them; and that a connexion exists between certain
morphological characters, notably the type of venation of
the mature lanceolate leaves (Fig. 81), and the chemical nature
of the oil. A 'feather' venation (as in *E. corymbosa* and *E.
calophylla*, the Red Gum of Western Australia) denotes the
presence of pinene and possibly of bornyl acetate (Group
I); an intermediate venation (as in *E. globulus*, *E. smithii*,[2]
and *E. polybractea*) is a sign of the occurrence of pinene with
cineole (Group II); and a 'butterfly-wing' venation (as in
E. piperita, *E. radiata*, and *E. dives*) points to phellandrene
and possibly piperitone or geranyl acetate (Group III).

A wider survey of this phytochemical parallelism reveals
that each of the three groups is characterised by a definite
type of anther in the flowers, and of venation in the leaves,
and also by special oils in the leaves and specific substances
in the kinos.

Hence, a large number of *Eucalyptus* species fall into one
of three main groups, of which the chemical characteristics
may be deduced from a mere inspection of the leaf-venation.
This is a startling conclusion, suggesting *inter alia* a revival
of the mediaeval doctrine of signatures,[3] according to which

[1] *Prelude*, 187.

[2] The leaf of *E. smithii* shown in Fig. 81 was 15·5 cm. long; in this figure the
negative sun-prints have been reversed, so as to give positive impressions of the
leaves.   [3] *Prelude*, 97.

'the president of *Nature*' conveyed valuable information to man by insculping 'notable and marvelous *Figures* upon *Plants* . . . and other inferior *Bodies*'. Other interesting extensions of the doctrine may be conjectured. Possibly, 'the president of *Nature*' suggested the boomerang to the Australian aborigines by producing sickle-shaped eucalyptus leaves capable under certain conditions of describing return paths in the air.

Again, there is the intriguing example of *E. gullicki* and *E. haemastoma*. These two species, sometimes found growing side by side, are much alike in the field, being trees of medium size with a smooth, white bark. Both the venation of the leaves and their odour, when crushed, indicate however that *E. gullicki* secretes cineole (Group II) and *E. haemastoma* phellandrene (Group III). More than this, the latter species, which is known also as Scribbly Gum, almost always shows insect markings, resembling scribbles, on the bark, while *E. gullicki* is innocent of such markings. A talented Australian artist has identified 'the president of *Nature*' responsible for these informative markings with an Australian pixie, or bush-sprite, whose activities are shown in a striking drawing (Fig. 82). *E. punctata* and certain other species exude warty masses of 'eucalyptus manna' from insect punctures in the bark and leaves: this curious product consists of a sugar, raffinose, suggesting that the bush-sprite has a sweet tooth!

Smith found that this sugary secretion was given only by certain species of *Eucalyptus*, and that it could not be induced by making artificial punctures in the bark or leaves of the favoured species. In all such details his practical knowledge of these Australian natural products was profound. Thus, long before the significance of 'trace elements' had been realised, he had emphasised the importance of minute amounts of manganese in the growth of eucalypts and Australian conifers.

In the laboratory, Smith's diagnosis of the chemical composition of a eucalyptus oil after a few rapid and almost perfunctory tests was a revelation. In the bush, the tall

trees were to him as familiar friends, and his intimate knowledge of their characteristics seemed to border at times upon
wizardry. His conversation abounded in bush-lore and in
anecdotes of the bush and of the pioneers of Australian
natural science. He cherished, for instance, a great admiration for Baron Ferdinand von Mueller, 'the Prince of
Australian Botanists', for many years the Government
Botanist of Victoria and Director of the Botanic Garden
in Melbourne. One of his stories related to an encounter
of this indefatigable botanist and explorer with some aborigines on the borders of New South Wales and Victoria.
Faced by the advancing band, and dubious about their
intentions, the Baron shinned up a neighbouring 'gum'-tree,
from which point of vantage, to quote his own words, he
'waved to them a green branch of *Eucalyptus dumosa*, in
token of ahm-eet-ee'. Since the gesture—or, as Smith
insinuated slyly, the species—met with the approval of the
natives, the refugee lost no time in relinquishing his un-
dignified position—unworthy of a baron even when he
was also a botanist—'up a gum-tree'.

AN EVOLUTIONARY THEORY

A larger outcome of these phytochemical researches,
which embraced the detailed examination of other botanical
and chemical features (including the morphology of anthers
and cotyledons, the colours of timbers, and the chemical
nature of exudations), was Baker and Smith's development
of an evolutionary theory, dealing with a geographical and
chronological sequence in the genus *Eucalyptus* (Fig. 83).
There is evidence that the genus may have occurred in
Tertiary, or perhaps Cretaceous, times in the northern hemisphere; but Baker and Smith's theory relates only to Australia.
According to this theory, the genus perhaps originated in the
sandy soil and warm climate of north and north-west Australia,
none but the oldest species being found in this region. These
belong to Group I, and have 'feather'-veined leaves yielding
a maximum of only about 0·5 per cent. of a pinene oil, often
containing bornyl acetate. The oils of this group have no
commercial value. The young leaves—often red in colour

—of most of the members are coated with a thin skin of rubber; this appears as a delicate elastic sheath when the leaf is broken by a longitudinal pull. A similar protective provision is found in most species of *Angophora*, a genus

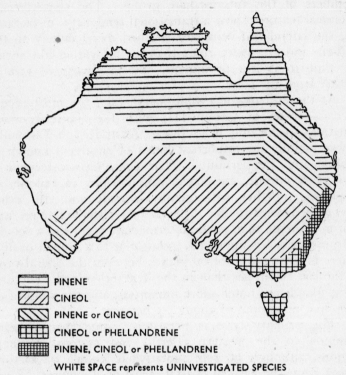

	PINENE
	CINEOL
	PINENE or CINEOL
	CINEOL or PHELLANDRENE
	PINENE, CINEOL or PHELLANDRENE

WHITE SPACE represents UNINVESTIGATED SPECIES

83. Phytochemical distribution of *Eucalyptus* in Australia. The map shows approximately the geographical limitation of *Eucalyptus* species according to the main chemical constituents in their oils

to which this oldest group of eucalypts is very closely related. The mature leaves have a thick mid-rib, with parallel lateral veins arranged close together (Fig. **81.**)

Chemical evolution is held to have accompanied botanical evolution. As the genus spread slowly eastwards and southwards, the evolution of new species was determined by changing conditions, due largely to more basic soils and cooler climates, and the pinene-cineole oils of Group II made their appearance. At this stage, pinene is still the chief terpene hydrocarbon; besides cineole, other constituents containing oxygen also made their appearance. The commercially valuable cineole oils are obtained from members of this intermediate group. The characteristic botanical features show a transitional tendency: in particular, the lateral leaf-veins are inclined more acutely to the mid-rib and are wider apart than in the feather-like form; the mid-rib is less prominent, and the marginal vein is farther from the edge.

At the end of the evolutionary scale, the most recent species—those of Group III, with the 'butterfly-wing' venation—occur only in south-east Australia and Tasmania. These include the important kinds of eucalypts known as 'Ashes' and 'Peppermints'. The characteristic terpene is now phellandrene, associated with cineole, piperitone, or terpineol, together with geranyl acetate and still other oxygenated constituents. The lateral veins are fewer and still more acute than in the intermediate type, and a second marginal vein has appeared, giving rise to a looped design. There is more room for oil glands between the lateral veins of the last two types than in the 'feather'-veined structure: these glands are much more numerous, and the yield of oil rises to a maximum of about 4·5 per cent.

The primary type is persistent, some species being common to the western (Perth) and eastern (Sydney) regions, although no representative is known in Victoria (apart from the eastern coastal strip) or Tasmania. Even the most recent species are very old: more than half of the indigenous Tasmanian species are found on the mainland, and it is concluded that these must have been distinct species long before the formation of Bass Strait.

Besides the three main groups of *Eucalyptus* included in this supposed order of evolution, the evolutionary classification takes into account such exceptional species as *E. macarthuri*, *E. citriodora*, and *E. staigeriana*, in which the chief constituents of the leaf-oil are geranyl acetate, citronellal, and citral, severally. Baker and Smith regarded such isolated species as botanico-chemical outliers, or end members of sequences in which the passage forms have disappeared in the course of evolution. Similarly, in the three main groups, dextro-pinene (which is the usual form) reaches a maximum in the oil of *E. dextropinea*; laevopinene in *E. laevopinea*; cineole in *E. polybractea, E. australiana,* and other species; phellandrene in *E. dives*; piperitone in *E. dives*; and so forth.

These extensive researches were continental in scope. The mere collection and verification of material was a task of much difficulty in widely separated regions of a sparsely settled land-mass, ill provided with means of transport, and measuring 2400 and 1970 miles from east to west and north to south respectively. Thus, in order to conduct a distillation of the leaves of *E. vernicosa* in Sydney, the material was collected in the Hartz Mountains of Tasmania, 4000 feet above sea-level, carried in bags for two miles on the shoulders of the collectors, conveyed a further twelve miles by pack-horse to Geeveston, and transported thence by boat to Hobart, and steamer to Sydney. Moreover, in order to establish the constancy of the oils from individual species, it was necessary to gather material from widely separated localities. But Baker and Smith[1] were men imbued with an extraordinary enthusiasm which no obstacles could daunt. They were apostles *par excellence* of the eucalypt. Towards the end of their labours they wrote: 'In the genus *Eucalyptus,* Australia has a commercial asset of so diversified and valuable a nature that it has no compeer in any other genus in the whole botanical world'.

MORE ABOUT AUSTRALIAN PLANT CHEMISTRY

Although the genus *Eucalyptus* overshadows the bush, there are many other Australian plants of great interest, both botanically and chemically. Here again, H. G. Smith took pride of place in the pioneering work of disclosing their chemical relationships. He was followed by various other investigators, in a field so wide and fruitful that nothing more than a bird's-eye view of it can be offered in this place.

Besides eucalypts, myrtaceous plants include the so-

---

[1] For portraits of Baker and Smith see *Endeavour,* 1944, **3,** 53.

called 'Tea Trees', an indefinite term applied to certain species of *Melaleuca, Leptospermum*, and other genera: the popular name is said to have arisen from Captain Cook's use of the leaves of *L. scoparium* as a substitute for tea. 'Tea Trees' are shrubs or trees with sweet-scented leaves: the leaf-oil of *L. liversidgei*, for example, contains 60 per cent. of citral; *L. citratum* secretes citronellal as well as citral. An even richer citral oil, consisting of the almost pure substance, is found in *Backhousia citriodora*; as an interesting exception to general experience, successful industrial use was made of aboriginal labour in the distillation of the essential oils of *B. citriodora* and *Eucalyptus citriodora* at Rockhampton, in Queensland. Of many species of *Melaleuca* that have been investigated, *M. uncinata* may be mentioned as the source of a good cajeput oil, containing cineole; *M. bracteata*, a species growing in New South Wales and Queensland, yields a leaf-oil containing methyl-eugenol.

Darwinia, an Australian genus named after the grandfather of Charles Darwin, includes the notable *D. fascicularis*,[1] a low shrub growing on waste sandy land in the coastal region around La Perouse and in many other localities. This yields a valuable leaf-oil vieing with that of *E. macarthuri* as a source of geranyl acetate, since it contains as much as 70 per cent. of geranyl acetate and 10 per cent. of free geraniol. Unlike *E. macarthuri*, this plant does not secrete eudesmol; its yield of oil, ranging from 0·4 to 0·5 per cent., is double that of the eucalypt. *D. fascicularis* could be cultivated economically as a source of geraniol for use in the manufacture of soap perfumes, synthetic attar of roses, and other fragrant products. Australia may well be regarded as the natural home of the perfume industry, although it has not yet realised that status.

The chief chemical interest of myrtaceous plants in Australia lies in their varied and bountiful selection of essential oils; at the same time, the kinos or resinous exudations which they also produce extensively have a

[1] For an illustration (about half natural size), see *Endeavour*, 1944, **3**, 54.

84. *Eucalyptus dives.*

This Australian tree secretes 'left-handed' piperitone.

(See p. 335.)

85. *Andropogon iwarancusa.*

This Indian grass secretes 'right-handed' piperitone.

(See p. 335.)

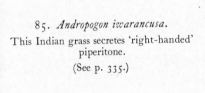

86. *dl*-Menthol from Piperitone.

Natural size. This specimen contains the finest crystals of the *dl*-form of natural menthol on record.
(See p. 336.)

limited application. Certain varieties are suitable for making medicinal extracts, or tinctures of kino; some yield good tanning extracts; formerly, also, the bark of *E. occidentalis* was exported to Germany in large quantities for this purpose. Other barks, particularly among the mallee eucalypts, contain crystalline deposits of calcium oxalate, forming sometimes as much as one-sixth of the weight of the air-dried bark; the bark of *E. salubris*, the tall Gimlet Gum of Western Australia, offers an excellent source both of oxalic acid and tannin.

Many of the kinos are deeply coloured, and some of them might possibly be used as dyes. The best-known dye furnished by the genus *Eucalyptus* is myrticolorin (quercitin rutinoside), which may be mordanted to yield fast yellow, khaki, and brown shades; the leaves of *E. macrorhynca*, a common species in New South Wales and Victoria, give as much as 8·5 per cent. when extracted with boiling water. 'The presence of this dye material in the leaves of *E. macrorhynca* at once distinguishes it from *E. laevopinea*,' wrote Baker and Smith, 'and is another illustration of the value of chemical evidence in determining differences between *Eucalyptus* species closely allied morphologically.'

Chemically, the family *Myrtaceae* takes pride of place among the indigenous flora of Australia; but there are certain other groups of considerable chemical importance, in particular the family *Leguminosae*, and also the *Coniferae*, a group much more ancient than the flowering plants.

The family *Leguminosae* includes more than four hundred species of Australian acacias, or wattles, having a wide reputation for their gay inflorescence and scented wood. Many of these exude gums, and certain species growing in the arid western areas yield a good gum arabic, although this cannot be collected economically. *Acacia pycnantha*, *A. mollissima*, *A. decurrens*, and other species give excellent tanning extracts. Some of these barks contain more than 30 per cent. of tannin, and at one time there was a considerable export of wattle bark at about £8 per ton; these tan-barks, however, can be be grown and gathered more economically in South African plantations than in their

z

native habitat, and there has even been an Australian importation from this source. In Australia, wattles give rise to great stretches of brigalow (*A. harpophylla*), mulga (*A. aneura*), myall, and other scrubs. The myall (*A. pendula*) is a small, graceful tree, with a violet-scented wood once much sought after for stockwhip handles. Another wattle, *A. acuminata*, is known as 'Raspberry Jam', on account of the curious odour of its wood. *A. melanoxylon*, or 'Blackwood', furnishes a valuable cabinet wood, close-grained and of a dark-brown hue, which Baker considered as unrivalled as an ornamental wood and for its variety of unique and gorgeous figures.

Many Australian conifers belong to *Callitris*, the genus *Pinus* being unknown in the indigenous flora. According to Baker and Smith, the genus *Callitris* also underwent evolutionary changes in traversing the continent from west to east. *C. glauca* (White Pine or Cypress Pine), a typical 'western' species, affords the best source of an Australian 'pine-needle' oil. This oil, obtained in yields reaching 0·6 per cent., contains pinene and bornyl acetate, and could be used in soap perfumes, sprays, and for pharmaceutical purposes. The timber also is valuable, and this is true for many Australian conifers. *C. tasmanica* (Oyster Bay Pine) gives up to about 0·2 per cent. of a leaf-oil containing 60 per cent. of geranyl acetate; in this 'eastern' species Australia possesses a strange and notable conifer which might be used economically as a source of geraniol. Other species, especially *C. calcarata* (Mountain Pine) and *C. arenosa*, produce rich tan-barks, furnishing up to 35 per cent. of tannin: Australia commands vast undeveloped sources of tannin in species of *Callitris* growing on land otherwise unproductive. Some of these trees also yield a good sandarac exudation, suitable for making spirit varnishes; but so far it has not proved possible to collect this material economically.

Of many other Australian conifers, *Araucaria cunninghamii* (Moreton Bay Pine or Hoop Pine) is a magnificent timber tree reaching 200 feet in height; *A. biawilli* (Bunya Bunya), another tall tree growing in the coastal zone of

Queensland, bears large cones containing edible seeds, to which the aborigines were very partial; *Agathis robusta* (Queensland Kauri) gives an oleo-resin which is the most economic Australian source of a turpentine; and *Dacrydium franklini* (Huon Pine) furnishes a timber very resistant to insects, possibly because it contains methyl-eugenol. Unfortunately, before the advent of scientific forestry in Australia, there was a reckless 'cutting out' by skilled axemen of these unique and magnificent species, without replanting.

To sum up: from the chemical point of view, the myrtaceous plants—*Eucalyptus* and its congeners—are remarkable for their wealth of essential oils; the Australian wattles and 'pines' are predominantly sources of astringent materials.

Finally, no more than a mere mention can be made of other flowering plants: for example, the dainty pink-petalled *Boronias* (*Rutaceae*), with their intriguing scents and interesting oils (containing elemicin, thujone, safrole, methyl-eugenol, etc.); the fifty or so species of *Prostanthera* (*Labiatae*), recognisable in the bush by their aromatic flowers and leaves (with oils containing pinene, cineole, cuminaldehyde, cymene, etc.); the sassafras and sandalwood trees; the 'Grass Trees', or 'Black Boys' (*Xanthorrhoea* spp.), renowned for a yellowish resin from which picric acid may be made; and the proteaceous tree, *Orites excelsa*, with its unique secretions of basic aluminium succinate.

It is unnecessary to detail the alkaloids, dyes, glucosides, saponins, starches, fibrous celluloses, and other important organic products which various investigators have isolated from Australian plants. The trend towards increasing specialisation in this field, as in science generally, may be illustrated by referring to such typical investigations, chosen at random from the chemical literature, as those upon trimethylamine in the Australian 'Salt Bush', *Rhagodia hastata* (Challinor, 1913); methyl laevo-inositol in *Heterodendron oleaefolium* (Petrie, 1918); cellulose from 'Marine Fibre' of *Posidonia australis* (Read and Smith, 1919); Rhodesian *Eucalyptus* oils (Carter and Read, 1925); cryptone, a second *Eucalyptus* ketone, in the oil of *E. cneorifolia* (Cahn, Penfold, and Simonsen, 1931); eremophilone, a new sesquiterpene ketone, in *Eremophila mitchelli* (Bradfield, Penfold, and Simonsen, 1932); the two varieties of piperitol (Read and Walker, 1934); the dihydrocryptols from cryptone of *Eucalyptus cneorifolia* (Gillespie, Macbeth, and Swanson, 1938); and thujene in *E. dives* (Birch and Earl, 1938).

The golden days of chemical pioneering in the Australian bush are past and gone; but alluring problems of mounting complexity still abound.

BIOLOGICAL, PHYTOCHEMICAL, AND CHEMICAL PROBLEMS

The isolation of Australia from the other great land-masses of the world has been the most important factor in the survival of its unique flora and fauna. In free contact with other continents, there is little doubt that many of these fascinating living forms would have perished long ago in the struggle for existence. With the advent of the white man from across the wide oceans, Australia's biological insulation was breached. Many new forms of plant and animal life were introduced into a fallow environment. Some of these were entirely beneficial; but others soon assumed the rôle of aggressive invaders, spreading at a rate which defied control. Australia thus gained an unenviable notoriety as a happy hunting-ground for plant and animal pests.

Among plant pests, the bramble, sweet-briar, and thistle became widely disseminated; in some regions the water hyacinth began to choke the rivers; in others, the St. John's wort was dispersed by stock over large areas. Most serious of all, prickly-pears, after gaining footholds in Queensland and New South Wales, began to spread rapidly from about 1900 onwards. Prickly-pears (*Opuntia* spp.) are indigenous in North and South America. While Dr. John White and his friends of the First Fleet were breathing 'their soft sighs through the lattice-work of a window or the grate of a convent' at Rio de Janeiro in

August 1787, Commodore Phillip took on board some prickly-pear plants, together with the cochineal insects which they harboured. Phillip hoped in this way to establish in his new colony a cochineal industry that would provide the red dye necessary for the military uniforms of those days; but there is no record of the plants or their insect parasites after their arrival at Port Jackson.

Although Governor Phillip introduced the first prickly-pear plants into Australia, the species was probably a comparatively harmless one (*Opuntia monacantha*), growing near Rio. The dangerous species were brought in later, from time to time, as plant curiosities. Some of them were used as hedges. Dissemination gradually followed, partly through the rooting of detached segments, but mainly through the distributive activities of emus, currawongs, and other birds feeding on the soft pulpy fruits.

The spread was slow at first, but by about 1884 the dangerous potentialities of the plant invaders began to be recognised. By 1900, some ten million acres had become infested. Soon, *O. inermis* and *O. stricta* became major plant pests; other species, although less prolific, assumed the status of noxious weeds in some areas. The rapid spread of *O. inermis* in Australia has been characterised as one of the botanical wonders of the world: in the later stages, its onset became almost explosive. By about 1917, prickly-pear had formed an almost impenetrable barrier over some twenty million acres in Queensland, and was advancing rapidly, like an irresistible tidal wave, into northern New South Wales. The infestation was particularly heavy in the brigalow (*Acacia harpophylla*) and belar (*Casuarina lepidophloia*) scrubs, in which areas the weight of pear rose to 800 tons per acre. Settlement retreated before the oncoming wall of prickly vegetation; land originally suitable for grazing, dairying, or general farming was overrun by the pest; holdings and homesteads lying in the line of advance had to be abandoned. Primitive methods of eradication had proved useless. The time had come for a scientific counter-offensive.

In 1917, the Executive Committee of the newly formed

Commonwealth Institute of Science and Industry[1] recommended urgently the inception of biological and chemical researches dealing with the problem of eradication. Among chemical methods, gassing with arsenical and other vapours was tried; but although sometimes successful on a small scale, both chemical and mechanical methods proved to be much too expensive for general application. A large monetary reward offered by the Government for a successful method of treatment stimulated the imaginations of inventors and others. Suggestions poured in, ranging from the proposed conversion of the pear into industrial alcohol to its extermination by means of tanks or flame-throwers. Latter-day Canutes arose on all sides. Even this formidable plant pest carried an element of humour in its train.

One morning in 1919, a letter, addressed to 'The Director of Science, Sydney University', was sent by the University sorting office to the Department of Organic Chemistry. It came from the head of a recognised firm of lawyers in Sydney, and read as follows:

Dear Sir,   *Re* Prickly Pear.

On behalf of a client I beg to submit following proposal with a view to the eradication of this land pest. My client asks for the use of a couple of acres of land near Sydney, so fenced that neither pigs nor goats can escape. He also asks for the use of about a dozen pigs (full-grown Boars), and the same number of goats. The two acres to be divided by a pear hedge which will decide the Boar and goat competition in the destruction of the Prickly-Pear.

The obvious expected result being that the pigs and goats having nothing else to eat will eventually become so hungry that they will consume not only the vegetation above the ground but that below it also, root and stump. It might be found that the goats will not be able to uproot the roots, but it is anticipated that they will eat the surface vegetation faster than the pigs, and the pigs may then be let in to eat the roots.

Personally I would recommend the proposition even as an experiment, the expense being nominal, and the pigs and goats being still marketable—the proponent merely claiming the reward for his alleged discovery. He assures me that the pigs and goats will survive

[1] Afterwards reorganised as the Council for Scientific and Industrial Research (C.S.I.R.).

the ordeal. At all events he claims that the Prickly-Pear will not survive.

Yours faithfully,   ——

P.S.—My client will, of course, superintend the animals during the trial, and if successful further arrangements will be made. Certainly it would open up a great industry in the pork line.

Fundamentally, the proponent whose fertile imagination shines through this letter had much in common with the alchemists. The principle of the unity of matter, underlying the alchemists' conception of goldmaking, was correct; but in the imaginary Philosopher's Stone they hit upon the wrong transmuting agent. Similarly, the principle of the biological control of prickly-pear, underlying the proponent's conception of goldmaking, was correct; but in his pigs and goats he hit upon the wrong animal organisms.

Prickly-pear still marched on. By 1925 it had spread between Mackay and Newcastle over some sixty million acres—an area exceeding that of Great Britain—of which about half was so densely infected as to be useless. This, however, was the high-tide mark of the prickly-pear invasion. In 1920 the Commonwealth Prickly Pear Board was set up with the specific task of attempting biological control by means of insect enemies which attack prickly-pears in their natural habitat. Of some 150 species of such insects, studied in America, about 50 were sent to Australia; of these, a dozen species were liberated and established after starvation tests had shown that their destructive activities in Australia would be confined to prickly-pears. By 1928 it had become evident that *Cactoblastis cactorum*, introduced in 1925 from Argentina, was able to bring about the complete destruction of *O. inermis* and *O. stricta* by rotting away the plant fabric. From 2750 eggs originally imported, it was possible between 1927 and 1930, through large-scale rearing in cages, to release some three thousand million eggs in the infected areas. The effect was phenomenal in its rapidity and completeness. By 1933, through the agency of *Cactoblastis cactorum*, the prickly-pear territory had been 'transformed as though by magic from a wilderness to a scene of prosperous endeavour'. The major problem having been solved, other insects were imported for the control of less prevalent species of *Opuntia*, including the so-called tiger pear and the tree pears.

Passing now from biological to phytochemical problems, it is evident from Baker and Smith's botanico-chemical researches on the Australian flora that the botanist, sometimes unable to go so far as the chemist in the differentiation of plant forms, may well ask when a species ends and a variety begins. An interesting example is provided by *Eucalyptus dives*, the type form of which shows a maximum proportion of more than 50 per cent. of piperitone in its oil. This is a species of high commercial value, and yet botanically the type form is inseparable from three varietal forms, in which the proportion of piperitone dwindles from about 20 per cent. to vanishing point, with an increase of phellandrene in one variety and the development of about 25 to 75 per cent. of cineole in the other two (Penfold and Morrison, 1927). To what extent can chemistry serve in the classification of living forms?

The admirable name *Eucalyptus* was synthesised by L'Héritier[1] in 1788 from the Greek *eu* (well) and *kalyptos* (covered), the allusion being to a protective lid or operculum which covers the inner part of the flower and falls off when the stamens reach maturity. For this and other reasons, Baker and Smith considered that cross-fertilisation occurs very rarely in the genus under natural conditions. Botanist and chemist alike would be interested to learn the effect of carefully controlled hybridisation upon the chemical composition of eucalyptus oils. How would the chemical factors be inherited? Would it be possible to breed forms producing essential oils of particular value?

Such phytochemical problems are bound up in turn with the close chemical relationships which are so commonly found to obtain between nearly related botanical species or varieties. Groups of substances found in their essential oils, for example, often appear to have been elaborated from

---

[1] L'Héritier founded the genus on the species *E. obliqua*, of which the original specimens came from Tasmania (p. 307).

a common chemical precursor through slight divergencies operating in a chain of simple processes. Thus, *Boronia pinnata* and *B. muelleri* both secrete elemicin in their essential oils; but in *B. safrolifera* one of the three methoxyl groups has been suppressed, so that both safrole and methyl-eugenol appear in the oil.

Some interesting chemical and phytochemical problems may be illustrated by referring to the ketone, piperitone, which H. G. Smith showed in 1900 to be the peppermint-smelling ingredient of John White's Sydney Peppermint. This substance occurs in more than twenty species of *Eucalyptus*, invariably in a laevo-rotatory or 'left-handed' (*l*) form, reaching its maximum proportion in the oil of *E. dives*. This species (Fig. 84), also known as the Broad-leaved Peppermint Tree, is common throughout the coastal ranges of New South Wales and Victoria.[1] In 1921, J. L. Simonsen, working independently at Dehra Dun, India, discovered dextro-rotatory or 'right-handed' (*d*) piperitone in the oil of *Andropogon iwarancusa* (Fig. 85); this Indian grass[2] is widely distributed in the Himalayas and outer hill zone from Kashmir to Assam, up to an altitude of more than 8000 feet, also in the plains from North-West Himalaya to Bombay Presidency. These two piperitones, of the southern and northern hemispheres, are identical, except that their molecules are related as object and distinct mirror-image.[3]

Thomas Hardy is usually regarded as a novelist; in select circles he is known as a poet; above all, however, he was a philosopher, and he had a broad philosophic interest in science. Thus, it was natural that one afternoon in the summer of 1923, at Max Gate, the two forms of piperitone should stray into a conversation dealing originally with climbing plants. 'In Europe', mused Mr. Hardy, 'the sun rises in the east and passes through south to west; in Australia through north to west. Here in Dorset the

---

[1] Fig. 84 shows (A) the early or sessile foliage, (B) the mature or lanceolate leaves, with flower-buds before flowering, and (C) the mature or lanceolate leaves, with fully formed seed-cases or fruits; the extreme length of (B) is 11 inches.

[2] The downward section of stalk shown in Fig. 85 is a foot long.

[3] Similarly, *l*-piperitol and *d*-piperitol, the corresponding secondary alcohols, have been found in species of *Eucalyptus* and *Andropogon* respectively.

scarlet-runner climbs in a right-handed spiral, following the sun. Does it climb left-handed in Australia? And would such a difference in the two hemispheres account for your two piperitones?'

To these shrewd questions it may be answered that right-handed climbers are right-handed on both sides of the equator, and that neither in climbing plants nor in molecules can right-handedness or left-handedness be ascribed to the apparent direction of motion of the sun. The asymmetry of the climber may perhaps be determined by molecular asymmetry of its chemical constituents; but the ultimate nature of the directive influence leading to a discriminative synthesis of right-handed and left-handed molecules in living organisms remains an unsolved problem of biochemistry.

A systematic study of the two forms of piperitone, begun at Sydney, in the southern hemisphere, and continued at St. Andrews, in the northern, has thrown much light upon chemical and stereochemical problems in the terpene group, besides leading to ideas of biochemical significance.

Firstly, by means of a network of delicate reactions, piperitone has been used as a source of the four kinds of menthols. Theoretically, each kind should exist in a 'right-handed' and a 'left-handed' form, together with a so-called dl-form composed of equal amounts of the two. As an outcome of this work, all of them have now been brought within reach of the chemist. One of the twelve forms (l-menthol) is identical with natural menthol from oil of peppermint (Mentha piperita). So, in the fullness of time, it has proved possible to prepare the chief constituent of 'English Peppermint' oil from the essential oil first drawn from the leaves of John White's 'Peppermint Tree' at Sydney Cove in 1788 (Fig. 86).

Secondly, it has been found possible to proceed, by laboratory processes, from the 'left-handed' Australian piperitone to the 'right-handed' Indian piperitone, a stereochemical achievement of great interest.

Lastly, these chemical and stereochemical researches offer a clue to the biochemical relationships of the Australian and Indian oils concerned. Baker and Smith held that the open-chain compound, geraniol, passed into *Eucalyptus* from the older genus *Angophora*, and probably runs through the whole genus, although often present only in small amounts. This view being accepted, geraniol may be presumed to function in *Eucalyptus* as the precursor of piperitol, piperitone, and phellandrene. A detailed theoretical scheme has been advanced, according to which the reactions take a slightly different turn in the Indian grasses, leading thereby from geraniol to piperitol and piperitone, with carene in place of phellandrene. The divergence is postulated as a consequence of two closely similar possibilities of migration offered to a hydrogen atom in the geraniol molecule. The migration in *Eucalyptus* species is limited to one direction; but in *Andropogon* species it occurs simultaneously in both directions.

The possibility of the two series of chemical reactions is clear, and some of the steps have been realised in the laboratory since the theory was first put forward; but in what way the plants discriminate between the 'left-handed' and 'right-handed' molecules remains obscure. The excessively delicate control of the molecular mechanism which is here implied appears to be a prerogative of the living organism. The organic chemist is powerless to effect such subtle differentiations by the artificial methods of the laboratory. At the present stage of our knowledge, the finer manifestations of organic synthesis appear to be inseparably bound up with vital processes.

ENVOI

A Spanish navigator named Alvaro Mendaña sailed westwards from Peru in 1567, in search of a golden continent. He would have found Australia; but by changing his course to the north-west he came to a group of islands which became known as the Solomon Islands, since they were supposed at the time to be 'those isles whence Solomon fetched gold to adorn the Temple at Jerusalem'.

Fifty years later, Count Michael Maier, in his *Contributions of Twelve Nations to the Golden Table*, linked the four known continents with the four elements: Europe with Earth, Asia with Air, Africa with Fire, and America with

Water. The Quintessence, or 'fifth existence', was left unallocated until the discovery of a fifth continent, which, in alchemical phraseology, 'God's Providence should make worthy of it'. The alchemists would have hailed Australia as the Land of Gold and the abode of the Philosopher's Stone (as symbolised by the eucalyptean *Sanguis draconis*); but with our fuller knowledge we may link the Quintessence with that Southern Land of the Holy Spirit (as Quiros designated the imagined southern continent in 1605) which is the natural home of essences and ethereal oils.

References

Baker, R. T., *The Hardwoods of Australia and their Economics*, Sydney, 1919.

Baker, R. T., and Smith, H. G., *A Research on the Eucalypts, especially in regard to their Essential Oils*, Sydney, 1902; 2nd edn., Sydney, 1920.

Idem.   *A Research on the Pines of Australia*, Sydney, 1910.

Banks, Sir J., Autograph letter, signed, to M. [P. M. A.] Broussonet, May 1 [1789], in the St. Andrews collection.

Dodd, A. P., *The Biological Campaign against Prickly-Pear*, Brisbane, 1940.

Hückel, W., 'Aus der Geschichte der Terpenchemie', *Die Naturwissenschaften*, 1942, **30**, 26.

Leichhardt, L., *Journal of an Overland Expedition in Australia, from Moreton Bay to Port Essington, a distance of upwards of 3000 miles, during the years 1844–1845*, London, 1847.

Maiden, J. H., *Sir Joseph Banks: The 'Father of Australia'*, Sydney, 1909.

Maier, M., *Symbola Aureae Mensae Duodecim Nationum*, Frankfurt, 1617.

Masefield, J. (ed.), *Dampier's Voyages*, 2 vols., London, 1906.

Read, J., 'Wizards of the Bush', *Sydney Morning Herald*, April 27th and 30th, 1921.

Idem.   'Henry George Smith', *J. Chem. Soc.*, 1925, **127**, 958.

Idem.   'A Chapter in the Chemistry of Essential Oils', *Nineteenth Streatfeild Memorial Lecture*, London, 1936.

Idem.   *Text-Book of Organic Chemistry*, London, 1946, 623.

Idem.   'Chemistry of the Australian Bush', *Endeavour*, 1944, **3**, 47.

Smith, H. G., 'Some Chemical Characteristics of the Australian Vegetation', *Report of the Australasian Association for the Advancement of Science*, Wellington, 1923, **16**, 201.

Smith, H. G., *et al.*, 'The Botanical and Chemical Characters of the Eucalypts and their Correlation', *British Association 85th Report* (*Manchester: 1915*), London, 1916, 97.

White, J., *Journal of a Voyage to New South Wales with Sixty-five Plates of Nondescript Animals, Birds, Lizards, Serpents, curious Cones of Trees and other Natural Productions. By John White Esqre. Surgeon General to the Settlement*, London, 1790.

CHAPTER XII

CHEMISTRY SUBLIMES INTO DRAMA

THE DRAMATIC ELEMENT IN CHEMISTRY

THE student of the human and humanistic appeal of science cannot fail to notice how often the dramatic note has been struck in the history of alchemy and chemistry. In alchemy, the story of James IV of Scotland and his court alchemist (p. 18) leads up to a moment of high drama when the stage is set on the battlements of Stirling Castle, in 1507, for Damian's flight to Paris: here is a dramatic story with interludes of comedy, but ending tragically in the classical manner of alchemy with the Death of the King. The Setonian episodes a hundred years later (p. 37) are still more highly fraught with dramatic interest: they constitute a veritable epic drama, leading from hazardous adventure, comedy and romance, to the final tragedy through a wide gamut of human experiences and emotions. The story of Seton and Sendivogius provides, without any embellishment, all the ingredients necessary for a thrilling novel, play, or film.

The dramatic element passed from alchemy to chemistry. Many examples could be brought forward in support of this thesis. Thus, Davy rose to fame through his dramatic experiments on the inhalation of gases (p. 205). 'Great Faraday, who made the world so wise', joined him at the Royal Institution because of an altercation between Mr. W. Payne, a laboratory attendant, and Mr. Newman, the instrument-maker, during which the former so far forgot himself as to strike the latter—thereby delivering one of the most dramatic and telling blows in the history of science, by creating a vacancy for the young bookbinding apprentice (p. 190). In more recent times, it is significant that the lives of Pasteur and Madame Curie have been represented with considerable effect on the screen.

Pasteur (Fig. 87)—one of the most human and humane of all great men of science—played at the outset of his scientific career an important rôle in developing our theories of molecular constitution. It is a striking reflection that these specialised and abstruse theories were elaborated over a long series of years to the accompaniment of a chain of dramatic incidents, beginning with the arrival of a travelling vendor of toy crackers in the market-place of Darmstadt early in the nineteenth century (p. 239).

The cheapjack's operations with silver fulminate attracted the attention of the boy Liebig. Liebig's consequent work on fulminates coincided in time with Wöhler's work on cyanates. This juxtaposition of action led to the recognition of isomerism (p. 124), and later to the development of the radical theory (p. 242). Soon after this position had been reached in unfolding the structure of the organic molecule, Pasteur, in 1848, discovered the spontaneous separation of sodium ammonium racemate into right-handed and left-handed crystals, distinguishable through the direction of slope of their hemihedral facets. The result aroused incredulity; and the veteran physicist, Biot, was appointed by the French Academy of Sciences to examine the suspiciously plausible claims of the young investigator. Pasteur himself has left an account of the ensuing dramatic scene:

'He [M. Biot] sent for me to repeat before his eyes the several experiments. He gave me racemic acid which he had himself previously examined and found to be quite inactive to polarised light. I prepared from it in his presence the sodium ammonium double salt, for which he also desired himself to provide the soda and ammonia. The liquid was set aside for slow evaporation in one of the rooms of his own laboratory, and when 30 to 40 grams of crystals had separated he again summoned me to the Collège de France, so that I might collect the dextro- and laevo-rotatory crystals before his eyes, and separate them according to their crystallographic character, asking me to repeat the statement that the crystals which I should place on his right hand would cause deviation to the right, and the others to the left. This done, he said that he himself would do the rest. He prepared the carefully weighed solutions, and, at the moment when he was about to examine them in the polarimeter, he again called me into his laboratory. He first put the more interesting solution, which was to cause rotation to the left, into the apparatus. Without making a reading, but already at the first sight of the colour-tints presented by the two halves of the field in the Soleil saccharimeter, he recognised that there was a strong laevorotation. Then the illustrious old man, who was visibly moved, seized me by the hand, and exclaimed: "My dear child, I have so loved the sciences throughout my life that this makes my heart leap with joy!" ["Mon cher enfant, j'ai tant aimé les sciences dans ma vie que cela me fait battre le cœur!"].'

Pasteur had discovered optical isomerism and laid the foundation of stereochemistry, or spatial chemistry. Stereoisomerism, a more delicate type of isomerism than that conceived by Liebig and Wöhler, had come to light. Soon after carrying out these classical experiments, Pasteur left this work for fields of scientific endeavour of more immediate benefit to humanity.[1]

Meanwhile, August Kekulé, a young *Privatdozent* at Heidelberg (p. 254), had been brooding over the problem of molecular structure; and the fundamental idea of the quadrivalency of carbon and the linking of carbon atoms came to him with dramatic suddenness as he sat one night in a reverie on the top of a London bus. A few years later, in 1865, as he dozed by his fireside at Ghent, a dramatic vision of a snake seizing hold of its own tail revealed to him in a flash the further secret of the benzene ring. So arose the fundamental theory of molecular structure. 'Lernen wir träumen, meine Herren,' said Kekulé, 'dann finden wir vielleicht die Wahrheit' ('Let us learn to dream, gentlemen, then perhaps we shall find the truth').

[1] Fig. 87, reproduced from a rare original photograph, shows the serious and intent expression so characteristic of Pasteur.

The work and ideas of Pasteur and Kekulé found their conclusion and logical sequel in 1874, in the theory of molecular configuration, or 'space theory', in which Le Bel and van 't Hoff translated the flat molecules of Kekulé into three-dimensional edifices. Here again a dramatic coincidence stepped in; for the theory was published independently and almost simultaneously by the young French and Dutch chemists. 'That shortly before this', wrote van 't Hoff, 'we had been working together in Wurtz's laboratory was purely fortuitous; we never exchanged a word about the tetrahedron there, though perhaps both of us already cherished the idea in secret. . . . Historically the difference lies in this, that Le Bel's starting point was the researches of Pasteur, mine those of Kekulé. . . . My conception is . . . a continuation of Kekulé's law of the quadrivalence of carbon, with the added hypothesis that the four valences are directed towards the corners of a tetrahedron, at the centre of which is the carbon atom.'[1]

The recurrence of the dramatic element in alchemy and chemistry leads naturally to the idea that even life and activity in a modern chemical laboratory may be romanticised and sublimated 'into something rich and strange' in chemical literature by presenting it in dramatic form. An experiment to test this idea was designed to mark the prospective centenary celebrations of the chair of chemistry at St. Andrews (Fig. 88), falling in 1940:[2] the outbreak of war interrupted the completion of the design; but the script of the drama may now be published, as a conclusion to this account of humour and humanism in chemistry.[3]

[1] For a fuller account of these theories, see P. Frankland, 'The Pasteur Memorial Lecture' (25 March 1897), and F. R. Japp, 'The Kekulé Memorial Lecture' (15 December 1897), in *Memorial Lectures delivered before The Chemical Society, 1893–1900*, London, 1901; also the author's *Text-Book of Organic Chemistry*, London, 1946.

[2] See Sir J. C. Irvine, *The Chair of Chemistry in the United College of St. Salvator and St. Leonard, University of St. Andrews: Centenary Lecture, 6th December, 1940*, Edinburgh, 1941.

[3] In introducing this play, it may be pointed out that although it contains some local colour, derived from the ancient University of St. Andrews, the characters, conversations, incidents and descriptions are wholly imaginary, and have no relation to actual persons, proceedings or institutions.

87. Louis Pasteur, 1822–1895 (*c.* 1875).

(See p. 341.)

88. 'Sanctandrois.' (See p. 342.)

THE NOBEL PRIZE

A Chemic Drama in One Act

PERSONS

AMY, *a melting bejantine* [1] OTHER BEJANTINES
ANNIE, *a caustic bejantine* SEMIES [1]
ETHEL, *a peroxide bejantine* A LABORATORY BOY
KATE, *a canny bejantine* A PAGE
BENJAMIN GREEN, *a white- SPECTATORS
coated research man*

SCENE: *A preparation room in the Chemistry Department of
an imaginary University*

TIME: *Eleven o'clock in the forenoon of a day in a Candlemas
Term, in the fourth decade of the twentieth century*

(*A loud buzz of conversation, punctuated by shrieks and laughter, is heard
as the curtain begins to rise. A gay group of* BEJANTINES *gradually
comes into view. They wear scarlet gowns, with caps bearing the blue
tassels characteristic of bejantdom. Some are busy making coffee; others
perch on tall laboratory stools and partake of coffee, shortbread and
biscuits. All indulge in the animated talk dear to the bejantine heart:
this centres upon a being of an Olympian order, named* BENJY GREEN.
*Soon a coherent pattern becomes audible in the babel, but this is still
punctuated as before.*)

VARIOUS BEJANTINES (*in rapid succession*):
Isn't Ben coming?
Yes—in a minute, he said.
He's immersed in a gigantic thriller.
Oh—what's it called?
Milestone, so he said. It looked pretty baleful.
One of Edgar Wallace's?
I don't know—but Ben said he was tracking something
down.
Sounds like foul play.

[1] See Glossary at end.

2 A

Ben the Broadway Bloodhound!

Had it got a skinny hand on the dust-jacket?

Oo-h—with daggers and automatics!

A bloated tome—I saw it.

So did I. Perfectly mountainous.

Deplorably massive. He called it a handbook of organic compounds.

Oh—you mean *Beilstein* . . . Beilstein's 'Handbuch'!

Annie, your knowledge of such matters is positively indecent—at your age!

But a *handbook*, my dears! Takes a professional weight-lifter to get it off the shelves. I ask you!

P'raps that's why Ben cultivates such a heavy hand.

I say, did you hear how he pulverised Bejant Kennedy yesterday when he forgot the metals of Group IIB?

Oh no, that's new. Let's have it.

'Look at their initials,' said Ben, 'and your difficulties will volatilise like ether.' So he looked at them—and they were . . . now, Amy?

Don't ask me. My memory's like a fluted filter-paper. Ethel?

IIB? . . . That's one thing I *do* know—strontium, chromium, and lead.

Exactly a hundred per cent wrong! Annie—you?

Arsenic, antimony, and tin—As, Sb, Sn—otherwise ASS!

Annie, my child, your familiarity with chemistry is really revolting!

I'm sorry. ASS—a tip for some of you, my dears! . . . Ben was really wild yesterday.

Was he—why?

Bejant Campbell asked him why the porous plates weren't glazed.

What did he say?

'Can *you* tell *me*,' Ben asked him, 'the difference between a moron and an oxymoron?' 'Of course,' said the Bejant. 'The oxymoron contains oxygen; the moron doesn't.' 'And yet *you* go on breathing air!' said Ben, in his most devastating tone.

Sorry, Annie; but I don't see the point.

Let it pass. 'Twould be a cruel kindness to explain it to you, Ethel my dear.

But to come back to those porous plates—why aren't they?

Why aren't they what?

Glazed.

Because they're not oxymorons.

I don't see that, either.

Well then, call it a dispensation of providence.

Apparently they never are. Ben foamed like a colloid at the mere idea.

Yes; but for a really rapid reaction give me Ben and the whale! Says Bejant Morrison, coming up to Ben with pencil and notebook, in his innocently anxious way: 'Why does the sperm whale secrete spermaceti in the crevices of his head?'

Aweel, Bejant Morrison's a clever wee mannie, wi' ilka shiny hair in place; but I jalouse he ended like Jonah, inside the muckle beastie!

Not a bad guess. 'A whale of a question,' says Ben, 'from one who secretes wax in the hollows of his own head every time he rubs his hair with Kurlykreme—and gets it from the overworked bee, instead of synthesising it himself. Go to the whale, thou sluggard!'

Good for Ben! . . . Ah, but were you there when Amy told him that a ketone was a kind of tuning-fork? That made him vibrate—didn't it, Amy?

Definitely—although he failed to tune in to the notion.

I wish I'd seen him with Bejant McGregor yesterday.

Oh—why?

Well, Mac returned No. 21 as a nitrate instead of a sulphate, and Ben found that he'd actually poured the conc. sulphuric down the *out*side of his test-tube.

Poor old Mac!

'The book said to pour down the side of the tube, so as not to mix the acid with the contents,' complained Mac. 'Who would have guessed that it meant the *in*side? Seems silly to me!' 'But where's your brown ring, anyway?'

asked Ben, raging. 'Here, unfortunately,' said Mac—and he pointed to the turn-up of his trews. Ben gained rapidly at that—leaving fuming HBr a bad second—and finally exploded!

Could you blame him!

Ben has a lot to put up with.

All research men have, I guess.

No wonder they used to become monks.

An awful life, I call it.

All the same, it has its bright spots.

And its intriguing moments.

Such as?

Well—take the bejantine and the borax beads, in Friday's First M.B. class!

The bejantine and the borax beads—that sounds promising—what was it?

A blushing bejantine, prompted by some knowing friends, came up to Ben and asked for a box of borax beads. 'I want enough to last the whole term,' she said. 'My favourite colour is pink.'

Ben must have felt like putting her on the shaking machine!

Then there was a semie who wrote down that the smell of beta-naphthol vapour reminded her of cows' breath. Ben advised her earnestly to go back to the land!

Did you ever hear the story of that 'verra canny' bejantine who never gave herself away?

Oh—'Maircury Macnaughton', she was called!

Yes—so she was—from the time that Ben drew public attention to an entry in her lab. notebook: 'Experiment— heated substance with powdered charcoal in a glass tube; observation—noticed globules of mercury condense on the cool part of the tube; inference—suspected presence of mercury'.

'Suspected' was good!

What did Ben say to her?

He advised her to take up Ph.D. work on 'The Estimation of Halogens in Theobromine and Chlorophyll'.

Pearls before swine, I'm afraid! Is that a joke?

Rather! It seems that the names are completely misleading. Theobromine is as innocent of bromine as chloro-phyll is of chlorine—at least, so I'm told by a research man who was obviously speaking in good faith.

There seems to be a lot of leg-pulling in chemistry.

Far too much, if you ask me.

I don't like it. I never know when Ben's pulling mine.

Nor do I. You never feel safe.

I suppose chemists put in these leg-pulls to brighten up their arid existence.

It's hard on us though.

I get terribly confused about a lot of things.

So do I. And quizzes terrify me.

One day I'm going to ask Ben to explain clearly and in as few words as possible—as they say in those repulsive exam. papers—the distinction between borax, thorax, and storax, giving illustrative formulae.

Is that important?

I expect so. I'm always stumbling across those abhorrent names in my text-books.

It's the sort of foul stuff examiners batten on.

I'll ask Ben at the same time if it's likely.

Ben loathes tipping, you know.

I believe he does.

Of course it puts a burden on Ben when one asks him leading questions, like that.

Such responsibility must be appalling.

No wonder Ben's apt to be short.

Well—Ben may be hard at times; but he can be very pleasant when he likes.

When he likes whom?

Annie, don't be so cynical!

Well, for example, the other day Beryl told him that if you burn *white* paper you get CO and if you burn *brown* paper you get CO_2. He simply roared with mirth for ten minutes on end—made a noise like a blowpipe flame!

Beryl—that deep-blonde semie?

Deep, my dear! A permanent wave on the outer fringe of the infra-red!

Ben *would* be soft with her—rather far gone, isn't he?

Ben seems to have a special affinity for semies.

Yes—look at Sadie!

And Meg.

Margarita, *he* calls her!

Not to mention darling Saccharissa!

He waxed quite poetic about *her* the other day.

Who was it said that a chemist is a poet who has taken the wrong turning?

I don't know—Saccharissa, I should think!

That would please Ben—one of his simple pleasures is declaiming poetry.

Or pseudo-poetry!

Ben's becoming alarmingly multivalent of late.

Yes—with Betty and Jean he gets his benzene ring!

With Ben at the centre?

I suppose so—is that sound theory, Annie?

Alpha-plus! 'The centric formula of Armstrong and Baeyer indicates a mutual saturation of the fourth valencies by directing them towards the centre of the ring or hexagon.'

What a marvellous demonstrator Nan would make!

Seems to me Ben has gone beyond the hexagon—at this rate he'll soon complete his octette!

Ben certainly has a blind eye for Beryl—although there's so much carrot in her hair that he can hardly suffer from night blindness!

Nan, you're caustic!

And at times acid.

In fact, amphoteric.

Think so? At any rate, Beryl has to make the most of her unusual wave-length.

Yes, poor dear—she's nothing else in common with the girl in the poem Ben was reciting the other day:

> 'Though I with the aid of a crammer
> Can only get beta and gamma,
> That girl over there, with the flaming red hair,
> Gets an alpha-plus every time, dam' 'er!'

A chestnut—but rather good! Couldn't be Beryl, though—positively not.

Her level's about gamma-minus.

I can't think what an intelligent man like Ben can see in her.

I expect he's literally dazzled by her strontium flame! But these very brainy men are often attracted by opposites.

Deep calling to shallow!

Alpha-plus neutralised by gamma-minus—keeps the average steady, I suppose. Nature's way!

Poor old Nature gets blamed for a lot!

Well, with all his faults, I dote on Ben.

And so do I.

He's just sweet—helpless as a babe!

I adore him.

Me too. (*Several voices.*)

I believe we all do—except Nan.

And even Nan may be camouflaging a secret passion!

Look here—isn't it time to set the wild echoes flying!

Nothing else will fetch Ben when he's sleuthing.

Come on, then. Let's get going!

> (*Some of the* BEJANTINES *now dismount from their lofty stools, shake the crumbs off their attire, set their caps at a jaunty angle, link hands, and dance around the coffee-making apparatus. Other* BEJANTINES *accompany the ensuing singing, upon mandolines or other instruments. At times the singers disengage hands and suit various actions to the words, in the different verses. Sometimes, as a variant, they break up into two rows facing each other, and the rows advance and retire in turn, either with linked or free hands.*)

CHORUS OF BEJANTINES (*singing to the air 'Here we go round the Mulberry Bush'*):

Here we go singing o' Benjy Green, Benjy Green, Benjy Green;

Here we go singing o' Benjy Green . . '. houp la, CH_2O_2!

The cutest chemist that's ever been seen, ever been seen, ever been seen;

The cutest chemist that's ever been seen . . . houp la, CH_2O_2!

He dwells on chemic peaks serene, peaks serene, peaks
    serene;
He dwells on chemic peaks serene . . . houp la,
    CH_2O_2!

(*The ring of dancers breaks and reforms around a* BEJANTINE
*who drops powdered crystals of Brilliant Green into a large
flask of water, 'with vigorous agitation'.*)

Bejantines call him Brilliant Green, Brilliant Green,
    Brilliant Green;
Bejantines call him Brilliant Green . . . houp la,
    CH_2O_2!

(*The ring ruptures and again undergoes closure around a*
BEJANTINE *who regards an open text-book of organic chemistry
with an air of worried bewilderment.*)

And well may Ben us silly call, silly call, silly call;
And well may Ben us silly call . . . houp la, CH_2O_2!

(*The ring now encloses a* BEJANTINE *who smells a specimen of
formic acid in a boiling-tube, and then pours it with a doubtful
air on to some solid sodium carbonate in a test glass; she views
the effervescing mass with intense surprise, and holds it aloft.*)

She thought the 'spot' was alcohol, alcohol, alcohol;
She thought the 'spot' was alcohol . . . och, 'twas
    CH_2O_2!

(*Another* BEJANTINE *enters the charmed circle, holding aloft an
examination book marked in red with a large nought.*)

Benjamin says we know next to nought, next to nought,
    next to nought;
Benjamin says we know next to nought . . . naughty
    Benjamin Green-o!

(*Enter* BEN, *carrying a large flask containing an acid solution of
phenolphthalein. The ring immediately suffers fission, and the
resulting open-chain twists and twines in snake-like motion about
him, as in Kekulé's vision. Then the motion subsides, and the*
BEJANTINES *stand rigid with admiration as* BEN *holds the flask
aloft and pours some alkali into it. The liquid turns pink. At
this sign the snake instantly seizes hold of its own tail and whirls
mockingly around the research man.*)

CHORUS OF BEJANTINES (*singing*):

But as for Ben, 'e knows it all, 'e knows it all, 'e knows it all;

But as for Ben, 'e knows it all . . . brainy Benjamin Green-o!

(*A* BEJANTINE *approaches* BEN *and fixes deftly into his flask a long condenser, or condenser tube, to the upper end of which are attached six gaily-coloured ribbons. Six* SEMIES *now enter in rapid succession and run lightly forward, smiling sweetly at* BEN *as they do so; each of them seizes the end of a ribbon, and a May-pole dance follows, to the singing and the music of the* BEJANTINES. *The* SEMIES *wear scarlet gowns and red-tasselled caps; each of them has on her back an artistic device bearing her name in large letters, the six names being, in order,* MARGARITA, SADIE, SACCHARISSA, BETTY, JEAN, *and* BERYL. *The last-named stands out by reason of her abundance of fiery-red hair. As the various verses are repeated by the chorus of* BEJANTINES, *the motion is now clockwise, now counter-clockwise.*

At the end of the last verse the six SEMIES, *still holding the ribbons, suddenly freeze in their positions, two* BEJANTINES *encircle them with a band of coloured ribbon, and* BEN *is surprised to find himself the centrepiece of a representation of the Armstrong-Baeyer formula for benzene. The* BEJANTINES *applaud enthusiastically, with chanting cries of 'Ben's in!'*

Presently the tableau dissolves, and the ring disintegrates. The SEMIES *make their exit in the above sequence,* BEN *bowing to each as she passes and blows him a kiss with a gay wave of her hand. A* BEJANTINE *relieves* BEN *of his apparatus, and he then bows elaborately to the* BEJANTINES.)

BEN (*smiling benignly*). How nice! I say, is my cup of morning coffee ready, Ethel?

ETHEL (*bluntly*). No, dear old buffer—I use the term in a purely chemical way, of course.

(*She busies herself ineffectually with the coffee-making apparatus. Her activities are marked by an occasional crash or exclamation, as the scene progresses.*)

BEN (*plaintively*). You keep me so long, Ethel. I'm pining for quarts of it. (*To the others*) Why is Ethel late?

ANNIE (*sarcastically*). I guess because her watch lacked tick—to use another purely chemical term!

BEN (*staggering*). O, for a retort; but all of them are gone!

AMY (*alarmed*). Look, Ben's ill! For shame, Annie! This is not what he cam' for.

BEN (*feebly*). Why does Annie lean that way? It's her great failing.

KATE (*sympathetically*). Yon chiel Ben's so innocent he'll know nane o't. The puir laddie can't absorb it all.

BEN (*despondently*). I guess my spiritual home's a rabbit hole!

ANNIE (*cuttingly*). O, Brilliant Green! Ben's a mean man—indeed, speaking chemically, he's no man at all!

BEN (*angrily*). If I may be permitted to speak chemically —you rate! Also, if you're not a Tartar, I'm a tick!

KATE (*dispassionately*). You're a militant bejantine, Annie—a bonny fechter!

AMY (*soulfully*). Ben's annoyed.

ANNIE (*hotly*). And so's Annie annoyed.

KATE (*aside*). I'll be creatin' a diversion. (*Exclaims*) Hist! I'd e'en jaloused I heard a catty call!

ETHEL (*pricking the bubble*). In a mice-'ell, I suppose? Silly sides! You but 'eard a catalyst mew, Kate.

ANNIE (*crushingly*). Notice her acid reaction—her mordant wit! Ben's so peroxide-conscious, or he'd sack 'er in a temper, since his coffee's still unready.

ETHEL (*angrily*). If I may make a chemical suggestion —economise your natural gas! You lack tone.

(*She swings round hastily and brings a pile of spoons to the ground with a metallic tintinnabulation.*)

ANNIE (*pungently*). I'd sack 'er right away! The coffee's still cold.

BEN (*impatiently*). Stop your alchemical music! Why's that gal late? I feel like a desiccator. Unless Annie lied, I'll go to a café in the town.

KATE (*taking command*). Hoots, laddie, fulminate nae mair. Forbye yer coffee tassie's fu' the noo.

(*She hands him a full cup.*)

BEN (*joyfully*). Is it in? (*Drinks.*) Angelic bejantine!

(*Drinks.*) Charming indicator! (*Drinks.*) I so preen myself that you're 'ere. In short, as Micawber would say, I'm lucky.

KATE (*severely practical*). Hae ye ony buns in yer pooch, the morn?

> (*She pats a bulging pocket in his attire.*)

BEN (*produces a paper bag therefrom and declaims*):

> I'll no' lee;
> Big yins they be;
> A'nt gi'ed 'em me.

(*He takes a bite.*)

KATE (*breaking a specimen from the bag*). Gude sakes, quicklime's wet beside yon yins! They maun ha' wandered wi' yer a'ntie mony a weary fute, in days o' auld lang syne! Try a lick o' treacle and some mair coffee wi' 'em, my mannie.

> (*She anoints one with golden syrup from a tin, which she produces from a pocket in her gown and opens deftly with a spatula. She proffers the confection to* BEN, *who literally eats from her hand.*)

BEN (*full of emotion*). I want no mo' lasses but you, honey.

> (*He licks his lips, however, and looks for more; but as none is forthcoming he empties his cup of coffee. The other* BEJANTINES, *who have been viewing the rapidly deteriorating situation with increasing alarm, now interpose in an attempt to detach* BEN *from* KATE. *Their efforts are in vain.* BEN *keeps his eyes fixed upon* KATE, *and sweeps the interpolators aside with one hand, in a manner compounded of impatience and absent-mindedness. Meanwhile, in his other hand he balances mechanically the empty cup and saucer.*)

AMY (*helplessly—producing an open laboratory notebook*). Ben, you're too much at Kate's beck, man. Also, you mark a sight too hard!

ETHEL (*jauntily*). Perhaps it's only temporary hardness, Amy. Wait till he gets heated!

AMY (*pleadingly—a beauty in distress*). Look, Ben, can't

you O.K. at least one of my six ways of spelling 'desiccator'?
I've known really nice men thole several of 'em.

(BEN *shudders and motions her aside. She moves away with a
pout and a toss of her head.* ETHEL *snatches a tube at haphazard
from a rack and rushes into the breach.*)

ETHEL (*with gushing gaiety*).   Ben, do look at this
perfectly adorable little powder-blue precipitate—isn't it
cute! I've been trying to find out whether it's KI or PCl_5
—could you lend me a borax bead?

(BEN *motions her aside, and a still stronger shudder pervades
his frame.* ANNIE *comes to the fore with determination and
drive.*)

ANNIE (*in a voice of great carrying power*).   Did that
blonde semie dine with you again last night, Ben?

(*She pretends to remove from his hair a hank of carroty-red
threads, which she has just abstracted from an adjacent specimen
cabinet. She dangles them accusingly before* BEN'*s eyes, and he
recoils with a wild surmise.*)

These were tangled up in your hair.

ETHEL (*with profound professional interest*).   What a
divine shade for a transformation! Who is the divinity,
Ben?

BEN (*hoarse with indignation*).   Good heavens! Are you
alluding to Beryl or Ruby? A semie'd e'en shun a transformation of so deep a dye! What a base insinuation—this
must be put to the acid test!

(BEN *is visibly moved—indeed he is more than mechanically
agitated. He takes the threads and runs them delicately
through his fingers. Then he examines them with a large lens.
The* BEJANTINES *watch him with breathless interest.*)

KATE (*defensively*).   You're a silly, Nan! 'Twas only a
dinner and a duty ride with old Miss Pickel—Ben's rich
a'ntie-body, ye ken. Yon blonde semie went oot the nicht
wi' Alan, in a Standard two-seater, for a night ride.

ETHEL (*with relish*).   I can well believe it—and, I tell
you, rides with Al aren't duty rides!

(BEN *now ignites one of the threads with a petrol-lighter, and
sniffs it as it burns. He breathes a sigh of relief, and his worried*

look fades out. Finally, he moistens some of the threads with a series of reagents contained in beakers. His self-possession returns completely as he faces his red-gowned audience and holds up the threads, which he afterwards tangles in his hair. Then he breaks into a variant of the old-time song, 'Silver Threads among the Gold'. The BEJANTINES *support him instrumentally throughout the song, and orally in each chorus.* BEN *beats time with the cup and saucer, which he has temporarily relinquished during his examination of the threads; but at times he exchanges them for appropriate pieces of apparatus concerned in the song. His attitude meanwhile is one of airy persiflage.)*

BEN (*sings*):

VISCOSE THREADS AMONG THE GOLD

(To the air of 'Silver Threads among the Gold')

> Bejantines, I'm growing old,
> Viscose threads among the gold
> Shine upon my brow to-day,
> Till the dyestuff fades away.

But though now my locks are few, are few,
Carbon still forms CO_2.
But though now my locks are few,
Carbon still forms CO_2.

(*Chorus*) Bejantines, I'm growing old,
Viscose threads among the gold
Shine upon my brow to-day,
Till the dyestuff fades away.

As I wander round the lab.
Mem'ry brings me many a stab
Of fair bejantines I've known,
Who have old and ugly grown.
But though bejants come and go, and go,
Water still is H_2O.
But though bejants come and go,
Water still is H_2O.

> As I wander round the lab.
> Mem'ry brings me many a stab
> Of fair bejantines I've known,
> Who have old and ugly grown.

Other lips sucked these pipettes,
Other eyes read these burettes:
Other eyes and other lips.
Gone are they who used these Kipps!
But the old-time smell remains, remains,
Reminiscent of bad drains.
But the old-time smell remains,
Reminiscent of bad drains.

Other lips sucked these pipettes,
Other eyes read these burettes:
Other eyes and other lips.
Gone are they who used these Kipps!

On this ever-changing stage
I have passed from youth to age;
But though others leave the scene,
I stay on with pyridine.
Antimony too I see, I see,
Coming down in Group IIB.
Antimony too I see,
Coming down in Group IIB.

Bejantines, I'm growing old,
Viscose threads among the gold
Shine upon my brow to-day,
Till the dyestuff fades away.

(*At the end of the song* BEN *bows, removes the threads from his hair, and hands them with another bow to* ANNIE.)

BEN (*affably*). Try a Lassaigne test next time, Nan, dearest——observation, no Prussian Blue; inference, no nitrogen, no hair, no blonde semie! A pretty little problem, Nan!

ANNIE (*sweetly, but devastatingly*). Which d' you consider your prettiest problem, Benjy dear: Beryl, Ruby, Sadie, Meg—or darling Saccharissa—'the sweetest thing on earth', I believe you called her the other day!

(BEN *falls back crushed, and again* KATE *comes to his rescue.*)

KATE (*suddenly*). Ben, you're alight. . . .

(BEN *jumps up in alarm, still holding the empty cup. He claps his free hand to various parts of his anatomy, as he dances about wildly.*)

BEN (*excitedly*). Am I? Where? It's that petrol-lighter again. Quick—tell me where, or you're a ninny!

KATE (*calmly*). You're all right. Set ye doon. (*He does so.*) As I was obsairvin' the noo, Ben, you're alight with ideas. (KATE's *manner shows* BEN *that he has not bluffed her over the episode of the blonde semie.*) But tak' tent, Ben—wi' yer unco' absorption in the infra-red—that the neon light ahead doesna' change to Green before ye've time to go into revairse. Ye'd rue it, Ben. Ah'm tellin' ye the noo!

(BEN *examines* KATE *intently from head to foot and back again for a full half minute. He is evidently considering still another pretty little problem. When he reaches his answer he jumps up in joyous abandon and walks around, motioning rhythmically with his cup and saucer.*)

BEN (*declaims*):

If I'd rue it, I won't do it:
I won't do it, if I'd rue it.
Here's a song, a lass (*looking at* KATE), but no wine!
(*He shakes his head as he looks at his cup.*)
Here's a song, but, alas (*again looking wistfully at his cup*), no wine!

ETHEL (*admiringly*). How divinely Ben orates!

AMY (*hopefully*). If I see right, he's going to sing us 'Wine, Woman, and Song'. That will be lovely.

BEN (*flattered*). Not without the wine. Couldn't do it without all the stage properties. But I'll give you my latest poem (*he clears his throat nervously*):

Said a lady one day
To a troubadour gay:
'Pray tell me, kind sir, why you flirt so.'
He replied, 'When I play,
Surely, madam, I may
Devote heart and soul to the scherzo!'

I call it, *Allegro ma non troppo*—fast, but not too fast.

OMNES (*enthusiastically*). Oh, that was rare, Ben! (*They applaud.*)

BEN (*modestly*). My original synthesis, you know. (*He clears his throat again.*) Perhaps I could now hit orf a song about semies, if you've an appetite for such—another synthesis of my own.

ANNIE (*with conviction*). It will certainly be authoritative if it's about semies. I should put it in for a D.Sc., Ben! (*She speaks as one reading from the University Calendar.*) See the University Calendar, page 1256: 'The subject matter of a D.Sc. Thesis should permit of extended treatment, and should form a connected whole indicative of the candidate's claim as an authority upon the subject.'

BEN (*placatingly*). Well, Nan, as you're so greatly interested, I appoint you external examiner!

(*He puts a few finishing touches to his voice.*)

AMY (*soulfully*). I dote on Ben's voice. It has a bell-metal quality, without being at all metallic—if you know what I mean.

(BEN *makes a false start.*)

ETHEL (*admiringly*). Ben's so manly! And he doesn't boom like a bittern.

(BEN *makes another false start.*)

ANNIE (*sceptically*). If he bellows, I shall put cotton wool in my ears.

(BEN *makes a third false start, and glares accusingly at* ANNIE.)

ETHEL (*reprovingly*). Nan, your tongue's ten times as active as it should be. Hold it, sister!

(*At last* BEN *starts off with his song, to the air of 'Clementine'. The* BEJANTINES *join in the chorus, and some of them provide an instrumental accompaniment.*)

BEN (*sings*):

TAUTOMERIC CHANGES
(To the air of 'Clementine')

In a corner of the Chem. Lab.,
Midst the fumes and tubes and twine,
Margarita, very sweet–a,
Bubbled gases into brine.

(*Chorus*) Oh my darling, darling semie,
    Wasn't Meg a lass divine!
    I was only semie-conscious
    Till I found my bejantine.

Substitution soon removed her,
And I thought the process fine;
For dear Sadie looked a lady
As she boiled a flask of wine.
    Oh my darling, darling semie,
    Wasn't Sadie just divine!
    I was only semie-conscious
    Till I found my bejantine.

Sadie soon evaporated;
But she left no vacant shrine.
Did I miss her? Saccharissa
Gave an answer saccharine.
    Oh my darling, darling semie,
    Saccharissa saccharine!
    I was only semie-conscious
    Till I found my bejantine.

One day she in tears dissolvèd,
As she thought of auld lang syne:
Dreadful' wetty—but with Betty
I sat down that night to dine.
    Oh my darling, darling semie,
    Wasn't Betty just divine!
    I was only semie-conscious
    Till I found my bejantine.

When dear Betty, tautomeric,
Wandered off to recombine,
Lassie Jean-a was my queen-a,
Or at least my columbine.
    Oh my darling, darling semie,
    Wasn't Jean a lass divine!
    I was only semie-conscious
    Till I found my bejantine.

2 B

With a coif-fure deeply coloured,
Like pyrrole when put on pine,
My last peril is dear Beryl,
And she brings my lives to nine.

> Oh my darling, darling semie,
> Wasn't Beryl just divine!
> I was only semie-conscious
> Till I found my bejantine.

AMY (*meltingly*).   What a lovely air!

ANNIE (*advancing with an official-looking document*).   Otherwise a perfect gas!   Bravo, Ben!   (*She puts on a large pair of spectacles and scans the document.   She then continues in formal and measured tones.*)   As a fully and completely external examiner, not even appointed by the University Court, I now beg to make my report to the Senatus Academicus on the Thesis presently submitted by Mr. Benjamin Green, B.Sc., in application for the degree of Doctor of Science in this University.

> (*As she speaks, there is a rustling isomerisation among the* BEJANTINES; *the scene dissolves, and recrystallises in a form strangely reminiscent of a graduation ceremonial in this imaginary University.   The* BEJANTINES *assume a semicircular orientation, with* ANNIE *standing at one end and* KATE *at the other—like two side-chains.* BEN *occupies a central position, and acts as conductor to the* BEJANTINE *choir, which now breaks into the opening verse of 'Gaudeamus'.*)

OMNES (*with spirit*):

Gaudeamus igitur, juvenes dum sumus:
Gaudeamus igitur, juvenes dum sumus:
Post jucundam juventutem, post molestam senectutem,
Nos habebit humus, nos habebit humus.

ANNIE (*continuing as before*).   The candidate has carried out a prolonged and delicate piece of work in an exacting field, in which he has constituted himself an authority.   In particular, the numerous semie-pinacolinic deaminations were brilliantly conceived and skilfully executed—no fewer than nine examples being described.   In each instance the migrational aptitude was very marked.   I recommend there-

fore that the candidate be promoted at once to the degree of
D.Sc., *summa cum laude*, without any further examination.

(BEN *acknowledges the ensuing applause by bowing to the* BEJAN-
TINES, *among whom a large certificate bearing a red seal is being
circulated at* ANNIE'S *initiative. They scan it—some earnestly,
others perfunctorily, or with an air of boredom—and append
their signatures in equally characteristic ways, using their
trenchers as writing-desks. After repeatedly falling to the floor
on the way, the certificate finally reaches* KATE, *who signs it
scrupulously and then rolls it up and pushes it into a cylinder
having a scarlet colour; she then holds it in readiness.* ANNIE
beckons BEN, *who approaches her and spreads his handkerchief
carefully on the floor in front of her. During this operation he
finds the empty cup and saucer an encumbrance: he looks round
helplessly for a suitable place in which to deposit it; but even the
waste-box is full, so he puts it on the floor by his handkerchief.*

A LABORATORY BOY *now enters from one side, pushing a
laboratory truck, fitted with rubber-tyred castors. Upon this
reposes the complete academic garb of a Doctor of Science. The
BOY is clad in a costume reminiscent of that in a woodcut[1]
depicting a mediaeval lab. boy, to be found on the reverse of
leaf xlvii of Brunschwick's 'Buch zu Distillieren'—a work
happily printed and brought to a close in the Imperial city of
Strassburg by Johann Grüninger on the eve of St. Adolphus in
the year of our Lord 1519. As the BOY enters, the BEJANTINE
choir breaks into a robust chorus, to the air of 'Cock Robin'.*)

CHORUS OF BEJANTINES (*singing*):

All the Profs. in their lair were a-hob-nob-nobbing,
When they put their names to the round-round-robin,
When they signed the decree for a D.Sc.!

Tra la, tra la-la-la-la, Tra la, tra la-la-la-la,
Tra la, tra la-la-la-la, Tra la-la-la-la-la, la!

(*The* LAB. BOY *helps* BEN *into the D.Sc. gown.* BEN *hitches up
his trews carefully and kneels down upon the handkerchief, facing
ANNIE expectantly with his head down and hands placed palm to
palm.* ANNIE *touches him on the head with the hank of carroty-
red threads.*)

ANNIE (*in a clear voice*). Et tu, Brute!

(*The* LAB. BOY *throws the loop of the hood deftly over* BEN'S *head
and makes a swift adjustment.*)

[1] See Fig. 9.

CHORUS OF BEJANTINES (*briskly*).   Tra la-la-la-la-la la!

(*The* BEJANTINES *applaud.*   BEN *rises, dusts his knees nervously with his hands, and bows to* ANNIE.   *She returns the bow and shakes hands with him in a congratulatory manner.*   BEN *then turns and advances precipitately towards* KATE.   *The* LAB. BOY *skilfully interposes and hands him the D.Sc. cap with an air of reproach.   Still maintaining this air, the* BOY *retrieves the handkerchief and the empty cup and saucer from the floor, places them on the truck, and then leaves, pushing the truck before him.*

BEN, *having donned the doctoral cap, resumes his impetuous way towards* KATE, *who bows and hands him the certificate.* BEN *returns the bow, tosses the certificate impatiently to the nearest* BEJANTINE, *and seizes* KATE's *left hand as well as her proffered right: drawing her towards him, he is on the point of proceeding to a distinctly unacademic greeting, but* KATE *draws back her face in the nick of time.*)

BEN (*purposefully*).   Say, K., I want no D.Sc. but you! I'm through my semie-final!   I've found my one and only bejantine!

(*The atmosphere of the Graduation Hall is now replaced by that of the chemical preparation room, previously obtaining, and the* BEJANTINES *undergo a corresponding rearrangement as the scene progresses.*)

KATE (*bluntly*).   What ye need, Dr. Ben, is neither a bejantine nor a D.Sc.—but a reflux condenser!   Ye're too volatile!

BEN (*persuasively*).   Don't be silly, Kate!   I'm aspirin' to have you share my home o' logs—my wee wooden hut, ye ken!

(*He places his arm experimentally round her waist. The resulting yield is by no means theoretical; but although she evades him, she does so with a significant lack of precipitation.*)

KATE (*delaying*).   Yer wee but an' ben, Ben?   But, Ben . . . but, but, Ben!   (*She becomes confused.*) . . . Ye ken, Ben . . . yon wee but an' ben, Ben!

BEN (*attentively*).   Yes, Kate—certainly.   But an' ben it shall be, if you prefer that nomenclature to home o' logs.

KATE (*hesitatingly*).   Oh—but Ben! . . . *Allegro ma non troppo*, ye ken!   Ye said it yersel', ye ken!

BEN (*gaily*).   Often passes into *Accelerando* in a really brisk passage, ye ken!

KATE (*at last reaching the necessary potential*).   Oh, but

Ben—in yon wee but an' ben, Ben—what—what—close-packing!

BEN (*apologetically*). I grant it's small: but *Poco a poco* —little by little—ye ken! I tell you, rates are so high nowadays. (*Persuasively*) We could start a home o' genius —even perhaps a new homologous series—oh, K.!

KATE (*yielding—decisively*). O.K.! . . . Ben, you're alight . . . (BEN *jumps round hastily, as before*) . . . you're alight with ideas. Dinna let yer reaction-velocity rin awa' wi' ye. (*Deliberately—emphasising her ultimatum by forceful stabs in the air with her forefinger*) But, gin ye ring-close yer notion—respectably, in a lum hat and a' that—mebbe I'll no' sigh an' 'ide in a corner! (*She crosses to the* BEJANTINE *holding* BEN's *certificate and restores it to him.*) Meantime ye've yer D.Sc. to carry on wi'!

BEN (*rapturously*). Sweet silly Kate! (*He emphasises his points by making appropriate motions with the certificate.*) We'll be co-efficient: like to a double sherry, but yet an onion in partition, as Shakespeare says. . . . Side by side we'll wander down the golden lane of life.

KATE (*concedingly*). Aweel, Ben, ye're by ordinar' preceepitate to mak' yer double bond. Gin ye're so bent on a race-mate, bide a wee, and I'll sing ye a song bearing on the subject.

AMY (*startled*). A race-mate! Oh, dear—Ben seems to have jumped out of the crucible into the Bunsen!

ETHEL (*soothingly*). Courage, mon amie! Perhaps she only means a racemate!

(*Accompanied by the* BEJANTINE *instrumentalists,* KATE *sings* 'The Mirror Song,' or Stereochemist's Love Song, to the old-time air of 'The Honeysuckle and the Bee'. The chorus of the first verse is sung by BEN solo, that of the second by KATE and BEN together.*)

THE MIRROR SONG
(To the air of 'The Honeysuckle and the Bee')

In a preparation room,
When the whins were in full bloom,
All the test-tubes lay at rest;

And each little Nicol prism,
Undeterred by inner schism,
Ceased turning in its snug half-shadow'd nest.
Came a labile lad and lass,
Who, migrating from their class,
Shared a single lab.-stool side by side;
As they sat there tight as glue,
Their infatuation grew,
Till he whispered to her thoughts he could not hide:

> (*Chorus*)
>
> 'You are my mirror, mirror-image, my looking-glass.
> I am your dextro, dextro-lad, and you my laevo-lass.
> We cling as dextro clings to laevo in a racemate:
> Nothing shall separate us as a conglomerate.'

These enantiomerides,
After many soft asides,
Thought it not at all amiss,
When a bold experiment,
With the lassie's shy consent,
Was sealed hermetically with a kiss.
As he gazed into her eyes,
He discovered with surprise,
She was optically active too;
So her head he did rotate,
And reformed the racemate,
As their lips became coincident anew:

> (*Chorus*)
>
> 'You are my mirror, mirror-image, my looking-glass.
> ⌠I am your dextro, dextro-lad, and you my laevo-lass.
> ⌡You are my dextro, dextro-lad, and I your laevo-lass.
> We cling as dextro clings to laevo in a racemate:
> Nothing shall separate us as a conglomerate.'

> (*The* BEJANTINES *applaud and call enthusiastically for an encore.*
> KATE *sings the second verse again, going through the appropriate*
> *actions with* BEN *on this occasion. The* BEJANTINES *group them-*
> *selves around and join in the final chorus.*)

KATE (*with an air of business to be done*). Ye can gather

frae a' that, Ben—by a process of inductive reasoning—
that whenever (*punctuating the conditions by wagging her
forefinger*)—that whenever ye fix the gowd ring, we'll purr
in a car away, and you can try steerin'.

BEN (*enthusiastically*). If you'll be my steric hindrance,
I'll steer all day!

KATE (*coyly*). *Ergo* steer all day, Dr. Ben—but what'll
we be doing in neutral when the wee car bides still?

BEN (*captivated*). You're still bein' silly, Kate! You'll
show such resource in all under the car bonnet that I'll
never make my beauty late.

KATE (*responsively*). Och, Ben, so I'll no' leave you, lose
you, nor malign you.

(*She pats her hair, using a large crystallising dish as a mirror,
readjusts her bejantine's cap with the blue tassel, dons a pair
of gloves, pulls her scarlet gown about her, and prepares to depart
with* BEN, *whom she now regards with a proprietary air. Her
companions eye these purposeful preparations in sombre silence.*
BEN *casts a half regretful glance at her fellow* BEJANTINES *as she
links her arm in his and urges him away.*)

ANNIE (*spitefully*). The jade!

KATE (*triumphantly*). Jade Green, ye ken!

(*Exeunt* KATE *and* BEN.)

ANNIE (*caustically*). Ben's a dam' silly man—she'll
make him pipe 'er in with the haggis! I'd like to see a
clumsy piper 'it one off the dish, all over her best costume!

AMY (*greatly troubled*). Poor Ben can say good-bye to all
his degrees of freedom now! He's done a jump clean out
of the crucible into the Bunsen! I saw it brewing.

ETHEL (*sorrowfully*). And when he cools down he'll be
like the heroine of his own pet limerick (*recites*):

There was an old lady of Ealing
Who jumped from the floe to the sealing;
    But when she got there
      A large polar bear
Unluckily chanced to be mealing!

ANNIE (*grimly*). And so the poor doggie had none!

ETHEL (*regretfully*). Kate's queered the pitch for us.

AMY (*mournfully*). She knocked spots off us.

ANNIE (*forcefully*). She ran him off like a bottom layer from a separating funnel! I never met a less orthodox candidate for wedded paradise!

ETHEL (*ruefully*). Why was I so late? She beat all of us with the coffee.

AMY (*sorrowfully*). And why was Amy late? Ah, if only Ben so ate treacled buns out of my hand!

ANNIE (*sourly*). You're a-b'ilin' over with self-pity—but don't say Annie's sick, even though Beau Nash of the Chem. Lab. has disintegrated into mere bone-ash!

OMNES (*with regretful admiration*). Aweel, she's no belle; but she gat 'er man!

(*Once again the* BEJANTINES *form a ring and dance around with linked hands, etc., as before, singing to the air 'Here we go round the Mulberry Bush'.*)

CHORUS OF BEJANTINES (*singing*):

Kate's no belle, but she gat 'er man, she gat 'er man, she gat 'er man;
Kate's no belle, but she gat 'er man . . . pray for Benjamin Green-o!

Benjamin Green was just sublime, just sublime, just sublime;
Benjamin Green was just sublime . . . till Ben sublimed with Kate-o!

And why did Kate volatilise, volatilise, volatilise;
And why did Kate volatilise . . . with Benjy, oh so Green-o?

Because she got the Nobel Prize, the Nobel Prize, the Nobel Prize;
Kate's no belle, so she got the Prize . . . alas, 'twas Benjamin Green-o!

(*The mellow lin-lan-lone of wedding bells, far far away, now*

89. 'The Golden Lane' (Zlatá ulička), Prague.

(See p. 371.)

90. 'A mediaeval damosel of high degree.'

(See p. 373.)

becomes perceptible; the sound swells and then dies to a single tolling note.)

Ben's only bells are those that ring, hey-ding-a-ding,
    hey-ding-a-ding;
Ben's only bells are those that ring . . . and toll for
    Benjamin Green-o!

(*As the* FIRST CURTAIN *falls slowly, the bell-music waxes into a merry peal, and then fades gradually away. Distant strains of 'Here comes the Bride' are then heard; these also wax and wane.*

    The curtain then rises to disclose the BEJANTINES *arranged in two ranks facing each other. There are also* SPECTATORS *with bags of confetti. The* BEJANTINES *support an archway of crossed retorts, beneath which* KATE *and* BEN, *with a train of bridal attendants, presently appear, to the triumphal strains of the Wedding March.* BEN'S *attire, impeccably up to date, includes a prominent lum hat which has evidently just been submitted to the equivalent of recrystallisation in the hatters' world.*

    KATE, *robed in bridal white, wears the conical head-dress and general costume of a mediaeval damosel of high degree, together with two braided tresses reminiscent of the legendary Lady Katharine Kennedy. She carries a bouquet. A small* PAGE—*the erstwhile laboratory boy—clad also in mediaeval attire as before, holds up her train. Her bridesmaids are six of the semie 'runners-up':* MEG, SADIE, SACCHARISSA, BETTY, JEAN, *and* BERYL, *the last-named with a fiery-red coiffure. The bridesmaids wear scarlet gowns, and their caps are adorned with the scarlet tassels of semidom: each of them carries a staff affixed to an ornamented heraldic shield bearing her name. As the procession passes slowly from view,* AMY *is seen to dab convulsively at her eyes with her handkerchief. The music of the Wedding March dies away as the* SECOND CURTAIN *falls slowly.*

    The curtain rises finally to disclose all the persons of the chemic drama grouped symmetrically about KATE *and* BEN. *Using his certificate as a conductor's baton,* BEN *induces the singing of two closing verses of 'Gaudeamus'.*)

OMNES (*with spirit*):
Vivat Academia, vivant Professores,
Vivat Academia, vivant Professores,
Vivat membrum quodlibet, vivant membra quaelibet,
Semper sint in flore, semper sint in flore!

Pereat tristitia, pereant osores,
Pereat tristitia, pereant osores,
Pereat diabolus, quivis antiburschius,
Atque irrisores, atque irrisores!

CURTAIN

Key to Chemical Terms

The text of the above chemic drama contains numerous chemical terms, some masquerading under a thin disguise and others more deeply concealed. A selection of these (in their order of occurrence and starting from the first dance of the bejantines on page 349) is given below, together with clues which might be substituted for them in a cryptic version of the drama, for use as a 'quiz' or test of general knowledge in chemistry. The attentive reader may unearth others. Only the very obvious examples should be stressed in the acting version of the drama.

Benzene. A hydrocarbon discovered by Faraday in 1825

Serine. A hydroxyamino-acid obtained from silk

Brilliant Green. A synthetic dye

Silicol. An alcohol which burns to sand and water

Alcohol. Originally 'eye-paint'

Inositol. $(CHOH)_6$

Gneiss. A stratified rock

Coffey. A hero of distillation

Ethyl. The radical of alcohol

Buffer. A pillar of hydrogen-ion concentration

Meso. Signifies internally compensated

Pinene. In oil of turpentine

Quartz. Often displays hemihedral facets

Ethylate. To get one, add sodium to alcohol

Lactic. An acid which turns milk sour

O. Dephlogisticated air

Retort. The alchemists called it a pelican

Argon. An inert gas

Benzil. $Ph·CO·CO·Ph$

Camphor. A ketone mentioned in the Koran

Aniline. A mother of coal-tar dyes

Fehling. A solution reminiscent of a French Atlantic seaport

Benzoin. $Ph·CH(OH)·CO·Ph$

No scent. Emphatically not SeMeEt

Nonane. A paraffin hydrocarbon

Cantab. Denotes the University in which $CHClI \cdot SO_3H$ was resolved

Sorbitol. A reduction product of glucose

Spirit. Often methylated

Arabitol. A pentahydric alcohol

O. Discovered on 1 August 1774

Benzamine. beta-Eucaine

Mannitol. A hexahydric alcohol

Urate. A salt of uric acid

Tartar emetic. Contains Sb and reduces Fehling's solution

Uramil. Aminobarbituric acid

Fecht. A chemist with a pugnacious surname

Benzenoid. Having an aromatic character

Anionoid. Character decidedly negative

Creatine. Methylguanidine acetic acid

Histidine. A heterocyclic amino-acid

Catechol. o-Dihydroxybenzene

Micelle. A colloidal aggregate

Silicides. Carborundum is one

Buttered. Smeared with a butyric fat

Catalyst. A chemical busybody

Mucate. A salt of mucic acid

Not ice. Water above 0° C.

Acid reaction. Makes blue litmus blush

Mordant. Used in dyeing

Benzo-peroxide. $Ph \cdot CO \cdot O \cdot O \cdot CO \cdot Ph$

Saccharin. 'The sweetest thing on earth'

Temper. Influences even the behaviour of steel

Coffey's still. Used in manufacturing rectified spirit

Natural gas. Chiefly methane and ethane

Lactone. Given by 1,4- and 1,5-hydroxyacids

Saccharite. A granular variety of felspar

Alchemical music. Composed at Prague about 1618; rendered at St. Andrews in 1935

Gallate. A salt of gallic acid

Desiccator. Left in balance-rooms by careless students

Anilide. $Ph \cdot CO \cdot NH \cdot Ph$ is one

Caffeine. 1,3,7-Trimethyl-xanthine

Fulminate. Sets off other sensitive bodies

Meyer. Had the same Christian name as Trumper

Baeyer. He synthesised indigotin in 1880

NO_2. Scots for 'now'; American for 'new'

Isatin. An oxidation product of indigo

Angelic. An acid, $Me \cdot CH:CMe \cdot COOH$

Indicator. Like an examiner, may be internal or external

Isoprene. Polymerises to rubber

Urea. Carbamide

In. An element with a brilliant indigo line in its spectrum

As. Detected by Marsh's test (soluble in hypochlorite)

Mica, W, Ber. $KH_2Al_3(SiO_4)_3$, atomic number 74, abbreviation for a chemical journal

Bunsen. Sometimes lights back

Liebig. He defined organic chemistry as 'the chemistry of compound radicals'

Quicklime. Often in the limelight

Wandered. What a tautomeric atom did

Antimony. 'Wolf of the metals'

Molasses.   Residual sweetness

Honey.   Bee-lines are made for this

Beckmann.   An overgrown thermometer

Marcasite. FeS_2

Temporary hardness.   Removed by boiling

OK.   Suggests that potassium is bivalent

Menthol.   Mint camphor

Borax bead.   This kind is not made into necklaces

Semidine. Transformation.   { An intramolecular change undergone by *p*-substituted hydrazobenzenes

Beryl. $3BeO \cdot Al_2O_3 \cdot 6SiO_2$

Ruby.   Red and mainly alumina

Semidine. Transformation.   } See above

Dye.   Possesses an auxochrome as well as a chromophore

Base.   Characterised by the formation of hydroxyl ions

Acid.   Characterised by the formation of hydrogen ions

Uracil.   A purine base

Mispickel. $CoAsS$

Anti-body.   An immunising substance in the blood serum

Alanine.   Aminopropionic acid

Standard.   Often decinormal

Nitride.   A binary nitrogen compound

I.   A substance named after the violet colour of its vapour

Tellurides.   Derivatives of H_2Te

Al.   Atomic weight 27

Deuterides.   Heavy water is one

Viscose.   Discovered by Cross and Bevan

Kipps.   Homes of H_2S

Lassaigne.   The reagent is sodium

Prussian Blue.   Ferric ferrocyanide

Uralite.   Amphibole

Uranine.   Sodium fluorescein

Urol.   Piperazine quinate, a uric acid solvent

Neon.   'New'

Rue.   Its essential oil contains methylnonyl ketone

Aurates. $KAuO_2$ is one of them

Cerite.   A rare-earth mineral

Hittorf.   Known for his work on transport numbers

Apatite.   Natural calcium phosphate

Rare Ben.   An epithet applied to the author of 'The Alchemist'

Bell metal.   Cu 80%, Sn 20%

Metallic.   Forming basic oxides

Manley.   An Oxford chemist who used a very fine balance in 1912

Bittern.   Mother-liquor of sea-salt

Bellows.   An oxidising agent depicted in Teniers' 'Le Plaisir des fous'

Cotton wool.   Seed-hairs used in making collodion

Tungsten.   Occurs in New Zealand as scheelite

Active.   May be either radio or optically so

Tautomeric.   Fond of changing partners

Pyrrole.   A base which makes pine-splinters blush

Air.   An alchemical term applied generally to gases

Perfect gas.   Amenable to gaseous legislation

Semipinacolinic deaminations.   Frisky behaviour of susceptible amino-alcohols with nitrous acid

Migrational aptitude. A measure of such friskiness

Reflux condenser. Takes care of the return journey

Aspirin. Acetylsalicylic acid

Homologues. For example, formic and acetic acids

Close-packing. Often cubic or hexagonal in metallic crystals

Tellurates. Salts of telluric acid

Homogeneous. Adjective applicable to all pure substances

Homologous series. A numerous family, in organic chemistry

K. The subject of Davy's 'Capl. Expt.' on 19 October 1807

Ring-closure. Leads to cyclic compounds

Not ion. Conductivity nil

Alum. An astringent double sulphate

Cyanide. Hydrolyses to a carboxylic acid

Körner. He devised a method of orientation

Silicate. Present in rocks and glass

Coefficient. In chemistry, often associated with partition

Sherry. A beverage from Xeres, containing methylcarbinol

Onion. An edible biennial bulbous root secreting a lachrymatory compound, $C_6H_{12}S_2$

Partition. Distribution of a solute between two competing non-miscible solvents

Golden Lane. The Zlatá ulička (Street of the Alchemists), at Prague (Fig. 89)

Precipitate. Always coming down

Double bond. Signifies inclination to undergo addition

Racemate. A combination of an asymmetric molecule with its mirrored form

Crucible. Chaucer called it a crosselett

Bunsen. One who brought chemical fame to Heidelberg

Nicol prism. May be a polariser or an analyser

Half-shadow. This angle may be altered by rotating the polariser

Conglomerate. The dextro- and laevo-forms are deposited in separate crystals, instead of in the same crystal, as with a racemate

Enantiomerides. Optical isomers, dextro- and laevo-forms

Hermetically. After the manner of Hermes

Optically active. Rotating the plane of polarised light

Gold. Often called Sol in alchemy

Ring. Symbolised by a serpent biting its tail

Purine. The parent compound of uric acid

Caraway. A source of carvone

Tristearin. Glyceryl tristearate

Steric hindrance. Spatial interference

Sterol. Found in the unsaponifiable residue of fats

Ergosterol. Yields vitamin D when irradiated

Wattle. An Australian source of tannin

Neutral. Neither acid nor alkaline

Carbides. One of them is used in making acetylene

Still. The alchemists called it a bear

Stilbene. Ph·CH:CH·Ph

Silicate. One of them is used for preserving eggs

Resorcinol. Used in making fluorescein

Carbonate. Effervesces with acids

Butylate. For example, C_4H_9OK

Benzoyl. The radical of benzoic acid

Laevulose. *d*-Fructose

Normal. One gram-equivalent per litre

Jade Green. A famous Scottish dye

Benzidam. The name given to aniline prepared from nitrobenzene in 1842

Silliman. Appointed Professor of Chemistry in Yale College, in 1804

Piperine. A peppery alkaloid

Piperitone. A celebrated Australian ketone

Degrees of freedom. The sum of phases and components less two

Brewing. Leads to beer

Sealing. Often done in a blowpipe flame

Polar. Applicable to ions

Bear. Alchemical emblem for a still

Pitch. Left in the tar-still

Ferrous. Readily oxidised to ferric

Spots. Informal for 'organic identifications'

Bottom layer. Governed by the Phase Rule

Separating funnel. Often associated with dropping in

Meta. Applies to DNB

Ortho. Applies to aspirin

Para. Applies to hydroquinone

Isolate. Obtain pure

Betol. beta-Naphthyl salicylate

Coffey. Christian name, Aeneas

Amylate. For example, $C_5H_{11}ONa$

Benzoate. A salt of Flowers of Benjamin

Urobilin. A yellow pigment of urine

Anisic. *p*-Methoxybenzoic

Bone-ash. Chiefly calcium phosphate

Nobel. He invented dynamite and founded a Peace Prize

Gattermann. The diazotised solution fizzed when he threw copper into it

Sublime. A solid changes its position by vaporising

Volatilise. Signifies behaviour attributed to the feminine in alchemy

Nobel Prize. Evidently the one awarded for chemistry

GLOSSARY

A', all
Ah'm, I'm
Aiblins, perhaps
A'nt, aunt
Awa', away
Aweel, ah well

Bejant (m.), *bejantine* (f.), yellow-bill (*bec jaune*), fledgling, or first-year student
Birkies, lively fellows
Bonny, fine, good, beautiful
But an' ben, a small house, consisting of an outer and an inner room
By ordinar', extraordinarily

Canny, knowing, shrewd
Chiel, lad

Dee, die
Ding, force
Dinna, don't
Doon, down

Ettled, intended

Fanged, caught
Fash, trouble
Fleech, coax
Forbye, besides
Frae, from
Fu', full
Fute, foot

Gait, way, road
Ganged, went

Gar, make, compel
Gat, got
Gin, if (*gif*)
Gowd, gold
Gude, good

Hae, have
Haggis, a famous dish, often piped in at ceremonial feasts in Scotland
Hilt and hair, completely

Ilka, each

Jaloused, suspected

Ken, know
Kenspeckle, conspicuous

Lady Katharine Kennedy, according to a legend in the University of St. Andrews, was a niece of Bishop James Kennedy, who founded the College of St. Salvator in 1450. In the annual spring pageant which the students still hold in her honour, Kate Kennedy, attired as a mediaeval damosel of high degree (Fig. **90**), is impersonated by a 'beardless bejant' in a picturesque procession representing kings, saints, knights, prelates, martyrs, and scholars whose feet once trod the narrow wynds and cobbled ways of the ancient city. A bell

373

which Bishop Kennedy named Katharine and presented to the College in 1460 still hangs in the tower of the original collegiate chapel of St. Salvator (the spire of which is seen in Fig. **88**) [1]

Lang-nebbit, long-nosed
Lee, lie
Lum, chimney; *lum hat*, topper

Mair, more
Maun, must
Mony, many
Muckle, great

Nae, no
Nane, none
Nicht, night
Nicky Ben, the Devil
No', not
Noo, now

Ony, any
Oot, out

Pooch, pocket
Puir, poor

Rin, run

Sae, so
Semi (m.), *semie* (f.), a second-year student. (In the University of St. Andrews, a third-year student is a *tertian* and a fourth-year student a *magistrand:* they wear caps with gold and black tassels, respectively. *Bejants* have blue tassels and *semis* red ones)
Set, sit
Swither, hesitate

Tak', take
Tassie, drinking-cup
Tent, heed
Thole, endure, suffer

Unco', strange, unusual

Wadna, would not
Wee, small
Whins, gorse
Worriecow, bugbear

Yer, your
Yins, ones

[1] See the author's *Historic St. Andrews and its University*, St. Andrews, Scotland, 1946.

INDEX